KING'S RUN

A maverick's tale of football, wine and business

RAY KING

'The transformation of the Australian Brewing giant, Foster's into a global beverage powerhouse began with the purchase of Mildara Blass. Ted Kunkel's genius was to get on side Ray King who had run Mildara brilliantly.'
Robert Gottliebsen, '10 Best and Worst Decisions of Australian CEO's 1992 – 2002'

'Mr King turned an unprofitable Mildara into an international success story.'
Nigel Austin, 'Adelaide Advertiser' 1999

Published in Australia by Sid Harta Publishers Pty Ltd,
ABN: 46 119 415 842
23 Stirling Crescent, Glen Waverley, Victoria
3150 Australia
Telephone: +61 3 9560 9920, Facsimile: +61 3 9545 1742
E-mail: author@sidharta.com.au
First published in Australia 2015
This edition published 2025
Copyright © Ray King 2015
Cover design, typesetting: Working Type Studio
(www.workingtype.com.au)
The right of Ray King to be identified as the Author of the Work has been asserted in accordance with the Copyright, Designs and Patents Act 1988.

All rights reserved. No part of this publication may be reproduced, stored in a retrieval system, or transmitted, in any form or by any means without the prior written permission of the publisher, nor be otherwise circulated in any form of binding or cover other than that in which it is published and without a similar condition being imposed on the subsequent purchaser.

Kings Run: A maverick's tale of football, wine and business
King, Ray
EAN13: 978-1-925230-81-9
pp490

About the author

From an early life in the family's bakery in a Victorian country town, Ray King rose to become one of the biggest movers and shakers in the Australian corporate world.

During a thirty-year, often controversial career that began in 1970, he brought a fresh way of thinking to a wine industry steeped in tradition.

He introduced to the world the now ubiquitous bag in box wine carton, initiated takeovers and mergers during the wine industry's most stormy years and lifted an ailing Mildara Wines Limited into the global wine industry's third largest profit earner.

He saw early playing days with Carlton Football Club, spent a number of years as an AFL central umpire, won four Australian Masters Road Cycling Championships and later served seven years as chairman of directors at St Kilda Football Club.

He lives in Melbourne with Dawn, his wife of almost fifty years.

Dedication

For my family and for my close colleagues who played vital roles in our wine industry adventures.

It was our children who encouraged me to think about writing this history. Not for them, but for their children. Some legacy was needed to complete the circle.

Dawn, the love of my life and my soul mate for more than forty-seven years, kept asking, "For whom are you writing it, who is your audience?" At times I wrote for this audience, sometimes for that audience but in the end I realised the audience was me. It became an indulgence, pure and simple.

I have not written much about our children or our children's children despite the treasure they represent to us. They and theirs should tell their own stories. At night I dream of their time as small children and still feel their pain as I recall the times I disappointed them. I still remember their particular smell and the times when I hugged them and kissed them, a habit that convention at the time suggested should be short-lived. It disappeared all too soon. I wish it had not been so but the philosophy of the unstaked tree had made its indelible mark. In some vicarious way I have tried to compensate for that by insisting on hugging and kissing our seven grandchildren without restraint. I think they enjoy it; at least I hope they do.

Our family has been the blessing. They are happy, they have good values and have all done well. We could not have asked for more and Dawn and I are enormously proud. Importantly, their values, aspirations and sense of achievement have been passed on to their own children. Again, I hope the burden will not be too great.

We all live in the same city and as a family meet often, repeating the same stories over and over with never a failure. Afterwards, Dawn and I look at each other and smile our gratitude. Hopefully, the tradition of regular family functions will keep going after we are gone, particularly the Christmas day speech that falls on the shoulders of the next youngest member. Tears, as well as laughter, are a wonderful binding agent.

Ray King, 28 April 2015

Contents

Section 1: Early Adventures

1	Bugger of a kid	3
2	Adolescence	55
3	University	97
4	Teacher in Bendigo	131
5	Single parent/A.F.L. umpire/business executive	141
6	Jumping the fence is worth it	163
7	The world changes	173
8	Children	181

Section 2: Wine Industry Adventures

9	Wynn Winegrowers Limited	199
10	Into the trenches at Wynn's	203
11	Come in sucker	215
12	Baptism under fire	223
13	The wine cask	233
14	Taken over	249
15	The dream run ends	259
16	Mildara: the beginning	273
17	Mildara audit	284
18	A bumpy start	295
19	The plan	305
20	The turnaround	333
21	Yellowglen	343
22	Krondorf	351
23	Jamiesons Run	367
24	The eclectic period	375
25	Mr Audacious	391
26	Wolf Blass	397
27	Wolf Blass merger outcome	411

28 Too many brands 421
29 Pre Foster's 425
30 Sold to Foster's 435
31 Second prize 471

Appendix 1   Earnings before interest and tax 1981 – 1990 . 475
Appendix 2   Earnings before interest,
             tax and amortisation 1991 – 2000 476
Appendix 3   Return on investment 1981 – 2000 477
Acknowledgements 479

Section One
EARLY ADVENTURES

1

Bugger of a kid

September 1943, the fourth year of the Second World War. Nanna King's withering glare was enough to make him stop drumming his heels against the worn piano stool in the bakery shop owned by his family. He pondered more important considerations. Did he really have Ned Kelly's blood running through his veins? He kind of liked that idea.

There were two customers, Hacker Finn's grandmother and Mrs Urquhart. Hacker, a friend of the boy and later a champion schoolboy athlete, lived with his widowed grandmother up the hill from the bakery in a dilapidated, sagging house in Milton Street. Hacker's grandmother was being served by Maudie Maddocks. Maudie had little claim to fame other than her strong and impossible to budge belief she was the bastard granddaughter of Ned Kelly, Australia's famous bushranger hanged in 1896. On the other hand, Mrs Urquhart was the mother of Keith Urquhart, the Western District Football League's champion fullback. She was being attended to by the boy's grandmother, Mary Louisa King.

Mary thought Maudie a few cents short of the full dollar but employed her because she was a friendly soul, good with the customers and, more to the point, a close relative of the boy's grandfather.

The doorbell announced another customer. Tall, wearing an unusual flat cloth cap, the newcomer strolled to the counter and waited patiently to be served. He smiled at the boy and in a friendly, quietly spoken but thickly accented voice proclaimed, less than accurately as it turned out, 'you're a nice little boy.'

The nice little boy considered his options for a while before responding. 'You're not, you're a bloody German.'

I had succumbed to the plethora of World War Two government posters that shouted, 'Beware, the enemy watches and listens.' Keeping an eye open for Japanese and German spies was a concern for a four year old because useful information seemed to lurk everywhere.

The Japanese Imperial Army, having announced its intentions in the attack on the US fleet in Pearl Harbor, had followed up its expansionist objectives with advances through China, Malaya and Burma, decisively and humiliatingly defeating and incarcerating in early 1942 the incumbent British, Australian and Dutch defence forces. Invasion of Australia by 'the yellow hordes' was everybody's feared expectation.

Decisively or perversely, a point of view determined by where you lived, the Australian Government developed a strategy to meet an anticipated Japanese landing that would concede all territory north of Brisbane to the invaders. It became known as the 'Brisbane Line' — hardly original but suiting the time's purpose. Elsewhere, the war was not going any better for Australia's allies as Hitler's juggernaut continued on its merry way across Europe and North Africa, obliterating everything in sight and often anything that wasn't.

With recruitment to the armed services gradually denuding Hamilton of able-bodied men, my father had felt it his duty to volunteer in the service of his country. His classification as 'food provider' exempted him from conscription but, like so many others, any concern for his personal safety was overridden by more noble and adventurous thoughts. He responded to Prime Minister John Curtin's exhortations and joined up on 2 May 1942. For three of my formative years — 'give me the boy for his first seven years and I will give you the man,' said the Jesuits — I did not see him other than in the small Baby Brownie photographs that intermittently arrived in the mail.

¶

1939 turned out to be quite a year. It heralded the start of the Second World War, Batman made his first formal appearance in a comic and it saw the longest game of Test cricket ever played. The Timeless

Test, as it was called, took place in Durban between South Africa and England, ran for twelve days and had finally to be abandoned to allow the English team to catch the boat back home.

It was also the year I opened my account: at the Hamilton base hospital on 28 February under the star sign of Pisces, the last and oldest of the zodiacal signs. According to the soothsayers I would be a daydreamer, impressionable, trusting, tenacious, instinctive and loving. They would add that those Piscean dreams would later acquire substance, that I would be of my own making and determine my own end, the unique capability of the doubled fish.

My parents hadn't messed about. I arrived 259 days after they took their marriage vows. I might have been the first cab off the rank for Ernest and Thelma's three children but more could have been done for my latent sporting ambitions. I could only wish for the prospect of being tall, lean and able to cover a hundred yards in ten seconds, or even eleven seconds. Instead, they produced a stumpy kid with a big head who, had he been a thoroughbred, would have remained friendless in the sale ring.

Thelma Edward, a mere 148 centimetres of pocket-sized fire and brimstone, was raised in Ballarat, the eldest of five children. Her father, a house painter and wallpaper hanger, had not been blessed with good fortune, disappointment being a continuing feature of his relatively short life. Unable to work for the final eight years because of a chronic heart condition, his life ended at the tender age of forty and the burden of his family's survival fell on the shoulders of my maternal grandmother, Nanna Edward. Her family of seven survived on a miserable invalid pension meagrely supplemented by what the children could contribute to the household's income. Upon my grandfather's early demise financial matters took a decided turn for the worse. The invalid pension ceased to arrive in the mail and it was not until six years after my grandfather's death that the Federal Government introduced the widow's pension. In that time Nanna Edward's unrelenting budgetary burdens incurred visits to local and presumably rapacious moneylenders in order to grace the kitchen table with sufficient food and keep the landlord at bay.

Thelma, like the rest of the Edward family, suffered those difficult years in resourceful desperation. There didn't appear to be any feeling of humiliation or injustice regarding their desperate circumstances (at least I never heard or have no memory of any grumbling) as their situation was all too common. They simply had to get on with their lives and overcome these financial inconveniences in any way possible.

Upon reaching the minimum school leaving age each of the Edward children was gainfully employed. The partial exception was my Uncle George who continued his education, a not uncommon aspect of family life in those days, when the brightest child's path was strewn with roses while the others had to fend for themselves. But, in keeping with the Edward family's financial travails, George's promising career and earnings prospects ended with an untimely and tragic death from a brain tumour at the tender age of thirty. He would not to be the last of his mother's children to die in her arms.

In the summer of 1937 Thelma Edward admired the form of 184 centimetre tall Hamilton ruckman Ernest Charles King. Ernest stood the tallest of the highly rated Hamilton Volunteer Fire Brigade's demonstration team. His mate, 'Chalky' Wishart, a 160 centimetre butcher, was the shortest. Fire Brigade demonstration championships were hugely popular events in rural Victoria at the time, providing spectacular and fearless displays of physicality and daring to their enthusiastic supporters. Ballarat residents were no exception. Running up a twelve metre ladder with no safety harness while handling a pulsating, writhing, eight centimetre hose bursting with water endeavouring to make its escape was no easy matter and was greeted by gleeful cries from the spectators.

Ernest was painfully shy but, like all the male members of the King family, well most of them, was highly admired for his star quality good looks; his handsome face complemented his broad shouldered tall frame more than nicely. Being a family member as well as an heir to the highly successful and moderately famous King's Bakery in Hamilton didn't do any harm either. He was considered quite a catch. And of course it was Thelma who made all the running. She eventually relocated to Hamilton where she delighted in a newly built house at 43 Alexandra Parade. But not for long.

After my father took his chances in joining the Royal Australian Air Force in 1942 my mother and I moved in with his parents, Nanna and Pa King, at the combined bakery, shop and residence on the corner of Hamilton's Brown and Lonsdale streets. The uncertain likelihood of our seeing my father again doubtless made our relocation seem like a good idea at the time. Although it was not something she had signed up for when she got married my mother had little choice but to become involved in a business in which she had little interest. Worse, she was now part of a household and a business dominated by my grandmother, the King family's daunting, or at least slightly daunting, matriarch. While Mum was no shrinking violet she didn't hold a candle to Nanna King in the machismo department nor in her ability to practice domestic politics. Nonetheless, she had a sufficiently decent bark to ensure an almost equal level of wariness on the matriarch's part, which was saying something. In any case, it was wartime. You did what you had to do, which was little consolation to a woman who had recently escaped from relative poverty and looked forward to a life without all the pressures relative poverty entailed. The fact that I placed Nanna King on a pedestal probably only added to the negative turn Mum's life had taken and fuelled her increasing pessimism over her husband's prospects for surviving the war. She very quickly had come to terms with the decidedly unpleasant realisation that life's pressures never go away, they merely change character.

I told Mum and Nanna King that I said a little prayer for Dad each night when I went to bed and Nanna said that she prayed for him and Uncle Stan every hour of every day which was a surprise to me given she didn't seem to be religious in the slightest.

King's Bakery, opposite Hamilton's major sporting arena, Melville Oval, sprang to life at 4 a.m. every day except Sunday when the bread makers kicked off at lunch time. With the lights turning on before 4 a.m. and generally remaining on until after midnight, the bakery buildings were a constant blur of activity.

If Mum's efforts to adapt to her new environment were accompanied by more than a degree of teeth grinding, then for kids it was easier. At least it was for this one. All grandparents indulge their grandchildren so living with them is an even better proposition. No doubt influenced by my new environment I became what Mum began to describe to others as 'that bugger of a kid'. But woe betide anyone who dared criticise her son within earshot.

King's Bakery was diverse and entertaining for an only child who from an early age had learned to rely on his own resources and his own company. For Mum, those adventures didn't come without a downside. The three hard-drinking, foul-mouthed, afternoon shift bread makers, 'Kelly' Grant, 'Motty' Mott and 'Boofhead' Mann became the bane of Mum's life. I was their malleable apprentice. They took great delight in regaling me with eye-popping dirty stories, regularly presented me with even more eye-popping artistic and not so artistic 'life' photographs and very successfully taught me, like the pirates' parrot, to swear in the vilest of terms. Four-letter words were their specialty. Anyone who had a conversation with a bread maker at King's Bakery knew half the words were not fit to print and the other half not fit to even think. As for me, I thought that enthusiastically embracing the Australian vernacular gave me an appealing, worldly aspect.

Nanna King didn't necessarily agree with Mum's description that I was a bugger of a kid but she did think I was a bit different. In any case, as her first male grandchild, she naturally had me earmarked for great things. I was evidently precocious as well as possessing a bit of an imagination, exaggerating some things and lying about others. Nanna believed that the lies I told were not always of evil intent, perhaps more often than not having their genesis in imaginative fantasy or a desire for the limelight, but I suspect even she felt that on most occasions I might have been leaning more towards my own interests than those of others. In any case, she liked my early signs of independence, a trait that mothers rarely embrace, and Mum was certainly no exception.

I was evidently a wanderer on my trike, a three-wheeled affair my parents presented to me at age three, which was the age at which most kids received them in those days. Invariably, I took 'Tiger', Nanna King's Australian silky haired terrier, on the trike's rear tray for protection. Tiger had an inferiority complex and had always been a bit on the evil side anyway, but more so now that he was half blind and on the slippery slope to senility. He didn't seem to be particularly riled by me, only by those who approached us. It was not unusual for us to be returned after dark by indulgent Hamiltonians who were aware I was 'that bloody kid from the bakery' and who also knew to keep out of the way of Tiger's nasty little choppers.

Nanna King was the information source about the day I insulted the friendly, foreign looking gentleman. She particularly remembered also my presence in the bread makers' change room where Ned Kelly, not the real Ned Kelly, was in the process of undressing. He had apparently grasped his penis in his fist, with plenty left to spare (based on my detailed anatomical response to Nanna's forensic questioning), and waved it at me. I had bolted, not in fright but in excitement to share this awesome and most impressive sight with my grandfather who was busily serving a crowded King's Bakery shop. 'Fardi, Fardi' (my mangled pronunciation of grandfather) I evidently bellowed, 'come and look at Kelly's big bum.'

Nanna also recalled an incident at the Hamilton Methodist Church in 1945. The red brick interior soared above my neatly combed hair and the air was filled with the smell of burning candles. We sat at the front, not because we wanted to be closer to God but because we were family. My Uncle Stan was being married. The minister mumbled strange words that were probably English but could have been anything and everyone seemed to be touched with the romantic spirit of the occasion. Everyone, that is, except me. As the minister mumbled away the hushed silence was starkly shattered. 'What's that silly old bugger saying, Mum?' Mum's default option successfully pinpointed the guilty party to the congregation as she leapt to her feet and dragged me out of the packed church while I compounded the crime with an aggrieved, 'Jesus, Mum, I was only asking, I was only asking.'

The radio was compulsory family listening ('shut up Ray, for God's sake, we're trying to listen to the news.') The boosters to improve radio reception in country areas were only moderately effective and it was my job to sit on the arm of the stuffed leather armchair next to the radio and fiddle with the station finder when the regular waves of static plunged out of control.

It is almost impossible to imagine now what a big deal radio was in the 1940s. The radio, or what we all called the wireless, was the television of the '40s, the wonder of the age and the centre of every Australian family's existence. We huddled around an appliance almost as large as a refrigerator, listening to the news, to sports of all descriptions, to quiz shows, talent quests and weekly radio plays. Some radio plays ran for years. Australia's *Blue Hills* ran for a difficult to believe thirty-one years.

At seven o'clock each evening we listened for news of Japanese armed forces in the Pacific Islands north of Australia where Dad was serving as a leading aircraftman with 75 Squadron. His job was to service, repair and re arm British-made Hurricanes and American-built Kittyhawks. These fighter planes, operating from crudely cleared and even more crudely levelled jungle airstrips, were often out-manoeuvred and out fought by the lighter, faster Japanese Zeros and those that survived required constant repairs and patching up. The jungle airstrips were under constant bombing attacks by the Japanese, particularly at night. It was only after Dad returned home safe and sound that we learned of his being bombed and of the juxtaposed terror and black humoured repartee as he and his mates huddled in a shallow slit trench sweating on whether the fast approaching whistling missile was to be the last thing they would ever hear.

We also listened for news of what was happening in Europe where my Uncle Stan, Dad's brother, a wireless air gunner on secondment to the British Air force, rolled the dice every time his bomber took off. They both survived the war, my uncle miraculously so given the low survival rate of bomber crews operating in raids over Germany.

¶

In 1943 I was introduced to a new and wonderful world; girls.

Alexandra Girls College provided education for day students and boarders and is still located on a large parcel of land diagonally opposite King's Bakery. Based on the English private school model, the college was established in the late 1880s to cater for the daughters of wealthy western Victorian sheep farmers whose parents' preference was to have their daughters closer to home than Geelong's enclave of more expensive private schools. Mum felt Alexandra College might balance the education I was receiving at the hands of the bread makers given that attempts to ban me from the bakehouse had inevitably proved futile. Nanna King duly negotiated my enrolment as the school's only male.

There was only one other pre-schooler, Judy McPhee, the sister of John (Dopey) McPhee, later to be a team mate of mine in the St Andrew's under-eighteen football team. The tuition for our preschool class of two was not charged with energy. We merely sat in with a combined class of years one and two, a baby-sitting job really, and had little choice but to learn by osmosis and pick up what we could. Contradicting all modern educational theory, it actually seemed to work. By the time I began primary school I understood arithmetic fractions and could multiply and divide.

My other educational advance was a practical introduction to the mysteries and delights of the female species. Judy McPhee's inviting proximity provided the opportunity to express my enthusiasm for the new world I now found myself in. It was an opportunity that would not go begging. I planted regular kisses on Judy's fair cheeks which, I was delighted to discover, were well received. I had not been inhibited by the presence of our classmates or by the fact that Judy was constructed along Amazonian lines, she being considerably taller than me and, if I remember correctly, also somewhat wider. But my bakehouse tutors, Kelly, Motty and Boofhead were less than impressed with my newly acquired Alexandra College rounded vowels — 'you little poofter'.

¶

In January 1944 Mum and I made one of our twice-yearly pilgrimages by train to Ballarat to holiday with Nanna Edward and my two aunts and two uncles. Nanna Edward always welcomed me with a raucous and elongated 'hello love', crushing me in her predictable and enthusiastic bear hug. I couldn't remember being hugged before and decided I really liked it — it seemed my parents were curiously incapable of showing overt affection either to each other (I cannot recall ever seeing them hug or kiss) or for that matter their children. I knew they loved us but they just didn't get around to showing it, a rule I thought to be standard for all parents.

The real attraction in Ballarat was my Uncle Bill. Only fourteen years older than me, Bill was an enthusiastic, irreverent, laughing cavalier. His image was stratospheric to his nephew courtesy of his having played for Footscray in the AFL (the VFL at the time). He later 'fessed up' that it was only four games, only a slight exaggeration given that the actual number was three, but who was counting? Far better to have been a has-been than a never was or will be.

I would wait in feverish, excited anticipation, hungry for his outstretched arms and his raucous, gleeful laugh which always announced his arrival in the gravelled, pot-holed side lane that separated Nanna's house from holiday playmate Bill Pedie's house next door. The only memories that survive of my friendship with Bill Pedie are of invariably being similarly clothed in the day's small boy's uniform of overalls and hobnailed boots and of our partnership one day on the steps of his mother's kitchen when we consumed a one pound (600 gram) bag of green cherries, each challenging the other, successfully as it turned out, to eat the pips as well. My friendship with Bill was a short one. He died of leukemia when he was nine.

Uncle Bill dinked me everywhere on his pushbike, presenting me with apparent pride to his bevy of colourful friends — a particularly large and colourful lot they were too — and indulged my every whim.

Bill (Curly to his mates) Edward had started his working life beneath the earth's surface in one of Ballarat's gold mines, or so he informed me. But after one day he told them to stick the job up their arse, a word picture that generated such hilarity for a four year old that I could always say without a word of a lie that I once laughed so hard I did actually pee my pants.

Uncle Bill supplemented his earnings as a fitter at the Ballarat rail yards by laying the odds with his work mates (illegally), practising as a licensed bookmaker on selected evenings and at weekends (legally), receiving one pound (two dollars) a week playing for East Ballarat in the Ballarat Football League on Saturdays and from coaching a local football team on Sundays (fee unknown).

Our mid-year visits introduced me to Ballarat's icy winter blasts and cemented at least in my mind the city's reputation as the coldest place in Victoria if not the world. Heating for the enthusiasts at the evening races was provided via converted forty-four gallon petrol drums filled with burning coke. On windy nights (most of them) swirling eddies provided spectacular displays of billowing sparks which you were more than happy to be enveloped in and you usually went home with little black rimmed holes in your outer clothing.

Uncle Bill's knowledge of and friendship with devious and murky racecourse characters was stuff of legend and that which wasn't he simply made up on the spot. He covered horse racing and 'the red hots' (the trots) but his special love was the dogs, the murkiest of them all. He usually took me along on his bookmaking ventures as his apprentice 'penciller' where he sat me on his bookmaking stand and introduced me to clients who had neither Christian name nor surname but names such as Spider, Adger, Moose and Holy Willy.

Uncle Bill became the father of three daughters and it seems I was the son he was never going to have. Everyone should have an Uncle Bill.

The day of the train journey to Ballarat was forty-five degrees Celsius, 1944's hottest day of the year. On cue, the countryside burst into flames. A scheduled two and a half hours train journey turned into an eight-hour adventure (but only for me) with the rail track's timber sleepers requiring regular replacement by hastily recruited local firefighters. The day's excitement was tempered somewhat by the worried faces of the mainly female passengers as well as the weeping despair of those who had fled their destroyed or about to be destroyed homes and who sought refuge on the platforms of the local railway stations along the way. I spent much of the journey on my own, wandering up and down the train's corridors as Mum, in her self-appointed role of Good Samaritan, offered glasses of water, wet handkerchiefs and encouragement to our fellow passengers.

Much to Mum's relief, I was accepted for enrolment at Hamilton Primary School, again due to some judicious arm twisting by Nanna King, as my birthdate fell four weeks outside the official starting age. On that first day I walked the six block journey from the bakery through the town's back streets to Gray Street Primary School unattended, albeit shadowed at a discreet distance with clandestine thoroughness by Mum. I might have been a bugger of a kid but I was still her kid.

I felt dismissively superior to my classmates in 'the bubs' who dissolved into tears at the prospective and then ultimate retreat of their mothers. After all, I was now an old hand at this school caper. But even for an old hand the bubs class was no easy meal ticket in 1944. Prep mistress, Miss Merlin, punished me vigorously with a wooden ruler to the back of my hand each time I failed to correctly spell the word 'eight', a tough assignment for a recently turned five year old. Miss Merlin believed in the positive aspects of pain for enhancing the learning process and most of the time she was right.

Things went from bad to worse with the rapid realisation that I had still not discovered the universal formula for romantic success.

Despite my pledging undying affection to desk mate Mary Coulter, the daughter of one of Dad's close friends, 'Spud' Coulter, she wasn't having any of it. Her right arm punching the air she yelled, 'Miss, Miss, Ray King keeps trying to kiss me,' resulting in my hasty relocation to Bruce 'Brasso' McGregor's desk.

Brasso was notable for having a multitude of talents, most of which, if not all, he ultimately wasted and I, like many of my peers, was drawn to his iconic differences. At the end of that first year Brasso and I left our classmates behind by jumping Year One and bobbing up in Year Two.

Nineteen-forty-five was a very good year. Rainbird won 'The Cup', I won twelve shillings in the King's Bakery sweep and the war came to an end. Dad survived the war and was discharged from the air force on 6 September.

We soon resumed our residency at 43 Alexandra Parade, a popular move as far as Mum was concerned, and life returned to some semblance of peace time normality. That relief for Mum was to be short lived — by 1949 we were back at the bakery, although she did have the consolation that Nanna King was no longer on the premises.

King's Bakery was home for most of my first sixteen years. And, while the time at the bakery was a great influence, the greater influence was the bakery's founder, Mary Louisa King, my paternal grandmother. Mary was a tearaway in her younger days, and in her later days too. Her brothers confirmed she threw a decent punch.

¶

Castlemaine, in central Victoria, conceived in the gold rush of the 1850s, was a town in steady decline. Gold production had fallen to an uneconomic trickle, the times they were a-changing and it was necessary to change with them or get left behind. The carpetbaggers, opportunists and thieves had moved on to greener pastures, businesses were closing and jobs were scarce. In 1906 fifteen year old Mary Louisa Burge joined the exodus. Only the lazy, the mentally paralysed and the not so smart remained as well as a few generous souls who felt it their duty to provide a helping hand. Mary headed for Hamilton, the centre of a booming fine wool industry. Judging by the small teaspoon I still possess, the Hamilton elders at the time were not beyond a bit of puffery. On it is stamped, 'Hamilton, the Wool Capital of the World'. And a thriving, vibrant town of more than 5000 people it was too.

Edie, the eldest of Mary's three sisters, actually a half-sister, had recently moved to Hamilton to marry Archie Bruce, the owner of one of the town's three bakeries. Bakeries, forerunners to today's fast food industries, were central to Australian family life and accounted for a high proportion of the average family's calorific consumption. And, conveniently for the King family, that level of dependence on their services would continue well into the second half of the twentieth century.

¶

Mary's first visit to her sister was all it took. Attracted by the vibrant, bustling town, Mary asked Edie to help her find employment. As she had hoped, she found a job in Bruce's Bakery.

By her first anniversary in Hamilton Mary was moving up in the world. The sixteen year old had departed Bruce's Bakery and become manager (manageress in those days) of the Hamilton Tea Rooms in Gray Street, Hamilton's main street. And she had begun stepping out with her fancy man, the bread carter from Bruce's Bakery, my grandfather to be.

Mary was charismatic, had a level of determination that was off the scale and was already a force to be reckoned with. Anybody who knew her stayed out of her way when she was on a mission. She was to become the centre of the King family's universe and the go-to person for anyone with problems, sometimes family related, sometimes not. She dispensed her practical home-spun philosophies to anyone who needed help and was prepared to listen. And they generally did. She had an instinctive business acumen. Nor did she care about or allow herself to be influenced by what others thought. She was tougher than old shoe leather but balanced those ingredients with integrity and a strong sense of what was fair. Whenever she had a job that needed to be done around the house she always offered it to the local tradesman she felt had the greatest financial need. Although she qualified for the pension when she turned sixty (there was no means test then) she didn't apply for it until she was well into her eighties when pragmatism finally won out.

She needed to bring all those superlatives to bear following the birth of her first child, my uncle Les. A sickly child, Les had developed a stomach ailment that both prevented the absorption of nourishment and frustrated the medical fraternity, not to mention uncle Les himself. Washing his hands of the case was the local medico with the unlikely name, Billy Kneebone. Billy was a tough customer, more than happy to give a noisy hysterical young kid a cuff behind the ear before grasping his arm and plunging a needle into it as quick as you like. Not a great believer in the subtlety of the relatively new concept of the bedside manner, Billy suggested that in uncle Les' case Nanna should prepare herself for the worst. 'Be damned,' was her retort, the worst word in her vocabulary. She developed her own program, massaging Les' body for thirty minutes three times a day with olive oil, believing it would be absorbed into Les' system by osmosis. They were Les' three square meals a day. Billy Kneebone was at least kind enough not to say she was wasting her time. Weeks turned into months but Nanna King and Les eventually won out.

Mary married Les King (born, Marangan Leslie King) in 1910 but not before my grandfather agreed to pay a substantial deposit to 'Attie' Gunn, Hamilton's leading builder, to erect a three-bedroom bungalow in Milton Street, the site of yet another subdivision in the still thriving town.

My grandfather came from a long line of itinerant timber cutters and sawmillers, few of whom could read or write and who plied their lonely trade in remote and generally inaccessible mountainous areas of western Victoria. Les was one of the luckier family members to get some schooling, an activity that encouraged him to the eminently sensible conclusion that there were better paid and certainly safer things to do than lead a lonely and perilous existence around the family's timber mills.

Pa King had personality. He loved people, he loved to talk. He was generous in spirit as well as in financial matters and was always a soft but willing touch for the town's derelicts. He was also no stranger to the art of public relations in furthering the fortunes of King's Bakery. It was a familiarity at least vigorously encouraged if not driven by my grandmother.

The week before my appearance in the Hamilton under-fourteen football grand final as an eleven year old my grandfather made an announcement that thrilled the hearts of twenty of the twenty-three members of the Patterson Park Football Club. The local sports store proprietor was even happier. My grandfather announced that he had acquired a set of jumpers and socks that would turn twenty members of the team into a mini version of the Geelong Football Club. While being decked out in the uniform of Geelong, the AFL's most successful club at the time, might have seemed sufficient reason for our feeling uplifted it wasn't the main reason. Any sort of uniform would have sufficed as our existing strip was somewhat rag tag and flexible. The unifying element was simply a thin piece of white calico material preferably sewn but more often than not merely safety-pinned diagonally left to right (sometimes right to left) across the front of any old jumper of indiscriminate colour. This lack of sophistication extended to footwear. I was one of the luckier team members to have real footy boots. My more deprived team members had to hammer leather stops into the soles of their school shoes or boots before the game and pull them out afterwards with the club's pliers so they could walk home.

To describe my role in that year's Grand Final as an 'appearance' was not to overstate the reality. My contribution to our victory, a triumph dominated by my near neighbour, the man-child 'Cackle'

Agnew, was a solitary possession, a registration of some flattery given that it was an insubstantial, glancing kick along the ground. While Dad was silent on my performance that day, Nanna King was far more effusive, as only a grandmother can be. She thought I had played really well. Nonetheless, the major pleasure I derived from the occasion was not the game itself but rather the night of receiving my new livery. I spent endless hours of indescribable pleasure in front of the full length mirror in my bedroom admiring myself from every conceivable angle.

¶

Mary continued to manage the Hamilton Tea Rooms to help reduce what she and Les owed on their newly constructed home. She recognised the benefits of debt but was not comfortable in being beholden to anyone, let alone lenders. The quicker it was repaid the better.

By 1912 it was time for the next phase, the creation of a family. In quick succession Mary produced Les, Ernest and Stanley; not quite one a year, until the First World War. Lucy, 'the last', arrived nine years later in 1922. It wasn't that Mary was holding out until she had a daughter. At the outset she had decided on four children and, having achieved her target, that was pretty well that. In any case, despite the fact that everyone in the world loved Lucy, not the least being Nanna herself, I suspect she would have been just as happy to have had four boys. She was more the Boadicea type.

Mary's children were all different.

My Uncle Les, a loquacious larrikin, had a soft spot for the disadvantaged and those in trouble with the law. He was the prime mover in gaining employment at King's Bakery for his wayward friend Eric Grant, better known as Ned or Kelly, which happily for all concerned appeared to subvert Eric's budding career as an incompetent petty criminal. Uncle Les was himself no stranger to the constabulary, often found influenced by the local firewater wherever he felt comfortable at the time.

Dad was the strong silent type, Ernest by name, earnest by nature. Painfully shy, almost to the point of invisibility, he spent his early years hiding behind Nanna's legs when outsiders were about. Until he reached the age of four every one outside the family thought he was deaf and dumb — they had never heard him speak. Tall and broad shouldered, Dad was a big man in every sense of the word.

He also had the patience of Job.

In February 1967, ignoring the haughty receptionist at Melbourne University who kept suggesting he should find something more constructive to do, Dad spent more than six hours patiently cooling his heels in the principal's postage stamp sized reception area waiting for the opportunity to prosecute the case of my brother, Peter to become a schoolteacher. Peter's Year Twelve results had been borderline and following Dad's quiet persistence as to the extenuating circumstances (it was the year Mum died) the principal, far more receptive than her bitchy self-important underling, felt she just couldn't shoot Bambi. Many years later when he was getting near the end I asked him, purely out of curiosity, why he had persisted in that endeavour for so long. It came as a complete surprise when he said that had been my strong advice at the time — apparently I had told him that if he sat there long enough, she would eventually see him. I don't know where that piece of advice came from or why he even took it. I must admit it made me feel pretty good when he told me that.

Rarely if ever judgmental, tolerant to a fault, Dad fully understood and was accepting of the inherent frailty of man. He was generous financially and in spirit to his small group of friends and had a level of intelligence that belied his formal education having ceased at the tender age of twelve. Never flustered, rarely angry, he was the epitome of the 'reasonable man', practicing common sense and exercising judgment as well as anyone I have known (with the possible exclusion of his mother). I wear on a gold chain one of his boyhood achievement medallions and I give him and Mum a wave first thing every morning by sharpening a knife with the old 'stone' that I commandeered from his kitchen drawer after he died (every knife in the King household was sharpened with laser like precision). Dad left this earth in the same relaxed fashion he had lived on it, dying in his sleep in Port Fairy aged ninety-four.

Uncle Stan defied death during the Second World War, surviving three crash landings and on another occasion being one of only three surviving crew members that returned to base — what was left of the others being hosed out of the severely crippled bomber. Stan was the toff of the family, dressed like a dandy, wore a carefully manicured Clark Gable moustache and was a great hit with the ladies. He became a highly successful hotelier and was the best friend of Reg Ansett, later to become Australia's first transport industry tycoon. He also taught his sister to smoke and to dance.

Aunty Lucy, an international class swimmer (Dad taught her to swim), excellent tennis player and single figure golfer, bubbled with effervescence and was loved by everyone.

¶

Over the years my grandfather continued the home delivery of Archie Bruce's bread using horse and cart. He had been delivering bread to his household customers for almost twenty years. Rising from his bed at three a.m. he rode his bicycle to the bakery, stacked the delivery cart with the previous night's freshly baked loaves and was on the road by four a.m. His delivery route gradually grew to more than three hundred households.

At the age of twelve I began what became my annual routine of spending at least two weeks during the Christmas holidays delivering bread with Dad via horse and cart, a routine I thought decidedly unfair to be inflicted upon a twelve year old boy. Rising at 3.30 a.m., being harassed in the dark by startled don't-mess-with-me dogs and lugging a large wicker basket of loaves that weighed a tonne did not exactly make it my favourite time of the year despite getting time to spend man on man with my father.

My grandfather was a good provider, loved his family, enjoyed his friends and life was good. But Mary had much bigger plans and in those plans he was to be a key player.

In a world dominated by small business it was always clear to Mary that the only way to get on was to own one. She also knew her husband would only be comfortable in a business he knew something about. The bakery business it would have to be.

Her particular focus was the Rob Roy Bakery, the newest and least successful of Hamilton's three bakeries. Its two competitors were far better located, one in Gray Street the other in Thomson Street, both surrounded by other busy retailers, whereas the Rob Roy was isolated on the corner of Brown and Lonsdale Streets, almost a full block from the nearest retailer. Its location seemed a serious disadvantage but not to Mary who saw things differently from most people.

The Rob Roy Bakery was distinctive for its smells, some seductively aromatic some not so. As well as the four-bedroom dwelling attached to the bakery shop there were two yards, a bakehouse, a storeroom housing stacks of fifty-kilo bags of flour (an excellent if dangerous kid's playroom), an open shed for the delivery carts, a shed containing tanks of rank smelling preserved eggs for the cakes that were baked daily, a stable for the horses and an extremely ripe, pungent, forever fermenting manure pit. There was but one toilet on the property and that was generally pretty ripe as well. Like most toilets in those days it was external, for the use of employees and family members alike, a total of around twenty personnel. It was a rare visit that didn't have your nose twitching but at least the seat was usually warm. Toilet paper consisted of squarely torn newspaper hanging by string attached to a nail hammered into a wall stud.

Mary became a regular customer at the Rob Roy Bakery and liked what she saw, particularly the fact that the proprietors displayed little interest in their customers. Despite the dearth of surrounding retailers there was plenty of passing foot traffic. Unfortunately it kept passing the door. But Mary already had plans to deal with that.

Having checked out the Rob Roy Bakery to her satisfaction Mary broached the subject of business ownership with Les. She was unsurprised at his initial resistance. He was happy with his uncomplicated, risk free life and he felt obliged to Archie Bruce — far too obliged thought Mary — and the idea of going into debt to acquire the Rob Roy Bakery made him more than a little nervous. But Mary was nothing if not daunting when she put her mind to something and already had her ducks in a row. It was agreed that he and Mary would put Mary's proposition to the owners.

The owners were happy to sell, in fact couldn't wait. They were not making enough to even pay themselves a decent wage and the value of the business was little more than that of the real estate. A deal was struck and Mary and Les agreed they would place their Milton Street property on the market and visit the Bank of New South Wales to seek the loan needed to fund the difference. Plain sailing so far but the storm clouds were gathering. Some things needed to be sorted out and not all of them would go smoothly.

That evening at the family dinner table a nervous Les announced to Mary that he was having second thoughts. His mother, Deborah, believed the venture to be far too risky. She had a point and by normal risk standards it was a very good point. By all accounts, Deborah was no slouch in the intimidation department as well as being more than a little churlish towards the woman who had supplanted her in her favourite son's life. But Mary was up for everything Deborah was likely to throw at her. She was the genuine article was Nanna King.

'Too risky be damned,' she exploded, again using her worst word.

Les was now in that most uncomfortable of positions — between a rock and a hard place. But Nanna realised she had a serious problem. Banks would not lend to females and she needed Les to sign the necessary papers even if the bank could be convinced to advance the loan.

Undeterred, Mary kept her appointment, visiting the bank manager alone and claiming Les had been delayed. William Cleland, the Bank of New South Wales' long-serving manager of the Hamilton branch, was impressed by Mary's bearing and by her forthright, confident manner that conveyed an expectation of success. The word failure didn't exist in Mary's vocabulary, let alone in her thoughts. Evidently, William already knew a bit about my grandmother, having admired her from afar, according to her unblushing account many years later. She claimed to have once had a sixteen-inch waist but I suspect by this time and after four kids there had been a degree of expansion. Nevertheless, she must have still been worth a look and William now admired her in the flesh, encouraging her to outline how she and Les intended to go about making the business successful.

Mary figured her husband was so popular and so trusted by his, or more correctly, Archie Bruce's home delivery customers of close to twenty years that most of them would be prepared to switch their purchases to the Rob Roy Bakery which, up to now, provided no delivery service. Presumably, Archie Bruce did not bank with the Bank of New South Wales.

She would turn the Rob Roy Bakery's passing traffic from a potential asset into a real asset by starting the afternoon's bread-making early enough for the first batch to be available to those walking or riding their bicycles home from work. The extraordinary seductiveness of the aroma of freshly baked bread would do the trick.

Then came her master stroke, simple but effective. Trading hours for all retailers, strictly enforced by the Hamilton Town Council, were from 8 a.m. to 6 p.m. In an act of low cunning she would inform all her customers that if they needed bread, cakes or pies after hours (biscuits and soft drinks were also available from King's Bakery) they should simply knock on the back door of the residence and from there they would be able to access the shop. Technically speaking, the shop, front-door locked, curtains drawn, would be closed. This ploy not only added cream to the takings but also over the years created enormous goodwill and customer loyalty.

As Mary's four children, Leslie, Ernest, Stanley and Lucy each came of age, deemed to be ten by Mary, answering the back door to late shopping customers became their job. Years later it also became my job once I attained my seniority. The sense of worth in wrapping bread, bagging cakes, slicing fruit cake and working the till was quickly obliterated by the intrusion of a regular stream of customers until 8 p.m. and sometimes as late as 10 p.m. You didn't dawdle towards a demanding knock if Nanna King was nearby unless you wanted a cuff to the ear as a forcible reminder that in her day they ran to the door in case the customer lost patience and left.

Les sat down to dinner that evening in a pall of silence he knew could only be the pre-curser to the coming confrontation. Before he had cleaned his plate King's Bakery was back on the agenda and he had again agreed to meet Mr Cleland. This time he did not change his mind and Deborah had to eat Mary's humble pie yet again.

On 17 August, 1924, under new management and heavily indebted to the Bank of New South Wales, the Rob Roy Bakery reopened for business. There was a minor glitch when it was realised there was no money to put in the till to begin the day's trading. Undeterred, Mary telephoned her new friend who despatched the bank's junior with five pounds in change. He had his money back at the end of the day.

Within five days of reopening, LES KING: BAKER appeared on the shop front, the first of countless injustices, symbolic and real, over forty-one years that failed to formally acknowledge the real founder and business driver of King's Bakery. But that was the deal and, anyway, appearances were largely irrelevant to this mistress of substance over style. She had achieved her objective of establishing what she was certain would lead to the financial security of her family. As usual she was right.

She told me some time later during one of our many discussions (she was not one for small talk) that her ambitions for developing King's Bakery into a bigger and more successful business were routinely undermined by my grandfather's and my father's conservatism. On one of those occasions, wishing to provide her with some idea of how much I admired her, I asked her why she seemed to be so good at getting things right when others didn't. She thought for a minute and then said words to the effect, 'if you are clear as to what you want to achieve and you set about doing that honestly (in expressing that word she always emphasised the 'h' as in honey) and with determination then more often than not you will succeed.'

'So, not always,' I said, a bit disappointed. I was looking for certainty, a guaranteed formula for success.

'No, not always, but it is better that way isn't it because otherwise if you could be certain about what was going to happen then life wouldn't be so interesting would it and you wouldn't have the satisfaction of finding another way if the first one doesn't work.'

On another occasion, during one of our philosophical discussions, she provided her greatest piece of advice. 'Find out what you believe in Ray and use that to guide you for the rest of your life. And till your dying day, stick to that view no matter what.' In my final year in Hamilton, Nanna King had upped the ante on philosophical discussions. She was still willing me to be destined for great things and she was going to leave no stone unturned in influencing that outcome.

As the years rolled on King's Bakery not only achieved increasing financial success but King's Corner also became one of Hamilton's established landmarks and a favoured meeting spot for sporting teams and anyone else. During my high school years, although King's Bakery was only one of three bakeries in the town, one in five Hamiltonians who were of school age or above consumed a King's pie or pasty every day, three hundred and sixty-five times a year. The business was sold to a large flour miller in 1966 and almost fifty years later is still called King's Bakery.

¶

Ern King and family returned to 43 Alexandra Parade towards the end of my grade two year. It placed me a further three blocks from the primary school, requiring me to amend my travel arrangements and become a commuter via the local bus service, known to all of us as the 'penny tacker'. It was a bus that had no seats. It wasn't until some years later I realised buses were supposed to have seats. The fare was a penny (one cent) irrespective of the distance travelled. It took me a while to get the hang of public transport in Hamilton and I quickly learned that shedding tears when things went wrong was a less than successful ploy. You sank or swam depending on your own efforts. The timetable was variable, there were no designated getting on or off points and the bus driver stopped when he saw you, or not, his state of mind often the deciding factor. You only needed to miss the bus a few times to become a proactively alert, determined and in-your-face commuter. Pragmatism and self- reliance were all the go for a six year old in 1945 and parents, like everyone else, were dismissive of complaints.

There was no limit to the number of passengers so by the time we reached school we were packed in like sardines, the smell of unwashed flesh strong in the confines of the vehicle's turbid air. The trip home was always particularly whiffy. Daily bathing was a custom yet to occur for most country kids and even a bath a week was a challenge too difficult for some to overcome, a week's worth of Western District grime and sweat clearly evident. Those of us who did manage a couple of baths a week still made a contribution given our objective to make our underwear and socks last at least a week. Often we had to beat our socks against the back of a chair to soften them up before putting them on.

The penny tacker was my daily school transport until the fourth grade when I was presented with a new Rainbow two-wheeler bicycle for my eighth birthday. The multi-coloured Rainbow was not a particularly cool looking conveyance, no doubt the reason for the almost universal derision the bike's appearance generated and probably the reason I never saw another Rainbow on Hamilton's streets. Or anywhere else for that matter.

¶

Corporal punishment for kids in Hamilton in those times was a fact of life. 'Spare the rod and spoil the child' remained the universal catchcry. Dad was particularly adept, with left or right hand, at the curling cuff to the back of the head. Any attempt at evading one cuff merely resulted in another coming at you from the other side, generally with a bit more grunt behind it.

Dad was more than handy with his hands, having at one time held the Western District heavyweight boxing title. The bout had been sponsored by King's Bakery, apparently the only time the title was contested. Nanna evidently thought that having a titleholder in the family would be good for business, the referee's decision taken for granted given that the prospect of defeat was not an acceptable option. Nanna King was adamant that one of Melbourne's leading boxing trainers, who had observed Dad's victory that evening and who at the time had the world rated light-heavyweight Ambrose Palmer in his stable, believed he could turn Dad into the heavyweight champion of the world. But Nanna wouldn't allow her favourite son to live in Melbourne with 'that lot'. She also boasted Geelong Football Club had left no stone unturned in attempting to recruit Dad in 1933 and again in 1934 but Nanna insisted he was needed in the bakehouse. From all accounts, Dad was a strong mark and a hit 'em hard and hit 'em low ruckman in the Jack Dyer mould. In the main, according to my informants, those that were hit generally stayed hit.

I was introduced to tripe, boiled cow's stomach, for dinner. It is unappetisingly white in colour, virtually tasteless and usually, as it was then, covered in equally tasteless white sauce. I was aghast at what it looked like and even more aghast at what it was likely to taste like. I suspect my facial rejection of this love offering by my mother started the ball rolling.

'Just try it,' instructed Dad.

I carefully scraped the glutinous, now cold, white sauce from the smallest piece I could find. Gingerly forking the repulsive piece of offal into my mouth I could not prevent my face registering a general feeling of revulsion, the tripe feeling and tasting like a piece of greasy, slightly burned rubber although I had never actually consumed rubber before, slightly burned or otherwise. Out snaked Dad's left hand. Undeterred by the blow, I continued staring at my plate and slowly poked my tongue out at the offensive mess. Again out snaked the ex-boxer's left hand, striking not once but this time twice in quick succession, jab, jab, the boxer's staple lead-up. Mum's contribution to the debate was the time's stock standard, 'the starving millions in China would love to eat it.' Dad threw up his arms in frustration and probably remorse (he told me later he didn't like tripe either) and stalked out of the kitchen. Realising our stand-off was at an end, I made myself scarce. Later, Mum came outside and surreptitiously gave me a piece of cake. Both were trying to square off. Fortunately for all concerned tripe was now off the menu.

¶

Someone must have given me a soft toy rabbit, light blue in colour. I used it as a football. Being heavier at the bottom it was ideally weighted for a little kid to learn the process of kicking an Aussie Rules football. This particularly applied to the drop kick. The drop kick, long disappeared from the game, not only required perfect timing (the football needing to hit the ground only a fraction of a second before being contacted by the foot) but also a perfect ball drop angle. A player of class always used the smooth travelling but still risky drop kick whereas others used the 'cow-yard' or 'mongrel' punt that ducked, floated and swerved and was difficult to mark. The drop punt was yet to make its universal appearance. It took me some time, in fact many weeks of what must have been disciplined and despairing perseverance, to master the coordination required for the dropkick's difficult technique. Once that was mastered our back yard became the Melbourne Cricket Ground.

'This is Merv Williams your sports-caller, live from the MCG,' intoned the imaginary radio, in between waves of static. Merv, who had a plethora of droll similes and metaphors to sprinkle on his commentary, continued: 'The siren sounds, Umpire Blackburn bounces the ball, King soars majestically into the air and palms the ball straight down the throat of King who has timed his run to perfection. King streaks away from the pack and at full speed launches a long, raking drop kick to the goal square. King rises spectacularly above the pack. YYYeeesss, the Carlton supporters roar, as he grasps the football in his vice-like grip. King lines up the goals (the pole of the rotary clothes line) and again kicks truly (with an inventive drop punt). With King in such good form, Collingwood is like the boy who fell out of the balloon. They're just not in it,' reports Williams, delivering another of his famous 'Mervisms'.

That day, Mum had the bed sheets drying at the Melbourne Cricket Ground and with me having naturally ignored her first warning one of the sheets now carried an almost photocopied imprint of my damp and grubby 'football'. I wasn't particularly concerned because I was sure Mum fully understood the training intensity required for me to eventually become a Carlton player and I had little doubt she was in full agreement that not a minute should be lost in that endeavour. Occasionally, I wondered what I would do if my football career didn't work out but any thought along those lines was generally dismissed as an idea too painful to contemplate or, better still, an event most unlikely to occur.

The back door banged followed by a stentorian, 'come here!' It looked as though there may have been a serious breakdown in communications. Dad had not only grown to Goliath-like proportions but was ominously wielding his nasty looking (rifle) bullet belt with what looked like very dangerous intent. I was not wrong. Grasped by the scruff of the neck I was spun around and held at arm's length to maximise his leverage as Dad whacked away at the backs of my legs. Each strike was accompanied by, 'I've,' grunt, 'told you,' grunt, 'before,' grunt, 'not to,' grunt, etc. etc. As he paused to rest he added, 'next time I'll use the (shotgun) cartridge belt,' which was a much bigger and heavier weapon. I thought the current one was more than enough, thank you very much. My cries were impressive but the neighbours' heads hadn't appeared above the side fences to observe the fun. They apparently felt they didn't need a personal viewing to get the full effect.

¶

Corporal punishment was not limited to the domestic scene. At Hamilton Primary School the strap was the persuader used to guide our educational development. From year two onwards the strap was the standard response not only to misbehaviour but also to poor academic performance. The strap was a piece of stiff leather approximately half a centimetre thick, five centimetres wide and around sixty centimetres long. Male teachers each had their own strap and were rated by the kids on how effectively they could employ it. The punishment was referred to as getting the cuts. In my six years at primary school I had a male teacher for only one year and that was Doug Stevenson in grade three. Three times I copped one cut and on one more memorable occasion, two. Doug was a devotee of the strap and his delivery particularly highly rated, his swing reaching all the way back to his calf before the strap made its impressive, whistling overarm descent.

The cut was delivered across the palm of the hand. Minor infractions earned one cut and major transgressions earned up to an Education Department regulated maximum of six, although the heaviest penalty I can recall having seen was four. The strap was not restricted to behavioural infractions. It was also used as a teaching aid and Doug was always even-handed in his sentencing. A poor result on one of Doug's tests generally earned at least one cut but if a really smart kid received nine out of ten on a test when Doug felt he should have scored ten then he copped one as well.

The punishment was always meted out in public at the front of the class. Ghouls to a man, we took vicarious and bloodthirsty pleasure in the process, the recipient earning respect both from Doug and the class if he took the punishment stony-faced and, moreover, delayed rubbing his hand until he returned to his desk. Doug believed strongly in encouraging macho responses to life's difficulties and in the main his teaching of manly values was highly effective. Anyone trying to pull his hand away or who cried was not only treated with humiliating scorn but also copped another one for being cowardly. There is always something in the misfortune of others that does not displease us — 'give him another one sir,' we would loudly and happily chorus.

Doug, a colourful character, was unpredictable, funny and different. In year two we all hoped we would get him the following year. He ruled like the mad Roman emperor Caligula, funny one minute and in a foul purple-faced rage the next.

He was a keen cricket fan and had us memorise the names of the sixteen Australian players selected to play England in the 1946 Ashes series. Doug outlined the engaging principles behind the success of the classic batsman; the logic of playing a straight bat rather than our favoured stroke, the cross bat slog towards mid-wicket. His sensible advice was that a straight bat (vertical) covered around seventy-five per cent of the stumps area whereas a cross bat (horizontal) concealed a much smaller share of the bowler's target. The protection of the stumps was sacrosanct in Doug's world. But to us kids the practice of stonewalling made for unlikely heroes and was starkly inconsistent with his football rev up address to 'remember, boys, faint heart never won fair lady,' despite its highly doubtful providence as we learned later in life.

My clearest memory of Doug is from Empire Day 1946. This was the anachronistic day set aside to commemorate the previous glory of a declining, frail, but still existing British Empire, now called the Commonwealth of Nations. On that morning we had all been issued with a small cardboard British flag, the Union Jack, the outcome of a merciless public relations campaign by some organisation called Friends of the Crown. I had creatively attached my flag to the highly chewed and splintered top of my wooden handled pen, the nib inserted in a ball of modelling plasticine slightly smaller than that of a tennis ball. It rested next to a piece of equipment that has since disappeared into education history, the ink-well, which sat in its prescribed hole in the desk I shared with Peter Humphries. Peter Humphries was a small kid, even smaller than me, a memorable fact in itself. But he was far better known for arriving at school each morning with his strikingly pale blonde hair set like concrete, the comb rows as neat as the lines in a notebook. The secret was a sugar solution invented by his father that ensured at the end of each day the comb rows were just as precise as when Peter arrived each morning.

Doug Stevenson was a great prowler, regularly patrolling the aisles between the rows of double desks looking, avidly we believed, for punishment excuses. One of his favourite acts when such action was deemed appropriate was to slam the heads of two boys together. It was quite painful. The sound was confusing and a common topic of conversation. To the onlookers it sounded like a dull thud but to the participants it always felt like a sharp crack. On this day of prowling Doug paused next to our desk. With only a couple of minutes to go to the end of the day Humph and I thought we were dead out of luck. Flinching in anticipation, we instinctively leaned towards each other, the standard practice for minimising the velocity of Doug's double head slam. But to our great surprise and even greater relief Doug merely snatched up my design piece, leaned back as if he were delivering a cricket ball from the boundary and hurled it towards the open window on the far side of the classroom. It didn't come even close. The plasticine missile exploded through the adjacent window pane with the sound of a rifle shot. As if portending the future in store for the British Empire, the Union Jack dislodged itself from the missile's shaft and in slow motion fluttered in an inauspicious death spiral to the classroom floor where it settled and lay still. The silence in the room was broken only by the peal of the school bell to end the day's proceedings. Doug quietly dismissed the class to a collective sigh of relief, the Union Jack subjected to the humiliation of being stomped on by the grubby footwear of a dozen snot-nosed, ignorant Grade three boys eager to exit the classroom. My classmates suggested I should sue Doug for the cost of the plasticine.

¶

In 1948, Don Bradman, the greatest Test batsman the world has seen, played his last Test innings. It was against England at the Oval. 'The Don', as he was called, marched in his unique bustling style to the crease to a standing ovation from the capacity crowd as well as generous applause from his on-field opponents. His batting average stood at 101.3, the highest of any cricketer in the history of Test cricket. He needed to score a mere four runs in his last innings to maintain a batting average in excess of 100. He didn't get them. Followed by a collective gasp, then dead silence, he was bowled second ball by England leg spinner Eric Hollies — out for a duck and his all-time average reduced to a seemingly disappointing 99.94.

That same week, the Gray Street primary school boys in grades four to six marched in formation, three abreast, a distance of approximately three kilometres, to the Old Cricket Ground for house football, the surroundings far less salubrious than those enjoyed by the Don for his swan song. It was a Friday. The Old Cricket Ground was on an ancient flood plain adjacent to the local creek. We entered through a small, partly fenced, grassy common used occasionally by neighbours to graze a few head of cattle and then descended through a line of planted oak trees down the steep, grassy and often slippery slope to the playing field. Like most of the playing fields in Hamilton (with the exception of Melville Oval) it was little more than a cow paddock, potholed and waterlogged in winter and without a blade of green grass in summer.

On this particular Friday, as the formation swung past the quietly grazing cattle, sixth grader, 'Joey' Pelchen (all the Pelchen boys were called Joey), front and centre of the marching column and never known for his intelligence, started flapping his red tie in an attempt to attract the beasts' attention. We all knew that bulls, particularly those of Spanish descent, would charge at anything red being waved in front of them. Those kids with an article of clothing even remotely red followed suit. The four escorting teachers, particularly those on the cattle side of the column, issued predictably harmless threats but a voice from the ranks yelled, 'don't worry sir, they're only cows.' We also knew cows were not supposed to be riled by anything red.

Even those kids without any red clothing were now flapping anything they could lay their hands on. Others hooted a challenging, 'charge, charge, (ya bastards)' in the direction of the startled animals. The cattle, disturbed in their grazing, trembled and stared wide eyed at this waving, laughing, hooting column of kids. They suddenly charged, or at least seemed to. Our previously tight formation exploded into a hundred and twenty-four screaming fragments, all trying to run flat out and look backwards at the same time. Being on the opposite side to the cattle and near one of the area's few fences I thought the kaleidoscopic explosion of panic stricken kids one of the funniest things I had seen, particularly after I had reached safety on the other side of the conveniently located fence.

The deathly silent aftermath saw every available tree branch and dried water course inhabited by those kids who had not out-distanced the still trembling cattle. Fatty Lambert, who was dangerously stupid as well as fat, had flattened himself on the ground in the idle belief that the cattle wouldn't see him. The incident was reported in the *Hamilton Spectator*, which declared the beasts were cows, a report we were all gleefully able to refute as unadulterated bullshit.

¶

Mum was a member of the Church of Christ whereas Dad's side of the family was supposedly Baptist, but there was no supporting evidence to suggest that the King family belonged to any institution that was even remotely religious.

The Church of Christ in Hamilton was housed in a timber dwelling without a steeple and paled into insignificance compared to the grand, imposing and magnificently steepled bluestone edifices of the Catholic Church, the Church of England and the Presbyterian Church, each of which had been sited on the highest ground available at the time. Even the mad Methodists had a far better church than ours, a church at least built of bricks. With the possible exception of the Baptists, who also worshipped in modest surroundings, everyone else felt sorry for us.

Mum insisted I attend Sunday school in the vain belief that it might teach me the error of my ways. This was a 2.30 pm commitment which involved Sunday best clothes and shiny shoes, a commitment that started when I was seven and sorely inconvenienced my social objectives. Nevertheless, I did enjoy the annual picnics where I usually won the footrace prize despite, or perhaps because of, the unreliable handicapping system.

I knew everybody at Sunday school and they knew me. For better or for worse, it was a family and we all loved one another, or at least professed to. But there were some special friends. There was Lenny Martin, notable for being a spectacular and acrobatic mark of the football and, with his unique round arm action, a very fast if erratic bowler of a cricket ball. There was also his younger brother, Charlie, who had never done anything memorable other than in 1949 defecate in an astonishing manner in full view of most of the young attendees at the annual Sunday school picnic at Byaduk.

Byaduk, around twenty kilometres south of Hamilton, is situated on an old lava flow. Millions of years earlier, Mount Nepean, a nearby extinct volcano (which we regularly inspected for ominous wisps of smoke) had spewed molten lava, hot rock and volcanic ash over more than a thousand square kilometres of Victoria's western district, infusing the region's soil with unbounded fertility.

The village of Byaduk is, or at least was at the time, notable for three things; the sea of scotch thistles and ferns that covered the area like a network of swaying multi-layered blankets, the snakes that sunned themselves on the rocky outcrops; and last but certainly not least, the most beautiful village cricket ground you were likely to see.

Bordered by a burbling, pebble filled stream and evergreen weeping willows, it was peaceful, green and sleepy.

In Byaduk's ancient, long condemned and crumbling bluestone flour mill Lennie's brother, Charlie, shimmied along a sagging beam twenty feet above the ground in preparation for his infamous act. For the open mouthed audience at ground level Charlie's rumbling bowels presaged a sudden evacuation in both senses of the word as his particularly nasty dose of diarrhoea exploded to all points of the compass. One horrified but highly observant attendee, apparently worried about Charlie's medical status, whispered in hushed, concerned tones to nobody in particular, 'Jesus, he's pissing out his arse,' before making his hasty exit.

There were also the three Dennett brothers who were memorable, as were the Pelchen, Agnew and Wishart boys, for carrying the same nickname. In this case it was 'Woolly' (a peculiarly Hamilton phenomenon) and each had the curious but much esteemed ability to fart in the most spectacular fashion, on demand and without apparent effort. But what the Dennett brothers were really good at was the ability to fight. Their father suffered an alcohol related brain problem and had developed the nasty habit of wanting to beat one of them up when he got home from the pub, so they made sure they were not around after he'd popped down to the boozer for a 'quick one'.

The word was that they had been taught to fight by their mother who could evidently go a bit and was something of a hard case herself. For good reason she felt some instruction in the art of pugilism for her sons might come in handy. Rumour had it that she had broken the nose of one of Hamilton's 'finest' who had attempted to arrest her husband for being drunk and disorderly. For patently obvious reasons the constable never brought the case to court. Despite their tendency towards violence, the Dennetts were all good fun and like the rest of my friends didn't want to be there.

Life was no treat for pious, well-meaning Margaret Mihill either. Margaret was our teenage, forever jovial, butterball church leader (why are they always so jolly?) who, in the cause of the greater good, tried with little success to make light of our smart arse, ambiguous and sacrilegious comments.

There was also Johnny Elston whose devout mother sought out Mum for solace explaining in between sobs that she had found Johnny in their lounge room clapping his hands, punching the air and singing 'hallelujah' as if enjoying a vigorous religious revival meeting. Johnny had won the lucrative first prize in that week's Tattersalls lottery. Surprisingly, this was not good news. Not only was gambling a sin considered worse than death by Johnny's parents (although not by Johnny) but they had taken a vow of poverty and been scrimping and saving to provide Johnny with an appropriate nest egg for his future.

We all enjoyed Boys Club on Tuesday evenings, a twenty-minute walk which I did both ways, alone, and in the dark, albeit with the aid of a torch. It wasn't that parents in those days were indifferent to their child's well-being by any means. It was simply that they believed everything would turn out OK in the end. And in the main they were right.

The Church of Christ took great pride in 'saving' people by getting them to commit their life to Jesus Christ. The cleansing process was by way of being dunked in a small wading pool positioned between the pulpit area where we all performed on concert night and the pews occupied by our parents. The annual concert was a favourite 'saving' night. However, most of us knew that those who lined up to be saved were invariably local deadbeats or their kids and we were very suspicious of the recruiting process. Rarely, if ever, were these saved souls seen in or around the church after the first couple of weeks. But as it was a sin to criticise your preacher, at least out loud, we held our counsel.

My successful argument as to why it was time for me to do something else on Sunday afternoons was based on my well-rehearsed outrage at not having won the best attendance prize in 1952. I had attended Sunday school fifty-one times for the year and provided the church with a note from Mum which verified my 'attendance' on the fifty-second Sunday. Based on the prize's ground rules, travelling on a Sunday counted as an attendance. To make matters worse the best attendance prize had gone to red haired, freckle faced, Margaret Hadden, the daughter of one of the church elders, who had again beaten me to win that year's western district bible competition prize.

Margaret soon gained an unsavoury reputation — promoted mainly by me — for not only consorting with boys old enough to have left school but in particular for granting her favours to vile Catholic boys. Mum, being rabidly anti-Catholic, seemed too easily convinced. I suspect she felt she had done well to get my religious education this far.

As far as religion was concerned, Hamilton was a town not much different from those in Northern Ireland in the 1930s. It was divided into two bellicose and bigoted camps, the Roman Catholics and the Protestants. The Catholics, who had drifted north from their original beachhead in Port Fairy, had gradually infiltrated the region's fertile, well watered flatlands. It was an incursion not appreciated by the largely Protestant business community or by the landed gentry who concentrated on growing the world's fattest sheep and its finest wool. This religious rivalry, which had existed since the earliest times, reached its feverish zenith in February 1948 when Fred Fanning was appointed playing coach of the Hamilton Football Club in controversial circumstances.

In 1947, the club had languished at the bottom of the ladder until mid-way through the season when new playing Coach, Jack O'Keefe not only revived it but miraculously took it to an unlikely 1947 Western District League premiership. To make it an even better story the winning behind was kicked in the dying moments of the game by winger Ted Kenna, local hero and Victoria Cross winner in New Guinea in 1945.

Ted was the ninetieth Australian to receive the British Empire's highest bravery award and one of only twenty recipients from the Second World War. He was rewarded for kicking the winning behind by being given the dubious honour of becoming the inaugural permanent caretaker of Melville Oval, the scene of his greatest moment of football glory.

We used to follow Ted around the oval firing questions at him while he moved the hoses — 'come on Ted, tell us how many Japs you killed that day?' Or, 'where did you shoot 'em Ted?' But Ted always shrugged off his Victoria Cross exploit as just another day at the office. He told us he must have been pissed at the time because he couldn't remember much about it.

There were two compelling reasons for the 1948 controversy. Fred Fanning was a giant of a man, built like a very large refrigerator and a superstar footballer. He held the record for the most goals kicked in a single game in the Victorian Football League — eighteen for Melbourne against St Kilda in 1945 — and had won the VFL goal kicking award in 1945, 1946 and 1947. Fred had married a Hamilton girl and was keen to settle in Hamilton and cash in on his reputation by becoming playing coach of the town's football club. In those days coaching a country team was the only way for a VFL footballer to make any real money.

The football club committee (Dad was a board member, a position at the time known as a 'committeeman') felt it had little choice but to sack Jack and replace him with Fred as it couldn't afford both. To rub salt into the wound Fred Fanning's fee was set at the seemingly outrageous level of twelve pounds a week, the highest sum so far paid to an Aussie Rules footballer in the history of the game. Fred had received three pounds a week playing for Melbourne and the premiership coach's fee the previous year had been five pounds a week.

The inconvenient and damaging issue was that O'Keefe was a Catholic whereas Fred Fanning was a Protestant. The decision was seen by the town's Catholics as a slight not only on O'Keefe's amazing and admirable feat the previous year but also on his Irish heritage. There's no doubt about the Irish. They're generally laughing, crying or fighting. They also love a melancholy song. It was therefore with no great surprise that all hell broke loose. A breakaway club, to be named

Hamilton Imperials, was formed with Jack O'Keefe at the helm, the Catholic players left the club and the state's most bitter rivalry became set in stone. The ferocity of the religious rivalry between these two clubs was truly something to behold.

There was to be nobody I hated more than Adolph Hitler, Judas or the members of the Collingwood Football Club but the Hamilton Imperials came very close. The feud, as feuds often do, turned out to be a lot of wasted energy. The two clubs amalgamated in 2014.

¶

The Saturday afternoon movie matinee, initially screened at the Hamilton town hall but later graduating to the newly constructed purpose built Regent Theatre further down Brown Street, was a special time for us kids. From the age of eight until we turned fourteen and started playing afternoon sport we were transported for two and a half hours to a fantasy land where the good guys (with the white hats) always won. We learned how criminals (with the black hats) operated, how cops caught them, how wars were fought and won and how history was made in America's Wild West. We hated the singing cowboys Gene Autrey and Roy Rogers as well as any kissing but loved the action movies and the weekly serials which ended each week in foreshadowed disaster but always resumed the following week in laughably stupid redemption.

The main feature occupied the second session during which we licked the ice creams and sucked the lollies purchased during intermission, each determined to make them last longer than the kid sitting next to him. The poorer kids and often the not so poorer kids chewed the second-hand and sometimes third- or even fourth-hand chewing gum stuck to the underside of every seat.

The intermission sustenance was usually procured at Henderson's milk bar, a full block further down Brown Street rather than at the Regent Theatre's kiosk, the extra distance being rendered redundant by Mr Henderson's two highly attractive daughters who worked behind the counter. The theatre's kiosk was run by a doddering and endearingly small couple who looked as though they were the parents of the theatre's equally minute proprietor, a man we all called Pinhead.

¶

Pinhead's parents, or rather their business, was another reason for making the trek to Henderson's Milk Bar. The kiosk's assorted sweets and ice creams looked as though they hadn't been renewed, or sold for that matter, in a very long time.

Pinhead was not only the proprietor, ticket seller and chief projectionist but he also policed the auditorium with his powerful flashlight, regularly ejecting over noisy kids on to the Brown Street footpath. Admission to Pinhead's theatre for matinees was threepence (three cents) for the five rows closest to the screen, sixpence for the rest of downstairs and a shilling for upstairs. Most theatres of the day had an upstairs with carpeted floors and more luxurious seats that were less likely to be dislodged from their worn fittings and crash to the floor to the emotional and physical discomfort of the occupant and roars of raucous laughter from those nearby. You soon learned to sit extremely still in a downstairs seat at Saturday matinees in Hamilton.

As soon as the theatre's lights started to dim the heads of the kids in the first five rows suddenly disappeared and reformed as a silent human chain of nose to tail bodies that slid smoothly under the demarcation ropes and continued up both aisles before bobbing up in any empty sixpenny seat that might be available. There was a small window of opportunity while Pinhead was setting up the reels in the projection room. The interlopers often had to make do with the unpopular empty seats directly underneath the upstairs balcony. These were subject to the near certainty of drips of highly sticky substances or rapidly descending four-a-penny gumballs, particularly after half time.

During the polio epidemic of the late 1940s parents were encouraged to keep their kids from congregating in places such as movie theatres despite the incongruous fact we were all congregating at school for five days out of every seven. If that advice made any sense it turned out that attending the Saturday afternoon matinee was the safest place to be. Polio was so rife and such a popular topic of conversation at the time that newspaper articles provided useful tips on how to reduce risks for children, including avoiding the gaining of new friends. One Saturday during the epidemic I counted a total of eight kids in a theatre with a capacity of eighteen hundred, a pretty impressive capacity for a town of less than 8000 inhabitants. But in those days, apart from the local dance and Saturday afternoon footy, going to the movies was the only game in town. The movies, or what we called 'the pictures', was such an important social event that families had permanent seat bookings, adult males wore suits and ties and their partners wore their best frocks. It was the weekly opportunity to see and be seen. The movies were so popular that the Regent Theatre was the source of weekly entertainment for around half the town's entire adult population.

¶

Three other kids around my age lived in Alexandra Parade.

Teddy and Jimmy Stokie lived at number twenty-nine, seven doors due south from our house. Teddy was a month older than me and Jimmy nearly three years older. Jimmy introduced Teddy and me to the study of anatomy. Having recently achieved puberty, Jimmy proudly presented his naked erection at every opportunity, which was generally on a daily basis. This was invariably accompanied by a vivid commentary and practical demonstration explaining what he would do with his newly acquired instrument when the occasion arose. Given that Teddy's and my age were still denominated by a single digit, Jimmy's pronouncements were of little more than academic interest. We merely rolled our eyes and suggested he might carry out that particular ambition on himself — one of the more colourfully creative phrases I had picked up from the bread makers.

Teddy was my best friend for the first part of my conscious life. Being sports mad, our activities comprised endless hours of backyard cricket, kick to kick on the gravel roadway (cars were a rarity, most people in Hamilton rode their bikes to work), our own version of fire brigade demonstrations, bike races and death defying canoe races in or on anything that floated in the deep open drain dividing the Alexander Parade north south carriageways. Also popular were running races and time trials up and down Alexandra Parade, the timing mechanism invariably causing heated debate, and occasionally a marathon run to Pedrina airport and back, our performances only slightly impaired by the work overalls and heavy leather boots that all kids wore at that time. The airport was little more than a large paddock with a windsock and a corrugated iron shed that saw five landings and take-offs a week by Reg Ansett's Douglas DC3 airliners plying the Hamilton to Melbourne run. Later Teddy and I learned to play tennis, although with a slightly different objective given that we had made the important discovery that girls played tennis.

Teddy's father had landed on the beach at Gallipoli in the First World War and survived that disaster despite suffering a back wound ('show us where that Turk shot you again, Mr Stokie').

I often had Sunday lunch at Teddy's house under the piercing gaze of a print of the Australian Army's most revered officer at the time, Major General Thomas Blamey, later Field Marshal Sir Thomas Blamey, who had been Mr Stokie's commanding officer. Teddy's mother was not a great cook or, if she were, then Sunday must have been her bad day. Sunday lunch was always roast lamb and without exception was invariably burned black.

'It's a bit burned,' she would say apologetically each week, 'but I scraped off the burned part,' overlooking the fact that was generally most of it.

Mrs Stokie had a wood stove with no temperature control but she never seemed to learn from the previous week's debacle. You had to soak the lamb in mint sauce to cover the carbon taste. Nevertheless, Teddy's mother's accompanying vegetables — peas to which she had added a sprinkle of sugar and crunchy double roasted roast potatoes — were first class and worth the lunch on their own. The most disconcerting thing was not the charred leg of lamb but the positioning of the dining table. Directly above it was a light fitting from which hung a ribbon of sticky fly paper encrusted with the black bodies of long deceased flies, the odd bumble bee and on at least one occasion a very colourful and large wasp, known to us all as a horse stinger. It was shaped like a small torpedo, had large, transparent, stained glass wings and when on the move made a noise like a small chainsaw.

Mrs Stokie talked a lot and Mr Stokie not so much. Mr Stokie appeared to have three major objectives in life; to ignore Mrs Stokie, to successfully produce his weekly batch of ginger beer and to prevent the garden pests from invading his strawberry patch in summer.

'How did you go this week, Mr Stokie,' I would dutifully enquire each Sunday.

Mr Stokie would proudly announce something like, 'well, only three bottles (of the usual twelve bottle batch) exploded this week,' which would rate as a good result given the dodgy yeast Mr Stokie used, 'and only one snail got through my defensive perimeter,' which was an even better result because I preferred Mr Stokie's strawberries to his ginger beer by quite a wide margin.

Teddy and Jimmy Stokie were always looking for new adventures and extended that thought to earning a healthy ten shillings a week by way of morning paper delivery rounds in the dark and on their bikes. Much to my invisible delight, my parents flatly refused to entertain the idea of me emulating my friends' efforts in the depths of winter at 6 a.m. When I reported this apparently disappointing piece of news I was met with sympathetic but highly concerned alarm at the limitations my parents were imposing on me. What other grave acts might they be capable of? I nodded my head in grave agreement. In all seriousness, and he was around nine at the time, Teddy pontificated that I was now doomed never to get on in life.

That was the same day that Stokie's dog, Tom, buried his teeth in my knee, presumably the result of having vigorously teased and enraged him the previous day with my cricket bat. Tom must have been a slow thinker because I had been patting him for some minutes as if trying to make up for my previous day's indiscretion. He wagged his tail and was having a wow of a time. I was about to put my face down to his as an ultimate expression of good faith and remorse when Tom eventually remembered he was supposed to be annoyed with me and took a mouthful of my left knee. Honour having been served he gave a woofy bark and started prancing around ready for the next game.

The next day, Tom's more than impressive puncture marks were surrounded by an even more impressive purple bruise, which provided a wonderful opportunity to exhibit my macho credentials by appearing to be completely indifferent to the previous day's trauma. These days, following endless enquiries, Tom would have been despatched to dog heaven for being a danger to the human race. But the sensible and pragmatic view that prevailed at the time was that if you were stupid enough to put yourself in danger by getting close to these almost feral animals then it was your own stupid fault. Dogs could bite kids every day of the week with impunity, which meant dog world was a great place to be.

Hamilton was a town densely populated with vicious, salivating dogs, most of them mongrels. There wasn't a kid I knew who hadn't been bitten at least once, so we all knew the drill. To my recollection this was my fourth. By the time I left primary school I was up to five, suggesting I was either a dog lover or really dumb.

I was quickly reintroduced to the tetanus needle. We all had a great fear of needles because at the time they were used more than once and always stood on the doctor's desk hidden in a milky looking solution before making their terrifying appearance. To make matters worse, the syringes seemed as big as bicycle pumps. In fact, if I remember correctly, they were as big as bicycle pumps. Multiple use caused the needles, always a sinister shade of black, to bend and become progressively blunt. We always knew we were going to get the blunt one which would hurt twice as much. Nevertheless, the tetanus injection was the one we were most prepared to face up to because we knew that if you contracted tetanus you ended up with lockjaw and would never be able to open your mouth. And we all knew if you couldn't open your mouth you couldn't eat, and if you couldn't eat you couldn't shit and if you couldn't shit then you died.

The other thing about dogs at that time was that you saw them humping one another left, right and centre. It must have been another Hamilton phenomenon because after I left Hamilton I did never see the humping thing again. When the promiscuous pair had finished their act –generally surrounded by a young, large and enthusiastic audience — they were for a time stuck together, the heavier dog dragging the other around as they endeavoured to separate themselves. We would all screw up our faces in sympathy, then in unison say something like, 'Jesus, that's not good is it?' On one such occasion Teddy thought he might add a touch of wisdom to the performance (he really did believe he was something of a sage did Teddy). 'You know Kingy that's how babies are made.' I stared at him in disbelief and abject horror. 'Bullshit,' I said, 'my Mum and Dad wouldn't do that.' Teddy might have been wise beyond his years but he certainly had that bit wrong.

During year six my parents and I returned to King's Bakery, swapping houses with Nanna and Pa King and breaking the nexus that had initiated and nurtured my close relationship with Teddy. At high school, Teddy pursued the technical stream that later introduced another fork in the road. We remained good friends (he came to Ballarat with me in year ten for the September holidays) but the serious and intense debates and the visions we shared for our respective futures faded into gradual obscurity as we extended our social networks. And as these things have a habit of turning out, after leaving Hamilton at the end of year twelve, I never saw Teddy again.

Billy Brewster, nicknamed 'Tanker' to some and 'Tonker' to others, lived at the other end of Alexandra Parade less than two hundred metres from the bakery. His house was very old, unpainted, eerily dark inside and hidden from the street by a dense row of rarely trimmed miniature cypress trees. Depressing things are cypress trees. Billy, the youngest of four brothers, was nearly two years older than me. There was no father in attendance. Unconfirmed rumour had it that each of the Brewster boys had different fathers. As Billy's house was close to the bakery I started spending more time with him, being particularly attracted to his backyard with its liberal sprinkling of high bearing fruit trees and a collection of long discarded, grass entangled pieces of machinery and other indiscriminate items of junk.

Unlike Teddy Stokie, Billy Brewster was shy, pudgy, no good at sport, not one of the popular boys and well outside the periphery of the movers and shakers. We played fantasy games among which war stories and cowboys and Indians were particularly popular. Billy played anything as long as it wasn't competitive.

Billy's mother lacked humour and didn't like me all that much. She was invariably dressed in drab black or grey, never wore make-up and her hair was usually done in an untidy bun. She also had moles on her face out of which grew unsightly tufts of grey and black hair. Mrs Brewster may not have looked so good but she was pretty smart and particularly good at crosswords. She didn't try all that hard to hide her feelings about me. Her major criticisms, which she voiced regularly, were that I was opinionated, always wanted my own way and did not appreciate what others did for me, all of which it might be argued carried an element of truth. I must also have been curiously incapable of feeling embarrassment because I kept going to Billy's house and was there most days throughout the year.

Jack was Billy's next eldest brother. He had served in World War Two as a truck driver and was now a carpenter. Having turned up at Billy's house when Billy was not at home — doors in Hamilton were never locked and standard practice was to just walk in — I took one of Billy's many war books from the bookcase and made myself comfortable on the worn couch. Jack wandered in, sat down beside me and began pointing out various things in the book that he knew about from his time in the army. I then felt this hand sliding inside the front of my shorts. Kids didn't wear underpants, at least none that I knew, until we started high school. I said to myself 'what the 'fuck', or words to that effect, and shuffled towards the end of the couch. He shuffled with me. I shuffled some more until I was up against the arm of the couch. This was starting to get serious so I decided to deal with the situation as conveniently as I could and casually, or at least trying for casual, trotted off home.

¶

Milton Thomas was also almost two years older than me and lived in the residence attached to Hamilton Aerated Waters, a soft drink factory directly across the road from King's Bakery. Milton obviously had a close relationship with his mother because after I told him about Jack's unwelcome attentions he said without a moment's hesitation that his mother had already told him Jack was a 'homo'. I didn't know exactly what a homo was but I now had a pretty fair idea and in any case Milton quickly filled in any gaps in my knowledge base. I didn't tell Mum or Dad of the episode because I didn't want to be banned from future visits to Tanker's joint. Interestingly, Milton's mother didn't seem to think it necessary to ban Milton from going to Billy's place despite her inside knowledge. Anyway, I made sure that I didn't get caught alone with Jack again.

On that note, Billy had sometimes suggested that if I were interested he would introduce me to a new game he liked called 'blackfellas'. I had no idea what he was talking about but had a strong feeling it was a game I didn't want to play. Milton was later to put me straight on that as well. I always ignored Billy's comment and not being the insistent type he never followed up. I was not particularly fazed by the fact that Billy, like his brother, was a bit different, particularly as it was Billy's back yard as much as Billy that I found attractive. Nevertheless, as our common interests begin to diverge,

I gradually saw less and less of him. Later, when I was indulging my obsession with sport, Billy was pursuing square dancing and ballroom dancing.

Milton Thomas attended Hamilton Boys' College, the brother school to Alexandra Girls' College. Although the school was very much the poor relation its buildings were beautifully historic, in particular having an impressive bell tower. During the depression years following the 1929 stockmarket crash the school had fallen on hard times and never really recovered. In 1950 less than one hundred and fifty boys attended across all twelve grades. Like the girls at Alexandra College most of the attendees were boarders destined to return to their grazier parents' properties. Academia it was not. Nevertheless, Hamilton Boys' College achieved one claim to fame with the arrival of Harry Zachariah as principal in 1954. Harry had bowled left arm spin for Victoria before the war and had two daughters worthy of attention as well.

Milton was a child of the senses and seemed to be remarkably familiar with every intoxicant known to man. He introduced me to the joys of smoking and attempted, unsuccessfully as it turned out, to teach me the drawback. He confirmed my suspicions that he had 'gone the whole way' with Billy but said he had no further interest in that particular department. Among other things, Milton was an enthusiastic petrol sniffer, regularly sticking his nose into the petrol tank of one of the soft drink factory's two delivery trucks. He tried to get me interested but after one hesitant attempt I thought he was out of his mind which, upon reflection, was probably the reason he did it.

One of Milton's early attractions was the supply of hot magazines that his father kept hidden in his bedroom in a secret spot known only to himself, Milton, half the boys at Hamilton College and of course me. We often wondered what Mr Thomas made of his obviously well-handled magazines and whether he was aware they were being enjoyed by a much wider audience. They were much juicier than the monthly magazines *Man Junior* and *Cavalcade* available from McCasker's Newsagency and with which most of us had quickly become strikingly familiar. The arrival of each new edition of these magazines at McCasker's seemed to correspond with a monthly spike in literary interest among the town's early adolescents. Each of the magazines had one and, if you were extremely lucky, two artistic 'life, by Everard' studies, featuring a nude woman from the waist up trying to get her bottom half to face backwards. These two magazines introduced us to the wonders of female anatomy and for years had been passed from grubby hand to grubby hand in Hamilton High's junior boys' locker room, generating indescribable and heated pleasure. But Milton's father's magazines were something else. He certainly hadn't bought them at McCasker's. They must have been good because Brasso McGregor gravely remarked one day with a straight face, successfully stifling any hint of enthusiasm — something Brasso was seriously good at — that, 'frankly I find them quite disturbing.' But despite promising stirrings I had not quite reached that stage at which every drop of blood in my body would suddenly rush to the pelvic region.

Milton and I regularly climbed one of the several mountains of empty wooden boxes used for storing and delivering the soft drinks and there we would reconfigure the boxes into a cleverly designed and constructed hut, complete with roof. With a supply of his mother's cigarettes, his father's magazines, soft drinks from the factory and cakes purloined from the bakery, we would put our feet up and agree that life in the fast lane was pretty good. We projected an aura of savoir faire as we leaned back, hands behind heads, attempting to blow another smoke ring through the previous one. He was good at it. I was the one doing the attempting. Milton was also the world's top authority on sexual matters, at least as far as I was concerned. However, as he was only twelve at the time, his knowledge was probably a little less encyclopaedic than I gave him credit for. He was adamant that girls not only enjoyed furtive glances at their tits but also were not averse to the accidently-on-purpose brush by 'feel' that he swore he had enjoyed hundreds of times. Despite Milton's experiments with Billy he declared his favourite subject was girls and we shared our colourful views on every female of interest. Often these were views our elders may not have warmly applauded.

¶

The soft drink factory's bottling equipment sometimes had a quality control problem, either injecting too much carbon dioxide or not enough and thus producing rejects that could not be sold. Those with too much gas were of particular interest, veritable hand grenades. We would shake the grenade vigorously above our head (just in case it exploded before release) and then lob it on to the concrete gutter adjacent to the wall of the factory. The resultant explosions were more than impressive, slivers of glass soaring as high as the roof of the double-storey building. Fortunately, God was always with us.

He was also with us on another day.

The soft drink delivery trucks were fuelled from a supply of forty-four-gallon metal drums stacked in one of the factory's wide open sheds. The petrol sniffer loosened the cap on one of the drums and proceeded to do his thing.

'You know, Kingy,' he said, 'there is only a little bit of petrol in this drum.' There were, however, lots of fumes. 'I wonder what would happen if we dropped a match into it.'

'I don't think that's such a great idea,' I observed, but nonetheless distinctly curious as to what sort of dramatic outcome might eventuate.

Milton proceeded to light matches, drop them through the bung hole and attempt to watch their descent to the bottom of the drum — Milton of course was seriously stupid. Fortunately, the matches extinguished themselves without causing any damage to either the drum or to Milton.

The genius then said, 'I know what the problem is. Get me some paper Tommy.'

So I lit a twist of paper and dropped it through the open bung hole. Instinctively, I quickly retreated, anticipating an outcome neither of us might appreciate. All hell suddenly broke loose, starting with a deafening, ear-splitting explosion. An impressive jet of white and pink flame burst into the air through the drum's small bung hole as the energy released by our clever experiment tried to drive the drum into the ground. When this failed the drum trampolined off the unforgiving earthen floor and headed skywards before being brought to a shuddering halt by the galvanised iron of the shed's roof. It then admitted defeat and registered its frustration and disgust with an impressive finale that sent great plumes of evil smelling grey black smoke spewing forth as it descended. Bug-eyed, comically covered in soot, hair standing upright, we stared through the billowing smoke and assorted debris to see whether the other had survived the blast. The adrenalin rush was followed by relieved, maniacal laughter. Safely back on the ground the drum's top had become a neatly split dome and its sides resembled the shape of the Michelin man.

We had detonated a forty-four-gallon bomb. Fortunately, sufficient fumes had escaped through the open bung hole while Milton was messing around with his stupid match dropping exercise to prevent an explosion with more dire consequences. Milton's father quickly appeared on the scene, directing his understandably hysterical queries to Milton but glaring fiercely at me. He was not amused, particularly when the police and the fire brigade took a keen interest in proceedings as well. Wiping the grin from his face, Milton attempted to describe the incident as a bit of bad luck. A carelessly thrown lighted match had somehow found its way in to an even more carelessly left open bung hole. I thought it far wiser to keep my counsel. Mr Thomas didn't take Milton's comment well nor my suspicious silence. Neither did the local policeman who, grimly, knowingly, nodded. He had been down this slippery slope before. I was banned from Milton's joint for two months — probably a lenient sentence given the potential for what might have happened. There were a dozen or so full and partially full forty-four-gallon drums in the shed and it was no surprise to anyone that this was neither the first nor the last time I was to be banned from Milton's.

As with Billy Brewster, my friendship with Milton gradually faded into obscurity as a result of my increasing interest in sport. The adventures of a new world beckoned.

2

Adolescence

In 1950, in a prelude to the outbreak of the Korean War, the price of Australian wool soared on world markets to an unprecedented level that has never since been seen, even closely. Within twelve months more than two million US defence personnel had been relocated to Korea warmed by Australian wool. The Korean War was under way.

The timing of the local graziers' unexpected largesse coincided with my arrival at Hamilton High School, a combined high school and technical school and one of Victoria's largest secondary schools. We were introduced to a multi-dimensional world that juxtaposed a new sense of independence and a daunting absence of the warmth and security that had comforted us in years five and six at Hamilton Primary School. Those comforts had come courtesy of the maternal, nurturing and wonderful Mrs Menzel with whom I had fallen in Freudian love and with whom I had diligently and shamelessly, attempted to curry unilateral favour. But Mrs Menzel was now comforting somebody else. In our new world we made uncertain stuttering choices, reversed some, made new ones, worked towards those that would ultimately define us and entered into friendships that would last forever.

In the second week of our new existence, fresh faced newcomer, Norman James Burgess interrupted an already chaotic session for first year geography teacher, Valerie Sprigg. The chaos was no great surprise; our year seven class of close to seventy students was a challenge for the most battle hardened teacher.

On the upraised platform at the front of the classroom, the new arrival was the focus of all eyes. Less than comfortable with this level of attention (it was one of the few times in his early life Norman had been in the close company of seventy human beings), Norman unburdened himself of the bag he had been hefting since amending his original decision to enter the technical school. His stress level, already uncomfortably high due to the sudden attention riveted upon him by his new peers, jerked into the stratosphere as his less than regimentally positioned school cap slipped from his head, avoided his desperate lunging grasp and in agonising slow motion spiralled to the floor. The room erupted in cruel, exaggerated laughter. Miss Sprigg rolled her eyes and sighed. She did a lot of sighing at that point in her career. My double desk at the front of the classroom was the only desk not already occupied by two students so Miss Sprigg had little alternative but to place the newcomer next to me. I had already decided I quite liked the cut of Norman's jib and the fact he looked a bit shorter than me as well. Ignoring the clear warning registered on Miss Sprigg's otherwise angelic face I welcomed the newcomer with an elbow to the ribs. He responded in kind. We both grinned. Miss Sprigg sighed. In years to come I was to provide my services as best man at Norman's three weddings. Having proven to be something of a handful for his first two wives, Norman had much better luck with the third, the wonderfully natured Jenny.

Burge, as he became known, lived in the village of Caramut (population 134 in 1951), midway between Hamilton and Warrnambool and each day travelled a 140 kilometre round trip on one of the numerous buses bringing country kids to Hamilton from all points of the compass for their secondary education. Burge quickly confessed to being a Catholic, the first Catholic kid I had met who hadn't been educated by the nuns at St Mary's, that downtrodden parish school for losers (all Catholics were losers) in Coleraine Road.

Mum had grave reservations about Catholics ('best you stay away from Catholics Ray otherwise they'll get you in the end,' was her on cue, adamant declaration). But I didn't care what Burge was or where he came from. What mattered most was where we thought we were going. Nonetheless, Burge felt his being a Catholic was an important piece of background information for me to have. In any case, he said he was a Catholic only once a month due to the district priest's allocation of a maximum of twelve visits a year to the area. As I didn't really know what a Catholic was he tried to explain things to me but Burge was at best shaky on the subject of theology. Having gotten the Catholic thing off his chest he delivered what he thought was an even more important piece of information. For reasons impossible to imagine, Burge thought his not having a father (his father had died when he was eight) might impair our growing friendship. 'Burge, I don't give a fuck about that either,' was my smooth, sympathetic reply.

Burge eventually introduced me to pretty well every member of Caramut's meagre population. Most seemed to be related to him, a not unusual phenomenon in small towns in Victoria or I guess anywhere else. Caramut was not exactly the pinnacle of sophisticated living. There was access to electricity but not to gas, running water or sewerage and Norman's mother's laundry had a unique floor of compacted earth that never failed to attract my snootily grinning attention. The twice weekly bath was taken, generally two kids at a time, in no more than two inches of tepid water. The water was warmed by a highly lethal heater fuelled by woodchips. It was attached to the end of the bath and operated like a small steam engine but without the safety valve. Attempting to have a bath in anything like hot water was only an invitation to trouble.

A visit to Caramut also required you to address your bowel habits. Opening your lunch box required restriction to daylight hours, a practice highly recommended because of the difficulty of safely negotiating in the dark, even with a torch, the minefield of dinner plate sized pats of steaming cow shit deposited between the house and the ramshackle lonely dunny down the end of the back yard. Burge's back yard was no ordinary back yard. It accommodated three cows, a dozen or so chooks, his mother's horse and the rural family's inevitable pack of dogs, each carrying variable strains of kelpie, healer and fox-terrier. Furthermore, a daylight bowel movement avoided the likelihood of stepping on the occasional opportunistic black snake keen on circumnavigating a still warm cow pat to lie in wait for the small birds trying to extract apparently treasured undigested grass seeds from the said pats. Even during daylight hours, the dunny, a rusting double handled large can emptied only on a weekly basis, was not exactly a great experience. Naive attempts to hold your breath to avoid the suffocating stench ascending in waves from the open, mess-filled can only succeeded in delaying the inevitable. The intake of invisible miasma that followed the ultimate surrender of your bursting lungs introduced you to the living certainty that every disease known to the human race had just been punched into your system.

The Caramut quarterly dance, attended by every human being within a radius of thirty kilometres, was also worthy of attention. On the regular occasions I accompanied Norman back to Caramut on the school bus determined to show the locals how it was done (I fancied myself on the dance floor) I found it hard to hide my sense of semi urban superiority. The Caramut dance band consisted of a generously bosomed woman who played vigorous if ordinary piano and an old guy who played the mouth organ and occasionally switched to playing the gum leaf or whistling.

Burge's mother, Kath, a horse-breaker and trainer, was the shire's highly respected ranger. She ensured that local farmers kept their herds enclosed in their paddocks and wily itinerant drovers, illegally grazing their herds and flocks on the good grass that sprouted on the verges of the shire's roadways, were moved on in timely fashion.

Kath had lost her husband and Burge's father, an elite two hundred a day shearer, from a heart attack. Life was tough for Kath with three children that had to be fed, housed and watered, not to mention the family's animals. Kath was a Caramut institution; droll, omnipotent, twinkling eyed, a tanned weathered face ready to break into a knowing grin, a smouldering hand-rolled cigarette inevitably stuck to her bottom lip.

Kath echoed Teddy Stokie's comments as to both Burge's and my future prospects; 'Norman, you and Kingy, you're both bloody well tarred with the same brush, bone lazy and neither of you will ever amount to anything.' There was little doubt that Burge and I were bone lazy as far as physical work was concerned but we were both fiercely aggressive rivals and heroically ambitious as to our future sporting careers. Backyard sporting contests were highly physical and it was a rare occasion that didn't end in jumper punching and threatened and at times actual physical violence. Burge went on to establish the Black Rock Pharmaceutical Emporium, one of Melbourne's most successful pharmacies, and Kath was happy to eat her words, proudly laying on a spectacular spread for the locals when Burge, Caramut's first tertiary graduate, made his garlanded, triumphant annual return to the town.

¶

On the first Wednesday of the school year, in keeping with decades of tradition, all Hamilton High School newcomers were formed into one continuous line in the school quadrangle, tallest to the left, shortest to the right. It was selection day. We were the new season's recruits and each was required to become a member of one of the school's four houses. House competitions were a huge deal, particularly in sport, a compulsory activity for every student, junior fifth's cricket being no exception. We were fanatically loyal to our houses and loyalty to a cause even of the unthinking indiscriminate kind had a magnetic, heroic attraction at Hamilton High. At least it did for me.

The selection process, based largely on physical appearance, was pure Darwinian. Midgets, the fat, the lame and the ugly would be among the last to be selected, embarrassment and inadequacy about to be exposed yet again. But they were the days when reality prevailed and those with physical deficiencies or who knew they were doomed to fail just had to tough it out. There were no pumped up, parent inspired, blinkered false expectations in those days. Some of us examined our shoes in great detail and others kicked idly at one of the many exposed islands of gravel that regularly leaked through the quadrangle's eroded asphalt surface. Some more creative individuals showed inordinate interest in the fading initials of decades of past students whose literary efforts had heroically defied the school cleaner's scrubbing brush and still adorned the walls of the adjacent toilet blocks.

Standing before us were the captains and vice-captains of each of the school's four houses. The captain of Sangster House, Graeme 'Pillsy' Ball had won first pick. Pillsy's parents had quickly become known to us as proprietors of that most excellent of institutions, the school tuck shop, located on the other side of White Street. We were delighted to be made aware of such a wonderful concept. The tuck shop initially survived the treachery of the school's parents' and citizens' association which, in the stated interests of developing healthy eating habits, initiated the establishment of a school cafeteria in direct competition to Pillsy's parents' business. It was never made clear to us whether the austere, clinically efficient cafeteria ever achieved its undisclosed economic objective of raising funds but what did become abundantly clear was that the association's culinary objectives went unrewarded. A King's meat pie (famous among the kids for its mythical rats' tails) and the number one seller in Ball's tuck shop remained at the top of the list in the cafeteria as well. Ultimately, despite the vocal outrage of senior students who had come to know and love the homeliness of the tuck shop and the challenge of getting served in its postage stamp sized premises (actually, it was no challenge, we merely shoved the little kids out of the way), reality delivered its cruel verdict and Pillsy's parents' previously lucrative business yielded to the march of progress.

One had to assume that Pillsy hadn't given the approaching selection process much thought or, if he had, then he hadn't formed any terribly advanced conclusions. Pillsy's vice-captain, Bobby Stevenson, a first class leg spinner, raucously advised him, 'pick King, pick King, I know him, I know him, he's good, he's good.' I suspect Bobby had been influenced as much by the fact that his mother was employed at King's Bakery as by the regular games of cricket we played in the bakery's back yard. My chest swelled in eager anticipation but Pillsy didn't seem to be all that certain. Having had King pointed out to him it was abundantly clear, at least to me, that Pillsy wasn't all that convinced. Nor should he have been given my stumpy legs had me much closer to the right hand end of the line and my oversized head was one more befitting that of a taller person. Nevertheless, Pillsy finally yielded to Bobby's advice and I become first draft pick. First draft pick had a wonderful ring to it, particularly to a highly ambitious if not so highly credentialed budding sportsman. Pillsy would ultimately rue Bobby's advice because my early sporting performances on the fields of Hamilton High School were inconclusive at best and consisted largely of trying to get as creatively muddy as possible in the winter months and as sweaty as possible in summer in order to present a heroically sporting vision to any female within half reasonable range. The drawing of blood and the development of a really bad limp were also highly thought of.

Pillsy had apparently quickly come to the disappointing conclusion that Bobby's advice might have been a bit on the dodgy side given what happened the following day.

'G'day Pillsy,' I yelled enthusiastically, as he and a couple of his year twelve mates approached from the other direction. I was seeking to impress my friends as to my new-found fame as well as being familiar with one of the school's big-noters. But Pillsy had something else in mind, violently grabbing the front of my shirt in both hands and lifting my 145 centimetres body off the ground — a decent lift it was too, given he was more than 185 centimetres tall. 'Listen you cheeky little prick, Graeme's the name to you,' Pillsy snarled through clenched teeth.

I was about to gasp, 'but I thought everyone called you Pillsy' then thought better of it, particularly as I was finding it difficult to breathe let alone talk.

'A bit fucken sensitive for a big kid, isn't he,' I muttered to my colleagues once he was safely out of earshot.

In 1950 the linoleum-floored 'sleep-out' at the bakery became my bedroom when I qualified as a big kid by turning eleven. The sleep-out faced on to a yard housing the mountain of partially split logs of red and white gum used for fuelling the bakery ovens. The logs had to be regularly and laboriously cleared to provide sufficient space for my narrow cricket pitch.

The sleep-out had been my grandparents' bedroom for more than twenty years. The top thirty per cent of one external wall consisted purely of fly wire, hence the name. The rest of the walls were adorned with pictures of sporting heroes cut from the weekly magazine *Sporting Life*. The fly wire was a more than generous invitation to cold biting winds in winter and to billowing dust in summer, with shafts of sunlight revealing untold millions of deadly dust motes in a swirl of kaleidoscopic colour.

In mid-winter the sleep-out seemed hardly separate from the outside world. After you had climbed into the icy sheets it was unbelievably cold but gradually your body heat took over and you became warm and happy in a way that had seemed most unlikely only minutes earlier. That is, until you stretched beyond your body template.

Exposure to the elements had its own strange impact on an early adolescent whose vivid imagination was colourfully stimulated and enhanced by bedtime reading. As well as being happy to invent scenarios and games in which I was the sole actor I was also a voracious reader, cutting my reading teeth as an eight year old on the *Just William* series written by Richmal Crompton. Then followed *Brown of the Lower Fourth*, a burdensome schoolboy to his teachers in some long forgotten mythical English private school, and *Danny of the Dazzlers*, a noble British schoolmaster who had taken the amateur oath and casually blended his teaching duties with remarkable match winning exploits in Test cricket in summer and world soccer in winter. Their sometimes mundane, sometimes heroic exploits were wonderfully outlined in the fully imported fortnightly editions of *Champion Magazine for Boys* which had encouraged my early passion for tales tall and true. By the time I turned ten I had graduated to the time's highly popular American Western paperbacks. Westerns filled most of the shelves at McCasker's Newsagency and had inadvertently but very effectively introduced me to nineteenth century North American geography and history. By the time I turned thirteen I had discovered the lascivious pulp fiction of the *Carter Brown* private detective stories. The hero's services were invariably engaged by an impossibly tall honey-blonde client who had legs wending their way all the way up to her neck, sported a jutting bosom and had such head turning good looks that cars kept running into one another in Los Angeles' busy thoroughfares. The *Carter Brown*s, originally *Peter Carter Brown*, were first published in the early 1950s. They were set in the US despite the author, an Australian by the name of Yates, never having visited that country. Yates was contracted to produce a seemingly impossible three novels a month. He died in 1983, presumably from exhaustion, and by then had reportedly sold more than 120 million copies of his books which, if this was to be believed, was a circulation in 1983 second only to the Bible.

The sleep-out provided a high level of independence for an eleven year old as a consequence of its door opening on to the outside world. This convenient design element also had its disadvantages. The key had been lost, the door could not be locked and it was not manly to complain. Resourcefully, until I became more comfortable with the security arrangements, I wedged a metal tipped cricket stump against the door and supplemented it with another secreted under the bedclothes. If these security arrangements failed I was in big trouble because there was no connecting door to the rest of the house.

Kids jumped the back fence at any time of the day or night and simply walked in. I was really popular and more than happy to encourage that happy state of affairs by prostituting myself with pretty well whatever King's bakery shop had to offer.

I had a spare bed in the sleep-out that was popular with Burge when he was copping grief from the school bus driver, which meant his sleeping over was a fairly common occurrence. I rarely got around to telling Mum that Burge was staying the night so when she finally caught up with us she was, understandably, less than pleased with my lack of common sense, let alone courtesy. Like Nanna King, Mum was not one for small talk. Having inspected both of us for potential criticism opportunities she would get stuck straight into it with something like, 'you've got a hole in your jumper Burgey. Here, take it off and I'll mend it'. Kath was not strong on mending and Mum didn't take no for an answer. Very bossy was Mum.

Apart from being on the bossy side Mum was never far from the difficult economic circumstances of her childhood. If she thought someone needed help she didn't ask, she just did it. When our family visited Portland for our summer holidays Mum would set herself up as the lost and found agent, marching up and down the beach with sniffling kids in tow until they were claimed by their less than enthusiastic parents who were either unaware or more likely delighted their kids had disappeared. She continued in that self-appointed role after Nanna King's prescient 1948 purchase of 'the shack' on the cliff overlooking Port Fairy's magnificent eastern beach that stretched as far as the eye could see. Incidentally, the shack had escalated in value 1000 fold by 2014.

At dinner time Mum would get even with Burge and me for our lack of respect by serving cauliflower to me and peas to Burge as one of our two vegies. Mum ignored the fact that I disliked cauliflower. No, in truth, I detested cauliflower and while Burge loved cauliflower she knew he wasn't a great rap for peas. He hated them, so the problem was easily solved as soon as Mum left the table.

On one of my holidays to Ballarat to visit Nanna Edward I discovered a photograph of Mum looking slim, extremely attractive and dressed in an evening gown with a sash that seemed to proclaim (following my close inspection with a magnifying glass), 'Ballarat Firemen's Ball, Belle of the Ball — 1932. She was seventeen.

'I'll be buggered,' I thought, 'how the hell did that happen?'

It had never occurred to me that Mum had ever been anything more than a scrubbed faced beach ball, she being, for most of the time

I could remember, almost as wide as she was tall. Her photo album was full of photographs with parts missing where Mum had chopped herself out. It was the custom in rural Victoria at that time for mothers to 'let themselves go' once they started bearing children. If it weren't the custom then Mum was certainly trying hard to establish it, which no doubt encouraged her to adopt her oft quoted 'mutton dressed as lamb' jibe for those women over thirty years of age who were otherwise inclined.

It is not overstating the case to say I detested cauliflower. But that did not deter Mum from including it in pretty well every meal she cooked — it was cheap you see. In those days one's culinary likes and dislikes were routinely ignored by parents and accompanied by colourful reminders about the starving millions in China as well as the time's other popular phrase, 'you'll sit there until you eat it', both of which have since disappeared from the English language. I addressed the cauliflower problem pragmatically. I generally ate alone so it really wasn't that much of a problem. Having resourcefully accumulated a supply of calico marble bags I made sure I always had one in my pocket in anticipation of the meal including cauliflower.

Despite our being surrounded by food at the bakery Mum still took great pride in being frugal and many of our meals consisted of leftovers. 'You know Ern, I got twenty servings off that leg of lamb,' she would boast to Dad as if vying for an entry in the *Guinness Book of Records*. Mum delighted in economy and was triumphant if she could re-use an envelope or a brown paper bag.

Another difference in those days was that kids lived their lives outdoors. We left home as early as possible and rarely returned before 6 pm. Life was unregulated, unsupervised and active. Life also happened to be highly accident prone, a characteristic treated with indifference by just about everyone. At Hamilton Primary School there was a four cornered monument in the middle of the playground and at recess and lunch times during the cricket season there were generally two but, on more perilous occasions, three cricket matches in progress, each using one of the four sides of the monument as the stumps. Cross bat shots invariably introduced an element of mayhem on one and sometimes two other batsmen and the position of wicketkeeper obviously had little appeal, requiring a high degree of creativity as well as an equally high level of stupidity.

Alarmingly, none of the teachers thought it necessary to ban the practice of simultaneous games. Then again, we all thought we were bullet proof. We didn't need seatbelts, airbags, smoke detectors, cricket helmets or even helmets for our bikes. Nor did we need written instructions that putting a plastic bag over our heads might cause difficulty in breathing, that bleach was not a refreshing drink or that petrol when exposed to a lighted match or cigarette might have a tendency to explode. We were in our pomp and couldn't possibly conceive of living beyond the age of forty anyway. Despite widespread views to the contrary, life for us kids moved pretty slowly. It is only when you get older that life moves at an exponentially increasing speed. Every year seemed to be better than the one before and you enthusiastically discussed with your mates the coming year which you knew was going to be even better. And that's why the years moved so slowly. You couldn't wait for stuff that was coming up and in the meantime prayed that you wouldn't get appendicitis or contract TB or poliomyelitis.

¶

Brasso McGegor, my desk-mate in year one, lived with his parents and his seedy looking, mysterious, loser of an elder brother (losers were not always exclusive to the Catholic Church) in an unpainted ramshackle house down by the creek. Brasso's parents left a lot to be desired in the opinion of the more straight-laced members of Hamilton society which of course happened to be most of them. Brasso's mother drank and smoked, activities that Mum regarded as near criminal acts for males but bordering on the heinous if practiced by women.

'Ern, don't think you're going to bring your mates around here drinking and smoking and stinking the place out,' she would caution my father.

To make matters worse, Brasso's mother also qualified for the mutton dressed up as lamb classification Mum so derided. Among other rumoured salacious activities that were never accompanied by specifics, Brasso's father was probably best known as the local SP (starting price) bookmaker, an illegal but highly lucrative activity given he was satisfying a strong market demand.

Brasso. Well, Brasso was Brasso — a modern day Huckleberry Finn, carefree, oblivious to what others thought and always doing stuff we knew our parents wouldn't approve of. I was more like Tom Sawyer, author Mark Twain's straight man to Huckleberry. As was the case for Tom, I was always being blindsided by Brasso's ingenious and razor sharp instinct for understanding and taking advantage of human nature. However, like Tom, instead of being pissed off when Brasso took advantage, I generally chalked it up as yet another lesson learned. Brasso was funny, street smart and had a level of rat cunning that was off the charts. Nor was there anything wrong with his intellectual apparatus either as it functioned extremely well. He regularly topped the class in primary school but, as was the case with my own academic performance after we entered High School, Brasso's transgressions began to catch up with him and his examination marks tailed off into the bottom half of the class. It seemed that Dad's ambitions for me to become the first member of the King family to attend university might have to be reassessed. Dad had liked the idea of my becoming an engineer, a profession with a touch of the mystical at the time. I wasn't so sure about that. I didn't want anything getting in the way of my future playing career with Carlton.

I had talked regularly and obsessively with Burge, Teddy Stokie and even Milton Thomas and Billy Brewster about what we were going to do when we got older but it was always different with Brasso. The future never seemed to enter Brasso's head. He had no interest in preparing in any way to ultimately earn a living or to be a productive member of society. Yet to be with Brasso was to know that life was full of glorious possibilities. Mum was particularly unhappy about my connection with Brasso, mostly, it must be said, because of his unsavoury parents but she was no great fan of Brasso either, believing he was too often up to no good.

At the beginning of our second year at Hamilton High Brasso discovered that a house next door to the Alexandra Girls' College hostel in French Street had conveniently become vacant. Convenient that is for what Brasso had in mind. Further investigation revealed that the girls were hungry for male attention, an even more important discovery that Brasso and I were happy to accommodate. As were man-child and outstanding junior footballer, 'Cackle' Agnew and his mate, 'Loppy' Ubergang, when we felt like inviting them along.

Brasso and I took full advantage of his opportunistic discovery in French Street and we chatted to the girls over the back fence most evenings. That was pretty much the extent of it but for young punks, particularly for trespassing young punks, it was excitement of heart pumping order. The Alexandra College girls were, or seemed so at the time, much more appealing than the Hamilton High girls; we were yet to learn that the grass on the other side of the fence only seems greener. The Alexandra College girls, hungry for male attention, were not particularly discerning. Anything wearing trousers would have done so, happily for all concerned, high levels of satisfaction were generated on both sides. Brasso and I were OK with Cackle and Loppy coming along because they were morons as far as girls were concerned and made us look pretty good in comparison. Then Brasso and I got really adventurous and really stupid.

Each morning, when the Alexandra College girls were being marched army style to school, Brasso and I were in close attendance doing tricks on our bikes, although it was really only Brasso doing the tricks as I merely basked in reflected glory. A fleeting, flashing smile from a favoured girl seemed to be worth its weight in gold, inspiring us, that is Brasso, to even greater heights. Brasso's antics seemed to entertain the ranks no end but the Alexandra College teachers who were riding shotgun to protect the girls from, in their eyes, unwanted attention, were singularly unimpressed. They eventually extracted from the girls not only our names but also the disturbing fact that we were connecting over the hostel's back fence after school. Could we also be making contact in the vacant house itself? That really put the cat among the pigeons, causing imaginations to run wild. What dastardly things could we be doing with them? The answer was not much, given that Brasso and I were still only eleven. But Cackle and Loppy were different propositions altogether. Almost two years older than us, their thoughts were already enthusiastically and imaginatively carnal.

One thing led to another and, in order to cover her backside, the Alexandra College principal contacted high school principal Mr Frencham and royal commissions were duly launched on both campuses. Mr Frencham, always looking for a moral subject to inject into his morning address, had the trace of a rare smile on his face at our assembly the next morning. In the deep sombre voice he reserved for expulsions and catastrophic sporting defeats, he announced he was the bearer of grievous news, news so grievous that certain happenings at the Alexandra College hostel in French Street involving some junior Hamilton High School boys may result in police involvement.

'Oooowah' was the grinning, thunderous response from the boys' side of the assembly. Every male head turned left, right and backwards seeking to identify the lucky culprits. A few of the girls seemed interested as well.

Brasso was called out of class at the beginning of the first lesson and on his return whispered, conspiratorially, as he passed my desk, 'they're on to us.' This, for eleven year olds, was shorthand for invisible ink and the dead letter drop. In other words, 'I've spilled the beans Kingy old son, and there's no point in your playing the innocent, who sir? Me sir? Definitely not me sir, kind of deceitful schoolboy bullshit.' I was evidently in enough trouble as it was without also trying for a bit of cunning subterfuge. Half the class picked it up. Then I was called out for interrogation, making it fairly obvious who the alleged sex maniacs were. By the end of the day rumours were running pretty wild, the stories becoming increasingly colourful as the day wore on. The more we protested the innocence of our involvement the more impressed the kids became at our obviously gallant attempts to preserve the honour of our new-found friends. In any case, who wanted to believe we were only chatting to them over the back fence? That blissful state of schoolboy wishful thinking seemed to be confirmed by Cackle and Loppy's colourfully embellished fantasies which were enthusiastically doing the rounds as 'cross your heart and hope to die' fact.

Our parents were called to the school but wondered what the fuss was all about and finally the innocent truth of the happenings was grudgingly accepted and the matter gradually died a natural death. Brasso and I continued to bathe in the sunshine of the boys' unjustified envy as well as being treated with a mixture of curiosity and skittishness by the girls.

Nearly four years later, having behaved with almost impeccable manners in dropping off Rick Winnell's attractive cousin at her doorstep one evening after 'the pictures', a first and last time event as far as she was concerned, the ghost of the matter raised its head again. Rick Winnell, along with Jeff Partington and Rex 'Porky' Staples (a good friend and a devastatingly wasted football talent) were team members of mine when the Hamilton High School four by 100 metres relay team finished second in the final of the under-sixteen Victorian all schools athletics championships at Carlton's Royal Park in 1954. Rick's sexy cousin, having entertained me on her doorstep with my first 'frenchy', a tongue down the throat job, sent me on my way with an enquiring, ambiguous and seemingly disappointed, 'you know, Ray, I always thought you were fast', my performance apparently having fallen a bit short of expectations.

¶

With Dad being a keen punter it was almost inevitable I would also become a student of the turf. I spent endless hours of pleasure studying the *Truth* racing form guide. At the time, the *Truth* newspaper was a highly popular publication specialising in sex crimes and juicy court cases, its feverish prose invariably accompanied by highly revealing and even more warmly admired page three photographs. Strangely, readership surveys indicated that ninety-nine per cent of subscribers purchased *The Truth* for its form guide.

I became quite knowledgeable about the so called sport of kings. I knew really useful stuff like being wary of horses second up after a spell, backing 1600 metre specialists first up over 1200 metres, particularly down the straight six (1200 metres) at Flemington and the 'get out' bet being on 'Last Race' Jack Purtell's mount.

My having suffered an ailment Mum always referred to as a bilious attack, ('Jeez Mum, the teachers say there's a lot of gastro going around') just happened to coincide with a mid-week race meeting at the Hamilton race track. I must have made a credible and miraculous recovery as well as catching Dad in a weak moment because he agreed to me accompanying him to the track that afternoon. This was far from the first time I had gone with Dad to a race track but it was the first time for a mid-week meeting on a school day.

Our usual routine was for Dad to stake me two pounds, the equivalent of around fifty dollars today. At country race meetings in those days the bookmakers were more than comfortable in taking bets from twelve year olds — in fact I placed my first bet when I was only ten. Dad would nominate a place near the winning post where he could be contacted after each race but only if it were an absolute necessity — if I needed to replenish my betting stake or if some random, desperate and unanticipated serious emergency arose. Anything less than my hair suddenly bursting into flames probably wouldn't have qualified. We both understood that making contact would occur only under dire and exceptional circumstances so, to all intents and purposes, I was on my own. This was right up my alley. Other than the smell, the noise and the excitement of the horse racing itself there were many fascinating activities to be observed for a twelve year old, particularly those of the exaggerated, hackneyed racetrack characters who made their living there, bearing in mind that country race meetings in contrast to today were always extremely well attended. I was now well into my thirteenth year and trying to ignore the increasingly regular crop of ugly volcanoes that had begun erupting all over my face. Related to this unfortunate state of affairs was a rapidly rising and out of control libido. I sometimes positioned myself in front of the most attractive female in the betting ring as I implemented a vain and fantasy inspired hope that I might be invited around the back of the grandstand and taught a thing or two.

That day I had had a reasonable day on the punt and in racing parlance was still 'holding folding' approaching the last race. At country race meetings there was always a lack of information and reliable form so Dad always waited until a few minutes before a race started and then followed the money. I had usually adhered to the same practice. This time, however, coming to the last race I decided on something different. I took myself down to the exercise yard where the strappers were walking their horses before taking them to the mounting yard. A magnificent chestnut carrying the number one saddle cloth towered over the other seven acceptors. A check of the race book revealed his name to be Maelstrom. With unbridled enthusiasm and mounting expectation I rushed to the betting ring to apply my research and there I was met with a more than pleasant surprise. Maelstrom's odds listed on the bookmakers' boards were twenty to one, the rank outsider in an eight horse race. The bookmakers were obviously crazy. I had yet to learn that if something looks too good to be true then it probably is. But not this time. God was clearly whetting my appetite in preparation for a more spectacular dumping at some other time in the future. Having placed my bet with local bookmaker, Ron (The Badger) Archibald, I hurried to take up a good position in the grandstand. The stars aligned and Maelstrom duly saluted the judge. He was last into the straight but one by one mowed down each of his rivals to win narrowly by a head.

As it was the last race I joined Dad and his mate Alan Steele at the appointed spot by the winning post and kept my cool.

Incidentally, 'Steely' was worthy of comment in his own right. He stuttered very badly and worked at the Hamilton Gasworks, an institution familiar to large towns at the time that produced evil smelling gas from heated coal and which have since been usurped by natural gas. Steely was best known however for being an excellent cricketer who refused to bow to convention by wearing an old pair of suit trousers and a grey shirt on the field. His only concession was to wear the time's 'runners', known then as 'sand shoes'. But even here he was slightly off-beat. Steely's apparently inexhaustible supply of 'white' sand shoes had ugly black toe-caps. And we all had a fairly good idea where they had come from. In 1945, on the declaration of peace to end the Second World War, the quartermaster at the Hamilton army barracks, in an act of drunken levity, had either inadvertently left the quartermaster store door open or had gone into business for himself. Steely had evidently 'cornered the market' for inexpensive size ten army issue sand shoes.

My enthusiasm getting the better of me I looked up at Dad and out of the side of my mouth in a fair imitation of a racehorse spiv murmured, 'back that?'

'Of course not,' Dad replied. He kept on chatting to Steely — anyone having a chat with Steely had to do most of the chatting — and then as an afterthought asked, 'did you?'

My big grin gave the game away.

'Jeez,' he laughed.

I delivered my rationale. He agreed that Maelstrom was by far the best looking horse in the race, but then put me straight. Maelstrom was having his first start in more than twelve months. More to the point, he was a three mile steeplechaser having a warm-up race over only five furlongs (1000 metres) against a group of flying sprinters.

'By rights Maelstrom should have been one hundred to one,' he added, just to make sure I wasn't getting ahead of myself. I didn't care, I had won today's equivalent of two hundred and fifty dollars.

The next afternoon I purchased my first watch but not before Mr Frencham had waylaid me in the crowded corridor. For reasons unknown to us all he had continued taking a keen interest in me following the Alexander College hostel episode, often seeking me out for a 'good morning King,' which intrigued us all. My flame continued to burn brightly.

On a totally different plane, unbeknown to others, I had become Mr Frencham's sounding board on such playground matters as the safety of certain games and whether various schoolyard activities relied on skill or chance. I was also his on-the-spot reporter for that common occurrence, the schoolyard fist fight.

Nothing electrified the schoolyard more than a good fist fight. 'Fight, fight, fight,' was the call to arms as we rushed around trying to find where it was. Invariably, someone would say, 'I bet it's one of the Dennetts'. Having located the fracas Burge and I would snake our way through the gathering mob eager to see some violence. There was always something noble about a Hamilton High fight. Almost without exception, once honour had been served, the two antagonists, having shaken hands, wandered off arm in arm to clean up in the dunnies.

Mr Frencham was particularly concerned about the evils of gambling. He considered games of chance to be gambling and not to be tolerated, it being immoral or, perhaps more accurately, amoral. To the dismay of my friends the particularly favoured schoolyard activity of 'two-up', played with swap cards rather than two pennies, became a banned activity. The decision was not met with universal acclaim by the two-up participants. With little conscience, I failed to reveal to my friends my covert role as Mr Frencham's stool pigeon, cleverly camouflaging my involvement by joining the loud chorus of protest that sought two-up's unlikely reinstatement.

The level playing field for swap cards (the odds were obviously 50/50) was about to be replaced with something not quite so level. Human resourcefulness was not unknown in the Hamilton High schoolyard and innovation and creativity soon came to the fore in response to the new regulation. This became my simple introduction to the incongruous but common outcome of society's well intentioned desire to protect the innocent while achieving exactly the opposite.

Within the blink of an eye the morally unacceptable and banned game of swap card two-up was quickly replaced by two apparent games of skill in which the opportunists, with carefree impunity, could fleece the unsuspecting lambs of their swap cards depicting leading cricketers, footballers and famous people and places. This turned out to be quite traumatic for the fleeced because it took forever to achieve a complete set of cards (a feat that I had never achieved) as well as accumulate a stock of spares for swapping. Only two cards came in each large packet of Kornies, a well-known but far from preferred breakfast cereal that always took a frustratingly inordinate period of time to be consumed. It was a constant source of wonder how some kids always had a full set within days of a new series of cards being introduced. Inevitably, you made a strong recommendation to your mother that Kornies be part of the menu for every meal. Alternatively, you embraced clandestine activities that saw perfectly good packets of Kornies, minus their cards, turning up in the most unlikely places. In other words, the cards generated exactly the kind of behaviour the manufacturers of Kornies had in mind.

The two new games were 'closest to the wall' and 'long distance'. Closest to the wall involved two or more players flicking their cards towards a wall from a distance of approximately three metres. The exact form of flicking was unregulated and depended purely on personal preference. On a winner–takes-all basis the player who flicked his card closest to the wall collected a card from each of the other participants.

The new games encouraged such innovation, ingenuity and creativity in the secret insertion of unknown performance enhancing substances into the participating cards that anyone who could not induce his skittering card to retain contact with the wall or, even better, cause his card to attach itself to the wall like Spiderman needn't have bothered to play. Similarly, long distance flicking resulted in the creation of cards that raised unmanned flight to a whole new level.

The point of these new games soon became lost. They had resulted in the creation of such superior and unbeatable products that ultimately only one player was going to be left standing. In our case that was 'Whiskers' White, a slightly shadowy and decidedly odd figure (as far as Burge and I were concerned anyone not actively involved in sport was shadowy and odd) who was a year ahead of us. Whiskers might have been odd but there was nothing wrong with his ingenuity. Swap card games quickly became meaningless, inevitably causing the swap card season to go into a steep and never-to-recover decline and the marbles season to arrive early.

The day after my successful punt at the Hamilton racecourse I was waylaid by Mr Frencham in the school corridor. Suspiciously, he enquired as to how I was feeling, my illness having been duly verified by Mum's sick note as required by the regulations. I detected a very large and smelly rat and quickly revealed to Mr Frencham how I had made a rapid enough improvement after my morning bilious attack to attend the races at the Hamilton track that afternoon. He smiled an apparently knowing, toothy smile.

'Good boy,' he said, adding, 'I would like you to take over as the bell ringer.'

¶

Hamilton High had a system of five-minute warning bells that preceded the bell to end each lesson. The warning bell was supposed to aid educational productivity by reducing delays and facilitating the speed with which kids and teachers could finish one lesson and move on to their next classroom, a process of jostling, enjoyable bedlam for the students and frustrating teeth-grinding exasperation for the teachers. Ludicrously, or so it seemed to me, the task of bellringer was rostered to a kid in year eight or year nine. Eight times a day that kid had to exit the classroom, collect the hand bell from Mr Frencham's office in time to ring the warning bell, return to the classroom and then repeat the process a few minutes later, a total of twenty-four interruptions a day. It turned the bellringer into a paranoid clock-watcher, an onerous task that played havoc with the learning process, which was not so onerous. The teaching staff did not take my appointment well. As far as they were concerned, having me as bellringer was akin to turning the lunatic asylum over to one of the inmates. It also caused them to raise their eyebrows as to Mr Frencham's state of mind as well. It was bad enough for a teacher's lessons to be interrupted by clattering metal tipped leather soles but another thing altogether for those interruptions to be legitimately undertaken by a grinning King. It did little to improve my already less than stellar standing with the teaching staff and we all breathed a mutual sigh of relief when my stint was up.

There was a worse aspect to the concept of the five-minute warning bell than my merely being the bellringer. Having recently burst through the doors of puberty the five-minute bell became the bane of my life. Out of control erections began to emerge and always at the most inconvenient times. Moving to one's next classroom location was certainly inconvenient, although being asked to demonstrate something on the blackboard at the front of the class was pretty hard to beat. It wasn't until I noticed other strategically positioned books and pencil cases, downcast furtive eyes and half embarrassed looks that I breathed a huge sigh of relief; my concern at having a unique problem was apparently unwarranted.

The sensitivity to the hormonal rumblings I was delighted to now share with others didn't apply to Ian Jacobson from Penshurst. Grinning like the imbecile he was, Ian strolled around proudly with what looked like a very large banana stuck down the front of his pants. On Sundays the kids from Penshurst congregated in one of the volcanic caves on nearby Mount Rouse where they amused themselves with a variety of personal activities. Anatomy lessons were apparently the most popular activity given Ian's regular comments about Freda Thessinger's sensational breasts. Freda was two years ahead of us and evidently suffered from the sin of pride because Ian said he couldn't keep his thoughts from occasionally drifting to Freda's breasts, although, based on Ian's physical condition, his thoughts must have been drifting towards Freda's breasts most of the time.

For me, the five-minute warning bell became a Pavlov's dogs' nightmare. As soon as the bell rang you knew if you had to change classrooms what was going to happen and your affliction was going to stay with you for what seemed like forever. One of the first rules that a new teacher of middle school boys learned was never to ask a boy to, 'bring out what you're playing with under the desk.'

¶

Until 1955 Hamilton did not have a public swimming pool and private swimming pools were like hen's teeth. There was only one house in Hamilton with a swimming pool that I was aware of and that was owned by the parents of a less than attractive but nonetheless highly popular girl who attended Alexandra College. Remarkably, Gray Street Primary School had a pool, albeit a small and pretty ordinary pool at that. It had been constructed with very coarse sand in the concrete mix and so left a nasty graze every time you attempted to climb out of it. Despite the pool's lethal tendencies it was a potentially useful but rarely used piece of infrastructure — few of the teachers were able to swim. Those of us who did learn to swim in Hamilton did so in the Grange Creek, a narrow, slow-moving often stagnant and decidedly unsanitary watercourse that meandered south-west of the town before reaching its destination in snake-infested marshlands. Naturally, we were banned by our parents from swimming in the creek but pressure to be part of the in group inevitably rendered those bans irrelevant.

There were two swimming holes: the 'log', frequented by the smaller kids and ingeniously named after the tree that had fallen in the middle of it, and the 'bank', a little further along and the domain of the big kids who used the three-metre high riverbank as a diving platform. The depth of the water below the bank's launch pad was rarely more than two metres, requiring one of a variety of highly creative mid-air manoeuvres to prevent your head making powerful contact with the admittedly soft muddy bottom. After one abortive, near death experience, gymnastics being far from my long suit, I resorted to the spectacular but nonetheless still piss weak 'honeypot', known these days as a 'bomb'. The muddy bottom oozed disconcertingly through your toes, we shared the water with the occasional eel or snake and regularly stubbed our toes on old bedsteads or stolen bicycles that mysteriously found their way into our swimming hole.

Upon exiting the soupy water you were likely to have three or four blood-sucking leeches attached to your body. A box of matches or a cigarette lighter was an essential piece of equipment if you were a devotee of the creek, standard practice upon exiting the water being to ask the nearest kid to inspect your back and any other body part you couldn't see and have him put a flame to the leech's tail. A seared tail encouraged the leech to let go. If you did not adhere to this practice and merely tried to pull the leech off, its head remained underneath the skin and resulted in a nasty infection and sometimes death. Well, at least that was the predicted outcome that had been handed down from generation to generation with no one prepared to test its veracity.

If there were dangers in the creek then its banks could be kind of interesting as well. Brasso and I had donned our Sunday best with the intention of hanging out at Strangio's milk bar, the most popular meeting spot for Hamilton's youth. Mum was visiting Nanna Edward in Ballarat and I had convinced Nanna King I needed a rest from Sunday school. Having failed to make contact with any females of interest in Strangio's we initially whiled away the time with Nancy, the proprietor's delightful but tragically overweight daughter, and headed to the creek to test our nerves. This involved allowing your bike to run down the steep grassy slope towards the creek's edge before you implemented the necessary evasive tactics. My nerve was particularly tested because the reviled Rainbow had now been replaced by Dad's ancient full sized Malvern Star with a fixed rear wheel. It was a matter of more than just inconvenience that Dad's bike, an old track racing bike, had no formal braking system. A reduction in speed was achieved by contorting the right leg and applying one's heel to the rear tyre, a practice that was risky as well as surprisingly effective as long as you got the process right. Nonetheless, it was still a twenty-five years old bike with an outdated and rusty head stem configuration occasionally causing the handlebars to slide forward off the stem, the forward press invariably encouraged by travelling downhill. Quite an adrenalin rush is riding along with handle bars no longer attached to the bike.

After a couple of fear-charged but injury free bail-outs designed to prevent our progressively higher levels of risk-taking ending up in the creek, we headed for Brasso's house, our grass-stained trousers now bearing the tell-tale evidence of our unapproved endeavours. On the way we ran into the very tall but very thin Geoff 'Goofy' Elkins, an exceptionally good cricketer a couple of years older than us. He had left school the day he turned fourteen to work for one of the local horse trainers as a strapper and was giving a big brown/black steeplechaser named Tramp slow work along the edge of the creek. Although Goofy often looked ready to inflict personal damage at any given moment and had a strain of something quite dastardly in his character he was generally quite friendly to us. Today was no exception. But one of us must have said something to rile him or perhaps he simply decided to have a bit of fun at our expense because we soon became aware of the ominous sound of drumming hooves.

' Fuck me, look out Kingy,' muttered Brasso, our worst fears confirmed as Tramp and the mounted Goofy came galloping straight at us. Brasso's rapier-like brain galvanised into immediate action and with a bound he was over the adjacent barbed wire fence that separated his parents' property from the banks of the creek. Lacking Brasso's alertness and response time and initially fazed by those rusty but razor sharp barbs my default option was less convincing. I did exactly what Goofy hoped one of us might do. I discarded the bike and charted a coarse parallel to the fence. The drumming hooves came closer and closer until I could feel the hot snorting breath of 550 kilos of runaway freight train on the back of my neck, the adrenalin spike of allowing our bikes to run down the grassy slope not having come anywhere near the intensity of the lightning bolt that electrified my system. With my flying feet covering the ground at a speed well beyond my previous personal best I was suddenly struck, paradoxically, by a moment of absolute crystal clarity. Twenty or so metres ahead of my increasingly despairing efforts to avoid an untimely end a sagging strand of barbed wire offered a suggestion of hope for possible escape. The world slowed, stopped, then stood perfectly still as my brain, feverish and cool at the same time, calibrated the combination of perpendicular, tangential and sideways angles required to execute a successful getaway. In full flight, my body jack-knifed, perfected an unlikely sequence of apparently brilliant acrobatic gyrations and, finally, as straight as an arrow fired with almost unerring aim, speared through that barbed narrow opening to the disappearing strains of Goofy's maniacal laughter as he galloped Tramp off into the distance.

Olympic gymnast I was not but in that slivered fraction of a second my brain had planned and executed a unique out of body experience. But those barbs could be pesky things. Having inspected my lacerated bare bum, a highly impressed Brasso ignored the fact that the cuts were caused by barbs covered in rust and assured me (I believed everything Brasso told me) that serious medical attention, in other words stitches, was not required. Brasso duly extolled my amazing acrobatic feat to all our friends, creating a heady glow in which I unashamedly basked for days.

Brasso left school at the end of year ten in 1953, devoting the next portion of his life to becoming a very good poolroom hustler and a not so good professional punter. He embellished his reputation for being more than slightly off beat by wearing a full length fur coat in all weathers and continually having a burning cigarette hanging from his bottom lip. He was running headlong into a shady world of questionable activities and slick, low level opportunists. I always hoped Brasso had made a right-angle turn in his life and perhaps become a property developer or an internet entrepreneur but I fear his skeleton lies at the bottom of the Hamilton reservoir with the weights still around its ankles. After I left Hamilton for Melbourne I never saw him again.

¶

Each year Hamilton High held a fair to raise money for charity. Unlike school fairs today, the Hamilton High School fair was largely run by and for the kids with only a sprinkling of parents ever attending. Its biggest money spinner by far was the boxing tent in the school gymnasium run by the senior level trade class. Burge and I were both keen boxing fans, often putting on the gloves and tearing into one another in our lounge room at home. We listened religiously to broadcasts of the fights at West Melbourne Stadium (Festival Hall) on Friday nights and at Sydney Stadium on Monday nights. My two all-time heroes, both Australian lightweight champions, were Sydney's hard hitting George Barnes and, later, the master of defence with the peppery straight left, Max Carlos from Shepparton. I was unbeatable in any quiz on boxing courtesy of my, or more correctly Dad's, subscriptions to the Australian and US editions of *Ring Magazine*.

In year eight Burge and I made our debuts in the Hamilton High boxing tent in front of around two hundred kids and a few parents. I fought as 'Killer King' the ring name that appeared on the various placards distributed around the school promoting the gladiatorial glamour and gore of Hamilton High's 'House of Stoush'. My opponent was a high profile, part aboriginal kid of doubtful age with an impressive sporting background. His name was John Reid but was known by all, including the teachers, as 'Abo' Reid. My agreeing to fight Abo over three one-minute rounds was initially met with a degree of concern for my welfare given the stark contrast between our sporting achievements as well as his greater size and maturity but I surprised everyone by holding my own and the referee couldn't separate us in a closely fought draw. Burge fought under the name of 'Bruiser Burgess' and lost to another part aboriginal kid, Rod 'Lothar' Lampard. Burge was certain Lampard was a man. The following year was the last year in which the boxing tent featured in the fete's activities before being banned by the school council. It was a particularly bloody boxing tent that year with a couple of bouts having to be stopped to enable the claret to be mopped up in order to prevent the more enthusiastic antagonists from slipping over. I fought another draw against 'Dangerous Dunbar' and Burge squared the ledger by outpointing a well hung kid by the name of Ray 'Donkey' Beavis.

¶

Despite my good relationship with Mr Frencham I was not popular with his staff and this strange dichotomy continued until year twelve when Mr (Charlie) Alexander arrived as principal. Despite the fact I quite liked most of my teachers they didn't appreciate what they saw as a smart-arse kid trying to create the impression he could not be knocked off his game. Fortunately, in contrast to his teaching staff, Charlie believed I had some saving graces. He seemed able to find some good in every kid. It was just his staff that he didn't seem to like, in particular those who had difficulty relaxing what he saw as an overly authoritarian stance. My report book at the end of each term consistently contained the comment, 'Ray is a distracting influence and could be more cooperative in class', with no mention of my can-do attitude or other indispensable qualities.

That categorisation came largely courtesy of Roy Paine who took us for British history in year twelve. Roy, a big man, had a number of memorable characteristics, two of them being a bad case of acne and a booming voice. He also drove a straight eight Ford, a car much admired by the local petrol-heads. Roy had an aggressive, haranguing teaching style suggestive of a failing football coach, often adopting a Leninist pose with his right arm sweeping across the class or an index finger pointed at an individual as though his words were aimed solely at them.

His major claim to fame, at least during that final year, was that he had to be the worst joke teller in creation. Pam Jones and Jennifer Standish, two of my year twelve classmates, who considered themselves more observant than the average bear, pointed out to me early on that whenever Roy cracked a joke he always seemed to focus on me as if seeking a reaction. This was when my major troubles with Roy began. Having had this acute observation pointed out to me I felt I had little alternative but to present a stony-faced response every time Roy tried to redeem himself from his previous failures — hence, presumably, the consistent 'could be more cooperative in class' comment. Having been extremely successful in this endeavour I began to ease off after a while, feeling that I had made a prick of myself for long enough. Nevertheless, there was to be a happy ending. That year Roy lived every year twelve teacher's dream and 'picked' the British history examination paper. Courtesy of five perfect answers learned by rote I received a high distinction (in those days a first class honour) as well as an early morning telephone call from a delighted Roy, as did Jennifer Standish who achieved a similar result.

In spite of these apparently self-inflicted hardships I loved my time at Hamilton High, enjoying the bonhomie of my classmates, the adrenalin of the sporting fields and that special uplifting glow when I managed to get the rhythm of school life to run in sync with my own. It was in year twelve that I made my biggest strides. Having been elected captain of Sangster House, a legacy of being the first draft pick in 1950, I quickly learned that as long as you went about it the right way kids didn't seem to mind being told what to do. This was a useful discovery because I realised I liked telling them what to do even more.

Going about it the right way had nothing to do with a flair for diplomacy but rather the manipulative process of kidding them into believing their house captain might be a good bloke. In the school's corridors I made it a practice of acknowledging as many Sangster

House kids as I could, sometimes with their name, sometimes with a grin and sometimes with merely a nod before graduating to that Churchillian gesture of the two-fingered V, which seemed to impress them even more. The process appeared to make them warm to me, particularly those of the lower ranks, the knowledge making me feel even warmer given what I had in mind.

Hamilton High had an honours board on which four new names appeared each year. These were the boy and girl head prefects and the boy and girl house captains of the year's best performed house. Points were awarded for sport, scholastics and, of all things, gardening. As I was not the head prefect, let alone any sort of prefect, I set my cap on being captain of the winning house, seeking registration of my gilded name on the honours board for all time. These were the days when every desktop was pitted with carved initials and names, the letters still discernible under decades of caretakers' coats of varnish. But I didn't want my mark to be merely one of hundreds seeking acknowledgement I had passed this way, I wanted official recognition.

The apparent anomaly of gardening being a key ingredient of the award was based on the school's historical policy of saving on gardening expenses by allocating the upkeep of twenty-five per cent of the school's garden to each house. Sangster won the gardening prize that year largely because I was more successful than the other house captains in pressing into service the necessary number of Sangster House members as well as implementing devious plans and activities to monopolise the availability of gardening tools.

The second leg to my ambitious plan was junior sport, which was held on Tuesday afternoons and just happened to coincide with my private study periods. I would stroll over to the playing fields and coach the junior Sangster teams, hopefully to victory. My house captain peers didn't care to waste their private study periods, thus giving me the opportunity to establish a competitive advantage. Gradually, my vanity inspired plan morphed into something else. The junior Sangster teams clearly appreciated the attention I gave them and were soon at the head of the sports table. That is, until my activities were brought to a sudden and disappointing halt.

English teacher Colin Cave, the father of weirdo rock singer Nick Cave, was umpiring a junior house football match and later objected at the weekly staff meeting to my being, in his view, off reservation. My witnessing his less than competent umpiring may not have been totally irrelevant to his stance. Colin Cave was interesting and different but he could also be a horrible prick when necessary and it seemed he thought it necessary a lot of the time. He had no problem calling a kid 'monkey face' if the kid looked a bit Neanderthal, 'bat ears' if he had big ears or 'stumpy' if a bit on the short side. It was Colin Cave who had led the inquisition into the French Street hostel incident in year eight and while neither Brasso nor I could have justifiably accused him of unduly roughing us up in encouraging us to divulge incriminating evidence he did get painfully rigid fingered around our chest area. You soon learned Colin Cave was the kind of teacher who was best avoided. He later became an inspector of schools and died in a car accident.

Given I had what the teaching staff considered to be 'form' the consensus at the weekly staff meeting was that my coaching duties were an obvious blind, that I was up to no good and that I should be banned from what they saw as unjustifiable off road activities. Although Charlie Alexander saw my coaching as a leadership initiative of some value he was new to the school. Not wanting yet another divisive issue with his staff he therefore felt he had little choice but to bring my coaching duties to a close.

Despite my best, or perhaps worst efforts, Sangster didn't win the house of the year. Following the ban on my coaching activities, coincidence or not, we were pipped at the post after leading for most of the year. I missed out to head prefect Roger Pope who therefore got his name up twice. But no one was complaining, least of all me. Roger was not quite saintly but went very close. We all admired his uncomplaining and stoic bravery after sustaining an eye injury in a freak accident during year eleven. It dashed a sporting future in which

Roger could have aspired to be absolutely anything, his membership of the school football team when just a year eight midget being an indication of his huge potential. With only one serviceable eye he was still an elite performer, remarkably and justifiably captaining both the school football team (I was his deputy) and the school tennis teams in year twelve. He became a successful pharmacist and died of cancer aged seventy.

¶

I was considered one of the smarter kids at primary school but my academic record at high school was distinguished only by its mediocrity. I was, however, a whiz at two subjects that didn't seem to be considered terribly important in the overall academic scheme of things — arithmetic and commercial principles and practice. I also did that other subject set aside for the mentally challenged, woodwork, generally receiving 'P-minus' for my creations, which presumably meant not quite a 'pass'. These three subjects were forced upon those who made up the highly disparaged 'non-professional' stream of students considered not smart enough to study maths and sciences. Nevertheless, to everyone's amazement, my stocks rose in year twelve, presumably in response to my greater efforts in ensuring I made it to Melbourne the following year to pursue sporting ambitions.

At the beginning of year twelve the prefects, six girls and six boys, were elected by the students in years eight and above. I was absent on the day of the announcement of the election results and received the news from Lyn Henderson, one of the bloke magnets from Henderson's Milk Bar, as we were riding to school the following day. Lyn always had a bit of an edge that either enhanced her attractiveness or detracted from it depending on your perspective. She also felt I was more than a bit ahead of myself anyway so she was not discouraged from giving it to me right between the eyes. Luminous eyes flashing and a big grin revealing her large, brilliantly white teeth, she casually mentioned the election results for the new prefects had been announced the previous day and that my name was not among them. Coincidentally, nor was Burge's. The general view was that we had been blackballed by the teaching staff, an event that was more or less without precedent and an action to which Burge and I took less than kindly.

Burge and I had looked forward to wearing the prefect's smart green blazer with its colourfully monogrammed pocket, the main reason we wanted to be prefects. Prefects were the only students who got to wear a blazer. The teachers, in mischievously attempting to divert blame for their intervention, leaked a story that Burge and I hadn't received sufficient students' votes. Our omission was one of the school's major topics of conversation for at least five minutes.

Ultimately, during one of my regular visits to his office, Charlie Alexander confirmed I had polled second to Roger Pope in the student elections and Burge fourth. Charlie was definitely different. He was a libertarian and a philosopher, more like a kindly grandparent than a school principal and he and I had many deep and meaningful discussions. I began to wonder whether Charlie was orchestrating some of my visits to his office in order to provide light relief from his strained relationship with his staff. He could give a very convincing impression that he was a bit doddery and absent minded but that was largely an act. Charlie was a master manipulator, invariably getting me to do exactly what he wanted and despite my recognising the game I thought he was playing, I always felt endearingly good about it.

Charlie seemed a little before his time in attempting to treat the senior kids as adults and sought my advice on whether I thought it a good idea for the boys to be encouraged to formally accompany a favoured girl to the end of year school 'social'. He was fully aware of the lascivious and less than gallant intentions of the boys in taking the girls home after the social but felt it would show greater honour, chivalry and good manners if these intentions were balanced by arriving with the girl in the first place. The highly polished and sophisticated Jennifer Standish had been the apple of my eye in year ten but following my having fallen out of favour in year eleven and being replaced by the ubiquitous Roger Pope, I had made a strong and determined comeback in year twelve and Jennifer and I had become an item. I was happy to agree with Charlie's thoughts and I had my first official date.

¶

Despite my lack of natural talent, sport was an obsession. In primary school I had always acquitted myself well in foot races but despite my continuing certainty as to my future playing career at Carlton I was still largely a nonentity as a footballer and cricketer, the only sports available. In high school, although only in year eight and at an age that normally would have had me in year seven, I had finished tenth out of three hundred boys of all ages in the school's annual cross country nine kilometre run (the competitive but similarly aged Teddy Stokie pipping me on the line in finishing ninth). My heart and lungs were clearly OK but the crucial physical skills required for anything more complicated than running left a bit to be desired. Then some light appeared at the end of the tunnel.

I had a tantalising but all too brief growth spurt between the ages of eleven and twelve which brought my height close but not quite equal to around average for my age. At Patterson Park's under-fourteen cricket practice I was thrown the ball and soon had the batsmen disconcerted by the pace I was generating. It was the first time I had emerged from the sporting ruck since my cross-country performance in year eight. I became the leading wicket taker in the competition, terrorising the little kids with my ridiculously long run-up.

The following year, aged fourteen, I graduated to the adult competition and did well enough to be the youngest player ever selected to open the bowling for the Hamilton and District Cricket Association at Country Week in Ballarat where towns in western Victoria competed for the honour of being the best. My selection was more of an encouragement award than anything else but I rose to the occasion and was Hamilton's leading wicket taker, causing me to talk of nothing else for at least a month. Over the next few years I was a regular in Hamilton's representative sides but by the age of sixteen, not having grown a fraction of a centimetre since turning fourteen, the end of the road was near. I didn't know it at the time but the party was over. Fully stretched at a very generous 171 centimetres, I would, in fast bowling terms, remain a midget.

¶

Despite my early success as a cricketer the adrenalin appeal of Aussie Rules football always influenced my preference. Kick to kick at recess and lunch times became the highlight of the school day. At junior level my moderate footballing talent was evident as a hard at the ball back man with limited peripheral vision; but by age sixteen I was playing in all the Hamilton and District under-age inter league sides as an on-baller, my name generally appearing as one of the better players albeit due largely to enthusiasm and determination rather than any sublime skill.

Kick to kick on the dry, dusty hockey field at Hamilton High School was excitement and war. With three footballs going and up to forty kids at each end all fighting and tearing at each other trying to get a kick, it was no place for the faint hearted. The scavengers and the smaller kids stuck to the perimeters, mainly in front of the pack or behind it, hoping for the easy one. But for Burge and me it was all about practicing the mark, particularly the leaping early, back climbing, reach for the stratosphere, spectacular 'hanger'. In contrast to the fighting that went on for the ground ball, any mark, clean or fumbled, was treated with reverential respect by all, the space around the successful aspirant quickly cleared, inviolate and sacrosanct. A corridor quickly formed allowing you to coolly drop kick the ball back down the other end or to casually, almost disdainfully, hand ball to a kid who hadn't had a kick all day. Striking a cricket ball to the boundary or hitting the stumps when bowling was always a great thrill but the stratospheric, acrobatic hanger was on its own for euphoric triumph.

From as early as I could remember I had always been a Carlton barracker. There did not appear to be any rhyme or reason for this choice because nobody else I knew barracked for Carlton. Dad was an Essendon supporter and pretty well everybody else I knew barracked for Collingwood. Each Saturday afternoon, in feverish, unrequited anticipation, I listened to the Carlton game on the radio despite the often dodgy reception and each year spent endless hours building a scrapbook of pictures and statistics of my heroes. It wasn't a great period in Carlton's history. Nevertheless, every relevant photo was lovingly cut from the metropolitan dailies and I dutifully ran my own best and fairest award based on each week's better player nominations. And whenever Dad travelled to Melbourne for the races I tried to grab a spot in the car. When successful, I found my way through the city to where Carlton was playing, no mean feat for a simple country boy armed with a page or two torn from the Metropolitan Street Directory. There I soaked up the atmosphere and fantasised about seeing myself in the Carlton jersey — one of the joys of youth where anything is possible and hope is the last thing to die.

¶

If there was a dud year at Hamilton High School it was year eleven.

For the first time in my life the world didn't seem to want to cooperate. Disturbing periods of unhappiness began to emerge which thankfully disappeared just as quickly. Perhaps hormonal, perhaps the psychological chaos associated with crossing the divide from kid to emerging adult; who knew what brought these mood swings about? The good thing was that despite having the weight of the world on your shoulders for a few hours the low disappeared without notice. After a while, like the dissipation of a headache, it was gone. This was handy to know because when the dark cloud descended you would say to yourself, 'just wait for a while and sooner or later it will lift of its own accord.' Or so I tried to tell myself.

There was a practical side to these lows. Compared to the year twelve boys who got all the spoils we year elevens, almost big kids but not quite, were gauche, timid, unsophisticated or too short and sometimes all four. It was the year my face reached its zenith as fertile terrain for spotty, sensitive-to-the-touch volcanoes. You couldn't help but peer at yourself in every reflective surface to see whether yet another eruption was pending.

My yardstick and mentor for social success was Bill Deacon. Bill had arrived at Hamilton High at the beginning of that year and was in year twelve. More than two years older than me, he was tall, urbane, wittily articulate and a state ranked tennis player who possessed the much admired asset of having spent all his life in Melbourne, aka, the Big Smoke, the source of all sophistication. Bill and I became firm friends although that did have its downsides because he made me look pretty ordinary when he was on a roll. Bill took a philosophical approach to life and pushed me to believe that principles should guide life's actions, all of which sounded good at the time but which did not resonate until some years later when I had read and been besotted by Ayn Rand's *Atlas Shrugged*.

Bill left slight pauses in our discussions that caused me to wonder whether he was engaged in subtle mockery or high seriousness. He never called me Kingy or King like everyone else but addressed me as Raymond rather than Ray, whereas in Burge's case, he shortened the unlengthenable Norman to Norm. Initially, I tried to ape his actions and to memorise and repeat his quips (which I dutifully learned by rote) but from the disdainful looks my poorly timed comments generated I soon realised this was an unlikely road to success. In Bill's mouth his lines seemed clever and sophisticated, in mine they were merely fatuous. Bill returned to Melbourne at the end of that year and we wrote letters to each other, as people — even the young — did in those days, often starting a letter with such words as 'being in receipt of your epistle of the 11th inst,' which to us seemed quite clever and witty. Bill settled in Brisbane, became a tennis coach, a world class masters squash player and joins us each year at the class of 1955 reunion.

As the end of year eleven approached I sat astride the bakery wall, chin in my hands, pondering yet again the solution to my lack of social impact. Morbid disbelief had hit me hard. The problem was my personality. I was too dull. Ignoring my recent lack of success I again determined to emulate my mentor. I would try harder. I would become vibrant and exciting. I would accumulate and disseminate at will a store of hilarious jokes and stories. I would become quick witted and seductively funny. I would become the person that everyone wanted to be with. At least it was a plan. Quite comforting is a plan.

On the inside back cover of the December 1954 edition of *Sporting Life* I discovered the solution to my problem, just what I needed. The advertisement titillated and challenged, *Develop a winning manner, learn the art of irresistible charm, how to act, speak and dress to achieve social success, how to strengthen your personality* — all for the equivalent of one dollar thirty, together with a money back guarantee. Wow! The advertisement also offered some other useful goals: *Develop a KO blow; Add to your height; Remove constipation; Tricks with cards; Become a ventriloquist; Beat the bully; Weld at home; Stop your rupture worries; Beat the bookies.* These advertisements were the innocent forerunners to emails from Nigerians who can't spell and who beg to put money into your bank account and to billboard advertisers offering improbable means of making your male parts longer.

Having spent the one dollar thirty I refused to acknowledge that what arrived in the mail two weeks later was somewhat disappointing.

But I had been worrying unnecessarily.

If almost being a big kid was frustrating and depressing then actually becoming a big kid in year twelve was an enlightening revelation. Magically, our problems disappeared, confidence suddenly materialising. No longer were we making dumb, moronic, unfunny comments. Girls seemed to be really interested in what we had to say or what we did. We were now heroes, idolised by the little kids.

We didn't care or even wonder if we were living in a dream world. It was our year in the sun and we were going to make the most of it. It was wonderful.

But nothing could be that perfect.

Rhamat was a mature age student from India, his age impossible to determine. During his exchange year he had the distinct misfortune to be allocated to Hamilton Boys' College. The cultural and age chasm that separated him from his fellow students was unbridgeable and no doubt the source of his desperate loneliness. He was as black as the ace of spades, had shiny black wavy hair and stood out like a sore thumb. I often saw him making his sad, meandering way to and from Hamilton's deserted Gray Street on Sunday afternoons, the sorry lot of the college boarders who had little else to do on their free half day. As Rhamat trudged relentlessly by I engaged him from my usual position atop the bakery wall where I watched the world go by. He was taken aback both by the fact I had spoken to him and, no doubt, by my smooth opening gambit, 'must be a bastard going to the College'. Rhamat was beautifully mannered and would not have thought for one second to criticise his circumstances. I ejected myself on to the footpath and completed the introduction. Following convention we shook hands, his pressure light. He quietly acknowledged he knew who I was. Like many born in India he was a cricket tragic and had been present when Hamilton High had overwhelmed the Boys' College in the annual cricket match between the two schools. I had captained the High School side and taken little pleasure from my seven wickets in dismissing the weak College side for a paltry thirty three runs.

One thing led to another and Rhamat responded enthusiastically to my suggestion that he might like to accompany me to the movies on the following Monday evening. It eventually became a regular thing and was my introduction to the homily, 'no good turn ever goes unpunished'. He soon made it clear in his quiet, cultured, beautifully spoken English that Monday evening had become the highlight of his week. Rhamat bombarded me with invitations to dine with him at the

College and to join him in other social engagements. Monday evening at the movies was not enough. By then, however, my objective of getting to Melbourne the following year had translated into three-hour study sessions, five evenings a week. My excuses sounded lame (which they probably were) and he showed petulance at my attempted explanations and excuses, all of which he took as a form of rejection. It was never going to end well. Our Monday evenings became increasingly strained and eventually came to a halt, a conclusion which may or may not have been inevitable. Heavy with guilt I occasionally caught his eye when we passed each other in Gray Street.

Melva Clayton was the eldest of eight children born to Valentine Clayton and his wife. Valentine, a highly qualified and accomplished chartered accountant, was the district's top wicketkeeper. He lived on a property on the outskirts of Hamilton with his equally highly academically qualified (reputedly in receipt of a PhD) but strange wife. Neither in appearance nor in nature did Valentine Clayton convey a great image. He was unpopular, ill-tempered, criminally short, not to mention fat, and his cricket attire invariably grubby. When his wife came to town she was accompanied by her large brood of children, all steps and stairs, straggling behind her trying to keep up. She invariably wore an outdated cloche hat and dressed in clothes of the same era. The kids looked snotty nosed, woebegone and in keeping with the era, dressed in hand me downs. Cricketing colleagues who had visited Valentine's home swore that a variety of farm animals and domestic birds had the run of the house, which itself was not exactly in pristine condition.

Melva was a year below me and if her parents left something to be desired and had something to answer for, she was also burdened by two other unfortunate characteristics. She suffered from epileptic fits that frightened the life out of her classmates and sometimes caused her to wet herself, which hardly encouraged close relationships. Just as burdensome was the nickname everyone attached to her, including me I am ashamed to say, of Ponger Clayton. Invariably alone in the school ground, shoulders hunched, eyes downcast, head turned to the side as if fending off slanting, heavy rain she was a tragic sight. I was too caught up in my own affairs to even think about doing something nice for her. Melva, wherever you are, a thousand pardons. I wish it had been otherwise and I can only hope that I would have been brave enough at the time to carry it through.

Despite these examples of why I would like to have another chance to relive that year I retain a life-long attachment to Hamilton High. After all, most of my development took place within that healthy, generally happy community and I reminisce each year with my remaining peers at the annual reunion of the class of '55.

Following the daunting final year's external examinations we whiled away the languid days of that year's long hot summer at Hamilton's newly constructed Olympic Pool in fear or happy anticipation of examination results that we were convinced would make us or break us. We worked on our suntans, inflicted permanent damage to our skin and discussed in eager anticipation how the next section in our lives might unfold. I spent much of that time with year twelve classmate and long-time friend, Pam Jones, comparing notes and providing mutual advice on the shadowy challenges that lay ahead.

In the main, 1955 was a wonderful year of promise, determined expectation and a world we would not see the likes of again.

Hacker Finn would never see it again either. In 1955 Hacker cut his highly promising sporting life short in a tragic level crossing smash on the Dunkeld Road.

3

University

'Sign up to be a teacher,' the smooth talking voiceover said, 'and we will not only pay your university fees but also pay you a living wage while you are having the time of your life.'

In September 1955 Hamilton High received a visit from the Victorian Education Department's recruiting team touting for secondary schoolteacher training candidates. They treated us to a seductive and mischievously misleading five-minute film depicting sport, playing fields and beautiful people. The last thing I thought I might do was teach. However, signing up would at least get me to Melbourne, and you had to start somewhere. Also, as I ultimately learnt, one's future didn't have to be defined by where you started. You just had to start. The recruiting team did well, signing up fourteen out of a possible nineteen members of Hamilton High's Class of '55.

In 1956 no more than two per cent of Australia's population successfully completed university degrees. To get to university the rule of thumb was simple; pass year twelve examinations and you gained entry to your university course of choice. You didn't compete with other students; you competed with the year twelve examiner.

My results were OK. I had timed my run nicely, neatly sliding across the line with just enough up my sleeve to be awarded entry to Melbourne University's commerce faculty and a teaching studentship. The studentship was the handy one. It came with a seven guineas weekly living allowance, around $225 today. The sting in the tail was that you were contracted to teach for three years.

Aged sixteen years and ten months, bright-eyed and bushy-tailed, I was delivered by Dad to the Big Smoke in January 1956, the year of the Melbourne Olympics.

'Take care of yourself,' was the sum of his fatherly advice as he shook my hand and looked deeply and meaningfully into my eyes. He didn't shed a tear but I suspected one was not far away. A few weeks later I was in that same boat myself, not quite the big bronzed Anzac I thought I was.

Despite my strongly voiced desire to be housed in one of the Education Department's student hostels Dad had received firm advice to the contrary. Having made exploratory enquiries he had quickly developed a somewhat jaundiced view of what university students could get up to. He concluded I didn't need encouragement from like-minded students to be any more foolish than my natural inclination suggested. His chief accommodation adviser, collaborator and occasional drinking pal at Hamilton's Caledonian Hotel, the eminent local businessman and jeweller Herbert Rizzo, had given him what I suspected was a very one-sided view of university life, in other words a bum steer.

Herbert's son Max, an intermittent out of control lunatic, was known by everyone outside the Rizzo family as Mad Max and had always required pretty decent shackles to keep him on the straight and narrow. Max was to become my unlikely and unfortunate benchmark. To everyone's amazement, Max had recently graduated in engineering at Melbourne University, apparently the early inspiration for Dad's fantasy for me to study engineering, and was now making new accommodation arrangements. It is said that sometimes the world needs its lunatics but this was hardly one of those times. I didn't hold a candle to Max in terms of his degree of madness but, in their consummate wisdom, Dad and Mr Rizzo decided that was beside the point. Spartan accommodation was what was required for young Ray, the more Spartan the better, and Mad Max's previous digs were about as Spartan as you could get. In any case, Dad had always subscribed to the pragmatic theory that the unstaked tree grows strongest and the eminent jeweller's advice was right up that particular alley.

Number 10 Allen Street, Coburg sat directly opposite the huge and bustling Tip Top Bakery. The address didn't have much going for it unless you considered the convenient twenty-minute tram ride via nearby Sydney Road to Melbourne University or its close proximity to three movie theatres, also in Sydney Road, that were to provide occasional rewarding solace.

As well as being the domicile of the Spartans, 10 Allen Street was the home of Mrs Smith, a nice lady but no less rabidly anti-Catholic than Mum, if not more so. She was adamant that the nuns' and priests' quarters at the local Catholic schools were connected by conveniently located underground tunnels, a commonly believed and enthusiastically communicated fiction among Protestants at the time.

Mrs Smith provided bed and breakfast and little else to her lone boarder who was accommodated in the small bedsitter attached to her equally small federation period home. Breakfast was served in my study, a small entry alcove just large enough to house a built-in desk and a useful hardwood kitchen chair. The adjoining bedroom was similarly small, dark and stark. In keeping with the rest of my accommodation, the bedroom had a small window no more than a stride from the house next door and which in all likelihood had never seen the sun. The combined wardrobe and clothes cabinet rested on well-worn brown hued linoleum that originally could have been any colour. There was just enough space for a narrow single bed and the smallest bedside rug you were ever likely to see but nonetheless large enough to enable you to wipe your feet free of the minute particles of debris that inevitably accompanied linoleum floors and which stuck to the bottom of your feet like iron filings to a magnet.

There was no access to the rest of the house nor was there any heating, which meant I spent a lot of time in bed in the winter months. Radiators, not without good reason, were banned as being too dangerous as were the even deadlier water immersion heaters that, if you forgot to turn them off, kept getting hotter and hotter until they burst into flame– which was the short term fate of the appliance I smuggled into my quarters. It had been worth a try.

The toilet was a converted dunny at the end of the property closely adjacent to the back lane originally positioned to facilitate the night cart's collections. Washing, body and clothes, was facilitated by an external cold water tap mounted over an originally brown gulley trap that over the years had become vibrantly stained in an artistic combination of vivid blue, green and red. I could shower wherever I could find one. Telephone calls could be made from the public phone box at the Moreland railway station, a five-minute walk from 10 Allen Street and meals could be had at the Greek Café in Sydney Road, again a five-minute walk, at a budgeted limit of three shillings a meal, equal to around five dollars today. My textbooks and small transistor radio would keep me company during the long dark hours.

The few student colleagues from Hamilton and the new university friends I was about to acquire all lived south of the Yarra River in premises generally considered by those north of the Yarra, erroneously as it turned out, to be affluent in character. Given one's reliance on the limited public transport infrastructure (everything closed down at midnight) my friends might as well have lived on another planet. Dad's unstaked tree theory was going to be sorely tested. The weekends proved to be depressingly long. Nonetheless, it was not all doom and gloom. The weekly highlight, courtesy of the more cosmopolitan girls from migrant families north of the Yarra, was in attending one of the hugely popular Saturday night town hall dances in Moonee Ponds, Coburg or Brunswick. The concomitant downside was the walk, jog, run, half-marathon back to 10 Allen Street in the early hours of Sunday, fifty-six tram stops being my personal best. The other downside was the five-minute break between dances that encouraged lone figures like myself to join the more than forty per cent of the population that smoked and thus soon became addicted to a habit that took me thirty-seven years to break. Four weeks of cold turkey torture and its associated nightmares and intense unanticipated depression was no doddle.

Social contact in 10 Allen Street, Coburg, male or female, was banned without approval by Mrs Smith, permission most unlikely to be granted if the visitor happened to be female. During that first briefing Mrs Smith articulated her concern about Wendy Saunders who lived only two doors away. I had already noticed Wendy and hoped that with a bit of luck Mrs Smith's concern might be well founded. Things had taken a major turn for the better and I was suddenly paying much closer attention. And, surprising as it may have seemed at the outset, 1956 turned out to be a pretty good year.

Wendy Saunders was the receptionist at the real estate agency on the corner of Moreland and Sydney roads. Wendy did not qualify as beautiful but nonetheless was definitely up to snuff and enlivened every space she occupied, particularly in the eyes of a simple country boy. She had wild purple hair, wore startlingly tight sweaters and adorned herself in equally startling short skirts. She loved wearing the highest heels a country boy had seen and had a tottering staccato walk that would later be epitomised as pure Bette Midler. Wendy was smarter than first appeared, schoolroom endeavour never having rated all that highly compared to her other interests at the time and we were to become good mates; almost, but not quite, very good mates. It was more than convenient that Mrs Smith vacated 10 Allen Street at 4 pm to clean offices in the city, returning around 9 pm; even more convenient that there were no houses on the other side of Allen Street to accommodate prying, tell-tale eyes. On the first occasion I smuggled Wendy into my digs she picked up from my desk an economics text book with the title *Monopoly* and asked what 'moan-o-poly' was all about.

At weekends Wendy was a 'widgie'. Widgies were the euphemistic gun molls to the era's 'bodgies'. Bodgie and widgie groups had sprung up all over Melbourne in response to the rock and roll craze set alight by Bill Haley and the Comets and Elvis Presley in the mid-1950s. Their members were from lower socioeconomic backgrounds and engaged in exaggerated 'look at me' behaviour. The bodgies were easily recognisable by their slicked-back, heavily vaselined duck tail hairstyles, black stovepipe trousers, ripple soled shoes and white sport coats. The widgies didn't go for a uniform but were keen on heavy black eye makeup and ultra-pale lipstick. In her quieter moments, Wendy was nothing like her external persona might have suggested and she looked as though she might become a late bloomer.

Much to Mrs Smith's disdain and even greater concern, in this case concern for my personal welfare, I began squiring Wendy to her weekend rock and roll parties when she was having trouble with her on again off again boyfriend. Wendy's bodgie friends seemed surprisingly middle of the road given their knife-carrying reputations. It was no surprise that they were highly suspicious of the first university student they had met and I breathed a longish sigh of relief when they ultimately and perhaps falsely concluded I was not the superior, up myself toff they had taken for granted at the outset. I could be adaptable, or at least appear to be adaptable, if human survival was at stake. This was quite fortunate because Wendy's intermittent boyfriend was evidently twice as big as me and rumoured to indulge in violence as a leisure activity.

¶

If the excitement of being in the big smoke was one thing then the intimidation of Melbourne University was something else. It was a far more confronting reminder of that first day at Hamilton High and even those who relished the university's unfettered freedom knew we were really out of our depth. Our self-doubt pulsed and pounded; the hurdles were higher, the challenges more complex and our metropolitan peers bigger, cooler and, of course, far better looking.

Not helping matters was Melbourne University's cloistered architecture with its ability to shrink mere mortals. We continually succeeded in getting ourselves lost within its impenetrable maze of buildings, arrived late for lectures and were forced to endure the wit and sarcasm of the lecturers. Added to all this was that strange phenomenon peculiar to Melbourne University at the time — a derisive and belittling hiss from our fellow students that rose to a crescendo as the blushing upstarts from the rural nowhere tentatively searched for an empty seat.

Our country bumpkin attire contrasted with the sloppy white sweaters, corduroy trousers, Viyella shirts, duffel coats and desert boots worn by our sophisticated city-bred peers, all attempting to look like off-duty polo players with an air of indifference and wealth. The whole campus seemed to be trying to give the impression it lived in Toorak. Within weeks we, too, were getting our hair cut college style at Peter Jackson's as well as being captured by the university look. But for many months, despite our new livery, we still felt like imposters.

But there was something good awaiting new arrivals to the Big Smoke, something we hadn't even considered. We might have arrived anonymously in this city of more than two million people but who we were about to become depended on the degree to which we sought to reinvent ourselves. And as some long forgotten wise person once advised — 'once you have the new image down pat don't go too strongly at it mate; go gentle, play it simple. Don't make the mistake of trying to convince everyone who you were or who you were not. Your job was to convince yourself.'

Peter Jackson's in 1956 in Melbourne's Bourke Street was the House of Cool; cool clothes, cool hair styles. The front of the shop was all dark wood befitting a gentleman's outfitter and smelt of richness, luxury and indulgence. The back room opened up into the barber's shop with six leather chairs in a line. On the walls were testimonials, photos of famous sportsmen and framed letters of thanks from the rich and famous, Henry Bolte, Lindsay Hassett and Laurie Nash among them. One could only guess as to whose eminent bum had warmed my chair before me and I was overcome by this cozy, gushing feeling about what a great place Melbourne was.

We were led to believe all the barbers were Italian, the best barbers in the world. Only scissors were used and electric clippers were nowhere to be seen. There were photos of highly ambitious hairstyles on the bench in front of us from which we could select our new 'do' if that were our inclination; bodgie with kiss curl in the front, brush back, buzz cut, college cut, the eastern cut-off, floppy fringe, Robert Wagner, James Dean. Certainly no short back and sides; that would never have done. The swarthy members of the mafia modelled our hair with a disdainful, bored flourish, our heads mere props in what amounted to a vaudeville act as they entertained themselves in a loud foreign babble we assumed to be Italian. My man was Gino and to complete his act Gino wrapped a hot towel around my head, vigorously slapped on a pervasive aftershave lotion, puffed my neck with talcum powder and spun the chair a couple of times with an exaggerated energetic flourish before providing intimidating grinning assistance in showing me where my feet were supposed to be. Silently, Gino gestured to a cup on the bench with coins in it, causing me to hesitate for a moment, unsure as to whether I should take one out or put one in. For what seemed an eternity but in fact only a fraction of a second the dumb country boy's fingers twitched in agonising uncertainty until the toff alighting from the adjacent chair casually flipped a coin into his man's, that is Roberto's, cup. Scarlet faced, I quickly fumbled for and found a threepenny bit in the folds of my trouser pocket and as casually off-duty as I could muster, flipped it into Gino's mug as if that had always been the accepted order of things.

I couldn't afford to buy my clothes at the House of Cool, that honour going to the less lofty, more down at heel Fairway Trading Company in Elizabeth Street, not far from Flinders Street station. I was there to load up on some good tackle, having been attracted by the red painted 'Closing Down Sale, Everything Must Go' sign in the window, more-so the '50 per cent off'. In one visit I purchased a year's wardrobe; a white sloppy jumper, a Viyella check shirt, two pairs of corduroy trousers, a duffel coat, desert boots and some smalls. The closing down sale was obviously less than a huge success because one Saturday morning six months later as I walked down Elizabeth Street to catch the train to Footscray Football Ground I noticed the same sign on the window. Sixteen years later it was still there.

We met Jews for the first time. Apart from Dad's drinking mate, Herbert Rizzo, who was Jewish and who I had always assumed to be some sort of Hamilton aberration, I thought Jews only existed in the Bible. It seemed in 1955 that news of the holocaust hadn't drifted as far west as Hamilton. Confident, colourful, abrasively candid, apparently insensitive to the views of others, sometimes likeable, sometimes not, my new Jewish acquaintances stuck mainly to their own but added another dimension to my understanding of personal style — their stepping aside to allow you to take the running was a rarely observed generosity. And under no circumstances was anyone permitted to stuff up their day, their time apparently far more important than yours. I applauded their self-belief and envied their 'chutzpah', their bullet-proofed individuality, their practice of sitting front and centre in the lecture theatres and their preparedness to not merely ask but to demand answers to fearless questions. In the meantime, I wrestled with my inevitable introduction to anti-Semitic dogma. Outside their own they seemed to have few friends, only occasional allies and many detractors.

The free spirited, charismatic, not to mention lascivious Germaine Greer, her followers dawdling along behind her hoping for some reflected glory, stalked the campus like a lioness. Attractive, loud, foul-mouthed, her colourful reputation becoming more salacious by the day, we admired her from afar.

We kept a keen lookout during lunchtime on Wednesdays for marauding bands of 'rag' obsessed, boiler suited engineering students who, in keeping with decades of tradition, on Wednesday afternoons flour bombed anyone foolish enough to come within range.

We attended free lunchtime jazz concerts in the Union Theatre and loved the hugely popular student reviews. The reviews added a challenging and intimidating dimension to a simple country boy's developing understanding of what young people were capable of.

We paid twenty cents to attend weekly lunchtime rock and roll classes where I was provided with the opportunity to strut my stuff. I could hold a beat and thought I was a pretty good mover on my feet, soon doing some good work with the Quality Street, well-bred rich girls with plummy accents who, popular belief had it, could even be up for a carefree ride over the jumps. Promisingly, they appeared to fancy a brash desperado who was a bit different to their usual private school lads. Tragically, these classes were banned after only four sessions in response to their discovery by the engineering students as well as the unrest caused by the inevitable flour bombing. It was of course a Wednesday. Following the demise of the dance classes, the plummy voiced girls disappeared, returning to those mysterious places from whence they had come, never to be seen again.

We were introduced to lunch at Jimmy Watson's famous wine bar and restaurant in nearby Lygon Street. There, on Wednesday afternoons, a half day off for students, we rubbed shoulders with those who purchased their clothes at Peter Jackson's and Henry Bucks and jostled with the business suits to cook our rump steaks, onions and tomatoes on the do it yourself hot plates. The original larger than life Jimmy Watson, leather apron attired, barged between bodies, splashing claret on each hot plate as hard as he could go. My introduction to Jimmy Watson's was by way of fellow student David Dole who, despite promising early appearances, knew as much about wine as I did, precisely nothing. Our steaks on that day were accompanied by my first bottle of wine, sweet sherry labelled as Australian Madeira. We thought it was great. Jimmy straightened us out the following week. We completed the process with a Craven A cigarette, Australia's then leading brand, pontificating that there was nothing better than having a good wine with your steak and finishing off with a smoke. I remember it was a Craven A cigarette because David had a class member the previous year at Christian Brothers Parade in Abbotsford whose surname was Cravanna but who was always referred to as Craven A.

We spent our spare time in the Union Building, the university's central hub. I hid in the men's lounge slumped in one of the many over-stuffed leather armchairs where I read discarded copies of the cleverly written weekly university newspaper, *Farrago*, and surreptitiously observed the moves of the cool dudes and those in the know.

Ralph Willis and I often had lunch, sandwiches only, in the billiards room where we admired the deft expertise of those who had graduated in billiards with honours. When we were game enough to emulate them we were embarrassed to find we shouldn't have.

To our dismay we learned that lecturers lectured, they didn't teach. On principle they seldom presented things simply if an absurdly demanding alternative happened to be available. It seemed they saw themselves above the mundane task of imparting knowledge to idiots. That was the Communist, Socialist intelligentsia for you who, having sat around blaming the capitalist system for the world's ills in the run up to the Second World War, still dominated the academic ranks. Mind you, in 1956 the densely populated lecture theatres, often holding hundreds of students, provided little opportunity to address the needs of such large audiences. We were supplied with few lecture note handouts and relied on our own improvisations in note-taking. For a while I tried to supplement my notes with summaries of the notes of my fellow students but soon became even more depressed, concluding that we must have attended different lectures. The most depressing part of all was an awareness of what you didn't know and, worse, not knowing enough to ask sensible questions about that which you didn't know — which always seemed like most of it.

The attitude of our contemptuous, recently graduated tutors whose task, we thought, was to fill in the gaps at the weekly tutorials, was even worse. It was hardly a consolation that everyone seemed to be caught up in the same vortex of frustration, desperation and despair. When misery and depression reached peak levels I took myself off to my regular safety valve, an afternoon session at the movies in the city. Afterwards, reinvigorated by a feel-good movie, I re-joined the battle, my problems seemingly more fathomable.

Usually, I arrived early at university and stayed late but that had nothing to do with my zeal to learn. The libraries were warm, the café was always open and there was electric light and very nice toilet paper in the washrooms. But these pleasantries did not prevent me from leaving university each day in what was usually a pall of gloom. The lonely, cramped, not to mention again, Spartan quarters of 10 Allen Street hardly beckoned. Miraculously, having achieved little understanding of what I was studying, I passed all four subjects.

In that first year university life was made more than bearable by:

Peter B. Lawrence from Lakes Entrance, as likeable a soul as the century produced, who mastered a serious speech impediment and later became a high profile sharebroker, chairman of the Victoria Amateur Turf Club (later the Melbourne Racing Club) and president of the Savage Club;

Wally Lawler, the tall, charismatic, hurdling heart throb from Geelong who just missed out on representing Australia at the '56 Olympics in the 110 metres hurdles and who later went bust in a Ford dealership;

Ralph Willis, the quiet, unassuming leg spinner from Footscray with whom, during my first year two years, I spent most time. Ralph's father was a union official and, unlike that of the rest of us, Ralph's politics were to the left. Ralph successfully mentored me in economics in first year but not so successfully in second year. He had initially planned to become a schoolteacher but made a right angle turn in his career path and followed Bob Hawke as research officer of the Australian Council of Trades Unions. He then ventured into politics and became a highly regarded minister in the Hawke Labour government and finally, Federal Treasurer in the Keating government;

The hyper active Bob Rees, who suffered from the worst case of facial volcanoes I have seen and who couldn't keep his mouth shut. Those who knew him less well could have been forgiven for under estimating his abilities. He played AFL football with Richmond (two games) and captained the university's third eleven;

I occasionally attended court room trials with law student John (Jack) Winneke, brother of Mike and son of the then Governor of Victoria, Sir Henry Winneke. Jack and Mike later became University Blacks team members of mine in the A Grade Amateurs in 1959. Big

Jack, a lively and hilarious storyteller, played fifty vigorous games as a ruckman with Hawthorn in the AFL before concentrating exclusively on the law. He became a judge in the Supreme Court of Victoria and later in the Court of Appeals.

The enthusiastic Alan Metcalf who, having been anointed as captain of Melbourne High School in 1955 seemed headed for big things. But leadership had been unfairly thrust upon him, brainwashing him into politically correct, limiting constraints. Alan's self-actualisation ambitions would have to be satisfied by having played first XI premier cricket with Melbourne Cricket Club given his later disappearance into the bowels of BHP never to be seen again;

Tall, thin and relaxed, Trevor Steer from Gippsland spoke with a slow, laconic drawl, walked with a long loping stride and inevitably was called 'Farmer'. Trevor later played Aussie Rules with University Blacks and went on to a very successful football career with the Collingwood first eighteen in the AFL. He also became a highly regarded high school principal;

The gentle giant from Yallourn, Peter Hutchinson, who was planning on becoming a science teacher and his mate, Ray Stallworthy, a more unpredictable but delightful character with whom I later shared a room in second year;

The hapless and increasingly tragic Herby Morrison, who, like most of my acquaintances in those early months, hid in the back row of the commerce lecture theatre. With the passage of time Herby became more forthright in his assertions and even less correct. I always suspected Herby had been building himself a permanent chemical shield against reality. He failed every subject in first year and soon found himself at the Victorian Titles Office in Queen Street, a well-known sump for the ambitionless, the temporary or permanently insane and a popular backstop for university students needing to supplement meagre incomes. It was an institution with which I, too, in the fullness of time, found the need to become acquainted.

And finally, the tall and athletic John Desmond from Warragul, also destined for teaching who by dint of his previous year's Aussie

Rules exploits had received an invitation to join Carlton in the AFL. The AFL draft system was years away and players residing outside the Melbourne metropolitan area were available to any club. John Desmond was one of a highly select group of 1956 AFL invitees and my friendship with him indirectly provided me with access to the potential dream.

John Desmond might have been tall, good looking and a promising high profile centre half forward but he was not as self-assured as might be thought. Aware of my passion for Carlton and uncomfortable about his turning up to training at Carlton alone John gently pleaded with me to accompany him to his first senior list training night at Princes Park. Not as an observer but as a player. I had apparently gone overboard in embellishing my football career highlights to John, giving little thought that these exaggerations might be revealed for what they were. In the fast approaching cold light of day my fantasised certain future career with Carlton took on a slightly different complexion. Gradually, the debilitating fear of failure subsided and Doug Stevenson's 'faint heart never having won fair lady' call to the barricades resonated in my ears and the more I thought about the idea the more I liked it.

John Desmond received a royal welcome at Princes Park, nobody bothering to question the credentials of the sixteen year old imposter with him. I must have either looked the goods or put on a good act on that first training night because I later learned that the Carlton officials each thought one of the other officials knew who I was.

Expecting to be ejected at any moment, I undressed side by side with players I knew only from photographs in my scrapbooks and from radio broadcasts. I escaped on to the hallowed turf of Princes Park with my heroes. In front of hundreds of early season Carlton supporters I strutted, preened, ran, jumped and brashly called for the ball from 1955 Victorian professional sprint champion and Big V state centre-man Laurie Kerr, as if I were a legitimate invitee. He must have thought so too because he put the ball, laces out, bang on my chest. The adrenalin added 'thirty centimetres to the height and a metre to the stride'. With sure hands and the running drop kicks perfected at 43 Alexandra Parade coming perfectly off the boot, I was not only acting legitimate I was legitimate. It was a fairy tale and a tribute to unjustified self-belief. And, climbing all over his back, I even took an arrogant mark over Carlton captain, Ken Hands, who was almost twelve centimetres taller than me. After training I casually shared a relaxing hot bath with 'team mate' Laurie Kerr who was happy to share some war stories with the cocky young pretender. That advice of only needing to convince yourself as to whom you might become had been right on the money.

I did enough on that first and subsequent training nights to be included in Carlton's first practice match of the season. The pre-season AFL competition of today was still decades away and pre-seasons consisted purely of intra club practice matches. Still pumped and playing in the midfield, I again over achieved and with the aid of my opponents' backs took a couple of Hamilton High School perfected spectacular marks. Not only was I back in my yard at 43 Alexandra Parade but I had also taught myself the most valuable lesson a good ordinary Aussie Rules footballer could learn. I had convinced myself to ignore teammates and competitors alike and to run to the ball as if they didn't exist. This practice would later be described as 'imposing yourself on the game', a handy practice if you were trying to be noticed. I was written up in that Saturday's *Sporting Globe* as one of the better players and a recruit from Hamilton worth watching. The journalist had gone to the trouble of making some enquiries of the club.

At the end of that first practice game the Carlton officials used one of the club's Form Fours to get my signature. Each club had a limited number of Form Fours that could be used each year. Signing one was formal acknowledgement that you were a potential senior player and placed you off limits to other clubs. Compared to the showy nature of some of Carlton's highly regarded invitees the officials said I had what they wanted. I was 'rugged'. I looked it up in Roget's Thesaurus. I was 'strong, robust, vigorous, herculean, built like a brick shithouse'. But I don't think the Carlton officials were acquainted with the thesaurus. I was now officially a Carlton player and living the dream. Outside the Carlton ground I coolly, authoritatively, shrugged my way on to the tram back to 10 Allen Street with the words 'the rugged Ray King' resonating in my ears. I stared into the eyes of my fellow passengers. Yes, they could see it too. I was definitely rugged. But I wanted more than that. I wanted to seem extraordinary in the eyes of those anonymous passengers — brilliant, adventurous, brave — I wanted them to see I was going to be a Carlton player.

Alongside the famous Sergio Silvagni, who went on to play 268 games with the senior team — exactly 268 games more than me — I became a member of the Carlton Under Nineteens, known then as the 'Thirds'. Over two hundred hopefuls had been cut to a final list of thirty-two. Ironically, prize recruit John Desmond didn't make it. Three times a week I was able to have a shower and three times a week I had regular social interaction other than at university. And naturally, every Saturday night, guilty of perhaps more than a hint of hubris, I wore my official Carlton blazer to the dance. As I had hoped it turned out to be a useful piece of infrastructure

In 1956 the 'Thirds', starting at noon, played the curtain raisers immediately before the senior AFL games. This arrangement changed in 1960 when the 'seconds' replaced the thirds as the curtain raisers. In order to protect ground conditions the curtain raisers ceased altogether during the 1980s and by the late '90s the Seconds, by then known as the Reserves, were also in the process of disappearing into a separate competition.

Not only did we have our names in the *AFL Record* each week (No. 17 — Ray King) but in the last quarter we were playing in front of as many as twenty-five thousand spectators. Occasionally, as I walked the streets of Coburg, I would hear a whispered 'that's Ray King', immediately bringing a spring to the step and an extension to the height. It wasn't the big time but it was extraordinarily seductive nonetheless.

Given the combination of the AFL's metropolitan zoning rules and the suburb of Carlton having become home to the influx of Italian migrants, I was one of a small minority of Anglo Saxons on the Carlton thirds' playing list. The others all had names ending in vowels — Bortolotto, Silvagni, Scarpella, Ruggerio, Puglia etc and with the exception of Sergio, who had no need to strut his stuff, they were all true to their hot Italian blood. I spent a lot of time on the field getting between them and opposition players.

I played the opening game of the season at Windy Hill, Essendon's old home ground, and ran on to the ground in front of at least five thousand spectators who had arrived early to take up good positions for the main game that followed. With the monogrammed CFC on my chest and first eighteen Doug Beasy's number seventeen on my back I thought my heart would burst with pride, the rest of life now an anti-climax, downhill all the way. I would be wrong but at the time I didn't think I would ever match that moment for pure, unadulterated exhilaration. My performance that day was pretty ordinary, needing the time of the uninitiated to adapt to the greater speed and intensity of the contest and thus winning only eight scrappy kicks. But despite my attempts to convince myself otherwise I now knew in my heart of hearts I just wasn't good enough. The chickens had come home to roost, truth always likely to win out; I was just a pretender. I poured my heart out to coach Ken Aitken after the game and he merely smiled. Three weeks later I took a Hamilton High hanger in the first minute at Princes Park and went on to be Carlton's best player against Collingwood, the crisis of confidence over.

I also became Ken Aitken's favoured 'tagger' when the occasion warranted, although that term was yet to be invented. In my day you were a 'stopper'. Later in the season I was promoted and played three games with the seconds. There was talk I was in line for inclusion on the following year's senior list but my name got no further than the 'to be considered' list. However, I did finish fourth in Carlton's best and fairest award and won the most determined player award. I also earned votes for the Morrish Medal, the 'Brownlow' of the thirds competition, in four games out of sixteen according to Ken Aitken, albeit for a total of only four votes. In those days there was no end-of-season awards' night; the AFL merely sent a typed sheet to each club with the outcome. Ken said I deserved better. It was a testament to good fortune, fantasy and unjustified self-belief.

The following year Sergio Silvagni was appointed captain of the Thirds and I was made vice-captain. Having upgraded my fantasies to more grandiose levels I couldn't wait for the season to get under way. Things were shaping up very nicely for an even better year and I again featured as one of the better players in all the practice games. It just goes to show how wrong you can be. The dream turned into a nightmare with a badly corked thigh in the final quarter of the last practice match, an injury that today would have been quickly dealt with by a wide bore needle. Unable to train for five weeks I was not back in the side until game seven. Only partially fit and down in confidence, I struggled against fitter and faster opponents. And it didn't get much better in the ensuing weeks, even being ignominiously dropped for one game, albeit being best on ground for Carlton Stars on the windswept open parklands adjacent to the Princes Park ground, and back in the side the following week. Suffice to say that the rediscovered self-belief with Carlton Stars that had been such a marvellous accomplice in 1956 was not enough to bridge the gap. My personal star gradually faded into obscurity and, inevitably, despite a couple of better games late in the season, my name was irrevocably removed from the potential senior player's list. The dream was over and 1957 was on the way to turning into a piece of shit.

I missed playing a third season with the thirds, turning nineteen on the twenty-eighth of February 1958, one day before the cut-off date, the first of March. Perhaps that was a blessing in disguise given my requirement to undertake National Service and my forgettable part season with Prahran in the Victorian Football Association.

1959 saw me playing with University Blacks, one of two university teams playing in the Victorian Amateur Football Association A division where I had sufficient enthusiasm to warrant being awarded a blue at the end of the season and to be selected to represent Melbourne University in that year's inter-varsity championships in Perth. It was an elite group, nine team members going on to play AFL at senior level. Of course, I was not one of them.

Meanwhile my cricket ambitions, like my height, also fell a bit short. I got as far as opening the bowling for University seconds in the Premier League competition but at 171 centimetres, fully stretched, I was never going anywhere as a fast bowler. A dwarf running in to open the bowling with a shiny new Kookaburra in his hand was not a good look; particularly for those who thought they should have been the one with the cherry in their hand.

For sport that was it; as we all learn all too quickly, a new life was unfolding. I was married in February 1960, a week short of my twenty-first birthday. By then I had completed a commerce degree and started studies for the Diploma of Education and beginning to focus on joining the ranks of the employed.

The isolation of a simple country boy in Coburg during that first year at university had produced some benefits. It had required the development of defence mechanisms and self-reliance in order to cope with loneliness and despondency. Perhaps Dad had been right after all. But it was time for a change.

¶

The year of 1957 saw the number of natural disasters around the globe rise to record levels. It was also the year I met Thelma Wright. She was a whiz with a sewing machine and worked as a part-time model with one of the fashion houses in Flinders Lane. She was attractive, easy company, uninterested in intellectual matters but nonetheless intelligent. I probably gave excessive weight to her looks. Apart from a disconcerting degree of assertiveness she was good to have around and we hit it off pretty well. I was a bit schizophrenic about that assertiveness. 'Introduction to Educational Psychology' had suggested that when both parties have the goal of establishing dominance the

115

ultimate result can get messy. Nonetheless within weeks, both having recently turned eighteen, we were a couple.

In October 1957, the night before my final financial accounting examination, a subject I thought I had pretty well under control, Thelma had a tear filled crisis which required my immediate attention. An intended short period away from the books fell into disarray while I played the Good Samaritan, although with little effect. Courtesy of my sleep deprived brain the examination result saw me fall two marks short of making the cut and 1957 continued to turn into the aforementioned piece of manure. Ominously, the grim reaper had also struck four weeks earlier when I misplaced my never to be seen again lecture and study notes for Economics B, largely based on the theories of John Maynard Keynes which even the lecturers had difficulty understanding. After my good year in 1956 God had balanced things up.

Murphy's Law, aided by self-inflicted folly, had bitten me on the backside well and truly. Now down two subjects, my Education Department salary about to be automatically suspended for twelve months, I now faced a troublesome 1958 quadrella; earning a living, finding somewhere to live, repeating two subjects on a part-time basis and starting the first stanza of national service — seventy-seven days at the Puckapunyal army camp in central Victoria.

¶

Nineteen fifty-eight was the first year of the national service ballot. My number had come up, along with approximately one thousand other less than fortunate Victorian eighteen year old males. We joined the twentieth intake of national (army) service on 3 January for 139 days of military training to be served in tranches over four years, largely at Puckapunyal but supplemented by periods at the discrete jungle training area known as Site Seventeen, also in central Victoria.

Number two platoon, home for me and my thirty-one colleagues for the next seventy-seven days, was one of four platoons in C

(Charlie) company. We were mainly university students with a few primary school student teachers thrown in. None of us wanted to be there, an irritation boosted by the deftness of lady luck and the doubtful pleasure of potentially dying for your country at some indeterminate time in the future.

I was issued with an identification disc (3/780713), ill-fitting work and marching-out gear, gruesomely stained bed linen, a variety of different sized equipment packs and a monstrously heavy and impossibly awkward First World War rifle. It was a Lee Enfield single shot .303 inch calibre rifle manufactured in Great Britain in 1913. 'Gallipoli' was scratched on the butt, presumably the creative adornment of some unfortunate sod who had fought in that never to be forgotten disaster. Courtesy of the quartermaster's dismissive hit or miss but mainly miss, sizing estimates few of us looked as though we belonged in uniform. That is, apart from Henry Kranz, a patrician if ever I saw one. Law student Henry was destined for the court room and his work clothes always looked as if they had come straight from the laundry. For the rest of us our army issued clothing fitted where it touched. The work day began at 6 am and lights out was 10 pm.

For two years at university we had been tutored to think for ourselves and to question everything put before us. But such a concept was not in accord with that of the army. The army preferred unthinking robots that followed orders to the letter. The scene was thus set for some predictable philosophical clashes. The trainees thought the army regulars narrow minded, ignorant morons and the regulars considered the university trainees arrogant, supercilious know-alls. There was a strong element of truth in both perspectives.

For the first few weeks we did little but drill on the corps parade ground in a gradually improving orderly manner hectored by less than original commentary from the regulars. Around and around we went in never varying circles or, to be more correct, 'squares'. The purpose of this seemingly mindless exercise was to hone our response times to the barked orders of our assailants who tried, mostly unsuccessfully, to remove any semblance of non-robotic thinking.

We then graduated to manoeuvres in the bush, war games and the firing of live ammunition on the move. I soon learned that military training was not necessarily a whole lot safer than combat, particularly when I felt the wind and heard the distinctive sound barrier breaking crack of a colleague's carelessly fired round as it exploded past my left thigh. I suppose I felt lucky. I don't know what else you call it when a missile travelling at more than 1600 kilometres an hour just misses you. Perhaps it was an omen, perhaps I was unkillable, because nothing said goodbye better than a .303 inch bullet from a Lee Enfield. I was obviously pleased to survive that piece of sloppiness albeit a little shocked that the situation had been allowed to arise in the first place. I thought a thorough investigation into the circumstances would not have gone astray.

The training was arduous and, for sedentary university students, unrelentingly and physically taxing. Like many of my colleagues I dropped around five kilos in weight despite the starchy food and having arrived pretty fit in the first place. I was now cut like a diamond.

It was no surprise that the regulars didn't like my style (described by others as irreverent) and that I was front and centre following an incident in the chow line in the mess (dining) hall at lunch on day two. Having received his very suspicious-looking culinary delight, Private 'Wild Bill' Harrison studied the contents of his mess tin with frowning disquiet. He turned to me in the long queue behind him and muttered, 'Jesus, the cook must be some weird sort of c—t' (after just two days in the army our language had gone up, or perhaps more correctly, down a couple of notches). My immediate and apparently louder response was, 'yeah, but is that weird 'c—t' really a cook?' a rejoinder to which the cook or whatever he was and who happened to be close by took immediate umbrage. That evening I had the first of a number of punishment guard duties, two hours on two hours off from 10 pm to 6 am.

Saturdays and Sundays were our days off, although we were required to attend church service on Sunday morning whether we liked it or not. And mostly we didn't like it. In a camp of more than a thousand frustrated young males, in every sense of the word, there was little to do at weekends other than wash clothes and repair and maintain equipment, with some recruits taking endless, mindless hours to polish the toes of their boots to a mirror like shine. On my first Saturday morning I was scrubbing away at my working gear in one of a row of deep troughs next to a cool dude. The cool dude was the first to relent and broke the ice with:

'Where're you from mate?'

'Hamilton. What about you?' I grunted.

'Warrnambool.'

'Warrnambool,' I replied, warming up, 'I've been to the dance in Warrnambool.'

'Uh huh,' he said. 'The Palais de Dance was it?'

'That's the one.'

'Do any good?'

To show I considered myself no slouch in that department and wishing to impress the cool dude, I replied 'I did as a matter of fact. I escorted this bird home, an especially nice bird she was too and we ended up in a vintage utility truck in her back yard.'

'Uh huh,' he drawled, 'not a bad bird that Vicki Pollock is she.'

We laughed, now soul mates, introduced ourselves and 'shook' according to convention. I matched his pressure, which was medium heavy.

Philip Shirrefs looked a little like actor Russell Crowe but acted more like Paul Newman of Butch Cassidy fame which, having had it pointed out to him, he had developed into a fine art. He was the Peter Pan of our platoon. People took to him. He was good for a laugh, great to hang with and drew companions like a magnet. I wanted his attention, his approval, wanted to be closest to him and told him my best stories first. He was to be my best man and I was to be his groomsman at our respective weddings.

Adrian 'Hank' Bennetto, father of playwright and media commentator Casey Bennetto, was also an original. Like me he fell for the three card trick. Foolishly raising our arms in response to a seemingly innocent out of context query as to whether anyone present had ever done any boxing, Hank and I were immediately pressed into trying out for C Company representation in the battalion boxing championships, a very large deal in national service at the time.

Hank, from Swan Hill in northern Victoria, was one of the students I had admired from afar in the Union lounge in first year at Melbourne University. Tall, well put together and with Hollywood good looks, he was a dead ringer for screen heart-throb Robert Wagner although later in life he morphed more into the heavily overweight, bald, Sydney Greenstreet mould. Hank always sat alone in the Union lounge and looked at best self-assured and at worst laid back arrogant. I must have been a great judge of character because he later told me he sat alone because he was shit frightened of talking to anyone.

Hank, blessed with wonderful sporting talent, could do anything with a ball, particularly a basketball and pretty good with a football too. His hand eye co-ordination was that of a conjurer, his hand speed capable of plucking a fly out of the air. He also threw a right hand like the kick of a mule. With lightning speed and evasiveness supplementing his explosive punching power, he could have been anything in the boxing ring had he turned to it professionally. He easily KO'd all his opponents, generally in the first round, to become the undisputed heavyweight champion of the battalion.

I was less impressive. In the final of the battalion championships I had the misfortune to meet a highly experienced light middleweight by the name of Lewis, who had deferred from previous intakes. Lewis was a mature twenty-two years of age, four years my senior. Over a period of seven years he had had fifty-eight amateur fights and was by a country mile the most seasoned and experienced boxer to pull on a glove in the championships and probably in the history of the Australian Defence Force's national service program. He was good enough to fight for the Australian amateur light middleweight title in 1959 which, had he won (he didn't) would have put him into the Tokyo Olympics in 1960. But, then, my two drawn fights at the Hamilton High School fete in years eight and nine were not to be sneezed at.

Stress and a heavy training schedule in the lead up to the final had caused more rapid weight loss than planned so by the night of the bout I tipped the scales as a welterweight, a full weight division less than my light middleweight opponent. I was seven kilos lighter than my last game at Carlton four months earlier. My being smaller, less seasoned and vastly less experienced than Lewis was unlikely to augur well. I had a seemingly endless six minutes in which I could run but not hide.

The first round was a predictable nightmare. Not for me because I was in something of a fog and didn't know what the hell was going on. The nightmare was for my friends who spent most of that first round with their heads down, eyes strategically positioned behind the seats in front of them wishing they were somewhere else. Having decided on an opening gambit of intimidating confrontation Lewis had hurtled across the ring at the sound of the opening bell, launched a whirlwind of blows and proceeded to hit me everywhere bar the soles of my feet. I had been very successfully confronted and intimidated. In that first round I was little more than a punching bag, my brain bouncing around like a pin ball. My embarrassed mates willed Lewis to permit me to mercifully melt to the canvas or, better still, for the referee to stop the slaughter.

Fortunately, or perhaps unfortunately, my thick and longish neck acted as a shock absorber. It not only saved me from an ignominious first round knockout but also allowed what seemed like a miraculous recovery in between rounds. My corner man and trainer, Corporal Tilbrook, a long term regular who had fought in the Korean War, was apparently disappointed with my less than sterling performance. He snarled into my battered face during the interlude, 'sit up straight and look good, you fucken girl,' fearing that the referee who was staring at me with great intent would stop the fight given the severe belting I had received. Burge, who had completed his first tranche of national service a year earlier and who, coincidentally, happened to be in Puckapunyal on a refresher course for medics put it more succinctly, if less than sympathetically, with, 'King, you had shit belted out of you in that first round.'

Corporal Tilbrook, a serial gambler, had invested a large sum of money on me. He thought I was a 'smokey' who had sneaked under the radar. Unfortunately for his pocket he had been unaware of my opponent's seriously impressive pedigree when he laid his bet so his exhortations did have some degree of self-interest. In the second round the effort of Lewis's whirlwind opening started to tell and his multiple punch onslaughts gradually, and thankfully for all concerned, waned. He was visibly tiring. Towards the end of the round I began to land some good punches. The second round was at least even, perhaps even slightly in my favour according to Corporal Tillbrook who was trying to think positively given the sum he had riding on me. In the final round an exhausted Lewis stopped to a stand-still courtesy of his first round heroics. It was now his turn to hang on for dear life. Urged on by Corporal Tillbrook's enthusiastic, spit-flying exhortations and the roar of the crowd I chased Lewis all around the ring trying to land the number of punches I needed to win the fight or to land the one telling blow needed to put him on the canvas. But it was not to be a fairy tale ending.

I was also tiring, with too many attempted blows glancing off Lewis's chin or curling ineffectually around the back of his head. The eight-ounce gloves now weighed a tonne. When I did snap his head back the audience roared its support in ever increasing volume as it always does when an apparently defeated fighter claws his way back into the contest. As the bell sounded the end of the bout the noble warriors fell into each other's arms, relieved, smiling and exhausted, the pain over and the endorphins pumping madly. That night we would both sleep the sleep of the just. I won that round clearly but not by as much as Lewis had won the crushing first round and despite my honourable comeback Lewis was awarded the fight. The audience sympathised with my grandstand finish, gratifyingly booing the judges' decision. Lewis became the battalion's light middleweight champion and I had the next day off in the sick bay nursing a giant headache, suffering memory loss and gracefully disappearing into boxing obscurity — a blessing in disguise given my ability to take a punch, too often the genesis of the shuffling, punch drunk boxer who refused to give the game away.

Despite my lack of popularity with the regular army staff I was one of a small minority of national serviceman to be classified with an A rating at the end of our training. In the event of a declaration of something approaching a Third World War I would be conscripted into the army on day one, as a commissioned officer.

¶

Four days after my return from Puckapunyal I was a member of the Australian workforce. It wasn't all that difficult to get a job. The world economies were booming with pent-up energy following nearly thirty years of depression and war. Australia, like most developed countries, had serious labour shortages and the Victorian Education Department was employing just about anyone as teachers as long as they had some form of tertiary education, failed or otherwise. For two weeks I taught arithmetic, geography and history to years seven and eight at Gardenvale Central school in East Brighton. My resignation was filed within minutes of receiving a pay cheque that was a little over half what I had been mistakenly led to believe by the person who had employed me. An hour later, following a hasty telephone call, I was a Victorian public servant again, now employed at that institutional fallback for the generally down at heel, the psychotic and needy university students, the Victorian Titles Office.

The titles office in Queen Street was a charming oddity. Not only was the building gracefully and inefficiently early Victorian in design but the processes and procedures of the institution were steeped in those of the same era. Upon stepping through the imposing, decoratively sculptured and arched entrance on to brown linoleum, with an underlay that deadened sound to morgue-like requirements, you were slightly disappointed in that hushed dreamy silence not to see top hats, frock coats and flowing beards.

Scratching away with pen and ink in my very best writing I strove to carefully transcribe the details of around forty land transfers a day. It was a cruel and difficult to resist invitation to slumber.

Our supervisor, Mr Davies, a severe looking but surprisingly kindly man, sat on a very tall stool at the front of a work hall that afforded him a panoramic and unimpeded view of his minions, all fourth grade temporary acting clerks. When the need arose he stepped from his lofty heights and patrolled the aisles separating our desks where he gently and sympathetically interrupted the slumbering dreams of those who had drifted off.

My fellow scribes were also part-timers, some working only one or two days a week. Retirees, out of work actors, alcoholics, the mentally unstable and failed university students working to repair the damage of misspent youth or mere brain fades made up the majority of its work force.

Hank Bennetto soon joined me. He, too, had had his teaching studentship suspended for twelve months for failing two second year subjects. Hank suffered from that heady feeling that caused him to believe he knew better than his lecturers and had proceeded to inform them of their inadequacies on the two examination papers he had been judged to fail. Unobtrusively, languidly and without apparent effort he entertained himself, me and our seemingly catatonic co-workers with nimble magician-like skills with balls of all sizes as well as slick sleight of hand tricks with cards and coins.

Attention to detail was not one of my strengths, nor was it one of Hank's. We made too many mistakes on our transfers. As the power of the Public Service Union prevented us from being dismissed for simple incompetence we were allotted what was deemed to be the worst task in the building, the burying of dead caveats in the cobwebbed dungeons way below ground level, all coated in more than a century's mite-contaminated dust. Oblivious to the dangers of the dreaded dust mite we found this to be a more than convenient change in our duties because no one else ventured downstairs unless under exceptional circumstances. We idled away our time on university assignments, two-handed poker, novels, listening to trumpeter Jonah Jones on Hank's smuggled in gramophone as well as on regular snoozes, daily for me, occasional for Hank.

At Hank's wedding I was his best man but we gradually lost touch as Hank wandered the state slowly climbing the Education Department ladder to become a highly successful school principal. In 2008, after almost fifty years, we reunited as if there had been no intervening period. The renewal of our friendship was tragically cut short by Hank's sudden heart attack in July 2013.

¶

For the two decades following the Second World War, the Miss Australia Quest was a big deal with the Australian public. It was a highly successful public relations exercise for Hickory, a foundation garments manufacturer and marketer and was largely a beauty contest although in the late 1950s personality and general knowledge were nominally introduced into the judging criteria to pay lip service to the increasing cries of derision from its critics. Ultimately, Germaine Greer and the rising tide of feminism, women's liberation and the emerging wrath of political correctness caused the practical death knell of beauty contests despite the contests raising hundreds of thousands of dollars for the Spastic Children's Society and other worthy charities. The late 1950s were probably the height of the beauty contest's fame and standing.

In order to qualify for the finals then perhaps go on to compete for the Miss World title with its movie and modelling contracts, the girls had to first win the state title.

At the 1958 Miss Victoria Extravaganza Ball, Melbourne's social event of the year, Thelma Wright was proclaimed Miss Victoria to an accompanying crescendo of trumpets and a deluge of predictable happy tears. Her photo took up most of the front page in the Melbourne *Sun News Pictorial* (now the *Herald* Sun) and because Thelma and I were about to become engaged to be married an even larger photo of the happy couple took up most of page three. For three weeks Thelma had a round of public appearances and enjoyed a fanfare of publicity befitting the aura of the event. I must admit I enjoyed a sudden spike of attention around the university campus myself. At yet another Extravaganza Ball that year's Miss Australia title was won by Miss Queensland and Thelma's three weeks of fame came to an abrupt halt.

Later in the year, benefitting from the stint in the titles office dungeons, I picked up the two subjects required to renew full-time university study the following year. In Thelma's case the spike in self-esteem due to her moment in the sun was followed by the inevitable anti-climactic plunge. She dismissed this as minor insecurity and was adamant she would be far more settled once we were officially engaged. So, in 1959, formally engaged we became.

In February 1960, two weeks short of my turning twenty-one, we were married in a high church, Church of England ceremony in Geelong. At the reception I asked Thelma's parents what I should now call them and they suggested that 'Mr and Mrs Wright would still be more than satisfactory thank you very much.'

Thelma and I honeymooned at the King family shack in Port Fairy. Each morning, having recently become an obsessed devotee of golf, I was out of bed long before the sun rose to get in a quick round at the nearby Warrnambool golf course before joining a still slumbering Thelma mid-morning. Again, there was not a minute to be lost. It may not have boded well for the marriage but I was able to telegram the boys that I was the first of us to break a hundred.

We rented a unit on the third floor of a walk up apartment block in the Melbourne suburb of Elwood. The unit reeked with a smell that was completely unfamiliar to me or anyone else who hadn't started life in Europe. It was called olive oil. Mum, like most proud Australian born mothers, had never used anything other than one hundred per cent pure animal fat in her cooking and over the years had diligently lined our veins and arteries with multiple layers of pure cholesterol.

Thelma and I were to become the neighbours from hell and we quickly learned to avoid the corporate body man due to the high probability of complaints. Without wishing to put too fine a point on it we were the sort of tenants upon whom the authorities needed to keep a vigilant eye. Three times we failed to turn off the hose that filled our landlord-banned washing machine and three times we succeeded in flooding the downstairs apartment. The third time was the final straw for the long term second floor residents who, in abject misery but showing remarkable restraint, gracefully accepted my apology but sensibly refused my half-hearted offer to repaint their walls before riding off into the sunset.

When two people are thrown together for the first time there is no greater test than their differences in domestic behaviour, particularly when each is still adapting to being a component of a couple.

Thelma was extraordinarily industrious, impressively creative and a first class seamstress, making all her own clothes, on occasions my trousers and shirts and sometimes even her hats for the races. But our preferences for order were at opposite ends of the scale. For Thelma, neat and tidy was not a priority, her things routinely stored randomly throughout the apartment. She also had the uncanny knack of timing the completion of her outfits to perfection. This meant immediately before needing to put them on. The concomitant downside was that her bursts of maniacal industry were followed by periods of complete paralysis. In the absence of any sustained energy, and it was mostly absent, our lounge room was generally a wind storm of cast off materials, threads, cottons, pins, paper templates, dirty ashtrays and the occasional half eaten sandwich.

The battle of wills as to who would act first to address the problem became leviathan. It was a fight that neither of us could win. I could no more prove it was her job than she could prove that it was not. It was at this point I realised that sometimes in a marriage you have to cut your losses and accept that the only option available is to acknowledge that there isn't one. Frequently, reason had to take second place to harmony. Thelma didn't bat an eyelid when friends dropped in, merely removing any detritus from a chair or table and casually dropping it on any other convenient surface. Our friends didn't seem to mind, no doubt allowing leeway for the true celebrity.

¶

The titles office may have been bad enough but there was no greater invitation to slumber than the diploma of education year, much of which was based on theory, opinion and guesswork, sometimes to a startling degree. Recommended educational techniques entailed principles that were as changeable as the wind. Theories that had been dismissed the previous year wafted back the next. Sixty years later nothing seems to have changed. However, the somnambulistic theories on education were a stark contrast to the stressful three week teaching rounds we all agonised over. Nothing could have adequately prepared us for the blasting baptism of fire in the classroom. The anxiety caused each of us to lose, on average, two to three kilos or even more in the first week alone. As if you needed any other source of stress there was an even greater one. In schools such as Melbourne High the students were so pissed off with student teachers that persecution had been turned into a finely honed and cruelly delivered art form.

Many student teachers buckled under that gleeful, enthusiastic onslaught, reversing their commitment to becoming teachers. With a relief that was as palpable as financially painful they agreed to repay the government the three years of salary received during their undergraduate years.

I was agreeably surprised to find that I was able to cunningly conceal my periods of abject terror and to present a persona to the kids that suggested I was not only comfortable in front of them but also their master in all senses of the word. After a few early stumbles

I also received the cautious plaudits of my teaching supervisors as being a natural teacher, a compliment that was as sincerely delivered as it was ambiguously received.

The diploma of education year staggered on at funereal pace accompanied by my fumbling and occasionally successful attempts at being a reasonable husband, my spending blissful hours on the nearby nine-hole Elsternwick golf course and, being the first of the group to be married, dealing with the inevitable conflict of determining how much time I should still be spending with my mates.

4

Teacher in Bendigo

The letter with the Education Department's logo said Golden Square High School, R C King. Where the hell was Golden Square?

It transpired it was a new school in temporary premises in an area of Bendigo with the less than inviting name of Gravel Hill. Looked down upon literally and metaphorically by its older and much larger neighbour, Bendigo High School, it had been established a year before my arrival. In 1961 it catered for years seven, eight and nine, a total of one hundred and twenty-three students. The year nines couldn't believe their good fortune. They would be the big noters and able to push the little kids around for another four years which, having already tasted blood the year before, they were more than happy to do.

The school turned out to be close to perfect. I was unsupervised and able to make my mistakes in private. With only seven staff members we were a close knit and mutually supportive group, felt a strong sense of ownership and were keen to place our stamp, albeit stamps of variable quality, on the new institution.

In most schools year nine students are in no man's land. Unsure of their real place, they are neither fish nor fowl; no longer new but not yet old hands. But at Golden Square High the year nines took a special pride in playing an integral part in what was being created. That pride related to the fact they were the seniors, the big kids. They were the prefects, the house captains, the leaders. Self-confidence quickly translated into responsibility.

While being a 'sage on stage' has a certain appeal teaching has never been an easy game. The outside world largely takes teachers for granted and sneers at the apparent need for thirteen weeks' holiday a year and a knock-off time of 4 pm. It has little appreciation of the pressure of needing to learn your lines before venturing into the spotlight for six very intensive hours each day, five days a week as well as dealing with demanding, unsympathetic parents.

Got a headache, don't feel like it today? Too bad, you're on stage son. You cannot pace yourself on your bad days or even on your good days unless you are prepared to be eaten alive by those little and sometimes not so little animals and their parents. Like their four-legged brethren they can smell weakness and insufficient preparation a mile off. For me, a business career ultimately turned out to be a doddle compared to the limited control over their career and daily environment that is the burden of a pro-active schoolteacher.

In addition to my weekly teaching allotment of thirty six periods out of a possible forty I was also the sports master, a full time position today, as well as responsible for the bookstall, effectively the school's retail business, also a full time position today. Despite Golden Square's small size it was still a heavy workload, even for an old hand, but I enjoyed being my own boss, soon learned to disregard the occasional stuff-up and became comfortable with making things up as I went along.

Plenty was happening in other fields.

On 12 July 1961, Jeremy Charles King was born. He was named after Jeremy Blade, a swashbuckling but noble and gallant comic book piratical hero from my childhood. He was statistically likely to reach the age of seventy, assuming no major change to the environment on which the statistics were based. As was the practice I was not permitted to be present at the birth and thank God for that. I had my first glimpse of his face along with those of all the other deliveries in the nursery an hour after he was born. Without doubt he was the best looking of all of them. It was indescribably thrilling as only a new parent can testify. I was twenty-two years of age and as the cynics say, 'I would grow up with my child.'

Jeremy was a placid baby and didn't often cry but occasionally had a bad night. I was far better at pacifying him than Thelma so when the need arose in the middle of the night that was my job. It was a job I was good at. With him in my arms we enjoyed the warmth of the still burning kitchen fire and I would be slightly sorry when he finally dropped off to sleep. The 'fire' was a recently introduced and highly fashionable kitchen appliance known as a slow combustion stove which provided us with hot water and on Bendigo's cold winter nights proved to be a highly seductive nocturnal companion. We were all intrigued with new home appliances in those days and were thrilled to own a clothes-dryer or a sandwich maker. If you acquired a new appliance you usually invited the neighbours in to admire it.

The kitchen was also the setting for Thelma's clandestine assault on me with a blunt object. An altercation post dinner had resulted in Thelma exiting the warm kitchen in a state of apoplexy that only a spot of mayhem was likely to satisfy. Matters did not get any better over the next half hour, particularly when I chortled at comedian Bill Cosby on the radio while Thelma cooled her heels somewhere else in the house. Actually, she wasn't so much cooling her heels as freezing her backside off in the unheated bedroom, a predicament to which her state of mind at the time had prevented her from giving sufficient consideration. It was too early to go to bed and she had no intention of crawling back into the warm kitchen with her cold tail between her legs. My laughter not only stimulated another bout of white line fever but also provided a potential solution to her problem. The kitchen door swung open mid laugh, followed by the sound of footsteps and rustling clothes rapidly closing the gap to my exposed back. The shoe descended on the back of my head not once but twice, accompanied by a shrill, 'stop enjoying yourself.'

For good measure the left side of my face copped four clenched finger nails as well. Thelma wasn't pissed off, she was seriously pissed off. Adding weight and momentum to the occasion, the assaulting shoe was not Thelma's but mine. Having taken the opportunity for release from the corner in which she had unintentionally painted herself she burst into tears and sought my solace. You had to make allowances for the hormonal rush of a young woman who was six months pregnant.

Shortly after Jeremy turned two he had a 'life'. I was called to the office by a stricken-faced principal's assistant in response to what was clearly a problem at home. I was already numb. Our next door neighbour was on the other end of the phone and, hackneyed expression or not, my heart actually froze. If he died I would also die. Then I heard the magic words, 'Jeremy is OK'. I was less interested in the follow up but still able to register, 'but he has been taken to the hospital to get some stitches.' Our next door neighbour may not have been particularly sophisticated but she had the common sense to know exactly what to say and when to say it. It was the classic neighbourhood disaster scenario. Jeremy had wandered next door to play with their daughter as her father started to back his utility down the driveway. Jeremy was less than happy about the exhaust smoke that had suddenly exploded into his eyes and instantly registered that fact with a loud cry. Fortunately, the neighbour heard the cry and hit the brakes but not before the exhaust pipe peeled back part of his scalp. Jeremy was chocked under the back wheel. God had again been exceptionally kind in deciding not to contradict the statistics on this occasion.

¶

Although comfortable with my retirement from playing Aussie Rules I yielded to aggressive encouragement by the local real estate agent, the self-appointed recruiting officer for the South Bendigo Football Club in the Bendigo Football League, to reconsider my football future. Early in the season, after been sold the dummy by an opponent's blind turn, I hit the deck clutching my left knee, the classic instantaneous response to a blown-out knee. The medial cartilage and the anterior cruciate ligament had been ruptured, my football playing days now definitely over. The medial cartilage was attended to but the damage to the more critical cruciate ligament was neither recognised nor repaired. The removal of the cartilage, which in those days required the knee to be dislocated, was carried out by a local surgeon of dubious repute, a useful piece of information I was unaware of at the time. To add a bit of colour to the occasion it was a Saturday night, which was rarely one of his better nights. I was back under the knife a week later, ultimately spending three weeks in hospital courtesy of his less than expert knife work. South Bendigo Football Club refused to pay for the operation or the hospitalisation on the basis of some long forgotten technicality and the cost pretty well cleaned out our rainy day savings.

Later in the season, having made a more than creditable recovery, I was invited to become an Aussie Rules central umpire with the Bendigo and District Football Umpires Association. The weekly fee would add approximately fifteen per cent to my annual teaching remuneration, a significant attraction given Thelma's status as a full-time housewife and our near virgin bank account.

The BDFUA was a dynamic, energetic and well run organisation, albeit at times bogged down in formality. Its president, Wally Boucher, ran a small but highly successful menswear business in View Street and the umpires' association reflected Wally's personal values and vitality. Its seventy umpires officiated at all the local minor leagues as well as the 'shirt-tearers' (the 'curtain raisers') of the major country leagues within a radius of a hundred kilometres of Bendigo. Most of my colleagues were clerks, shop assistants or tradesmen whose day jobs gave them little opportunity to express their views on organisational or administrative matters. The BDFUA provided that outlet.

The weekly Thursday meeting started at 7 pm. The agenda consisted of organisational formalities, a lecture on the correct interpretation of a tricky rule and finally the handing out of the next Saturday's umpiring appointments. Having fraternised almost exclusively with professional people over the previous five years I had developed the professional man's bias. It was an eye-opening and a salutary lesson to learn that one didn't need a university education to be impressive on his feet. The members of the BDFUA were not only well versed in meeting procedure but also highly articulate, quick thinking and invariably had their ducks in a row ('point of order Mr Chairman, member on his feet').

Each meeting began with the previous week's minutes, always a hotbed of controversy and disagreement as members attempted to rewrite history. Constitutional and organisational issues followed, interspersed with numerous points of order, the moving and seconding of motions, the moving of amendments to motions and sometimes the moving of amendments to amendments. It was the BDFUA's version of Parliamentary process and there was always some creative member trying to break the record for the number of times an amendment could be moved to the preceding amendments.

Wally Boucher would enjoy the early fun of comedy night but then quietly pilot us back through the motion minefield and restore order. The camaraderie was wonderful, the meetings unintentionally hilarious and the evening always one of the highlights of the week.

My big opportunity came in my second year with the BDFUA. I had umpired the curtain raiser at Cohuna in the Grand Central League and was in the process of showering when a stressed local official charged into the change room and announced that the Melbourne umpire handling the senior game was 'down' and unable to continue. Would I mind saddling up again? I was more than happy to re-don my sweaty whites and take over the 'big' game, my marathon performance receiving a complimentary run in the *Bendigo Advertiser*. It was as much appreciation as I was to receive. I was never paid for the game.

¶

In 1956 television was introduced to Australia, coinciding with the Melbourne Olympics. Penetration of the Australian market was slow with a television set costing as much as a small car. For years crowds lined footpaths watching flickering TVs in retailers' windows. Even six years after its introduction, less than fifteen per cent of Australian households owned a TV set. That year Thelma and I joined them.

Our set was paid for by Victorian punters via the recently established Totalisator Agency Board (TAB) which made its debut in Bendigo in 1962. I had maintained my interest in horse racing, continuing to study the form each weekend like a true student of the game. On the day the stars aligned one of my two disciplined and carefully budgeted five shilling (fifty cent) wagers was placed on the daily double (the quadrella and other creative bets were yet to be invented). Gay Waaf, a dour but bonny mare, won the Navy Handicap at Flemington over 2400 metres at 14 to 1 and Victorious, a handy but notoriously unreliable sprinter, won down the straight six (1200 metres), starting from the outside barrier and coming 'down the roses' at the glorious odds of 50 to 1. The return represented more than three months' salary and funded us into the minority of Australian households that owned TV sets. (This was not to be my only windfall courtesy of the TAB. In 1977 another carefully budgeted winning quadrella provided the funds to acquire a highly admired Datsun 240Z sports car for the love of my life).

The following year, our last in Bendigo, we moved to new rental accommodation in California Gulley, one of Bendigo's most recently developed suburbs. The area had little to say for itself other than that it was, like most of Bendigo, a giant gravel pit, treeless and honeycombed with old gold-mining shafts. Surprisingly, it was deemed safe for human habitation. Next door, on our right, lived the depressed wife and her unsuccessful insurance salesman husband who seemed to do little else but read Dale Carnegie's *How to Win Friends and Influence People*. On the other side we had the young couple associated with Jeremy's near driveway disaster and two doors down on the left was the huge and engaging slaughterman from the local abattoir who, according to regular reports from his wife, was obsessed with sex as well as her generously exposed and impressive breasts. With her superior social skills and readily available ear,

Thelma was the recipient of an endless supply of lascivious gossip from her equally housebound counterparts.

One Monday morning after heavy overnight rain we awoke to a driveway that had been replaced by a bottomless, gigantic hole. A hasty telephone call to the Bendigo Council saw a team of workers appear, casually drop timber beams into the old mine shaft until they snagged, deliver loads of sand into the gaping chasm until the hole no longer existed and without further ado or comment just as casually drive away.

In July 1963 I received notice from the Education Department of my promotion in 1964 to Melbourne's Bonbeach High School. At Nanna King's prompting (she didn't believe in paying rent) Thelma and I purchased a block of land in a new subdivision in the market garden suburb of Cheltenham for the princely sum of $2,000. Funded by a loan from Nanna King, we commissioned the building of our twelve squares dream home for the equally princely sum of $11,000.

The delightful prospect of building and owning our first home was tempered by late breaking news a few days before we were due to leave for Christmas in Hamilton. Thelma had evidently had another iron in the fire and thought she might like to remain in Bendigo. I hadn't seen it coming but quickly put two and two together. During the year we had become friendly with a very pleasant guy who made home deliveries from his family's butcher shop. Thelma, believing I was taking her for granted and not paying sufficient attention to detail, had evidently become particularly friendly. My days were pretty full and Thelma's hadn't been full enough — the burden of a city girl becoming a full time housewife in provincial surroundings.

The blow was as monumental as it was unsuspected, not to mention more than a little embarrassing given the apparent ease with which I had so easily facilitated a liaison that had gone seriously off-road. My first thoughts were what to do about our near completed home and what my Bendigo friends might think of my having been given the arse, to quote Uncle Bill Edward. Eventually, I cut through the mess churning away in my head and focussed on the most important issue, Jeremy. I made it clear to Thelma that, as much as I did not want her to remain in Bendigo, if that became her decision, I would not be leaving Jeremy behind. I had no idea how I would manage a two year old child but manage I would.

Belatedly, Thelma decided to make the trip to Hamilton. It was a long, long day. Within a couple of months we were able to put it behind us, our ex mutual friend soon forgotten; he had been playing outside his league anyway.

5

Single parent/A.F.L. umpire/ business executive

Mum died in 1966. She was fifty-one.
Seven years earlier she had been diagnosed with breast cancer. Never one to complain, she had got on with her life and I had tried not to think too much about it. Other than our annual visit to Hamilton I hadn't seen a lot of Mum since Thelma and I had become an item. From the start Mum had made it fairly clear to all and sundry, particularly to Thelma, that she thought Thelma's family values were a bit short of the mark. Mum wasn't all that easy to please and didn't believe in keeping things to herself. I guess to some extent that evened the score because Thelma's stiff upper lip English parents didn't think I was quite up to scratch myself. Nor had they been the best role models in the world for a budding parent based on the fact they couldn't wait to kick Thelma out of home as soon as she left school. Mind you, at sixteen she had evidently been a bit of a handful.

Two years after Thelma and I moved into our new home in Remer Court, Cheltenham, Thelma had arranged one of her regular get togethers. As our friends began arriving I received a call from Auntie Millie, Mum's sister. Mum's cancer had returned with a vengeance. She was in a bad way in the Ballarat Hospital and may not have long to go. I had figured from Dad's occasional evasive comments that Mum wasn't going all that well but I had had no idea of the seriousness of the recurrence and it came as something of a bolt from the blue. Communication was still not Dad's long suit and he was certainly not one to share the pain around either.

I made the hospital in less than two and a half hours. Dad, my sister, Jennifer and brother, Peter were already there. Mum looked awful, her morphine dosage having been progressively increased, always a bad sign. The resident medico was unequivocal that Mum would die within the next twenty-four hours. We all stood around with classic long faces not knowing what to say and were of little comfort either to Mum or to each other. That's the thing about hospital visitors: sometimes you wish they simply hadn't bothered to come along to try to cheer you up. Jennifer, planning to become a pharmacist, was just starting year twelve, a subject that was front and centre for Mum. She kept saying, actually more of a mumble, that she wanted to be there to help Jennifer through her critical year twelve studies. Mum had had something of an each way bet in case she didn't make it by having her hair tinted and set at the hairdressers before entering hospital. If need be she would enter the pearly gates in tip top style. But, a contrarian to the end, Mum decided she wasn't ready to meet St Peter just yet. She walked out of hospital a week later, returned to Hamilton and resumed her life, or what was left of it. A little over a year later, within weeks of Jennifer starting at the pharmacy college in Melbourne, Mum went to meet her maker. She had honoured her part of the bargain.

Forty-five years later, Aunt Millie was visiting that same hospital where her husband, Graeme, was gravely ill. She thought she recognised an ancient, frail, palliative nursing nun. 'I think you may have nursed my sister many years ago,' Millie said. 'What was her name dear,' the nun whispered. 'Thelma King.' Remarkably the old nun asked 'was she from the bakery dear?' Millie nodded. The old nun smiled and whispered again, 'Ah yes I remember her; it was a miracle wasn't it?' Well, that was her take on it.

How did I feel? Not so good. Mum and I had had what I thought for the times was a normal relationship between mother and son, more workmanlike than affectionate. But it takes two to tango and I hadn't done near enough.

Bonbeach High School was one of the larger Victorian high schools. It drew from a blue collar catchment area and catered for more than eight hundred students. I asked for and was given year twelve economics and accounting and was again appointed sports master but didn't cop the bookstall. The quid pro quo for the year twelve classes was a plethora of year ten classes, classes nobody else wanted. No great surprise there. They were the lower streams, the bottom quartile by academic ability and heavily weighted towards girls with behavioural issues who were not devoted to the classroom. The major objective was to keep them occupied and hopefully quiet, a goal achieved by devious and creative means that kept the kids working on activities that were generally only remotely related to the set subject. They didn't mind colouring in but for some even this seemed to be something of a struggle. One also learned to turn a blind eye to their written home assignments which invariably showed a suspiciously high level of imaginatively camouflaged but nonetheless crystal clear unanimity.

My approach with the two year twelve classes was somewhat different. Again, my approach was pragmatic, all about the end of year examinations. Past examination questions were the key and every topic structured to that end. The forensic approach was hardly unique but in terms of technique I was probably at the head of that particular queue and the results ultimately spoke for themselves. I had learned more than something from my firebrand British history teacher, Roy Paine, in year twelve.

This was also the year I coached and umpired a little kid in year eight at Bonbeach High who impressed me with his ability to find the ball on the football field. Confident little bugger he was too. 'I thought you umpired quite well today, Sir,' he told me on one occasion. 'Too bad he is too small and too slow to get anywhere in football,' I mused. His name was Leigh Matthews.

Towards the end of that first year at Bonbeach High the wisdom of making a long term career of the teaching profession became a subject of increasing relevance. I enjoyed teaching, the relationships

I had with the kids, their apparent respect and the ego pleasing process of doing something I thought I was reasonably good at. But my major sense of satisfaction came from competitive instincts — the challenges associated with getting more kids through external examinations than anyone else. This was as much for my sake as theirs and having reduced teaching to a series of definitive pragmatic steps I was clearly no Mr Chips. But for how long was this challenge likely to be sustaining? Hovering in the background was also the imagery of George Bernard Shaw's damning observation, 'those that can, do and those that can't, teach'.

The bigger question was, did I have the right stuff to make it in the outside world?

¶

In Bendigo I had read *Atlas Shrugged* by Ayn Rand. I liked the book's principles of small government, unregimented economic freedom and rewarding the individual for hard work and preparedness to take a risk. I liked her ideas so much I was little short of inspired. Not being particularly interested in politics at the time, I had little appreciation that the author's philosophies were somewhat to the right or that the author was a woman. *Atlas Shrugged* placed the businessman on a pedestal and I had started to fall in love with the idea of becoming one.

To help determine whether I was wasting my time in considering a future in the business world I decided towards the end of that first year at Bonbeach to pay today's equivalent of nearly $3,000 for two half days of psychological and aptitude testing with psychologists Chandler and McLeod. Thelma and I could ill afford the expense but if I were considering making a right angle turn in my career path I didn't want to end up in the fire if I jumped out of the frying pan.

The results when they arrived were somewhat lopsided. In a couple of key areas, numbers and problem solving, there were aptitude spikes that placed me in the top one per cent and three per cent respectively, of the total adult population. The report also indicated a high level of drive and a desire to lead, something else I had in common with that other dynamic dwarf, Napoleon Bonaparte. As well, I was evidently one of those feared inhabitants of the contemporary world, a unilateralist. I could be a team player as long as it was my team. Communication skills were no better than average for university students at the time (top thirteen per cent) and my attention to detail or should I say inattention to detail had me either in the bottom or the top fifty per cent of the adult population depending on which way you wanted to look at it.

I was unaware that you did not need to be really smart to be successful in running a business. It came as something of a surprise to learn that in the real world not only did the typical CEO of an Australian public company have an IQ no higher than the top fifteen per cent of the adult population but also be too smart to begin with. It appeared the head-hunters had a list of criteria they deemed far more important than intelligence. Apparently, you didn't need to be smart, just smart enough. What's more, you could be too smart. And if you were too smart the odds were you couldn't understand or get on with the average person.

Towards the end of that first year at Bonbeach it was time to test the water and answer some job advertisements. I focussed on the emerging fields of computers and market research. Computers proved to be a non-goer, my test results embarrassingly poor. Chandler and McLeod had been right on the money, inattention to detail and impatience coming home to roost. My aptitudes were far more consistent with market research's more intuitive requirements but the responses to those applications were equally predictable. Schoolteachers were not prime candidates on the Australian job market, secondary candidates either, my applications regularly drawing the damning response of 'overqualified'. The value of being a member of a very small minority with a degree was more than cancelled out by the stigma of being a schoolteacher.

By February 1965, my pleas to the business world having gone unanswered, I was faced with a serious dilemma. Did I continue to pursue the elusive path to the new world once the new school year began only to walk away from the year twelve kids if I were lucky enough to hit the jackpot? I decided to defer any departure for another twelve months.

Despite the disappointing reaction to my spate of job applications I was nonetheless blithely confident that the breakthrough would ultimately come. But rather than ignoring my objective for another twelve months I put the time to practical use and embarked on becoming a champion interviewee. I would then be super impressive when the right opportunity arose. It also satisfied a psychological need to not stand still.

I applied for any and every position that might have been remotely relevant to a commerce graduate without having any intention of accepting an offer. This was something I needn't have worried about because I didn't get any, not even a bite. But I did become a very experienced interviewee. I learned that company interviewers, who dominated the job market at that time, liked the idea of a candidate being keen on a job that might challenge him and take him out of his comfort zone. In early December, after my year twelves had completed their examinations, I hit pay dirt. The offer had nothing to do with my being a champion interviewee, but who cared?

¶

I was offered a position as a market research officer with one of Australia's largest and most venerable companies at that time, Australian Consolidated Industries (ACI), a manufacturing conglomerate with a blue blood board of directors and interests in paper, cardboard packaging, plastics, fibreglass insulation, glass containers and flat glass. There was only one problem, the job came with a twenty per cent pay cut. I approached that problem as simply as I could. I ignored it, the problem, not the job. I had no idea how Thelma and I would deal with the financial shortfall but rationalised that with luck it would be made up in the fullness of time. Having decided to accept the job I made the telephone call from the packed Bonbeach High men's staffroom. Clumsily informing the ACI person on the other end of the telephone that 'I had decided to make a decision,' my teaching colleagues, most of whom had taken a vicarious interest in my attempt to jump the metaphorical fence, erupted in hoots of undignified laughter. It was an inauspicious beginning.

My introduction to the business world via ACI fell well short of my grandiose *Atlas Shrugged* expectations. At ACI there was no driving ambition, no sense of purpose, no clash of steel and the roar of battle disappointingly absent. The ACI businessman was unimaginative and limp.

ACI had established a market research department in 1962 under economist Dr Kevin Prouse. He had earned an enviable reputation for accurately forecasting motor vehicle sales trends (an important determinant of ACI's flat glass production), was a loner and only interested in his vocation of statistics. Dr Prouse socialised a little but poorly and we rarely saw him.

The rapid build-up of ACI's market research department to a total of five analysts appeared to have been board-inspired because nobody, including the managers of ACI's operating divisions, had any idea what value the analysts might bring to their businesses. We couldn't make a contribution to that debate either, partly because we were not permitted to become acquainted with the operating divisions in other than a superficial way and partly because we were still wet behind the ears. More to the point, the divisional managers didn't want to have anything to do with us. They had risen through the ranks the hard way and saw a university degree as a decidedly uncomfortable threat. University graduates at ACI emitted the frighteningly paradoxical odour of being the elite of the elite.

While the ACI board's idea of introducing new blood and fresh ideas into their business made eminent sense in principle those good intentions were always going to be wasted without a clear plan of implementation. Lip service was ultimately paid to such a plan by giving the analysts an orientation week with each of the divisions. But the divisional managers didn't know what to do with us and considered us to be little less than damn nuisances, allocating tasks (or non-tasks) that would keep us out of the way. In one instance I was given a large cardboard box of out of date customer invoices to read. In another I was supplied with an asbestos suit, hard hat and goggles and given the task of observing the process of molten glass being drawn from a furnace, with a view to making suggestions as to any productivity improvements that might occur to me.

With the exception of the plastics division, where a sympathetic and helpful sales manager took me under his wing, I didn't bother to turn up after the first day and took four days off instead, finding the time far more useful in taking day trips to Mt Buller to learn to ski. There is no doubt about it, stolen pleasure beats most things particularly when you are supposed to be doing something else. Almost certainly, the divisional managers breathed a sigh of relief. We spent most days cocooned in a communal office whose clear glass walls had been painted over and we were subjects of only vague but nonetheless intimidated curiosity to the other employees.

Part of each morning was taken up by the few inconsequential tasks allotted to us, usually the recording of manufacturing and import statistics and the calculation of monthly market shares, none of which seemed to generate much interest outside our painted walls. Then we filled the vacuum with newspapers, crosswords, other puzzles, jokes, business magazines and the wonders of that unregulated casino at the time, the Stock Exchange. I spent much of my time trying to read market research journals.

In eight months at ACI I learned only three useful things. To successfully carry a cup of tea from the cafeteria down two flights of stairs without spilling it you must not look at the cup and to bark an assertive, don't mess with me, 'Ray King' when answering the telephone. I learned both these gems from Barry Watts who was our first amongst equals and who, many years later, became ACI's managing director. And finally, my mastery of all the important market research buzz words. Having them on the tip of my tongue proved to be more than useful before the year was out.

¶

In the meantime, another problem had arisen on the home front. Three months into my career change, the week before Easter and two months after we buried Mum, Thelma dropped her second bombshell. She had apparently been having another bet each way. I still wasn't paying attention or at least sufficient attention. As in Bendigo I hadn't seen it coming and the circumstances were remarkably similar. Thelma and I had become friendly with a vibrant young couple, the male member of which was a dashing, fast rising lawyer. Thelma had evidently become infatuated with him. I must admit I was pretty impressed with him myself, albeit for different reasons. I was beginning to look as though I might be a foundation member of that loser's club, the injury prone.

Thelma had evidently convinced herself that if she were less encumbered her lawyer bloke might be available to her on a more permanent basis — never one to die wondering was Thelma. My stomach lurched. Jesus, here we go again. When my head finally cleared I again made it clear to Thelma that under no circumstances would I agree to Jeremy going with her, a response she was almost certainly relying upon in order to achieve what she had in mind.

It now looked as though there was little choice but to accept that the marriage was doomed. 'Twice bitten thrice shy' seemed the only logical reaction. We did what we thought was the civilised thing and agreed to share the few tangible spoils we had. I estimated we had around $4000 equity in the house so I borrowed $2000 to get her started. I kept Jeremy, the house at Remer Court, half the furniture and got the better side of the deal.

Jeremy aside, the separation was far from my preferred outcome but sometimes, as I tried to convince myself, that is how it is between a man and a woman: something gets in the way, like real life, human nature and a whole lot of other stuff that isn't compatible with marriage's conventional set of rules and emotions. After the first few difficult weeks I realised I was down but far from out, neither grief-stricken nor paralysed. I had done the audit, liked what I saw and decided to get on with the rest of my life. I had my own house, made the transition to the business of business, was making my way as an elite AFL central umpire and, most importantly, I still had the joy of my life, Jer.

That was all well and good but in retrospect why was I able to adopt such an apparently measured, rational approach to one of life's greatest earthquakes? That didn't apply to the first few weeks following the split because I was little short of an emotional wreck but I gradually concluded that the marriage was really over. And there were other considerations. Thelma was a party girl and loved being in a crowd whereas I was more of a one on one person. Despite having the ability to get on with people I was something of a loner. I lived a lot of life in my head. I also had lots of things on the go and many outside interests, again, not always the path to a happy marriage with someone who craved plenty of attention. The reality was we were not all that compatible. I genuinely liked Thelma, probably even loved her, but if I did love her I clearly hadn't loved her enough. I had never felt sufficiently 'touchy feely' with her despite promising signs at the outset. The emotional side had fallen short of the mark. So for a raft of reasons one had to conclude the problem was partly of my own making. But how were eighteen year olds supposed to know what love is?

Some weeks after our separation I received a strange request from Thelma. The script was not proceeding to plan, her friendly lawyer not having come to the party. Perhaps he had never intended coming to the party. Thelma asked me to contact him and clear what she thought was the likely road block. It seemed a farcical request but why not agree to it? Thelma had made her definitive road to Damascus decision and, after all, the object of her attention was a friend of mine or so I had thought. The application of any sense of logic to the situation we found ourselves in suggested any thought of a positive future together as little short of delusional. And if that were the case, why not help each other out? And I had inherited Dad's strong view that there was little currency in implementing a desire for revenge, a dish which as the saying goes 'is best eaten cold'. Which I guess is just another way of saying, 'don't get angry, get even,' which, on reflection, also didn't seem all that relevant as I was neither angry nor wanting to get even.

The lawyer and I met at the hotel on the corner of King and Dudley Streets in the city, now known as Witches in Britches. He was somewhat on the uncomfortable side, keeping his cards close to his chest and admitting nothing. We had a few drinks, talked over old and unlikely to be repeated good times and he ultimately relaxed, slightly. But the meeting didn't result in the outcome that Thelma was hoping for. He might have been sensitive to the remote possibility he was being set up — the divorce laws at the time were particularly onerous for someone seen as contributing to a marriage breakdown. He was a lawyer after all and a lawyer with great ambition to boot. On the other hand there was more than a distinct possibility he had quickly and sensibly accepted the stance of buyer's remorse. He went on to become highly successful in the law, culminating in his appointment to the bench and a high profile career as a quirky but highly regarded Supreme Court judge.

The next few months were a period of extreme pain and bewilderment for Jeremy ('Dad, why can't we all live together like we used to'?). Initially Thelma saw him once a week, then the gaps got longer, defence mechanisms starting to kick in. Later in the year Thelma continued down her road to Damascus, this time literally via Rome where she was unceremoniously dumped, copping a couple of black eyes and a broken rib in the confines of a building elevator which generated a spike in her letter writing activities to Remer Court. Not having received an encouraging response she continued to reside in Rome for the next few years, writing the occasional letter to me and sending the occasional postcard to Jeremy.

Jeremy was brave, non-judgmental and battled resourcefully to get on with his life. This was long before the term single parent family came into use. Back then it was a broken home and Jeremy seemed to be the only kid he knew who came from one. Not only that but he was with his father rather than his mother, a most unusual outcome at the time. The broken home label ought to have given him a store of existential rage but somehow it didn't or at least didn't appear to. And what were the odds that a twenty-seven year old father could provide all the answers when he didn't even know what the questions should be. What little I knew of parenting theories at the time were a bit different from the more child centric flavours of today. A four year old child being cared for by his father was a rare circumstance and as usual I tended to make things up as I went along. And with life presenting so many temptations and problems there wasn't enough time to get everything right. I didn't seek counselling assistance or enquire whether such advice existed. It was my problem and I had to deal with it. I didn't even have a copy of *Dr Spock*. It was a far too narrow perspective. I wanted to believe that Dad was right in believing the un-staked tree grew strongest and what doesn't kill you only makes you stronger. But sometimes the simplest answer is not always the best answer.

As imperfect as I obviously was, I nevertheless thought I was doing a hell of a job as a housewife and mother, even allowing for the more than considerable help I was given. As if by magic a support network evolved. Nanna King, now seventy-five and still a force to be reckoned with moved in and took control for the first three weeks. Gary Butcher, an ex-Hamiltonian and a school friend of my brother, Peter, who had recently moved to Melbourne with the National Bank, was happy to become my house mate and principle backstop. A next door neighbour whose son was a playmate of Jeremy's was available for emergencies. Robin Chambers, a member of 'the group' who had recently started her own family was wonderfully supportive for the best part of three years, picking him up from school two or three times a week, teaching him simple fundamentals such as tying shoelaces and feeding him his evening meal. Thelma's sister, Judy, who had four children of her own, was unstinting in having him most weekends during three football seasons. We also received a lot of sympathy votes from concerned neighbours, friends and acquaintances, including some nervous and well intentioned single female ex-colleagues from Bonbeach High School. Although we didn't receive too many casseroles (thankfully, as far as Jeremy was concerned, for he hated anything more wet and mushy than sausages and chips) we did receive many generous dinner invitations which made Jeremy even more anxious given his strong preference for his normal and very limited menu. However, he didn't seem to mind the sympathetic attention of the various and mysterious aunties of variable quality who passed through our lives. By sheer luck or more likely his DNA resilience he came through the ordeal extraordinarily well.

It would be easy to conclude that Remer Court must have been a chaotic existence for a young child but if so then it was a chaos that Jeremy not only adapted to but also had a hand in shaping solutions to. Resourcefully, he organised his father with constant reminders and by surreptitiously rescheduling prescribed arrival times for his various activities to ensure I had him there on time, effectively countering my just in time strategy that was often a bit hit and miss.

And, surprising as it may seem and perhaps disappointingly to some given the pressures on my time of being a home owner, single parent, budding businessman, postgraduate MBA student and social butterfly, I still found time to continue my sporting career as an Aussie Rules central umpire.

¶

On our return to Melbourne in 1964, I had applied to the AFL to join the Australian Football League Umpires Association. My motivation was to do the best I could in what had become my sporting outlet and to supplement my earnings as a schoolteacher even though I probably would have done it for free. There were three umpiring lists. There was the elite panel of twenty from which the umpires to officiate at the AFL firsts and seconds were selected, the senior list and the reserves list. The senior list handled all the major Victorian country leagues and the subordinate group, the reserves list of around two hundred and fifty umpires handled the minor metropolitan leagues.

Favoured by a good reference from the Bendigo Football League and also from Cohuna, the scene of my double game the previous year, I become the first country-bred umpire to go straight on to the senior list.

Although umpiring continued to provide a handy supplement to the household income there was a downside, the time involved away from home. Travelling to the country took up most of the weekend, generally with overnighters on the Saturday evening at the local pub. The local officials always felt obliged to kill us with kindness after the game, a problem for me because at that time I didn't drink, something almost unheard of among umpires. For most, this was often seen as being the best part.

Under the single umpire system operating at that time it was estimated that the distance we covered in a game each week was equivalent to a half-marathon — most of it in short bursts, some of it running backwards and with lots of energy draining propping, stopping and re-accelerating in the opposite direction. If you were having an ordinary day the game felt as if it were going on forever. Given our limited two hours a week official training regime I prayed for the wet days that significantly reduced the speed of play.

The feeling of isolation and desolation, not to mention panicked desperation that occasionally besets all umpires, could not have been more striking than during a game between the two local clubs in Wagga in the South East League in NSW, a league with a healthy reputation for violence. The local derby in any league is always a recipe for a bit of blood-letting and the South East League was certainly no exception.

Following an incident requiring a free kick down field I dashed to the distant goal square to nominate the player to receive the benefit

5 Single parent / A.F.L. umpire / business executive

of my largesse. The virtual silence was suddenly interrupted by an almighty roar from the crowd. Looking back over my shoulder I was not exactly delighted to see a pack of more than a dozen players wrestling in a classic melee almost a hundred metres away. The goal umpire at the other end and the two boundary umpires, all members of the local football clubs were, as usual, standing there enjoying the fun. I charged back down the field and against explicit AFL instructions never to physically handle players, bored into the centre of the writhing pack of players, pushing and shoving, attempting to separate them. Tempers appeared to cool. Inconveniently, according to the rule book, I now had to return to the other end of the ground to grant the original free kick. As soon as there was sufficient distance between diddums and themselves the antagonists started into one another again. They had their images to maintain. There was an even greater roar from the crowd this time and there in the same spot was an even bigger writhing, pulsing melee. I was in real trouble. Losing control of a game is an umpire's worst nightmare. Again, 'illegally', I charged into the fracas, man-handling the players in order to separate them. Two of them I didn't have to worry about, each flat on his back and out cold. By the time I arrived the others were probably delighted to have an excuse to stop the mayhem, honour having already been served. But as their anger began to ebb mine was rising to full cry. A mind under siege can do a lot of things and mine seemed to be doing most of them. I was not plain angry; I was foaming at the mouth angry. How dare they stuff up my umpiring future? I jumper punched the two captains and snarled into their faces that I was going to call the game off as well as put them on report unless they restrained their players. I was not permitted under the rules to call a game off nor to report them but I guessed they didn't know that.

I then broke another rule. I couldn't risk moving away from this simmering hotbed of testosterone-charged ego so, instead of returning to the other end of the field to restart the game as I should have done, I informed the captains I was going to bounce the ball and restart the game where we stood. Obviously, the side that had been awarded the original free kick down field was being unfairly penalised.

'That's a trifle inequitable,' ex-Hawthorn player now Wagga captain and coach Graeme Cooper, suggested, although I think his comment might have been somewhat stronger and less articulate at the time. But I was on a roll. With my index finger less than an inch from his nose, I snarled again, 'fuck the rules Graeme, I'm running this show'. Nonetheless, I made a mental note of his height and the width of his shoulders and resolved to stay well clear of him once the game was over.

I bounced the ball to restart play and immediately paid a free kick to the player nearest to the ball, following up with half a dozen free kicks in less than a minute for highly technical if non-existent infringements and finally the players remembered what they were supposed to be doing on a Saturday afternoon. The burst of free kicks was standard (unofficial) practice in such circumstances. Sometimes it worked, sometimes it didn't. Unfortunately, the side that had been unfairly penalised lost the game by the barest margin, one point.

At country grounds there is no protection for umpires, no police and no enclosed race leading into the change rooms. I had faced some tough looking crowds in my time as an umpire but this one looked dangerously violent. I had little choice but to walk the gauntlet, the very nasty looking 'acme thunderer' knuckleduster still clipped to my fingers at the ready for whoever was prepared to break the line first. But as it turned out, as elsewhere, in Wagga spit was the most practical and favoured weapon in the disappointed supporter's armoury. The umpires' room was, as usual, a small three metre by three metre corrugated iron shed attached to the local grandstand which had access to the players' showers. Their outrage yet to be assuaged, the irate supporters of the losing side proceeded to give an excellent impression of trying to kick the door in. This was a not uncommon pleasure after a country game. Apart from causing the heart rate to spike a few times I imagine it was a bit like sitting inside a base drum.

Based on what I thought the local reaction would be I came to the logical but sad conclusion that my umpiring ambitions would have to be reassessed. It was therefore with some surprise I found two days later that the local Wagga newspaper had printed a laudatory article on how umpire King had saved the game. The South East League administrator wrote a similarly worded letter to the AFL, citing the league's need for strong umpires, not exactly how I felt at the time, recommending I be appointed at the end of the season to umpire the South East League grand final.

¶

When Thelma made her decision to seek greener pastures I had just begun my third season of umpiring in Melbourne. The previous year, after only one year on the senior list I had been added to the panel, the final step to 'making it'. It was unusual for an umpire with such little experience to be appointed to this panel and my appointment caused much shaking of heads among the old timers.

In 1967 I umpired the first three rounds in the AFL seconds and then, bingo, 'the big time'. In seventy years of the AFL (starting as the VFL) I was the 250th central umpire to officiate in a VFL game. Given the single central umpire system that prevailed at the time, a new umpire being appointed to the 'big six' was headline news. I arrived at training on the Wednesday evening to be met by three journalists. Two were from radio stations and the third was Jack Dunn, the senior sports journalist for the *Sun News Pictorial* (*Herald Sun* today) together with his photographer.

The following day my photograph and sporting and occupational background filled most of the back page. Jack Dunn had also contacted Wally Boucher in Bendigo. Never letting an opportunity pass to promote Bendigo umpires Wally was succinct and to the point. 'Yes, Ray's very good but we have at least half a dozen up here better than him,' said Wally. Congratulatory telegrams arrived from near and far. At the weekly AFLUA meeting that evening everyone wanted to shake my hand and slap me on the back. It was breathtakingly exciting for an umpire and I could not deny that in a wave of indescribable pleasure I soaked up every ounce of that admiration.

In 1967 there were only six AFL games each week and, given the single umpire system, only six umpires had the opportunity to perform at the elite level. Weeks, sometimes months, would go by without any change to this leading group. It was rare at the time for more than two or three new umpiring faces to appear each season and membership of the big six meant you were a member of a very exclusive club. It also meant you had a far greater potential impact on the outcome of a game than today's system of three umpires. We were almost as well known as the players, 'Oh shit, we've got King,' was a common response from the supporters when I walked on to the ground.

South Melbourne (the Swans) versus Richmond at the Lakeside Oval in Albert Road was the scene of my first big game. Ex-St Kilda Brownlow medallist Neil Roberts covered the game for the *Sporting Globe,* which ran an Umpire of the Year award in addition to its weekly award for the players. Each week the six umpires were awarded points out of ten for their performance. I was awarded nine out of ten in that first game, the highest number of points to be awarded for any performance that year. Among other uplifting comments, Neil Roberts wrote, 'a breath of fresh air on the umpiring scene and will go a long way.' Hmmm.

As an indication of how much the game has changed I awarded seventy-two free kicks that day, more than double the average number paid today. My record was ninety-eight in a game between Fitzroy and Carlton, admittedly on a muddy glue-pot, both performances paling into insignificance when compared with the number paid by the man considered to be the doyen of central umpires, Jack McMurray senior, in 1928. The *Sporting Globe* lauded McMurray's remarkable performance with, 'today Jack McMurray gave the greatest exhibition of umpiring ever seen on the Melbourne Cricket Ground. He paid one hundred and twenty-six free kicks'.

My performance that day at the Lake Oval was beginner's luck and from those lofty heights there was only one direction in which I could go. In the next season and a half I umpired twenty games before my unstable, unrepaired left knee went its predicted, wicked way. I could still run OK but a limping umpire was not a good look so after having had a season and a half in the big time, the AFL Commission suggested it was time I did something else.

It was a short but not uneventful career.

Not long after my debut game I umpired South Melbourne and Carlton, again at the Lakeside Oval. It was not one of my better games, needing to be escorted off the ground by a posse of policeman after Carlton won by a single point. The police cordon was no match for one dissatisfied customer, a female South Melbourne supporter who, easily evading the smiling coppers, stabbed me with her furled umbrella before following up with a hammer blow to the head. Presumably, she had disagreed with the free kick I paid to Carlton rover Terry Board, as the siren sounded when the scores were level. This provided Board with the opportunity to kick the winning behind. Inevitably, my having been a past Carlton player received plenty of air play. The *Sporting Globe* awarded me two points out of ten for my performance, one of which was for turning up, the other for the perfect bounce to begin the game. Alan Miller, the South Melbourne coach, when asked to comment on umpire King's performance — coaches were permitted to say what they liked about umpires in those days — responded with, 'Umpire King had more dreams in two hours than Walter Mitty had in a lifetime.' His comment received plenty of space in that night's *Sporting Globe*.

At Carlton on another day, Wes Lofts, Carlton's famous fullback, was not having the best of days on arguably the game's best ever full forward, Hawthorn's Peter Hudson. Just before half time, Hudson, having been infringed by Lofts (according to umpire King) was about to line up in the goal square for his fifth goal. Lofts, beside himself with embarrassment and rage screamed, 'King you're nothing but a little c—t.' Umpires were under strict instructions by the AFL board to report players for abusive language. I was highly conscious of my AFL board man sitting less than twenty metres away in the Robert Heatley stand. 'Report him ump,' grinned Hudson. Eyeballing Lofts from centimetres away (I had to crane my neck, he was at least twenty centimetres taller than me) I snarled, 'what did you say?' Lofts, who couldn't help himself, repeated his earlier spray. I now had a real dilemma because I didn't want to report him, given his highly emotional state — the free kick had perhaps been a little doubtful anyway — but nor did I want to be dropped the next week for failing to follow instructions. I then had a brainwave amending a similar line I had heard in a recent movie, 'Wes, I object to the word, "little".' Wes frowned and his mouth dropped open while his brain slowly tried to recall what he had said. He finally got it and smiled in spite of himself. Hudson liked it as well. Given the relaxed outcome the board man's suspicions melted into inaction. After the game I socialised with the players, enjoying a sausage roll and a soft drink — it was standard practice at that time for umpires and players to get together after the game — Wes strolled over and with a smile apologised for having used that terrible word, 'little'.

On the second last game of the 1968 home and away season I had a seconds' round at Carlton. Thelma's sister Judy couldn't have Jeremy that weekend so I took him to the game with me. It was against the rules but as I had a maximum of two games to go I didn't worry too much. Jeremy was seven. Wide-eyed, he held my hand as we strolled across the hallowed turf that he had seen only on TV replays and on which I had played a decade before. He was amazed at the seemingly monstrous size of the stands and the cavernous change rooms with their old photographs of ancient teams and action scenes. He was chuffed when the goal and boundary umpires made a fuss of him and used the game balls to trade little kicks with him. He walked down the race and stood with me on the boundary line as I waited for the goal and boundary umpires before stepping on to the ground to start the game.

Ron Barassi, Carlton's famed captain and coach, was doing warm-up laps before the main game. 'G'day Ray, g'day son,' said Ron casually as he trotted past. In open mouthed and wide-eyed wonder Jeremy stared up at me. Written all over his beaming face was, 'not only does Ron Barassi know my Dad but he actually SPOKE to ME,' He couldn't wait for Monday morning's 'show and tell'.

Later in my business career when I was addressing business conferences I would often be questioned about the controversies of being an AFL umpire, enabling me to immediately fold in my favourite. 'Collingwood supporters are just animals. I've been spat upon, sprayed by soft drink and beer cans and on one memorable day at Victoria Park I was actually pissed upon. But the day was excruciatingly cold and at least it was warm.' It never failed. Attribution goes to umpires' advisor Bob Nunn, who had a wealth of such stories.

My most infamous act as an umpire was my unwitting attempt to rewrite the voting rules of the Brownlow Medal in 1967. Collingwood had defeated Hawthorn at Victoria Park and I was feeling pretty happy with myself after having had what I thought was a good day. I was about to ruin it. The first thing the central umpire had to do after a game was record the votes for the Brownlow. I was having difficulty deciding on the third vote between Len Thompson of Collingwood and Ian Bremner of Hawthorn. The AFL board man at each game not only assessed the umpire's performance on the day but also collected the envelope containing the Brownlow votes. On this particular day the board man was in a hurry to get away and pressured me to complete the voting slip. I allowed my euphoria to get the better of my judgment. In a sudden rush of creativity I thought, 'bugger it, I'll give 'em half each.' I sealed the envelope and handed it to the board man. Although Len Thompson had won the Brownlow a few years earlier neither he nor Ian Bremner were in the running in 1967. This was just as well because the split vote was not counted, the first time in AFL history that a vote had been disregarded. Among my umpiring mates I became known as 'Kia Ora', a well-known brand of cordial at the time which was fifty per cent lemon and fifty per cent orange.

With my left knee continuing to deteriorate I managed only seven senior games in my second year in the big time before being forced to quit when the AFL finally suggested that a limping central umpire was not quite the look it wanted. I wasn't too sorry. In fact it was a convenience given I was beginning to make my way in the business world.

6

Jumping the fence is worth it

The advertisement appeared in *The Age* in October 1966.

> Market Analyst
> E. R. Squibb & Sons, research based pharmaceuticals.
> $5,000 pa plus benefits and car

This was a new position at Squibb, a US-based manufacturer and distributor of prescription pharmaceuticals. Having made it on to the short list of three selected from the thirty-seven applicants I attended Squibb's Franklin Street headquarters in Melbourne a week later.

The interview was with Frank Irving, the Australian marketing and sales director, who would be my boss if I got the job. Frank Irving was about to return the image of the businessman to my mythical pedestal. He proved to be articulate, persuasive, an excellent public speaker and a charismatic and dynamic leader. The chemistry between us, while pretty good, rose to another level after I extolled the philosophical virtues of Ayn Rand's, *Atlas Shrugged* which, more than usefully, Frank had been quite taken with as well. But he knew absolutely nothing about market research. I didn't know all that much about it either but I knew more than him and was successful in getting his attention with my enthusiastically articulated and designed-to-impress buzzwords. As well as appearing to be impressed by my other indispensable qualities, Frank particularly liked my noble desire to have a job that would challenge and take me out of my comfort zone. Those twelve months of studying to become the perfect interviewee may not have been such a waste of time after all.

I waited in nervous trepidation for Frank's verdict. The Squibb branded envelope that arrived a few days later began gloriously, 'I am delighted to …' I took in the whole of the letter in a single instant. Bathed in delight I folded it, unfolded it, read it more slowly, laughed out loud, made a pirouette, paced around the lounge room chuckling as I did so, sure this was the key that would open the door to my business future. How wonderful it was to be alive.

The job included a brand spanking new Chrysler Valiant, at the time a rare inclusion in remuneration packages for businesses other than those based in the US and all up the package was around $6000 a year, almost two-thirds greater than my ACI remuneration and around forty per cent more than I had been earning as a schoolteacher nine months earlier.

Squibb was business utopia. Besotted by the job, thrilled to the point of addiction, the romance and the glamour of it far surpassed anything I could have imagined. I was like the kid in the lolly shop. I couldn't wait to get there in the mornings and loath to leave in the evenings, the dream employee. In contrast to ACI it was as if everyone were on steroids. Executives rushed urgently through corridors clutching mandatory pieces of paper and I regularly jumped on and off silvery aircraft and felt absurdly self-important sitting with the other 'suits' in clouds of cigarette smoke (my own contribution not being insignificant) in the passionate belief we were not only keeping the wheels of industry turning but driving them forward.

At the end of most days I would join in enthusiastic discussion with other middle ranking ambitious colleagues as to how we could and would better run the company — everybody talking, nobody listening. Given we were part of an elite business we all wanted to believe we were a cut above the average and central to a dynamic culture that thrived on making an elite business even better. We even had plaques on our walls, like footy clubs, exhorting us to be better. Mine was 'The Secret Ingredient — the honour and integrity of the man who makes it.' This was all part of projecting an aura in which the pursuit of excellence was key. It was mostly bullshit, of course, and inevitably business life morphed into reality but while the fantasy lasted it was wonderful. Nonetheless, as reality inevitably began torpedoing my self-encouraged myths one after another I still saw Squibb as a second to none arena in which to learn the practical art of the business of business.

Within four months of my joining Squibb we relocated to purpose built, luxurious premises in the outer Melbourne suburb of Noble Park. The building had so much marble it could have been the Taj Mahal. I had my own three by four metre teak-lined office with a clear glass wall that looked out on to a flowered and beautifully manicured central garden. You were almost disappointed not to see peacocks wandering aimlessly through the grounds in background support to flaxen haired nymphs in flimsy, flowing costumes dancing to strains of gentle, heavenly music.

The imagery immediately brought to mind Hamilton High's awards day at the Regent Theatre in December 1953, an annual event always referred to for fairly obvious reasons as speech day. It was unanimously acknowledged as the most boring day on the school calendar for those not receiving an award, which was just about everyone. Midway through the most boring day on the school calendar, Burge's and my covert, cleverly camouflaged game of battleships and cruisers was gently interrupted by the dulcet strains of recorded violins and the mounting admiring murmur of the junior boys in the front rows of the boys' side of the theatre. Three ranks of barefoot, flimsily dressed year ten girls had drifted, floated and jiggled their way on to the stage from the adjacent wings like slightly uncoordinated golden butterflies. It wasn't all that professional but who cared about professional. This was just what the doctor ordered and we all sprang to life — at least the boys did — and studied in minute detail the writhing, grinding, surprisingly scantily clad bodies.

As I stepped into my teak scented Squibb office for the first time a warm glow of high and mightiness descended and I shamelessly, delightedly, compared such opulence to my allocated space of one and a half metres by one metre in the crowded men's staff room at Bonbeach High School and the smoke filled communal office at ACI.

It was the era of the hugely profitable pharmaceutical company's golden years. The stellar price-earnings ratio of its Wall Street listed shares reflected its superior returns on investment and fifteen per cent annual growth rates.

It was at Squibb where I learned to worship at the altar of gross margin. It was the key to the company's incredibly high return on investment and I was treated to a plethora of training programs as to why gross margin not only needed to be front and centre in every discussion but also how it could be maximised. Squibb did not carry a product that earned a gross profit of less than 80 cents in every sales dollar. These high profit margins were essential to encourage the large investments required to research new drugs that would heal the sick and the dying. Or so we were told. Apparently, everything was not quite as it seemed.

In reality, the 'research based' nomenclature shouted from the roof tops by every pharmaceutical company was a persistent myth propounded by the industry's political lobbyists and public relations hacks. Squibb, like its global counterparts, purchased potential new products from small experimental laboratories. These laboratories absorbed most of the research risks and the related costs. Ultimately, governments woke to the industry spin and applied the brakes to what until then had been monopolistic pricing policies underpinned by iron clad patent protection. Squibb's propaganda as to its business expertise and excellence was shown to be more apparent than real. Once monopolistic pricing went out the window pharmaceutical executives were soon seen to be made of flesh and blood like everyone else. Nevertheless, this turn of events was yet to occur and while the focus on gross margin engineering may have been far less important reasons for Squibb's success than monopolistic pricing, the principles covered in those early educational programs were still rock solid and ultimately worth their weight in gold.

¶

Frank Irving was Hollywood's version of the classic businessman. He was the most decisive executive I have known. However, while decisiveness was one thing, judgment was something else. Frank was great at making decisions but as often as not his decisions left something to be desired. Nevertheless, in the world of fool's gold that existed at the time Frank was just what Squibb headquarters in New York thought it was looking for. We were sorry to see him go but we were delighted for his sake and for the reputation of the pint sized Australian operation when he was promoted to a senior marketing role in New York. He must have done OK in the New York snake pit because a few years later he was promoted to an even more senior role in Europe. Tragically, but unsurprisingly given his driven nature, he died of a heart attack in his mid-forties and I often wondered whether the smoke he ingested from my sitting next to him (Frank didn't smoke) in the confines of Ansett Airlines flights had been a contributing factor.

¶

Monthly reporting at Squibb was a big deal. My monthly report on product performance provided Frank with much of the content of his report and his report made up the majority of managing director Robert S Gardiner's report to New York. And our sense of self-worth caused us to ignore the fact that Australia represented less than two per cent of Squibb's global business.

Robert S Gardiner had been Squibb's first medical detailer in Australia (the term salesman was too crass for the pharmaceutical industry) and Frank Irving hadn't been too far behind him. As a consequence, they had the inside running for the senior positions when head office decided to establish its fully integrated Australian operation. Robert had been a stage actor of some note — somewhat in the James Mason mould according to my older peers — and his acting ability also had a practical side. Robert combined sugar-coated charm with Hollywood good looks, both of which had helped him gain his stellar reputation as an inveterate 'player'.

Needing to have Robert approve a presentation I was to give on the coming Monday I called at his home on the preceding Saturday afternoon. Robert's face, when it appeared at the door, displayed the particularly nasty after-effects of what were obviously very seriously raked finger nails. I knew all about finger nails. Large as life and with great chutzpah he ignored the elephant in the room (and the dark, thunderous looks of his wife as she did the occasional walk-by) for the next half-hour. Robert, like Frank, was a quick thinker, articulate and wonderfully persuasive. He had perfected a cultured English accent whereas Frank was true blue to his lower middle class roots and Robert's brand of bullshit was absolutely first class. You knew it and he knew that you knew it but it didn't bother him because he knew he could out bullshit anyone. And although you knew you were being manipulated you could never think of a worthwhile counter argument, until it was far too late. Frank, who was pretty straight-laced and reputedly unimpressed with the exploits of the pantsman, was not short of manure either but the difference was that Frank, a more driven character, largely believed his.

I began to realise that Squibb Australia was less about substance and more about style and appearance. And those factors were being raised to a new level.

An unending cycle of sales training programs, sales conferences, public speaking and one-on-one personal enhancement sessions was aimed at developing and extracting every last ounce of our personal development and particularly our persuasiveness potential in an attempt to 'move the immovable' medical profession. I learned to my chagrin that persuasiveness was not one of my strengths. I couldn't have sold hot pies to hungry men.

Actually, that wasn't quite correct. Although I couldn't think quickly enough to outsmart my Squibb peers in role playing exercises, I had made better than good wages when operating as a commission salesman during my final year university vacation. Selling is a horses-for-courses exercise and the holiday job was right up my alley, at least for a time.

It was a door to door job, cold-calling parents of kids aged eight to fourteen to whom I delivered a canned sales pitch extolling the virtues of texts published by Australian Visual Education, a privately owned producer of educational publications. As the door was opened to my confident knock, there I was, in jacket and tie, sporting a university college cut and an enthusiastic smile. 'Good morning Mrs Jones, my name is Ray King. I am a university student (university students were still highly admired by the general public) studying to be a secondary schoolteacher and during the university vacation I have been selected to present the very latest in educational literature for children aged eight to fourteen. I believe, Mrs Jones (recounting more of the inside information that I had so cunningly gleaned from the neighbours) that you have a child in that age bracket. Is that correct?' Of course Mrs Jones had little option but to answer, 'yes' and once that hurdle was cleared I was in the lounge room in a flash surrounded by the unique pictorial/comic form of educational literature on every subject under the sun likely to be taught to this age group. A description of my life in teacher training at Melbourne University was usually delivered mid pitch adding even more convincing and credible evidence that this extremely likeable young man was an obvious expert on education. Almost without exception there was at least one if not more subjects that Mrs Jones thought her kid could be better at. The whole exercise obviously played on a parent's conscience. The neat thing was that I genuinely believed, at least I think I did, that what I had on offer would make a serious difference. A successful con almost always requires the con artist to at least partially believe his story.

My success rate was four in every five houses and the commission-only remuneration was more than double the weekly wage I had earned working behind the counter in retail stores in previous university vacations. But as good as the leaders at Australian Visual Education thought I was, not to mention my own personal rating, I realised towards the end of the third week that I was no natural. I was running out of juice, the work requiring extraordinarily high energy levels. For three weeks I had fired on rocket fuelled adrenalin after which I just keeled over and died. Mentally exhausted, I spent the last few weeks before Christmas recovering on Sandringham beach with my mates.

At Squibb it was a rare occasion that Robert S Gardiner and particularly Frank J Irving failed to take advantage of even the least likely opportunity to deliver an exhaustively prepared and enthusiastically delivered speech aimed at inspiring the troops to even greater heights. And those speeches were delivered with complete conviction, even when it was evident there didn't appear to be much to be convinced about in the first place.

Regular staff get-togethers were held in the homes of the state managers, the national sales manager and the sales and marketing director in an orchestrated campaign to facilitate bonding and blur our personal and corporate selves. But our inflated sense of self-worth, the necessary focus on presentation and the strength of the resistance of the medical profession to our efforts led, inevitably, to grumblings in the ranks. It was virtually impossible to identify superior performance by way of results. Predictably, when the too few promotional opportunities arose, executives of substance were often overlooked in favour of those who could talk the talk. With no sales background and little business experience I was seen by my colleagues as representing little or no threat to their ambitions. As a consequence, I became the sounding board for the relieving of frustrations, the airing of petty grievances and strangely, for tactical advice on how to get ahead. It was my introduction to the reality of human frailty and organisational politics.

While I had moved on from being the wide-eyed enthusiastic amateur and adopted a more cynical appraisal of the world of business, I still genuinely enjoyed turning up to work every morning. I enjoyed the vibrancy, the apparent esteem of my colleagues, felt as if I were well on the way to learning the art of business and more importantly, in how it could be most effectively applied to a broader canvas. While I was beginning to believe that I might have something to offer another business, I was in no hurry to tempt fate by even thinking about where I might go from here. Then a potential opportunity for the opening of further doors appeared.

In 1967 Monash University established its four-year part-time master's degree in business administration in opposition to Melbourne University's more restrictive two-year part-time, one-year full-time MBA, the only MBA available and which had been on offer since 1960. MBAs were in very short supply and I figured having one might compensate for someone making a late start in the world of business. Given the demands on my time as a single parent, central AFL umpire, budding businessman and those of an active social life it was going to be a significant challenge but I figured the fifteen hours a week study requirement could be found. I evidently satisfied all the academic requirements as well as the minimum two years' business experience and my application was duly accepted for the 1968 academic year. Squibb had been more than considerate in allowing me to leave work early to attend AFLUA training two nights a week and the firm was good enough to also acquiesce to my taking a few extra hours of normal work time to attend early morning lectures.

7

The world changes

In 1968 the world changed.
With one exception, the Monash MBA course content was a distinct disappointment. This in itself was not a problem given all I wanted was a piece of paper. But Monash had tacked its new MBA on to the duties of existing staff, all of whom were academics with little or no practical experience. It was no surprise that the content was straight out of the textbook. The exception, and it was an outstanding one, was corporate strategy, a subject presented by two graduates of the Harvard Business School and now consultants with PA International Australia, a leading consulting firm. They used the case study approach.

Each month we were presented with the financial and strategic history of an actual US firm and asked to analyse the business' past performance and provide a recommended strategy. The report was to be submitted a fortnight later and our findings critiqued by our peers and by the course leaders during subsequent class sessions. The critiquing sessions were little short of gladiatorial contests. The course members, all competitive bastards, cut, thrust and parried in an endeavour to be last man standing, the sessions more intellectually challenging and stressful than anything I was to later encounter in the boardroom but worth their weight in gold.

Having been handed our first case study, we complained predictably and bitterly to our two instructors about the insufficient information. How could we possibly develop a forward strategy to address the firm's issues and plot its future on such flimsy information? Smiling broadly, the course leaders dismissed our complaints and welcomed us to the real world of incomplete information and uncertainty. We were to introduce some imagination to the process.

In arriving at the strategy to solve the firm's problems I outlined my discarded options together with the rationale for their eventual dismissal before presenting a carefully honed, impossible to be improved upon final recommendation. The reality was that our instructors couldn't have cared less as to our specific recommended strategy. To them everything was relative. They were not interested in correct answers but rather whether we knew what the right questions should be. After all, choosing a strategy is little more than a value judgment. And who can predict the future anyway? What our course leaders were looking for was a plan that addressed the key questions and made some sort of overall sense, in other words, a plan with consistent elements. The revelation, at least to me, was that there were as many strategies presented for that first case study as there were class members. I thought the logic behind my impossible to be improved upon recommendation to be so compelling that all the class members would have recommended exactly the same solution. Of course it wasn't and they didn't. As we would eventually realise, there is always a solution to a business problem and invariably more than one.

But commencing my MBA in 1968 was not the world-changing event.

¶

On a Monday evening at 1 Remer Court, Cheltenham, in August 1968 I was eagerly looking forward to Melbourne's favourite 'reality' television program, Monday night's *TV Ringside*, two hours of boxing at Festival Hall, starting at 9.30. Jeremy had been watered, washed and fed and, following the ritual bedtime story, was sound asleep. The dishes had been done, dirty clothes whirring away in the washing machine and I had already put in a constructive hour of study.

Head resting against the back of one of my leather wing chairs, eyes closed, I pondered with a glow of satisfaction my almost perfect life. Due to a dodgy left knee I was coming to the end of a relatively short umpiring career, a sport in which I had satisfyingly if not necessarily enjoyably reached the elite level. I had a son — the joy of my life — our own home, a good job which I loved, a free company car, a pending MBA which held out promise for even better job prospects, two or three unbanked pay cheques in the cookie jar at any one time and a pretty good social life. My good friend Philip and I had often speculated when we were in our late teens as to who it was that was getting all the good birds. By the time we were in our late twenties we thought we knew the answer. Then again, Philip was never one to give up any sexual opportunity; good, bad or indifferent.

The self-indulgent reverie was abruptly interrupted by the sound of the telephone.

It was Neville Garner, a member of the group. He was to be married the following Saturday. The matron of honour was coming from Sydney unattended and Neville was planning, for the coming Thursday a night at Melbourne's hottest restaurant at the time, the Top of the Town. He wanted me to partner the matron of honour for the evening.

'Jeez, Nevvie, don't do this to me,' I complained, 'I don't have enough hours in a day as it is.'

I had met a heavily pregnant Dawn Dallas-Conte, albeit fleetingly, more than two years earlier in February 1966, only weeks before Thelma took her sabbatical. The connection was Margaret Battisti, Neville's bride-to-be. Dawn, a Bathurst girl, had originally intended to become a spy with ASIO but upon learning that would require her to be located in another sleepy, cold satellite city (Canberra) she had made a right angle turn in her thinking, attended university and became a schoolteacher in Sydney instead. She and Margaret Battisti had taught at the same school. At the time of our earlier meeting Dawn and her husband, Barrie had been visiting Margaret in Melbourne and Margaret had run out of good ideas, lousy ones as well, on how to best entertain them. Margaret brought them to Remer Court. The evening was not a great success, at least for me. Barrie was quiet and seemed ill at ease. When he and I realised we were not going to make a useful connection I had gradually withdrawn, probably much to Barrie's relief and for the rest of the evening had left the social niceties to Thelma.

As Neville continued his selling job I began to dredge from my memory images of that first meeting with Dawn. What was coming up on screen was a confident, heavily pregnant, striking, delightfully feminine, apparently intelligent, refined young woman surrounded by an aura of star quality that could only be described as 'presence'. Not only must she have been worth a look but it appeared I must have been paying a bit more attention than I had given myself credit for at the time. And it wasn't that she was all that tall but she walked tall, like a ballet dancer with something on her mind. In what turned out to be overkill, Neville just happened to let drop that Dawn's marriage had been a mistake. It was not going well and he believed there were significant compatibility problems. Perhaps it wouldn't be such a completely dud evening after all. Or was it a set-up?

I put the phone down. For only the second time in my life the hairs on the back of my neck stood bolt upright, the other time being when I finally discovered the answer to that dogged question, 'who is John Galt?,' in my prescient reading of *Atlas Shrugged*. The little man standing on my shoulder was yelling at the top of his voice, 'come on Raymond don't be completely stupid. Ten minutes ago you were contemplating your perfect life. You hardly know this woman. She's married, she has two young kids, she lives in Sydney and there was absolutely nothing that came out of her visit three years ago to justify this mounting tidal wave of excited anticipation.' In fact, as Dawn later pointed out, I had not only withdrawn from the conversation that evening but also compounded the crime by watching TV while the others chatted away. It just didn't make any sense to even think about going down this road. But as it eventuated it was a road I was to be drawn down as if incapable of rational thought.

Ten minutes late, following one of my last umpiring training sessions for the season, I hurried eagerly from the lift into the lounge of the Top of the Town restaurant. The foreshadowing was right on the money. I caught Dawn's eye and on cue I was struck by a thunderbolt. Somehow managing to grasp her extended hand I gently lowered myself on to the adjoining, strategically vacant seat. An instant bubble insulated us from the rest of the group who were bemused by the electricity that crackled for the rest of the evening. But it was no figment of the imagination and I was introduced to the exquisite pain and nausea that only real infatuation can provide. For the next few days I couldn't eat, I couldn't sleep and felt as if I were likely to throw up at any moment. Handily, it appeared Dawn felt the same way. I was struck by her inexplicable decision, given the circumstances, to choose me as her partner and the fear that one day she would realise her error.

Within forty-eight hours we had agreed to pursue the impossible dream. It was a whim of gigantic proportions and off the scale impetuosity. The risk of disaster and its consequences, particularly for Dawn, were enormous. But neither logic nor sentiment was permitted to stand in the way and my relentless persistence over the next six weeks overcame Dawn's inevitable cold-light-of-day spikes in apprehension.

Dawn, Danielle and Brook arrived on Melbourne Cup Day, 1968, the day Rain Lover won the first of his two Cups. To the neighbours' astonishment, given the comings and goings of the previous three years, we became Cheltenham's 'Brady Bunch'. Jeremy was seven, Danielle, two and Brook, ten months.

The kids adapted quickly to their new environment. Given their ages Danielle and Brook adjusted almost seamlessly. It was a little more difficult for Jeremy (now Jer) who, at age seven, was happy now to be part of a normal family and delighted to have Dawn picking him up from school rather than wending his own way to the close-by child minding centre on busy Warrigal Road. But there were hurdles. He faced the dilemma of having two mothers as well as having to share me with three intruders, a substantial adjustment after three years of having me to himself. It was never going to be all beer and skittles but Dawn's patience, sensitivity and common sense, not to mention the seductively happy family environment he now found himself in, were able to win the day.

As for me, I was in heaven. I had this wonderful creature I could touch and feel on a daily basis. As always, there was a slight downside, at least initially. She was smarter than me and had this disconcerting habit of not only thinking for herself (no surprise there given she had satisfied ASIO's requirements to become a spy) but also articulating views that were not always in accord with mine.

I hadn't experienced this before, particularly from someone I had gone for head over heels. Her incisive energy focussed on winning a debate rather than exerting dominance, which could be either exciting or a bit of a worry depending on how you were feeling at the time. Of course it helped if your opponent looked pretty good and had the wherewithal to salve your wounds at a not so later date. Up to now I had lived in a man's world and hadn't been used to contradiction or having my best thoughts trashed by a woman, often the case when I regressed to that ever comfortable position of defensive male thinking. Dawn was one of those feared women who titillated and challenged and who was described, inaccurately at the time, as a 'women's libber'. Gradually I learned to adapt, albeit somewhat grudgingly, to a new perspective on life. I must be a slow learner because forty-seven years later nothing much has changed. Nor has the excitement.

¶

Dawn regularly took Danielle and Brook to Barrie's mother in Sydney to provide Barrie the opportunity to spend time with them but the visits became increasingly awkward for Barrie and some of them didn't go well, particularly for Brook. Danielle and Brook eventually adopted the name King and as far as they were concerned I was their father. And Barrie's development of a serious blood condition while still in his thirties, which prevented him from full time employment, made life increasingly difficult for him and it seemed he had little interest other than whiling away his time in front of a poker machine. In 1992 Dawn learned from Barrie's mother that he was dying of cancer, with only weeks to live. She and Danielle travelled to the Gold Coast (Brook was overseas, managing a pub in St Johns Wood) and cajoled the hospice into allowing Barrie to have an evening out at the local sporting club, promising to have him back in time for his next morphine shot. Barrie invited his best friend, a young man with a deprived background whom Barrie had taught to read. Happily reacquainted with his favourite pastime of playing the pokies Barrie had a wonderful evening, proudly and with obvious pleasure, presenting Dawn and Danielle to all his old mates who were not only surprised to see him still alive and in such high spirits but also more than suitably impressed with his beautiful entourage.

¶

Christmas 1968 I took the new family to Hamilton to meet Dad and his new wife Tess. Tess's mother had died when she was a teenager and she had subsequently become the surrogate wife, mother and housekeeper for the rest of her large family and which for many years she had feared might have been her destiny. Dad and Tess had married earlier in the year and I had been Dad's best man. They were an excellent match and delightfully happy. Tess, like Dawn, was Catholic, confirming Mum's droll and oft quoted prophecy that you needed to be wary of Catholics because 'they would get you in the end'. Tess was much softer than Mum and had been brought up in a world in which a woman's key role was to please her man. Tess had also been brought up in the world of horse racing, a rearing of some convenience given Dad's keen punting background and given both loved a beer they had plenty in common. Marriage to Dad was Tess's idea of a dream come true and Dad was more than pleasantly surprised at marriage's new dimension.

Dawn was a big hit in Hamilton. Nanna King's loyal and pithy comment that Dawn was much better than 'that other one' (Nanna was not into forgiveness when a family member's interests were at stake) was complemented by Dad's view. Rarely one to run off at the mouth he suggested Dawn was probably the best thing that had happened to me. Tess was delighted to have another Catholic in the family and in many ways Dawn become the daughter that Tess never had. The real tragedy was that Mum never got to meet Dawn. Mum would have basked in the glow of Dawn's refinement, selflessness and almost excruciating need to do the right thing by her family and been delighted, if not amazed, that such a person could have been attracted to her bugger of a kid.

8

Children

Every day during the rollercoaster ride of being a parent you cannot help yourself. You look for indicators that the hopes and aspirations for your children will be realised, taking a ticket in that great lottery of parenthood, never knowing how they will turn out once they become themselves.

Among this plethora of daily value judgments there will occasionally be a standout that convinces you your child is not going to be merely OK but really OK. That standout may not make sense to anyone else but it would make sense to you.

¶

Brook was in no hurry; he came into the world three weeks late. He was a happy child, popular with his host of friends and every day was a good day. He rarely complained, was undemanding of his parents, generous in expressing appreciation and had few expectations of others. He was blessed not only with high emotional intelligence but also wonderful hand/eye coordination that enabled him to be good at all sports. He excelled as a relaxed, elegant century maker and wicketkeeper in representative junior cricket, was a standout in his first game of Aussie Rules and on his way to becoming a quick thinking, sure ball-handling, high marking forward. But it all came a bit too easily and he was not to take full advantage of a God given sporting talent that should have enabled him to play at the elite level with AFL club St Kilda. Nevertheless, without apparent effort, he kicks seventeen goals for Beaumaris in a single game in the South East Suburban Football league and became a key player for Old Collegians in the A Grade Amateurs. At that time being the best that he could possibly be was not all that important to him. He wanted only to live his life without unnecessary pressure — a view of the world that would ultimately change.

In keeping with Brook's relaxed approach to life was his diffident attitude to schooling. It was not all that important, at least not to him. Whilst this approach was not too much of a problem at primary school it became increasingly so at Mentone Grammar where, following in his brother's footsteps, he began in year seven. We were yet to discover that Mentone Grammar was probably the worst school for Brook at that time. Principal Keith Jones, was a blast from the past and a stickler for draconian discipline redolent of nineteenth century English education. The school's senior master, 'Boof' Lewis, was also a firm believer in discipline and would have been well placed running a correctional facility. The Mentone model was epitomised by the school's policy on hair length. Hair was not permitted to reach one's shirt collar, a policy that played very nicely into the hands of George Gardner, the local barber who provided his services one day a week to the authoritarian campus. Any student whose hair transgressed or at least looked as if it was about to transgress was tapped on the shoulder to immediately present himself to George who, no questions asked, proceeded to butcher the unfortunate student's hair in record time. The 'Brigadier', an ex-army type who ran the school's cadet program, was also a firm believer in 'short back and sides' and did the shoulder tapping, providing George with a steady stream of reluctant paying customers, the cost being added to next term's account.

A student with a relaxed view of education that did not fit the school's unilateral mould was a challenge that could not and would not be ignored. So it was with little surprise the staff set out to whip Brook into shape, literally as well as metaphorically. For months he was required to cool his heels outside the senior master's office for thirty minutes preceding each morning assembly, a punishment neither Brook nor the school believed his parents needed to know about.

Brook endured his privations without comment or complaint, at least to his parents, and tried to make the best of things as a high profile sporting identity on Saturdays and Sundays and by enjoying the bonhomie of his mates as well as their enthusiastic admiration of his skills at Space Invaders. Space Invaders was a highly popular and lucrative machine game for the proprietors of milk bars, hamburger joints and other dimly lit venues of doubtful repute, many of which have Brook's name posted in bright lights as the current record holder. His superior hand/eye coordination and quick hands were right up that particular alley. Again, this achievement was unknown to his parents and one in which Brook didn't take a great deal of pride given his belief that expertise in Space Invaders and similar games was the domain of losers.

While those glimpses of sunshine momentarily eased Brook's pain they were not enough. Inevitably he fell behind in his studies, the walls began to close in and the pressures took their inexorable toll. After two years of physical and mental purgatory the dam wall broke and he poured out his heart to Dawn. The Mentone machine had finally broken him.

How could we have been so blind? How could we have got it so wrong? The days of every day being a good day had gone. Of course Dawn and I wanted to take the conventional and easy way out, believing that Brook's negative attitude to school was a transitory thing that would finally right itself. But by now the pressure of daily conflict during school hours appeared to have been joined by the insidious pressure of self-esteem. Brook had what he saw as successful parents, a high achieving brother and a sister totally unfazed by anything the world might throw at her. He began to see himself as the odd man out, a square peg in a round hole. He was not to know that at that precise moment things were not going all that well for his so-called successful father either.

The dilemma was what to do. Should we persist with Mentone Grammar, try the more free-wheeling St Leonard's, the half-way house of Beaumaris High School or go with Brook's choice, Sandringham Technical School where he had a number of mates. Logic suggested the more free-wheeling St Leonard's as the better choice and Sandringham Tech as the worst. Dawn and I agonised for weeks, weighing the pluses and minuses of the various alternatives. It finally came down to a very simple premise. As a parent, if you could be granted but one wish for your kids what would it be? The answer is always that multifaceted, tenuous concept of happiness. We decided it was best in the short term to go down that road so Brook could recharge his batteries in a less pressured environment and live to fight another day. Sandy Tech it was and we crossed fingers, toes, in fact everything.

The revelation came in year ten, 'you know Dad I'm not so dumb after all.' He didn't mean academia; he meant personal values and had realised that his own were pretty good compared to those of some of his acquaintances, of whom he was nonetheless fearlessly protective. Everything is relative. That was the defining moment. He had climbed off the canvas and self-esteem was in the process of being restored. But life is rarely quite that simple. At times it is two steps forward and one step back but he goes on to gain his year twelve VCE and diploma in real estate as a prelude to embarking on a successful career in business.

Selling was always going to be Brook's go, his intuitive social skills his long suit. But not, as it turns out, in real estate. After three years in that field he decided it was not for him; he had better things to do with his life. In the meantime the lure of overseas travel worked its captivating magic. Now in his mid-twenties he spent fifteen wonderful months working his way around the world, largely as a hotel bar manager. Naturally, he returned without a penny to his name together with the mind-set of the carefree lotus eater. He couldn't wait to return to that wonderful life as soon as possible. But his family had no intention of facilitating a continuation of that seductive lifestyle and he gritted his teeth in acknowledging the need to get back into normal society. He accepted the first 'earner' that came along, in this case a lowly job in the warehouse of Jasol, a chemical supplies business. He began at the bottom, progressed to salesman, to sales manager and finally to state manager before jumping ship and buying his way into a business competitor of Jasol as one of four equal principals. His big brother negotiated the terms. Many of his previous clients came with him together with a number of key Jasol staff members. People still liked having him around. He later facilitated key career changes for his sister and brother-in-law. The new business boomed. He married Marni, built two substantial houses in the popular suburb of Hampton and produced high achieving and highly popular identical twin boys with superior social, academic and sporting skills; two burgers with the lot who will not be permitted to become lotus eaters. The poacher has become the gamekeeper.

¶

Danielle had an insatiable thirst for life. Fearless, wilful, compassionate to a fault, creative, impetuous, an imagination with all the colours of the rainbow, a passion for the underdog, never able to keep a secret, Danielle had to do everything now. Nothing was impossible and the concept of boundaries was neither acceptable nor even acknowledged. She was impatient to be born and arrived three weeks early.

Passive Danielle was not. She didn't crawl; that was too slow. She graduated from sitting up to using a 'walker' and finally walked at ten months, quickly. She put sentences together at twelve months and soon had the vocabulary of a two year-old. She either enjoyed or endured colourful dreams at night, the legacy of an over-active mind that didn't turn off. Dawn and I didn't get a full night's sleep until Danielle was seven. She also had a sense of observation and a photographic memory as acute and as accurate as a North American Indian.

Not yet three years of age, Danielle accompanied Dawn to the recently opened Southland regional shopping centre, an approximate fifteen minute winding, indirect journey by car from Remer Court. It was only her third visit to the busy shopping centre. Dawn's first port of call was the post office. She had Brook on her hip and released Danielle's hand in order to engage the post office shop-assistant. Suddenly there was no Danielle; she had decided to do her own shopping. Frantic, Dawn contacted an irritated shopping centre management which had to deal with yet another irresponsible mother. Nevertheless, they went through the motions of putting Dawn at ease by explaining this was an everyday occurrence and no doubt Danielle had gone to sleep in some inaccessible spot.

'Don't worry, happens all the time,' they said.

Hardly comforting was their normal routine in such cases. They would wait until the centre closed for the evening before beginning the search. However, Danielle is no dozy child. Dawn knew she was not asleep under the counter somewhere. Every nerve in her body screamed abduction. She knew Danielle's overwhelming confidence and being as friendly as a puppy would cause her to speak to or to engage with anyone, friend or foe.

An hour after Danielle's disappearance a distraught Dawn telephoned me at Squibb and asked me to 'phone home and tell Jer, who by now should be home from school, that she will be late home because Danielle is missing at Southland. 'No she's not,' said Jer, 'she walked in the door ten minutes ago.'

Danielle had not only been observed by a very nice lady as being unattended (hardly a flash of intelligence given that Danielle, not yet three, was wandering around a busy car park looking for Dawn's fourth-hand Morris 1100) but had also deflected any personal responsibility for her situation by explaining that her mother and brother had gone home and deliberately left her there.

Nonetheless, the Good Samaritan took Danielle in hand. Directed by Danielle's almost impossible to believe laser-like GPS accuracy (she was only two years and ten months old), she retraced the fifteen minute journey to Remer Court including navigating the labyrinthine housing estate before allowing Danielle to casually trot to the door unattended and disappear behind it, no questions asked. This was not the last time Danielle was to wander off to be returned by Good Samaritans, some of whom were smarter than others, but it was certainly the most impressive.

There were times when you wanted to kill her. There were other times when your mouth fell open in amazement.

For two years during the snow season the family spent every second weekend in the snow at Falls Creek, travelling by car, six riotous hours each way with me waving an extended violent arm into the back seat area, making blind, indiscriminate contact with the innocent and the guilty in roughly equal proportions.

On the slopes Danielle, aged seven, was her usual wayward, impossible self, doing her own thing, being a royal pain in the neck and refusing to embrace or even acknowledge my obviously expert ski instruction. About to explode with rage I banished her to practice by herself. Then we observed Danielle providing instruction to an obviously distraught, middle-aged female beginner who repeatedly fell over and rested immobile in the snow until provided with outside assistance. The seven year old pain in the arse was patiently, maternally, nurturing the middle-aged woman and parroting word for word the instructions she appeared to have completely ignored earlier in the day, together with practical demonstrations.

The woman, embarrassed but nonetheless grateful to have anyone provide even some passing respite to her torment (anyone who has learned to ski as an older person knows that torment extremely well) was fully accepting of and clearly saw nothing wrong with receiving instructions from a seven year old, albeit unaware that Danielle was having only her third day on the snow herself. It was a revelation that was soon obliterated by a continuing raft of misdemeanours and eventually written off as an aberration. It shouldn't have been.

Danielle loved Mentone Girls Grammar but regarded learning as irrelevant and an unnecessary impediment to her social life, an attitude that prevailed in all subjects with the exception of art. She wasn't interested in anything else. Nonetheless, while she exasperated her teachers by not meeting her apparent potential and her non-recognition of boundaries they could not help but admire her big smile, boundless energy and bubbling individuality.

In year twelve Danielle was elected a house captain and had evidently developed into a strong, responsible and proprietorial leader, although we saw little or no evidence of this development at home. We were more aware of her worrying discovery (at least for us) that bedroom windows were not only useful for letting in light but even more useful for ingress and egress during the nocturnal hours. Her 'on the one hand but on the other hand' life of contrasts was epitomised by an incident late one afternoon at school. Danielle, captain of school softball, invited us to attend an inter school final where she was the self-appointed manager, coach and cheerleader, enthusiastically encouraging and coercing 'her' team to success. This is a bit more like it, I mused. Then came the defining moment. Danielle was the 'catcher'. The batter hit a foul ball that looped high, high in the air over Danielle's head and ominously headed towards the brick wall of an adjacent building. She shrugged off the catcher's mask and, never taking he eye off the skyed ball, charged backwards towards the wall. Every eye focussed on Danielle, then the ball, then the wall, then back to Danielle, then the ball, then the wall, calculating, calculating, calculating; 'Jeezus, look out.' As in a feelgood movie, with the back of Danielle's head inches from the wall, the ball landed in her fearless, selfless, outstretched mitt and the crowd, well, the dozen or so parents in attendance, spontaneously leapt to its feet, arms in the air as her shoulder bounced safely off the wall with the ball still in her mitt. I knew then she was going to be really OK. She was prepared to go not just the extra mile but an extra ten miles for a cause she believed in.

And so it turned out. Somehow, largely with the benefit of an outstanding result in year twelve art, Danielle achieved her VCE and commenced fine arts at Monash University, which she quixotically deferred after two years in order to earn some money, before resuming her university studies. She completed these successfully and went on to complete an outstanding diploma of education at the Catholic university in Chadstone in Melbourne. She made such an impact during her three teaching rounds that she received job offers from each of the schools for the following year whereas the university was adamant she should continue academic pursuits and complete a master's degree in education. What the hell had happened? The caterpillar had turned into a butterfly albeit there was an ominous element appearing.

Still a person of extremes, Danielle had become a perfectionist and sets the bar impossibly high. She was now married to her 'rock', David O'Leary, had two children and was spending twelve hours a day at Kostka Hall, Xavier's junior school in Brighton where she was in charge of art and the principal's ever-willing go-to person when he needs things to happen, which was generally most of the time. In just four years she became a living legend with parents and kids alike. She taught every child in the school, all of whom are addressed as young 'gentlemen', and took a deep and abiding personal interest in each of their lives, helping to solve their academic, personal and sometimes family related problems.

Even more impressive, she not only knew the name of every student but filed away for future reference never to be forgotten personal details of every kid she taught. She raised money for one group of parents by painting (free) a work to be auctioned which was so successful that everyone jumped on the bandwagon. She was now head of money-raising as well and painting like a fiend into the small hours. She just couldn't say no. She was asked by an eleven year old who had just lost his mother if she would help him paint her coffin which they duly did late at night so the boy would not be embarrassed by other students or staff.

The Jesuit elders decide she could do more. Now at the senior Xavier campus in Kew she became accountable for art, design, drama, media studies, music, dance and anything else remotely related to the arts. She was responsible for sixty-five staff members across three campuses. She had high expectations of her staff including the inevitable minority who still attempt to take full advantage of the system and she performed no mean feat, given the institutionalisation of mediocrity in educational establishments, in creatively and determinedly ridding Xavier of its half-hearted, self-indulgent efforts.

She was now working even longer hours. It was a bottomless pit and her family rebelled. Reluctantly, she acknowledged they had a point. At age forty-one she resigned and was lost to education forever. Future generations of young gentlemen will be the losers. Seemingly without exception when Dawn and I come across her ex-students or their parents we get, 'my favourite teacher, my best ever teacher, my captain, my captain' in all their various forms. It is heart-warming but a sense of loss prevails.

She badgered her younger brother to pave the way for her to become a sales representative in his chemical supplies and cleaning business. This led to vigorous family debate as to potential dangers to family relationships. It was not the first time Brook had to consider providing the solution to a family problem and this was even more sensitive than the first time. Again, it was a close run thing. Brook accepted that family comes first and in any case he knew Danielle would always deliver. He embraced the challenge and it was no great surprise that Danielle's vibrancy, enterprise and energy led to outstanding success. Within three years she significantly improved the performance of her 'territory', was earning fifty per cent more than her teaching salary, working half the hours and had a prodigiously happier family life. However, her facility for being a pain in the neck had not subsided and she piled pressure on management to improve processes and procedures for more effective satisfaction of Hunter Industrial's clients' needs. After five years her remuneration was eighty per cent ahead. Unsurprisingly, she missed the challenge and satisfaction of her natural calling but acknowledged and accepted that you cannot have it all.

Her children were also doing OK. Her son took after her and regarded the impossible as purely a state of mind. Out of eleven hundred applicants he is one of three university graduates selected to intern with consumer goods giant Proctor and Gamble. He took up a full time role at the end of it and in less than three years was one of a small minority being fast-tracked for the future in Singapore. He then received an offer to join Google in San Francisco for a job that in theory required ten years' business experience. Danielle's daughter completed an arts degree at Monash University and set her sights on either a senior position catching criminals or in advertising.

Danielle's husband, David, continued to be driven to distraction by his energetic, creative and predictably unpredictable wife but he was her ever-present rock and had been since she was a sixteen year old and he a self-employed carpet-laying, Porsche driving, eighteen year-old DJ. We called him the apprentice millionaire. David left school at the end of year ten to get among the money and was self-employed until his early forties when he decided it was time for a more secure source of income.

David is hard working, highly computer literate and especially adept at solving technical and process related problems. But he has no academic qualifications and long term self-employed loners do not have a lot of immediate appeal to recruiters or human resources personnel. Danielle raised the spectre of Brook providing an opportunity for his brother-in-law. The family was evenly divided as to the wisdom of employing family members but Brook's strong sense of family again prevailed. He made the call and it was the right call. Four years later David was running Jasol's operations and this turns out to be a walk up start to a much bigger role as manager of operations at L'Oreal, the French owned cosmetic, fragrances and hair care monolith.

¶

Jeremy was dealt a cruel hand at the tender age of four. It didn't kill him but would it make him stronger? It was hardly likely. His paternal grandfather's calm, resilient genes might kick in and enable him to absorb the pain without psychological damage. I was heroically hopeful of such possibilities. I tried to explain to him why sometimes it is better for parents to live separately but it was a hopeless task. There was no chance he would comprehend a concept where both parents do not live with their child. I had a bit of difficulty comprehending it myself.

After two months he stopped asking why Mummy couldn't come back and eventually made the pragmatic suggestion that I might consider marrying his teacher, Miss McGeedy a buxom, caring young woman who had taken him under her wing. However, while Miss McGeedy might be wonderfully pastoral and a delightful young woman she was no Betty Grable. He needed to think again.

He had a father and major carer with lots of things going on in his life but was the quality of his father's budgeted attention sufficient to make up for the lack of quantity? Jeremy introduced a level of self-sufficiency and control into his life. He developed a program of prompts and reminders to keep his father on the job on matters pertaining to the proper functioning of his solar system and with well disguised exasperation tidied up when his father let him down. He had to grow up quicker than God intended. On the surface he seemed to have more than survived but what was happening psychologically?

Conveniently, his father concluded that if it could not be seen then it wasn't a problem.

At seven, suddenly and without warning, he suffered another major disruption to his life. After having had his father to himself for three years he not only had to learn to share me with three new faces but also had to struggle with the burden of how to keep two mothers happy. Hopefully, the pluses of the Brady Bunch would more than cancel out the minuses. Again, he had to apply quiet resourcefulness and resilience. Fortunately, he was smarter than the average bear having, like his father, presaged that worthy state by successfully skipping grade one and perhaps this again greases the wheels of adaptation despite the intrusions into his old life.

His bewildering new sister, Danielle, smashed a mug over his head to attract his attention from the comatose concentration he always paid to the television set. Without complaint he endured Danielle's regular need for security to not sleep alone as she regularly slid into her new big brother's bed in the early hours. Despite the age differences, Dawn's astute, careful and patient handling of the potential conflicts of the extended family led to him, Danielle and Brook building enduring relationships and becoming normal siblings.

At age ten he competed in his first Little Athletics in, of all things, the 800 metres. The field sprinted away and after 200 metres they were on world record pace. By 600 metres most of the field could hardly walk let alone run. Jeremy had three runners/walkers behind him. He staggered, vomited and laid down on the track. One of the stragglers passed his prostrate body. It took a few seconds for him to react. Strangely energised, he leapt to his feet and gave chase, passed the straggler comfortably and finished fourth last. He vomited again. I'm not sure what this says but it says something and my eyes stung with tears of pride.

Impetuous he was not. Jer was measured, well organised and thought things through, preferring to have a base covered before committing himself to the next challenge. He removed the risk from risk taking. He was strong academically and enjoyed the admiration of his teachers although he refused to take the compulsory school cadets seriously and fell foul of the brigadier who sought him out for a Mentone special haircut. Dawn was spitting angry and determined to take her displeasure to the principal, Keith Jones, but Jer successfully convinced her it was no big deal.

Like his father and grandfather before him he had a love for the sport of kings and provided that interest with a practical touch by taking advantage of his strength with numbers in becoming the Mentone Grammar bookmaker. He learnt how to 'set a gaming book' from his great uncle Bill Edward and was reeling it in until taking a bet from one of his teachers who foolishly made other staff members aware of Jer's bookmaking skills and the enterprise was quickly closed down by senior master Boof Lewis.

He was good at sport without being outstanding and like his father relied on determination and application rather than natural talent. He played full back for the combined Associated Grammar Schools football team and each year finished mid-field in the hurdles in the Victorian All Schools Championships. He survived the weekly cut and made St Kilda's under nineteen AFL team. He had a successful season with the Saints before moving on to play with University Blues and then Old Camberwell in the Amateurs.

In year twelve at Mentone Grammar he was overlooked for appointment as prefect. Midway through the year he made an impressive, thoughtful public address which convinced principal Keith Jones that Jeremy King has a philosophical side to him that outweighed his reputation as an amoral bookmaker and in an unusual mid-year appointment he was added to the prefects' list.

He began a commerce degree at Melbourne University and midway through the course took up residence at Trinity College. He interned at Peat Marwick & Mitchell, a major accounting practice, and took a job there on completion of his degree.

He married Lyn, an audiologist and this pretty good gene pool produced three sports active children who in year twelve achieve average enter scores in excess of 97 and go on to high level university degrees. Jer qualified as a chartered accountant and spent two years in receivership and liquidation before joining investment bank Potter Warburg in mergers and acquisitions. When the firm was taken over by Swiss global investment banking giant, UBS he switched to investment research. Five years in the pressurised ego driven cauldron as managing director of research with responsibility for more than sixty analysts and commuting to Sydney three days a week was as much as he could stand. The catchcry of the highly intensive investment banking business, 'forty and fucked' rose again.

Conveniently, he had earned sufficient from his personal investing to retire from full time employment at forty years of age. He continued his successful investing, maintained his interest in the sport of kings and reduced his golf handicap to five.

9

Wynn Winegrowers Limited

Dale Johnson had evidently done well for Squibb in South-east Asia but his critics believed he had talked the talk and managed upwards extremely well. In other words, they thought he was a brown noser. But he was exactly what Robert Gardiner was looking for and it was a welcome relief for Robert to not have Frank Irving still snapping at his heels.

It was also in 1969 that I made my first direct contribution to Squibb's bottom line. The successful new product introduction suggested I might have a future in marketing as opposed to the more backroom, nerdy activities of market research. In October 1969, encouraged by this token success, I was tempted to chance my arm and pursue a job opportunity that could only have been described as heroically ambitious.

It was the newly-created position of marketing and sales director for Wynn Winegrowers Pty Ltd, a family owned wine company planning to list on the Melbourne Stock Exchange. It seems hard to believe now but its listing would, at that time, make Wynns, a company earning little more than $450,000 before interest and tax, one of the largest three hundred public companies in Australia.

I knew nothing about wine other than having consumed the occasional glass, I had never sold anything other than during my three-week door to door stint and I had never been responsible for marketing anything other than introducing my recent new product idea. Nor did I know anything about managing a sales force other than my vicarious observations at Squibb. It seemed like a hurdle of monumental proportions and the chances of my application being successful had to be at cricket score odds. And in the unlikely event of a miracle occurring then the odds of successfully managing the task had to be open to even wider speculation. As things turned out in respect to the first miracle I had St Jude, the hope of the hopeless, in my corner and I was to gain assistance from some unlikely quarters.

The Wynns appointment was being handled by PA International's Bill Browning, who happened to be one of my two MBA course leaders in corporate strategy at Monash University. Also helping matters was the fact that David Wynn, the chairman of Wynn Winegrowers, was Jewish and like most of his kin believed strongly in the powers of higher education. He believed the wine industry was facing serious challenges that required a new brand of thinking and had decided that MBA studies provided a uniqueness that made me a candidate of interest. At least it got me an interview. Moreover, David believed that success often came from the most unexpected places and an outsider who brought a fresh perspective was likely to slot into that category more than nicely. Nevertheless, a long shot is still a long shot and, as my father used to say, 'you'll never get rich backing outsiders.'

But David was definitely an outside the square man. Many years later, William Thorndyke of Harvard Business School studied eight bosses whose firms outperformed the USA's S&P Index by more than twentyfold over their business careers. They were all outsiders who brought fresh perspectives.

David Wynn was a refined man, mixed in artistic and intellectual circles and over the years had very successfully applied instinct to an unsophisticated wine industry steeped in tradition. He was no textbook CEO, believed that the right people could make a difference, prided himself in having a unique ability to identify them and was prepared to take long shots whenever he felt the occasion demanded which, fortunately for me, was much of the time.

I had listed my Squibb boss, Dale Johnson, as my sole referee simply because I couldn't think of anyone else. For obvious reasons I hadn't expected my application to get very far and it was a more than pleasant surprise even to be granted an interview. It was still more surprising that David Wynn liked the cut of my jib to such a degree that after only one interview he decided I was his man. But Bill Browning had not followed normal protocol and cleared with me their intention to contact my sole referee.

Dale Johnson, having received the call from PA to check me out, descended on my office like a mini tornado close to hysterical as to what he saw as my lack of loyalty. Admittedly, Squibb had been more than generous in giving me time off for umpiring training and for my MBA studies. Nevertheless, I did think Dale's reaction was a little excessive. He entered the realms of the bizarre by proceeding to inform PA that I was not the sort of person they should be employing given I was living in sin with a married woman. Dawn and I were still waiting for our respective divorce applications to be granted, a process not without giant hurdles in those days. In 1969 being unmarried and living together was, in stark contrast to today's cultural mores, an uncommon practice and deeply frowned upon by many people in the community. But Dale's attempt to spike my guns apparently only reinforced Bill Browning's view that I must have had something to offer. Browning was evidently not only impressed by my approach to the thorny subject of corporate strategy but also by my apparent ability to multi task as a single parent. And what were the odds that David Wynn had not only lived in sin himself but had also spawned a child out of wedlock — we were unlikely soulmates.

Section Two
WINE INDUSTRY ADVENTURES

10

Into the trenches at Wynn's

Shlomo Weintraub, a Polish vineyard worker with radical views, took life very seriously. Then again, there wasn't much in his life to smile about in 1914.

Apart from being only 155 centimetres tall, a depressing thought in itself, Shlomo was facing four years of conscription. With the Germans straining at the leash to get the First World War under way Shlomo realised full well that a sojourn in the Polish army was unlikely to end happily given Poland would almost certainly be Germany's first port of call. Skipping the country seemed the simplest solution and he succeeded by turning up in London a week later. He improved the odds of staying alive even further by purchasing a third class boat fare to a distant land called Australia.

Seven years later, at the top end of Melbourne's Bourke Street, Shlomo established his first wine shop, adding a second in 1924 on a site occupied today by the Grossi Florentino restaurant. Having developed good relations with winemakers in gaining access to their product for his own shops he came to the eminently sensible realisation there was considerably less risk and more money to be made by satisfying the wine needs of other retailers rather than those of consumers. Shlomo anglicised his name to Samuel Wynn, sold his by now three wine shop operation and spent long hours building a successful wholesaling business called Wynns Wines, later to be known as Wynn Winegrowers.

In 1945 Samuel turned his boundless energy to his new passion, Zionism, becoming a significant contributor and prime mover for the foundation of the Jewish State, Israel. Of Samuel Wynn's three sons David was the commercial one, his two siblings preferring to pursue high-minded careers as eminent physicians. David was soon running the wine business and like his father was an outlier with good instincts. In particular, he had a feeling for wine consumers, understood their psyche and how best to appeal to them. He was an adventurous thinker, had little fear of failure and was prepared to experiment with different ideas, mundane as well as extreme, in order to deduce what made money and what didn't. He called it testing the soft underbelly of the market. What's more, he was brave enough or arrogant enough to be prepared to put his thoughts down on paper and happy to accept the plaudits of the crowd or ignore its ridicule. He was Jewish after all and instinctively didn't much care what others thought. He had also proved himself not only to others but to himself, having created an even better business than the one he had inherited from his father. Two years after I joined the company and had initiated the successful introduction of the wine-cask David told me he had believed I had similar instincts.

David's first major move upon taking over from his father had been to purchase in 1950 a vineyard in a little known region in South Australia called Coonawarra. He was impressed by the fact that Coonawarra's climate was almost identical to that of the famous Bordeaux region in France. His foresight was instrumental in boosting the family's fortunes because Coonawarra was soon vying with the Hunter Valley for the title of Australia's leading premium wine region of the day. David had a classic label designed for Wynn's Coonawarra Estate, which was a very early Australian example of linking a brand to a wine producing region. The classic label is still in use today and while Coonawarra is now only one of many recognised premium wine regions in Australia the Wynn brand is still the Coonawarra region's most successful winery by far.

Following a string of forgettable new product ideas David's second and even more lucrative initiative was to introduce to the market the half gallon (2.25 litre) glass flagon. It was not an original idea. David had picked up the concept during a trip to Italy's Chianti region but it was, like many apparent innovations, new to the Australian market.

David's creativity was in recognising the opportunity. He coined a new brand name, Wynvale.

The Wynvale flagon was a proprietary glass container in the shape of a barrel and David promoted the new product with the by-line 'three bottles for the price of two'. David's equally clever idea was to introduce a deposit system and offer to repurchase from consumers the empty container at a cost considerably less than producing a new container, encouraging in the process a repeat purchase. It involved establishing an initially complicated but ultimately efficient logistics system for collecting the empties from the retail trade. Now on a roll, David further developed the initiative by not only emblazoning his newly established fleet of delivery/collection trucks with the green Wynvale logo but also by providing free Wynvale neon signs that jutted over footpaths above retailers' entrances for all to see. The Wynvale sign soon became synonymous with the identification of a licensed retail outlet, in the process cementing public awareness of the Wynvale brand name. Retailers were yet to wake up to the free advertising they were helping to facilitate. Another innovation was to introduce movable free standing merchandising units that provided instant shelf space in retailers' walkways, their wheels adding a unique form of flexibility to retailers in allowing them to regularly reconfigure their floor space to better advantage.

David's new product was an instant success and quickly raised the new kid on the block's sales volume to number five in an industry in which the other major players had enjoyed a healthy head start of almost a century. Initially, David's more snooty competitors had been dismissive of Wynvale's 'watery' wines being sold in the jumbo container but soon changed their tune in banding together and commissioning the manufacture of an industry flagon to compete with the Wynvale product as well as replicating David's deposit and collection system. By 1970 the half gallon flagon in its various forms accounted for around fifty per cent of wine industry sales volume and had been largely responsible for the industry's nine per cent a year growth rate over the previous five years.

Even a cocky MBA undergraduate recognised that the role of marketing and sales director for a company about to be listed on the Stock Exchange was one of far greater consequence than his background deserved. On the drive to Wynn's office on that first day, January 3, 1970, not yet thirty one years of age, pulse racing, there was more than a hint of trepidation. The idea of the job had been seductive and salacious but now, in the cold light of day, the daunting task ahead had suddenly become very real. Was I up to it? I couldn't have felt less like the marketing and sales director of a wine company if I'd been wearing a dog collar.

As I parked my (second hand) company car there was something else, something undefined, clouding my thoughts. It took a while but I gradually realised what it was. I was no longer one of 'us'. I was now a 'they,' one of 'them,' someone who had to make decisions, someone who held the lives of others in his hands. 'It is the price that has to be paid,' I tried to tell myself 'AND BY GOD IT'S GOING TO BE WORTH IT,' I finally thundered.

My company car had been Samuel Wynn's much-prized but much panel beaten Chrysler Valiant before being confiscated some months earlier by David. Samuel, then in his eighties, his eyesight failing and his neurological capacity sapped by dementia had, like Mr Magoo of early movie cartoon fame, developed the habit of exercising three, four and five point turns by running into things before beginning the next stage of the process. David had resolved that problem by removing the car and convincing his father his car had been stolen. And on the day I turned up in 'his' car he was on to it in a flash, announcing in an aggrieved screech to all and sundry that not only had his stolen car miraculously turned up in one of the company's parking bays but there was the thief standing before him as large as life. Samuel lived to be ninety-one and never in the whole of his life as far as can be told experienced anything approaching a moment's real joy.

Having made the decision to leave Squibb and join Wynns I had been subjected to Robert Gardiner's first class persuasive bullshit as he endeavoured to head me off at the pass. He tried to convince me that I was nowhere near ready for the daunting task at Wynns, a task which would only railroad a promising future career at Squibb. He referred to me as one of his two 'stars', the other ultimately taking over from him as managing director and, consistent with the highly political environment at Squibb, being subsequently sacked for alleged malfeasance.

Robert Gardiner's cautionary comments made a lot of sense and the only rejoinder I could come up with was, 'oh, I think I might be able to pull a few rabbits out of the hat,' drawing a healthy, disbelieving and belittling laugh. But I really did think I had two things going for me — my belief that the invaluable lessons I had learned at Squibb were transferable and that my equally passionate belief in my corporate strategy MBA studies would ultimately lead to a successful action plan.

On arriving at Wynns I immediately set to work analysing the company's balance sheet and profit and loss statement and was startled to discover its appallingly low return on investment. In seeking a solution to this problem and still wanting to believe in simple solutions I turned to my Squibb acquired obsession of gross margin analysis as the likely key to the problem. I proceeded to spend much of my first three months trying to calculate the contribution made to the bottom line by each of Wynn's products. My ultimate objective was to focus the attention of the sales force on the more profitable products and to de-emphasise those that were less profitable. That was not what I had been directly employed to do but I had taken David's comment about the need for a new brand of thinking a little more literally than I suspect David might have had in mind. Wynn's accounting resources were limited so I undertook the task myself. It almost cost me my job.

Frank Devine had the title of managing director but was effectively chief operating officer. I reported to Frank and had very little direct contact with executive chairman David, who seemed to be spending less and less time in the business. Frank was a strong leader and in New Guinea in World War Two had been promoted in the field to the rank of captain in the Australian Army, a lofty position for a twenty-two year old. His management style was that of an old style accountant and he focussed mainly on the cash as well as on accounting's mechanical aspects rather than its analytical ones. Business development and financial analysis were certainly not his go and like many general managers at the time he saw his role as largely that of the administrator. He kept his finger on the business's pulse by approving every creditor's invoice and by signing every cheque. His other focus was as president of the Victorian branch of the Australian Wine and Brandy Producers' Association.

The Wine and Brandy Producers' Association was a powerful body. It was cartel of all the major Australian wine producers, its unstated objective being to minimise competition between its members. It did so by adopting the policy of what was euphemistically referred to as 'orderly marketing'. If a retailer sold products at less than an association member's recommended retail price then that retailer was in danger of being blacklisted and refused supply by all the members of the association. Similarly, if an association member were proven to have discounted his products or to have offered promotional inducements to the retail trade to purchase his products in preference to those of other members he was in danger of being drummed out of the association, a fate seemingly worse than death.

The formal rules of the Wine and Brandy Producers' Association were reinforced by such quaint innovations as Wine Week, a week set aside and lovingly looked forward to by the wine industry's leaders. It was a week of socialising and bonding for the CEOs and their vainglorious wives and only one of the reasons the wine industry seemed more like a club and its senior executives boasted of the industry's unique niceness.

With few exceptions the vast majority of the wine industry's products at that time were generic. There was little product differentiation and very few wine labels displayed the name of the grape variety or the regional source. Claret or burgundy described most red table wines and hock, Riesling, Chablis or white burgundy described white table wines, often exactly the same wine. Fortified wines, mainly sherry and port, were similarly labelled along generic lines. As with Wynn's white wines, many of its fortified wines, for example, cream sherry, sweet sherry, white port and Madeira were generally out of the same tank. As elsewhere throughout the wine industry Rafferty's Rules was all the go at Wynn's.

List prices of the major companies were similar if not identical and most competitors' wines could have come out of the same generic tank. In other words, there was no real product differentiation or price competition, a situation the market leaders were happy to maintain in order to shield their dominant positions.

I continued to work on my plan of analysing individual product profitability but had a brain flash after I learned from Frank Devine that Wynn's low return on investment was apparently not unique. A low return appeared to be universal throughout the industry. I was struck by the irresistible thought that there was a seemingly simpler solution to solving Wynn's low ROI problem than the exercise I was still laboriously ploughing through. Until now the Wine and Brandy Producers' Association members had not thought about the potential they had at their disposal to leverage the association's formal rules and informal practices to more profitable advantage. If they had, then they had proceeded to ignore it. I found it hard to believe I was the first person in the history of the wine industry, or at least since the formation of the Wine and Brandy Producers' Association, to consider what was running through my head but I found it equally difficult to believe that there was a rational reason such an idea had been neglected.

Although colluding on wine prices would be declared illegal, following the passing of the 1974 Restrictive Trade Practices Act, you could, in 1970, collude to your heart's content. It was the obvious key to solving what I now believed was the wine industry's key problem — its embarrassingly low return on investment. Compellingly, to me at least, it seemed that the association's rigid rules for membership and its supportive conventions such as Wine Week were the path to happiness along which the members could casually stroll to a level of profitability at least commensurate with that earned in other industries. In other words, there already existed a mechanism by which price collusion could be efficiently and effectively implemented and, what's more, enforced. All that had to be done was convince the association members to raise prices by something more than what they might otherwise have considered (in fact a big something more) and Bob's your uncle.

The wine industry was apparently not ready for a good idea let alone a new idea. The concept of a significant industry wide price rise did not go down well and Frank quickly dismissed the suggestion out of hand. While raising prices in unison had long been the association's practice, those price increases had generally been at less than the prevailing rate of inflation. Bumping prices by significantly more than the rate of inflation was too radical a thought not only as to the perceived brake it might apply to the current and impressive growth rate in sales but also in terms of accepted industry niceness. Moreover, managers of wine companies apparently didn't accept the fact there was a problem with a return on investment often less than one-third of that of other Australian manufacturing industries. If they did, then they presumably dismissed it on the basis that it was an industry-wide phenomenon and outside their control. They didn't seem to accept or even acknowledge the possibility that their major aim was to make money for their shareholders. In any case, if everyone else were in the same boat, one manager couldn't be singled out and made to pay the price for his company's poor performance.

Frank was well aware of why I was locked away in the board room buried under a mountain of statistics but while he appeared to be supportive of my analytical efforts I had to assume it unlikely he attached the same level of importance to product profitability as I did. If he had, the exercise that I thought so important would already have been completed. I also later realised that Frank had not kept David informed as to what I had been spending much of my time on. Nor can I recall Frank having mentioned to me that David was becoming increasingly agitated about the time I was not spending on the more conventional aspects of the role I had been appointed to carry out.

The decision to create the role I had undertaken had been David's alone. David was no devotee of the industry's clubby nature and he suspected that the wine industry cartel would eventually be brought to an end. He believed it was essential to strengthen the company's sales and marketing as a critical first step in any transition to a more competitive market environment. Frank, on the other hand, loved the wine industry the way it was and at fifty years of age he was keen for the industry's comfortable culture to continue, at least until he was ready to retire. It irritated Frank that all the state managers now reported to me, an organisational change he felt to be more than premature and a point of view consistent throughout the company with the exception of David Wynn and, of course, me. On the other hand, independent thinker David was determined to accelerate my journey up the learning curve by deliberately holding my feet to the fire. And despite some early misgivings he turned out to be right.

Having been kept largely in the dark by Frank as to my focus on the numbers David, had, unsurprisingly, developed the impression I had been sitting on my hands. He at last galvanised into action.

David sat behind his office desk, grim, unsmiling, his face cast in stone. In front of him lay a foolscap pad on which was a long list of questions. I knew they were questions because I could discern from my upside down reading very large question marks at the end of every line. David broke the silence, irritable and uncomfortable, his aggravation elevating as he continued painfully down the list, his infallibility in judging people and his cavalier approach to my appointment now under serious bombardment. Having been warned by Frank as to David's disappointment and the serious and likely prospect of a potential end to my short career in the wine industry I was ready.

Apologising for disappointing him as to his apparent expectations and for my not having more vigorously sought an audience with him to explain a less than orthodox approach to the job, I attempted to convince David of the logic of first determining the company's most profitable products and then focussing on those as a means of improving its poor return on investment. Such a course of action, if successful, would mean higher profits and dividends for David and the rest of the Wynn family. I had at least attracted his attention as well as unsettled him with my talk about ROI, a subject with which he was less than familiar. Despite David's initial agitation it seemed that the bones of our original connection still existed. Human nature was now beginning to will David into giving me the benefit of the doubt. And while the concept of return on investment and its significance was largely lost on David he was at least prepared to acknowledge that there was perhaps some promise in where I was now coming from — the image of my MBA studies still relevant. He decided to postpone sacking me. We agreed that for the next three months I would spend at least sixty per cent of my time on his stuff and the balance on my stuff and that we would meet once a week to discuss progress. We both breathed a sigh of relief.

The upshot was that after the first couple of meetings David either cancelled the meetings or didn't turn up. Perhaps my days were numbered after all. But I later learned David had sought the counsel of two of his fellow board members who did understand the significance of information based decision making and who had advised him to be patient. Conveniently for me, David's antennae had also come to the fore in the selection of the two independent non-executive directors he had appointed to the Wynn's board in preparation for its listing on the Stock Exchange. Both were savvy operators as well as highly capable businessmen. Victor Gibson shared David's love of the arts but was a tough hombre (he loved TV Westerns) and had established and then built Gibson Chemicals into a major Australian public company and David Hume was a swashbuckling sharebroker with a twinkle in his eye who had a soft spot for mavericks. Nonetheless, despite the support of these influential businessmen, it seemed that my analytical endeavours might have been barking up the wrong tree after all.

It was one thing to determine individual product profitability but altogether another thing to use the results as the basis for plotting a more profitable future. Wynn's operating dynamics, like every other company in the wine industry, did not cater for sharp right hand turns in marketing strategy or indeed in any other kind of strategy.

Wynn's conformed to standard wine industry practice as to the size of inventories. It held around three and a half years' supply of maturing red wine and fortified wine (sherry and port) in bulk and around one and a half years' supply of white wine that matured more quickly. There was also the need for between three and six months' supply of bottled wine to allow for the inherently delicate nature of wine to recover from the bruising impact of the bottling process. But the lack of flexibility had other contributors. Given the company's extensive vineyards and its long-term contracts to purchase grapes it could be argued that the period of rigidity extended to around seven years. Effectively, the wine industry was making production decisions based on what consumers might want seven years into the future. The scope for disconnection between supply and eventual demand and the risk involved was potentially enormous, the risk exacerbated by the significant investment required. The fact that all wine companies were in the same boat was of little consolation.

The practical significance of this supply inflexibility was twofold.

Individual product profitability analysis appeared to be irrelevant. There was not the flexibility in product supply to place greater focus on high margin lines or to de-emphasise low margin products because the wine to supply all products was not only already in place but in place for years to come. In effect, those decisions had been made years earlier. It was the classic problem faced by any business but particularly for a consumer based business that paradoxically, focussed on production rather than demand.

The other problem was that the funds tied up in inventory, storage facilities and plant and equipment were huge, around four to five times that for the average manufacturer. The financially unsophisticated, family dominated wine companies had either not taken that fact into account in arriving at the appropriate level of pricing for their products or, if they had, they had become complacent and happy to run their businesses at sub-optimal price levels. The huge investment in assets without a compensating pricing regime was the apparent reason the return on investment in the wine industry was only one-third to one-quarter of that earned by manufacturers in general, a return that was hardly impressive anyway.

When the wine industry's poor return was pointed out to long-term participants most were quick to hide behind the claim that the industry was more about lifestyle than profitability. Their thoughts were consistent with those of the landowners in Jane Austen's early nineteenth century England who looked down their noses at those 'in trade' who were sordidly buying and selling as a means of making money as opposed to receiving rent. One could understand such views being espoused by third and fourth generation family members who didn't know any better but it was pretty alarming when the professional managers they employed to run their businesses espoused similar views.

These barriers, behind which many of his peers hid, were those David Wynn intuitively wanted to challenge. While David's views on the means by which these challenges might be addressed were poles apart from mine, our broad philosophical principles were much more aligned — we controlled our own destiny (within reason), we had freedom to act (within reason) and we wanted to believe that in a free world we would win more often than we would lose. More importantly, we believed the battle was worth the prize.

But those ambitions were not ours alone. High profile fast moving consumer goods companies were turning their acquisitive eyes towards the wine industry. These companies were attracted by the wine industry's high growth rate as well as by its reputation for being commercially backward and financially unsophisticated. As far as the predators were concerned, the industry was ripe for the plucking. The barbarians were indeed gathering at the gates.

11

Come in sucker

Pounce the barbarians did.

The titans of the Australian tobacco and food and beverage industries made their moves. Fancy prices were paid for leading wine companies, topped by Philip Morris, the world's leading tobacco company paying almost twenty-seven times after-tax earnings for Lindeman's. The multiple was more than double the average earnings multiple for companies listed on the Australian Stock Exchanges.

The acquisition of the wine industry's then two largest players, Lindeman's and Penfolds (acquired by brewer Tooth & Co), turned out to be unmitigated disasters for their purchasers, a fate that has dogged the various subsequent owners of those famous brands to the present day. There were a number of smaller players who got in on the act as well but two other major players who had initial success were multinationals, H J Heinz and Reckitt and Colman, although neither company was able to achieve its targeted returns and ultimately decided it was better to ride off into the sunset.

Heinz had purchased the Stanley Wine Company and Reckitt and Colman, another highly successful global fast moving consumer goods company, had bought Orlando Wines. And while Tooheys, a brewer, was happy for almost a decade with its 1972 purchase of Wynns, its wine investment turned sour during the recession of 1981 – 1982 and the business disposed of in 1985. By the mid-80s all the wine companies that had been acquired with such heady optimism had seen their new owners heading for the exit.

Why did the wine industry seem so attractive?

The major appeal was the rapid growth in consumer demand for wine. From the 1960s wine had gradually but inexorably increased its share of the alcohol beverage market. Wine's association with food was the key, this happy and fashionable combination providing a new dimension to the consumption of alcohol. More cosmopolitan attitudes to dining out following the influx of European migrants stimulated the demand and the introduction of more liberal licensing laws saw the establishment of new retail outlets in facilitating the supply. In the five years to 1970 annual wine sales in Australia had grown at close to ten per cent a year. The introduction of the wine-cask in 1971 provided further stimulus and the successful introduction of the greatest packaging innovation since the invention of the glass bottle three thousand years earlier underpinned high growth well into the 1980s.

Ironically, the industry's poor profitability record was another attraction. In 1970 the wine industry was still dominated by family-owned companies, some of which were into their fourth and even their fifth generations. With few exceptions the latter generations not only lacked the missionary zeal of their forebears but also saw their inheritance as a right rather than a privilege to be embraced and nurtured. Modern business practices had largely been ignored in the Australian wine industry and there was an automatic presumption among the acquirers they would bring a far more profitable level of expertise to an industry that was seen as financially unsophisticated and commercially backward.

So what went wrong? Why couldn't these apparently highly successful businessmen make their acquisitions work?

Philip Morris, Reckitt & Colman and Heinz were prime examples of sophisticated multinational companies and their highly profitable operations in Australia were no exception. However, there was a fly in the ointment. And that fly was the conveniently ignored truth that their Australian businesses were little more than mere branch operations that slavishly followed the instructions of their overseas masters. Head office was where all the key decisions were made. Senior managers at the local level were in place not for their entrepreneurial skills, creativity, problem-solving abilities or their understanding of financial dynamics. They were there for their ability to implement and to follow head office's book of rules, rules that were invariably characterised by cast iron rigidity.

Even today, Proctor and Gamble, arguably the world's most highly regarded and successful consumer goods business, has its Australian operation focussed purely on meeting sales targets. Strategic areas such as diversification, new product development and the financial dynamics of return on investment are not only areas of no-go for the locals it is almost as if these concepts do not exist — remarkable in a company that prides itself on its in-house training programs. However, decades earlier, Proctor and Gamble had worked out its most successful strategy for success in the boondocks — keep it simple and stick to the company's rule book at the operational level.

The seemingly incongruous but nonetheless practical reality was that the Australian managers of the acquiring companies were simply not up to the task of dealing with an industry that had a totally different set of financial and operating dynamics.

Similar deficiencies could also be attributed to the brewers, although for different reasons. With the exception of New South Wales, where Tooths and Tooheys operated a duopoly and made decisions in unison, the brewers in the other states enjoyed what amounted to monopolies. These monopolies were based on informal agreements not to cross state boundaries and had been in place for almost a century. It wasn't until the passing of the Restrictive Trade Practices Act in 1974 that legitimate competition was encouraged in the Australian brewing industry and not until the late 1990s that actual competition began to reflect anything like that which we know today.

Having operated in a monopolistic environment for more than a century the brewers were highly profitable because of the ruthless exercise of power that monopolies invariably encourage. Moreover, the brewing companies had been successful for so long they had come to the understandable but nonetheless erroneous conclusion that their success came from superior business acumen. It didn't. Success came from their controlled business environment. Outside that environment they were not only mere mortals but actually had very little idea.

If these so-called titans of the business world had thrown away their rose-coloured glasses at the outset and wondered whether there were any reasons they should not have become involved in the wine industry what might they have found?

They would have learnt growing grapes is subject to the unpredictable vagaries of climate as well as to the natural tendency of a plant to 'revert to the mean', that is, to average its yield over a period of years. Bumper seasons tend to follow poor seasons and vice-versa. And the extreme variability in annual yields has serious practical implications. Poor seasons lead to shortages and spikes in prices that have an obvious short-term impact on production costs and product profitability. More critically, price spikes encourage financially unsophisticated growers to plant more vines — the timing of increased production (around five years later) often coinciding with nature's balancing act. As a consequence, over-supply of grapes has bedevilled the wine industry for most of its life and exerted inevitable downward pressure on wine prices in the market place.

The potential acquirers would also have found that favourable tax treatment by the Federal Government was counter-productive. It indirectly encouraged winemakers to carry stocks and plant grapes that arguably they didn't need in order to enjoy the up-front tax benefits. This tied up funds they could ill afford. Little thought was given to whether a use might be found for the added production. It was yet another example of tax driven poor behaviour.

Irrespective of poor government policy there has always been a natural tendency for growers to plant more vines each year on any spare land (because that is what farmers do) and in disregard of the needs of the market place. To make matters even worse, every second retired professional seemed to want to become a grape grower and to establish his own generally unsuccessful wine brand. As a consequence of all of these factors the wine industry over the past hundred years has suffered an over-supply of grapes in more than ninety of them. This has been accompanied by inevitable and unrelenting downward pressure on grape prices, wine prices and profitability. If these factors were not a sufficient deterrent to the invaders' confidence worse was yet to come.

It didn't seem possible but there was an even stronger and more compelling reason not to get involved in the wine industry. A simple comparison of a wine company's balance sheet and profit and loss statement with those of its acquirer would have revealed a startling contrast.

In 1970 a wine company's invested funds per dollar of sales revenue was significantly higher than that of its acquirer. This ratio, known as the capital intensity ratio, was around four times higher for a wine company than for a general manufacturer. Whereas a general manufacturer might have had forty cents per dollar of sales revenue invested in land, plant and equipment and in working capital, a wine company's invested funds per dollar of sales revenue was closer to one dollar sixty and often much higher.

This comparison should have begged at least two related questions.

Q. 1 Why was the capital intensity of the wine companies so much higher?

A. Wine companies at the time carried an average of around three years' inventory of maturing wine in bulk and in bottles and they needed a significant investment in expensive infrastructure to first of all make the wine (a once a year activity) and to house that production until it matured. On the other hand, the standard Australian manufacturing business needed to carry no more than three to four months' finished inventory.

Q. 2 What was the significance of this differential in capital intensity ratios?

A. The significance was twofold.

1. First, the key reason for the acquirer's interest was the wine industry's high level of growth. The acquirers should have been smart enough to realise that the wine industry's high capital intensity ratio was relatively fixed. This meant that for every dollar of anticipated

growth in sales revenue in its wine business the acquirer would need to invest around one dollar sixty before that was achieved. On the other hand, in its existing business, the financing of another dollar of sales revenue required only forty cents. A much higher level of investment — in fact four times as much — would be required to grow its wine acquisition compared to its existing highly profitable business; presumably the prime reason for making the acquisition in the first place.

2. Second, to produce the same return on invested funds in the acquired wine business, as in its existing business the profit for each dollar of sales revenue in the wine business would need to be four times higher than in its existing business. It works this way.

Assume the acquirer's existing business had net assets per dollar of sales revenue of $0.40. In order to produce a twenty per cent return on investment (most of the acquirers were already earning well above that in their existing business) its profit on sales needed to be only $0.08 for each sales dollar (twenty per cent of $0.40). However, given the wine industry's $1.60 of invested funds for each dollar of sales revenue, a twenty per cent return on investment required a profit of $0.32 cents for each sales dollar (twenty per cent of $1.60). If the fixed nature of the capital intensity ratio was a blind spot then it was unlikely that the acquirer would have understood the need for a much higher return per sales dollar in its new wine business — particularly so when the most common key performance indicator in its own business (as ordained by head office) was return on sales.

The blind spot was apparent because the acquirers made little effort to increase the return on sales ratio of their acquired wine businesses, a ratio only one-quarter of what it should have been if they were to produce an ROI anywhere near that of their existing businesses. The acquirers' major focus was on ramping up sales growth in the mistaken belief that this would automatically solve the problem. The result of more rapid sales growth would certainly have produced a much bigger business (and perhaps slightly reduced costs due to economies of scale) but unfortunately the business would continue to generate the same lousy return on investment as before. The problem could only be solved by significantly increasing prices.

If those carrying out the due diligence on the wine businesses had understood the significance of these points it is doubtful they would have proceeded with their investments. The barbarians would have had to raise prices by up to twenty per cent to achieve the same return on investment being earned in their current businesses. That the acquisitions did proceed suggests they were either prepared to throw caution to the wind or were ignorant of the significance of the contrasting sets of financial dynamics.

12

Baptism under fire

It was no great surprise that the early days of the inaugural Wynn's marketing and sales director were not without drama.

The marketing and sales department consisted of forty personnel, one of whom was marketing services manager Bill [Gunter] Stevens, my one and only ally.

Gunter had been born in Germany and lucky to be alive. As a fourteen year-old in 1943 he had been conscripted into the German army and placed on a train bound for the Russian front, a journey almost certain to end in an early demise one way or another. As the fledgling soldiers sat in fear and trepidation in a railway siding waiting for a more important train to pass Gunter decided he didn't have much to lose by taking matters into his own hands. Ignoring the exhortations of his older colleagues as to the prospect of his being shot sooner rather than later he casually stepped off the train. Somehow avoiding detection — conveniently it was night time — he simply walked back down the rail-track to freedom, or so he said, a trivialisation of what surely happened.

And what happened can only be imagined because he did never talk about it. No food, no money, Germany and Europe in increasingly dangerous chaos, likely to be shot at any tick of the clock for 'desertion', one can only marvel at the determination and resilience required to get away with it. And he was only fourteen years of age. Like Sammy Wynn, Gunter eventually found his way to Australia and anglicised his name. Despite rejecting all things associated with Hitler's regime Gunter (now Bill) could never quite rid himself of the Teutonic trait of clicking one's heels in coming to attention in formal circumstances. Nor, fortunately for me, did he rid himself of his other Teutonic traits of long hours, determination, discipline and resoluteness.

The other thirty-nine sales and marketing personnel were deployed throughout Victoria, New South Wales and Queensland. Each state branch had its own sales force, serviced its orders through its own warehouse and was responsible for debt collection. The Western Australian and South Australian markets were serviced through distributors, receiving little direction and even less supervision.

The managers of the three state branches, old hands in the sale and distribution of wines and spirits, had learned their craft the hard way, starting at the bottom. Predictably, they were not delighted to learn they no longer reported to managing director Frank Devine, who was now my boss. This was a situation they would have been unhappy about irrespective of the person appointed to be their manager. So it is easy to understand their feral reaction when they were informed that their new boss had spent most of his short working life as, of all things, a schoolteacher. Insulting and unworkable, they cried to Frank. Not unnaturally, Frank left the door open for them to call him at any time with the dual purpose of providing a safety valve for their frustrations as well as keeping abreast of whatever damn fool decisions the silly young bastard might be contemplating. They needed little encouragement to take Frank up on his offer and embarked on a well-planned tactic of destabilisation that had them caucusing regularly to keep their sense of moral outrage on the boil.

It was obvious to all, me included, that the more conventional sales management functions had me out of my depth. What would a reasonable man do? I did what I thought was common sense, although there is only one problem with common sense — it isn't all that common. I put the cards on the table and asked the state managers to bring me up to speed on what they thought the company's sales and marketing policies should include. But they hadn't read that particular textbook and were singularly unimpressed with my cunning attempt to encourage their cooperation. Their primal and instinctive reaction was to keep me in the dark for as long as possible in the hope I would fail, that sanity would finally prevail and that they would be back reporting to Frank in no time. It was hardly an ideal place to be.

The drama continued, like it or not, and mostly I didn't like it but had to accept it was part of that mythical price that had to be paid. I developed a simple plan that I discussed with no one other than my own conscience. I put up two fingers, added two more, and came up with four fingers. But I would have to bide my time.

It was no accident that David Wynn had thrown me to the wolves. He was confident his intuition was right on the money and that I would eventually come up trumps. He had warned me that the New South Wales manager, John Parkes, who had a minor business studies qualification and thought he was a cut above the rest, was likely to be the most difficult and he certainly wasn't wrong about that.

Having inherited his role from his father David seemingly floated above the business's more mundane and practical organisational issues. He had always had Frank Devine to deal with those. And while David was not ignorant of the possibility of poor inter personal relationships leading to a dysfunctional sales operation it was apparently not all that high on his priority list. He took it for granted that things would ultimately work themselves out. But it soon came to a point where the problem could no longer be ignored.

As Frank gradually tired of the state managers' complaints he began refusing to take their calls. Gnashing their teeth, the state managers finally accepted there seemed little choice but to accept their unhappy lot. And unhappy they still were, continuing by dumb insolence to make me aware of just how unhappy.

When you are learning on the job you manage by trial and error. As some supposedly wise person once said, 'getting things wrong is an important part of getting things right.' If that were correct then based on my early decision making I was going to be in particularly good shape in the future.

In my various discussions with the three state managers I had tried to get a fix on the dynamics of their role. What were their key objectives and how did they go about achieving them? How did they fill in their day? You would think that would be a simple process of information exchange. But spontaneous and sensible answers to the question, 'how do you spend your average day,' were not forthcoming. These days you would open your desk drawer and hand over a copy of your position description. But like most businesses in those days Wynns didn't use position descriptions.

With an instinct for ordeal that characterised my early decision making, I requested the state managers to fill in what were effectively time sheets, producing a brief description of what they were involved in every fifteen minutes. World War Three broke out. They appealed to Frank. 'Insulting and a waste of valuable time,' they chorused again, 'and merely emphasises King's ignorance and unsuitability for the job.'

Nevertheless, Frank supported me, or at least he said he did. The first week's results showed a preponderance of fifteen minute blocks in which the word, 'managing' had been recorded. I threw in the towel, again looked at four fingers, and reverted to my default position of mentally planning their terminations. It marked a low point but worse was around the corner.

Around six months into the job I again blotted my copybook, a book that was accumulating quite a few blots. In 1970 only half of a wine company's sales were made directly to retailers. The remaining fifty per cent was via general wholesalers who promoted to retailers the efficiency benefits of having one supplier rather than multiple suppliers. This was long before wholesalers established banner or buying groups to advertise 'specials'. Retailers paid the same price irrespective of whether they purchased direct from a supplier such as Wynn's or through a wholesaler. Interestingly, most retailers who had accounts with wholesalers also retained their direct accounts with suppliers. It didn't make immediate sense why this might be so, other than the retailers having a bet each way to ensure product availability. For me, it was an encouraging piece of information and supported what was rolling around in my head. And what was rolling round in my head had the potential to entirely upend the accepted order of things.

The cost to Wynn's of the retailer purchasing through the wholesaler, rather than direct from Wynn's, was most of the wholesaler's 12.5 per cent allowance. As Wynn's average profit margin was around thirty per cent I figured, somewhat simplistically, that if we could cut the wholesalers out of the distribution equation most of the wholesalers' allowance on fifty per cent of our sales revenue would be saved. Without there being any additional cost (our sales representatives already called on all the retailers irrespective of whether they placed their orders directly with us or indirectly through a wholesaler) it would lift our average gross profit margin from thirty per cent to more than thirty-five per cent once the additional servicing costs had been taken into account. It would be equivalent to a five per cent price rise. This gain would lift our net profit margin before tax from eleven per cent of sales revenue to more than 16 per cent, an instant relative profit gain of forty-five per cent. But to achieve that we would need to replace all our existing sales to wholesalers with direct purchases by the retailer.

Another way of looking at the problem was to say that as long as we converted at least two-thirds of our business through wholesalers we would at least break even. Anything above that would be cream. My objective was to convert a minimum of eighty-five per cent of wholesale business and be around twenty per cent better off in terms of profit. My plan, while being arrestingly specific, not only flew in the face of conventional wisdom but also decades of industry tradition and represented a serious challenge. Nonetheless, I wanted to believe it had potential. Only a dumb newcomer could have thought that way.

I decided to test the temperature of the water with just one wholesaler to see how much business we were likely to lose by attempting to re-channel that business from the wholesaler to ourselves. Austral Wines Pty Ltd was the wholesaler I figured had the least number of captive retailers (those few retailers who did not have an account with Wynn's) and who I felt was therefore the best wholesaler to try with my experiment. What I wasn't to know was that Austral Wines was probably the last wholesaler I should have considered as my guinea pig. Austral Wines was controlled by the Cody family, earlier members of which had been acquaintances of the fearless and ruthless John Wren.

John Wren had achieved a high level of notoriety in his heyday due to his ability to call on a squad of equally fearless and ruthless Melbourne citizens prepared to act in his best interests. Wren evidently controlled the lion's share of organised street crime in Melbourne's inner suburbs in the '20s and '30s and probably the lion's share of the disorganised street crime as well. What I didn't know was that some members of the Cody family were rumoured to be somewhat on the ruthless and fearless side themselves and not beyond issuing instructions for a bit of biff, either literally or metaphorically, when things were not exactly to their liking.

I made an appointment to see Pierce Cody, the third generation family member who was now managing director of Austral. Ushered into his office I was met by an impressively tall, nicely suited-up executive who had obviously been around the block a few times. I immediately cut to the chase and informed him that I was cutting Austral's allowance from twelve and a half per cent to ten per cent. He smiled, disarmingly. It was an expression entirely without humour and the knowing smile of someone who saw himself in the ascendency. As I anticipated and wanted, he made matters starkly clear. Wynn's would be put to the sword, our products out of his warehouse in no time. Unaware of the risk to my personal safety I suggested somewhat dismissively that it was up to him how he ran his business. By this time he had developed a strange, nasty gleam in his eye and I was wondering if there were something I should have been aware of.

In arriving at my strategy for profit improvement I had been encouraged by David Wynn's overt disdain for wholesalers, unaware that he felt they were probably still a necessary evil. I had also been encouraged by Frank's apparent ambivalence as to the importance of the sales and marketing functions in general. It was a fairly selective rationale on my part but a classic example of greenness. Not being completely stupid I had already kicked my revolutionary proposal around with Frank. While he had suggested that perhaps it wasn't such a great idea he hadn't appeared to be particularly adamant. At least that was my convenient interpretation at the time. Nor had he brought me up to speed on the rumoured proclivities of the Cody family when things didn't quite go to their liking. I had also discussed the Austral idea with my pugnacious Victorian state manager, Bernie Bartlau. Bernie, of Dutch extraction, was not enamoured of the possibility of losing a major customer overnight.

When Austral Wines contacted Bernie that same day and instructed him in no uncertain terms to come and collect 'his' stock and to close the account Bernie suffered what could only be described as a nuclear meltdown. Arms flailing, Bernie loudly brought Frank up to date as to my disastrous lack of competence and unsuitability for the job. Bernie followed up by storming into my office and berating me in full view of the rest of the staff. Without waiting for a response he retreated down the corridor continuing to utter a plethora of unflattering grunts and snorts. While Bernie's frustration was understandable it was also clear that our working relationship had now hit a new low from which the relationship was unlikely ever to be redeemed.

'No.' I mused, 'Bernie it looks like you are going to be the first to go.'

It was perhaps a bit unfair but under the circumstances I thought it was the best way forward, at least for me. I gave it another three months before striking. I held my breath but Frank remained silent. Surprisingly, Bernie didn't see it coming, suggesting how ineffectual he thought I was. I may have imagined it but following Bernie's disappearance the other state managers seemed to become less overtly hostile.

Within seconds of Bernie's outburst Frank had me in his office. He was less than happy. I reminded Frank that the exercise was an experiment to test the effectiveness of my profit improvement theory. Austral Wines' reaction, while immediate and dramatic, was merely part of the plan. Unless we were thrown out we would not get the opportunity to see whether our sales representatives could replace that business at a higher profit margin. Frank didn't quite see it that way and, in any case, broader issues were at play. Frank's previous calm and fatherly, albeit opaque, advice on the subject changed to a stone faced, direct order. He brought me up to speed in great detail as to the proclivities of the Cody family and the potential stick of dynamite that was now sputtering away in my fingers in regard to my personal welfare.

This was a state of affairs which would have been handy to know about in the first place and I was beginning to think I might need the services of a bodyguard or even a small arsenal. Frank also pointed out that Pierce Cody was his vice-president at the Wine and Brandy Producers' Association and a close buddy, an important piece of information it would have been even handier to know.

'No', said Frank, 'it will never do,' quickly torpedoing my clever experiment. I was forced to acknowledge, if not exactly admit, that perhaps I had been a bit too adventurous. Frank placed a slightly different interpretation on it.

The next morning I called on Mr Cody. Cut down to size, cap in hand, a little nervous and at least trying to appear remorseful (I wasn't) I took my medicine and restored the previous allowance. With a grin of shit-eating proportions, Frank's buddy informed me that he could have informed me of the likely outcome the previous day but had decided to let nature take its course, adding for good measure, 'you know what you are don't you,' large pointy finger in my face, 'you're just too bloody smart for your own good.' I got out of there quick smart before I found that finger rammed up my nose.

But these errors paled in comparison to my real doozie, which was the sacking, or at least the timing of my sacking, of New South Wales manager John Parkes. Of the three state managers, John Parkes, as David Wynn had predicted, had been the most difficult. Almost eighteen months into my time at Wynn's he was still being prickly and disdainful even of those of my ideas that were beginning to bear fruit. John hadn't been able to overcome the blow to his self-esteem in not getting my job in the first place but that blow was about to be compounded. He was to be pushed even further down the pecking order.

In the meantime, I had got something right. An idea that had worked extremely well was the establishment of our own sales operations in Western Australia and South Australia, states where we had previously used distributors. The result had been a dramatic and almost instantaneous improvement in our performance. Again, Frank had been unhappy about my disturbing the established order of things. Predictably, our distributors, in place for decades and with close personal ties to Frank, had given him a hard time in attempting to forestall the implementation of my plan but Frank, to his credit, did not stand in my way.

With the company now having five state managers it had become necessary to appoint a national sales manager to manage them. Or so I argued. John Parkes, to his chagrin, had again not been considered for the role. It said something about him that he complained bitterly at not being appointed as my right hand man. I had offered the job to an engaging, charismatic figure by the name of Rod Blake who was an experienced national sales manager from the pharmaceutical industry. And he was certainly no intellectual lightweight, the consultants' tests having estimated his IQ to be at least ten per cent higher than mine. His appointment enabled me to concentrate more time on the things I thought I was better at, the creation of new products and the application of ideas to develop the business in general.

Rod's relationship with John Parkes fared little better than mine, in fact decidedly worse. Within three months it had deteriorated to a level little better than toxic. Rod then presented me with the old 'him or me' ultimatum. Although John reported to Rod I felt it was more appropriate for me to accompany Rod and do the deed given

Rod's relatively short time with the company. It was not irrelevant to my thoughts at the time that the word on the street was that John was already deep in discussions with a major competitor. I had soon learned that much of what went on in the wine industry was an open secret.

We made an appointment to see John at his Sydney office at 10 am. John would have guessed what was coming. That evening at my Sydney hotel I received a telephone call from Frank informing me that John Parkes' wife had been involved in a car accident and was in hospital. Although not life threatening the injury was serious enough and Frank wondered whether we might postpone the next morning's meeting. A difficult decision was called for, another example of what I had soon learned management was all about. I weighed it up (for about two seconds) but with my instinct for ordeal still loud and clear I decided to go through with John's termination, an outcome that wouldn't look too good — which turned out to be something of an under-statement. I had convinced myself that it was a brave and correct business decision given that the relationship between John Parkes and Rod had become untenable. To some extent I was a victim of circumstances but those circumstances would soon be banished as irrelevant and not get in the way of the popular and quickly disseminated story as to what a nasty, horrible prick I was.

I added another month's pay to the severance arrangements to at least pay lip service to my conscience. In less than a week John was appointed national sales manager for Australia's largest wine company, Lindeman's, a position he had no doubt been negotiating at the time. Had I held out for another week he would have walked without any help from me. It was an outcome that would ultimately come back to bite me in no uncertain terms.

Nine months before my becoming the worst person in the wine industry I was exploring with the head of a promotions company creative ways of merchandising wine in retail stores. It turned out to be an epiphany.

13

The wine cask

In 1967 a strange looking container appeared on wine retailers' shelves.

It looked like a small metal barrel trying to emulate a small wooden barrel, which is precisely what it was. It was the most revolutionary wine container since the invention of the glass bottle three thousand years earlier. But the world wasn't to know that just yet. As often happens with first generation products the wine cask iteration that was first cab off the rank didn't quite cut it. It would be left to others to bring the revolution about.

The one gallon (4.5 litre) barrel contained a wine-filled flexible plastic bag. When the bag was punctured by the special spigot (tap) provided, a glass of wine could be drawn off without a backflow of air spoiling the remaining wine. Its principle was similar to that of the flexible wineskin of ancient times that more or less (generally less) achieved the same objective. The container's advantage was that it provided a higher level of convenience for regular wine consumers by keeping any unconsumed contents fresh for up to three months. On the other hand, the wine in a conventional wine container needed to be consumed within forty-eight hours of being opened — a limitation not always seen as a problem by wine's more enthusiastic devotees. The real commercial opportunity appeared to lay in the wine cask's potential to encourage the occasional consumer to imbibe more regularly by enabling him to consume small quantities more often. But perhaps an even greater opportunity lay in the possibility that the wine cask would encourage new consumers to enjoy the benefits wine had to offer. The overall potential appeared to be significant given that industry surveys showed that less than one in twelve Australian adults had consumed wine in the previous week.

At that time most wine industry insiders appeared to be oblivious to these opportunities and dismissed the new container as nothing more than a mantelpiece novelty. Neville Garner, a member of the social group I had joined through Philip Shirrefs, had had one on his mantelpiece and I was sufficiently impressed to try to buy one the following day but learned that its producer, Penfold's, Australia's largest wine company, had been forced to recall the product because of serious leakage problems.

The idea of selling wine packaged in a flexible plastic bag was not new to Australia. Angove's, a company based in South Australia's Riverland, had launched a wine-filled plastic bag in a cardboard box in the early 1960s but the product gained little traction in the market place because of its lack of a tapping principle. It was the tap that provided the Penfold's product with its real benefit.

Three years later, in early 1971, having unsuccessfully racked my brains in search of an innovative point of sale merchandising concept that might provide Wynn's with an advantage over its competitors, I sought external assistance. I had been thinking vaguely along lines similar to a vending machine but got no further than filling the waste paper basket with a plethora of weird and impractical diagrammatic creations. Resorting to outside help didn't get anywhere beyond a vague suggestion from a packaging and promotions consultant that if I were interested in new ideas then octogenarian Charles Malpas, the inventor of the original Penfold's wine cask, might be the man to speak to.

As it turned out, Malpas was not the inventor of the wine cask. But he was the inventor of the all-important tapping principle which he had licensed to Penfold's. My source believed significant progress had been made in solving the technical problems that had bedevilled Penfold's, a belief that turned out to be something of an exaggeration. He also informed me that Malpas had almost given up hope of finding a serious player in the wine industry who might be prepared to give the concept another chance.

13 The wine cask

Recalling the impact the Penfold's wine cask had made on me almost three years earlier I began to fantasise about the potential it might have for lifting Wynn's performance in the marketplace, not to mention the even more pleasant thought of financial gain and glory for me. I picked up the telephone and called Malpas at his home in Leopold on the Bellarine Peninsula.

Since the Penfold's debacle Malpas had left no stone unturned in attempting to resurrect his creation. He had retained Brian Grant and Associates, a marketing consultancy, to work on the major wine companies to convince them the product's problems had been overcome. But no wine company was prepared to again embrace the revolutionary idea, the baggage was just too great. Penfolds' leaking casks had so angered retailers at the time that they had not only refused to continue to stock the wine cask but in an act of narrow minded retaliatory revenge — a characteristic not uncommon among retailers — had also cut back on purchases of Penfold's other products. The disaster had remained fresh in the minds of every wine industry CEO and no one, with the exception of one retailer, was prepared to even consider the cask's potential for reinstatement irrespective of what improvements might have taken place. In any case, wine company CEOs believed the Penfolds wine cask hadn't been much of a winner in the first place.

In the light of these rejections my telephone enquiry to Charles Malpas must have seemed like a call from heaven. Spontaneously, and with unbridled enthusiasm, Malpas invited me to join him and his wife and son for lunch at his home the following day.

I arrived at the impressive country homestead in Leopold on the Bellarine Peninsula. On the front lawn was a small, wizened figure wearing an English hacking jacket and plus fours chipping golf balls into a large wicker basket. Most were finding the target. Charles Malpas had 'shot his age' on the golf course more than once. He pointedly ignored me until he completed his exercise, getting his head lower and concentrating even more determinedly once he was aware of my presence.

Malpas was a curious oddity. His quick-fire and creative brain made him a fascinating character but there was a downside. His overt passion and obsessive single mindedness made him a crushing bore, a not uncommon characteristic among inventors. An engineer, Malpas owned a once successful plastic injection moulding business in nearby Geelong, the management of which he had turned over to his son, John. Malpas now spent most of his time on his true vocation of dreaming up new inventions and applying for patents. Believing that the only ideas worth talking about were his own, Malpas was susceptible to the most extreme forms of flattery. This was a susceptibility I was not beyond attempting to exploit, although one wondered to what end given that no other wine company appeared to have any further interest in his invention. The reality was that I was the one being drawn into the spider's web.

Malpas dominated the lunch time conversation, boasting how his inventions had turned the complex into the simplex. He was angry with Penfold's for not having reintroduced the wine cask now that the problems were solved (they weren't) and he was certain that Wynn's would sweep the market with an obviously highly intelligent person like myself at the helm, a statement to which I gallantly bowed my head. Wynn's success would also prove the 'law of compensation and retribution', another Malpasism: Malpas would be compensated and Penfolds would suffer the retribution of Wynn's success.

He treated his wife who served the meal like the hired help, continually snapping his fingers to not keep his important guest waiting. And if I had needed any further convincing of his being an antiquated but nonetheless abhorrent bully that doubt was quickly dispelled when he started berating his forty year old son, John, who was handicapped by an unfortunate stammer, for making stupid comments. Further investigation revealed that Charles Malpas had more or less dismissed almost everything John had ever said or done, routinely belittling him in front of others and countermanding his decisions.

I learned that Dan Murphy, the high profile retailer and the name behind Australia's now most successful liquor retail chain, had installed a small wine cask production line in the back room of his then only store in Chapel Street in Melbourne. Murphy had been granted a restricted licensing agreement that prevented him from selling the product other than at his Chapel Street premises, making it fairly clear that the leaking problem was not exactly a thing of the past.

Daniel Francis Murphy was an opportunist and an affable rogue who must have hated his father because in 1952 he set up in competition only a hundred metres from his father's liquor store in Prahran. Dan had worked out fairly quickly that his replicating what every other retailer did was unlikely to lead to a road paved with gold. He decided to largely ignore the products of the wine industry cartel members and to concentrate on the non-members whose prices were unknown in the general marketplace. He also began importing wines from France, Spain and Germany. Dan could charge whatever he liked and still claim consumers were getting a bargain.

He also tried something else that was different. In the early 1980s, aided by some obscure legal hocus pocus, Dan had avoided paying the Victorian Government's ten per cent retail license fee by sourcing much of his wine from interstate. Unfortunately for Dan, the Victorian Government's lawyers proved superior to his and in 1988 the court ruled Dan's tax avoidance was in fact tax evasion and very much against the law. Dan was hit with a hefty fine and made to repay the Victorian Government what its lawyers believed he had filched from taxpayers' pockets. The judge also gave Dan a holiday for two and a half years at taxpayers' expense in Melbourne's Pentridge Prison where he became a cost item in Victoria's correctional system.

In the 1960s Dan had quickly recognised the opportunity that was presented by the early adopters of what was to become the Australian wine phenomenon. He established the Vintage Club, which in 1970 was a rapidly expanding group of more than 13,000 generally pretentious wine consumers who provided Dan with a very lucrative meal ticket. Possessing a little knowledge about wine was a dangerous thing and made the members an easy target for Dan's special brand of sophisticated wine bullshit. But like many high profile entrepreneurs Dan would not have been the success that he was without his business partner and right hand man, Tony Leon, who joined him in 1985. Tony not only held the business together by mortgaging his house to keep the business afloat but for many years rode shotgun in protecting Dan's interests and fashioning Dan's ideas into the practical aspect of making money. Dan had evidently promised Tony a half share in the business at the time he played the role of the Good Samaritan and Tony had to jog Dan's memory of that arrangement by threatening legal action a couple of years later.

Instead of using tinplate as the outer container for his wine-cask as Penfold's had done, Dan in 1971 was using cardboard as recommended by Malpas, inevitably leading to the wine-cask becoming known as the 'bag in a box' or 'soft pack'. Erroneously, as it turned out, Malpas argued that Penfold's leaking problem had been caused by the contrasting co-efficiency of expansion of the metal barrel and the plastic fittings, which Malpas registered under the patent name of Aerlesflo. Unlike other taps and spigots available at the time, it prevented air flowing back into the container during the turning on and off process and therefore prevented the wine from oxidising. Thus it allowed an 'air-less flow' (hence Aerlesflo) of wine. Malpas maintained that cardboard rather than tinplate would remove the problem. This technical mumbo jumbo diverted attention from the fact that his Aerlesflo fittings were not always perfectly machined, information he had decided to keep to himself until he solved the problem.

I was initially disappointed that the concept, even in such a minor way, had been re-embraced by someone else but I was nonetheless encouraged by the fact that the free-spirited and market savvy Murphy believed the wine cask had potential.

At our luncheon Malpas revealed that Dan Murphy's wine-cask sales in the first three months accounted for around three per cent of his total sales volume. This compared with Penfold's having achieved a market share of around one and a half per cent before the leaking problem led to the product's recall. Given the obvious consumer benefits of the wine cask, albeit only obvious to Dan and me, I was surprised and even more disappointed that the wine cask had not been embraced by consumers to a greater degree, particularly given Dan Murphy's captive market and his significant influence. It was a curt reminder that the wine industry and its consumers were still steeped in tradition and that Dan's special brand of manure had made only a limited breakthrough. Only a small percentage of wine consumers had been adventurous enough to even experiment with such a revolutionary idea.

On the drive back to Melbourne I kept rolling the numbers around in my head trying to make them work. While the market penetration rates may not at first have seemed particularly impressive they were better than merely interesting. Wynn's had less than five per cent of the Australian wine market and a replication of either Penfold's or Dan Murphy's initial penetration rates would still provide a significant boost to its performance in the marketplace. I was sufficiently encouraged, admittedly underpinned by a large dose of self-interest, to become the self-appointed champion that new and controversial ideas invariably need. As ex-Prime Minister Paul Keating famously said, 'if there's a horse in the race called self-interest then you should back it.'

The day after my visit to Leopold I sat down with Frank Devine and David Wynn and recommended we pursue what I had now convinced myself to be a great opportunity. David and Frank were adamant we should not. They regaled me with the details of the Penfold's disaster that had seen retail stores 'awash' with wine from leaking wine casks. That was an exaggeration but it did hold sufficient truth to suggest the argument could not to be entirely dismissed. Before my appointment as marketing and sales director David had been so negative to attempts to revive the wine cask he told me he had refused to even grant an interview to Brian Grant who was vainly trying to open a door, somewhere, anywhere. Frank's only contribution was, 'as every other wine company had rejected the opportunity surely they couldn't all be wrong.' Of course that begged a very large question given my views on the quality of management in the wine industry but for once I kept my mouth shut. As far as Frank was concerned I was about to become the epitome of the loyal mother who, in the way that mothers are, ignored the reality of her out-of-step son in the army's marching out parade, and mused, 'look at my son, isn't he wonderful, he's the only one in step.'

With the rabbit in my hat now in danger of making 'no appearance your worship', self-interest morphed into desperation. I presented David Wynn the next morning with a handwritten paper setting out my projections as to what I believed the wine cask could do for Wynn's bottom line. The key and not insignificant assumption was that the technical problems had been overcome. The second and equally significant assumption was that the cask's competitive advantage could enjoy a significant price premium. I proposed that the 4.5 litre container carry a price premium over that of two 2.25 litre flagons of twenty per cent. This would provide a profit a litre approximately two-thirds higher than the pedestrian gross margin we earned on two half-gallon flagons. Wynn's annual profit would more than double if we achieved no more than the same penetration rate as Penfold's. I had figured reading on a piece of paper numbers that might double his already not inconsiderable fortune was going to be difficult for David to ignore; and so it turned out. David stared at the numbers for what seemed like an interminable period then looked at me and nodded.

Listing Wynn's on the stock exchange had been a prelude to David's real objective of placing the family business on the market. His aim was to retire to that micro climate area in the Barossa Valley known as High Eden where he would establish a boutique vineyard and winery with his son Adam. Essentially, he just wanted to enjoy retirement and spend more time on his real love, the arts, in that city of the arts, Adelaide. The possibility, remote though it may have been, of David being able to more than double his anticipated retirement fund was too much of a temptation for him to ignore. In any case his natural and strong instinct to try different things had again been sparked. He was up for the challenge and we were on our way. Frank now thought David was as crazy as I was.

After a number of hiccups we finally negotiated an exclusive licence to use Malpas's patented tap for three years. Malpas had been awkward to deal with. Five minutes after saying yes he was saying no, successfully driving David to distraction. But the biggest hiccup turned out to be Malpas's iron-clad commission agreement with Brian Grant and Associates (which we hadn't known about) and which Malpas preferred to treat by ignoring it in order to cut Brian Grant out of the deal. When Malpas learned otherwise and we in turn learned we would have to pay a higher royalty than David had first anticipated, David's patience, already wafer thin, finally collapsed. He decided to call the deal off. It resulted in some panicky moments for me but my enthusiastic, albeit less than deft, arguments ultimately succeeded in overcoming David's emerging pangs of buyer's remorse. I had been introduced to the emotional rollercoaster ride to which major business deals are invariably hostage.

More than eight months were to elapse before we finally launched the Wynn's wine cask. Wynns' production manager, the highly capable Noel Davey, who saw me as a serious threat to his CEO ambitions at Wynn's, had been confident that an automated filling machine could be developed to meet the wine cask's specific needs. Like all production managers he was less keen on spending money on labour than on equipment. His determination to automate the filling process not only blew the cost budget sky high but also frustrated the rest of us because he couldn't get the damn thing to work, ultimately having to resort to a more labour intensive production line that is still the basis for wine cask filling lines today. His star had slipped a little further from the ascendancy. However, we needed all that time to deal with the problem of leakers that Malpas had never previously overcome. To his credit, Malpas worked like a terrier or at least gave the impression of working like a terrier in dealing with each new challenge as it arose.

It was Malpas's creativity that ultimately led to my luncheon engagements with Visy Industries boss, philanthropist billionaire and at times Australia's richest man, Richard Pratt (born Ryszard Przecicki in Poland). Richard's own creativity was later to get him into a highly publicised altercation with the authorities over a bit of price fixing. It was a spot of bother that would get him fined $36 million and lucky not to serve significant jail time. I was also a friend of his so-called partner in crime, Russell Jones, CEO of Visy's major competitor, Amcor.

Ironically, Russell was one of the nicest and, in my opinion, one of the most honourable businessmen you could meet. He was also one of the most heroic and brave Aussie Rules footballers I have ever seen. He was just unfortunate in being caught in the wrong place at the wrong time with the heavy guy that Graeme Samuel, head of the Australian Competition and Consumer Commission and his merry men had been trying to nail for a long time. It was collateral damage and Russell's life, certainly his business life, was ruined as a result. Nice guys find that sort of thing difficult to swallow. And as the words of the Joan Baez song go, 'there but for fortune go you or I.' It was one that God definitely got wrong.

Richard Pratt was that revered rarity, a billionaire who was a 'good bloke'. He hadn't lost the common touch of his early years and was worshipped by his Visy Industries employees as well as by a succession of high profile needy, sporting souls for whom he found (created) jobs in the Visy organisation. And it wasn't that Richard Pratt and I were necessarily close — I couldn't have held two intertwined fingers in the air and justifiably proclaimed to the world at large that, 'Richard and I are just like that mate' — but he apparently enjoyed my company. Richard's favourite watering hole at lunchtime in the '80s and '90s was the Stokehouse in St Kilda, which happened to be only a hop, skip and a jump from my office in Albert Park. When one of Richard's preferred candidates cancelled at the last minute or Richard couldn't think of anyone better he would give me a call around twelve o'clock and say, let's do lunch, just the two of us,' causing me to drop everything and hotfoot it over to the

Stokehouse hoping for a few crumbs to be brushed my way. The luncheon engagements were invariably embellished by a succession of highly attractive young women who presented themselves at our table in paying homage to the great man. A bit of a pants man was our Richard and what's more, evidently very generous into the bargain. It seemed to be a game he had down pretty well pat. And no, these were not the metaphorical crumbs I had in mind when I answered Richard's call.

When I first met Richard in 1971 he was running a small and only moderately successful cardboard box business he had inherited from his father. Ironically, Richard's father had initially abandoned hope that his son would ever amount to much in the business world due to Richard's aggressive pursuit of the good life and his equally aggressive pursuit, at least for a short time, of a singing career in musical comedy. The connection with Malpas was somewhat oblique.

During the almost nine months that passed between our signing the exclusive licensing agreement with Malpas and our launching the wine cask into the general marketplace we continued to be plagued by an unacceptable level of leakers. Malpas had ultimately solved that problem by employing a seemingly crude but nonetheless ingeniously simple solution. A number of reasons for leakers had been identified but the most common one appeared to be the sometimes ill-fitting components of the aerlesflo tap, the inconvenient reality that Malpas had finally come to accept. Rather than dealing with his quality control problems directly (a prohibitively expensive and lengthy process) Malpas's solution was to suspend an extremely thin piece of plastic film in front of the housing ring that attached the bag to the cardboard through which the spigot would broach the bag. The film would wrap itself around the 'male' tap as it entered the 'female' housing ring, blocking any small unintended gap that might have existed between the two components. The problem then was one of process — how to evolve a mass production system that would be effective as well as meet our cost constraints. This was where Richard Pratt came in.

Richard had been brought up in Carlton and like me had been a reasonable footballer but not quite reasonable enough. He had also played for Carlton Under-Nineteens as well as Carlton Seconds (albeit five years earlier than me) and so we had a connection that transcended the traditional demand and supply relationship. Richard, ultimately the patron of Carlton Football Club, never forgave me for becoming a director of rival club St Kilda where my two sons had played in under-age teams.

Richard supplied all Wynns' cardboard boxes but much to his own surprise he had also developed a love for using cardboard in creative and unconventional applications. He was particularly enthusiastic about cardboard coffins, an enthusiasm that, disappointingly for Richard, was not to be shared by the population at large. He also believed in applying the marketing concept in its simplest and purist form. And that was creating a competitive advantage for himself by rigorously meeting his customers' needs more effectively than his competitors. After all, a cardboard box is just a cardboard box. More importantly, he agreed the wine cask concept had the potential to revolutionise the way wine was presented to the consumer, along the way creating a nice little earner for himself.

Visy could supply not only the outer cardboard box 'shipper' but also supply the container the wine was packaged in. He could see the big picture. Richard believed the wine cask had the potential to open up a whole new market for him and was the sort of opportunity right up his iconoclastic alley.

Richard's major problem (and ours) was in finding a way in which a minuscule piece of fine plastic film could be introduced into a process in an industry that was fixated on automation. It was a mark of the man that he went back to the early days of mass production by employing an army of women who slowly and laboriously attached by hand fiddly little bits of plastic film to pieces of cardboard. Richard supplied the product to us at the right price but the process cost Richard's business a 'bomb', at least initially. Without his preparedness to wear the cost as an investment in the future the wine cask phenomenon may never have got under way.

The big day finally arrived, December 3, 1971.

I was on the 8 am flight to Sydney to welcome the first semi-trailer load. It was not to be a warm welcome and I was met with a mess of collapsing pallets. My stellar career in the wine industry seemed to be in the same boat. I thought I detected a slight smile on the face of John Parkes, who, having been subjected by his Penfold's counterpart to the ramifications of Penfold's earlier failure had been dead against the project from the start. Failure would of course provide further evidence of my unsuitability for the job. I telephoned Noel Davey to give him the bad news. He coolly asked me to have the leakers isolated as the first step in the investigation process. Tail between my legs I scurried back to Melbourne to participate in the crisis meeting I was not looking forward to.

But when I walked into Noel Davey's office later that afternoon I was met by his beaming face. 'Why the long face,' he asked laconically.

Whereas sales and marketing directors are more intuitive production managers are more methodical. Whereas my brain and courage had turned to mush, Noel Davey's had gone into overdrive. Like all production managers a high proportion of his time was spent on investigating, identifying and solving problems that hindered his production line.

The leaking casks were all from the same batch, the last to go down the line. Part of that batch was still in the warehouse in Melbourne and, as with their Sydney counterparts, didn't look all that flash. Within minutes of my telephone call Noel had got to the bottom of the problem. The heat bands that sealed the plastic bag had simply worn out. They had been tested and retested to unintended destruction. The casks had not been properly sealed. Noel had already installed new heat bands and had run some casks down the line. The difference was like chalk and cheese. Problem solved. Eat your heart out John Parkes.

Our market research suggested, at least conceptually, that around forty per cent of wine consumers would be prepared to test the product. But that that would only be the case if their favourite wine brand had access to the concept, that their favourite retailer stocked it and it was priced little more than that of two flagons. That price would not produce the return on investment I was looking for so we ignored the market research findings by sticking to the twenty per cent price premium over two flagons — surely the product's competitive and functional advantage had to be worth something. Our sales targets were based on an initial one per cent share of the table-wine market rising progressively to two per cent at the end of the first twelve months and that was pretty well how it turned out. By month eighteen our penetration had risen to three per cent and we were selling at the rate of one million casks a year. Wynn's profit had close to trebled rather than doubled and David rewarded me with a one-off bonus equal to a year's pay.

Dawn and I used the bonus to purchase a much bigger but it must be said, pretty ordinary looking ex beach-house in leafy Beaumaris in which we all lived very happily for the next fifteen years. In 1973 the name Ray King was inscribed on the Hoover Marketing Award, Australia's then most prestigious marketing award for the successful introduction of the wine cask. However, that was about as happy an ending for the wine cask saga as we were going to get.

Our having stolen a march on the rest of the wine industry with our exclusive licensing agreement was always likely to be too good to last and that was how it turned out. Eighteen months after the launch of the wine cask all our major competitors had gained access to an unattractive but more effective and slightly cheaper tapping system than that provided by the Aerlesflo tap.

The new tap had been invented by British engineering company Waddington and Duval and is still the tap of choice today. Whereas the Wynn's wine cask was priced to the trade at around $2.80 and produced a gross profit of close to $1.40 a cask our competitors undercut us by around a third with a price to the trade of around $2.00, which produced a return on investment of less than ten per cent. Typically, our competitors believed their wine casks needed to be cheaper than the market leader, totally ignoring the fact Wynn's had no more than three per cent of the overall market. It was overkill and to me, sheer madness. Our subsequent market research had shown that if all major companies had matched our price the potential for the segment was still thirty per cent of the total market. There was plenty for everyone but with our competitors focussed on sales revenue rather than profits human nature took its inevitable course.

We made some concession to the price competition but still retained a price for the Wynn's wine cask around ten per cent higher than our competitors and continued to sell around one million casks a year. But of course our growth stalled. Our gross margin of around $1.00 a wine-cask was still roughly double that being earned by our competitors but frustrated by our competitors' pricing policies I gradually lost interest in the cask and began pursuing a number of other potential growth areas.

The wine cask revolutionised the Australian wine industry and was a major contributor to more than a doubling of wine consumption in Australia from around eight litres a head in 1971 to around 18 litres a head by 1990. By then, more than thirty million wine casks were being sold annually and the wine cask accounted for close to sixty per cent of all wine sold in Australia. Unfortunately, it did not revolutionise the industry's profitability as it had the potential to do, a failing that was to be repeated during the latter two decades of the twentieth century following the sudden and phenomenal success of Australian wine in overseas markets.

It is an apparent mystery as to why, with the exception of South Africa — where I spent time in 1974 playing an admittedly far more modest role in that country's successful introduction of the wine cask — that the concept has not achieved success in any other world market. Penetration rates in markets other than South Africa and Australia have never exceeded four per cent.

14

Taken over

The directors of Tooheys Brewery in New South Wales had been wary of embracing the herd mentality that had seen otherwise sane men rushing headlong into the wine industry. But not so wary that they weren't at least tempted to have a look at what they might be missing out on.

In 1970, as a walk-up start, they agreed to purchase a small winery in McLaren Vale in South Australia by the name of Seaview. The winery's subsequent performance under its new owner was at least promising.

Sufficiently encouraged by their Seaview experiment Tooheys' directors in 1972 cast their eyes towards Australia's largest wine company, the mighty Penfolds, controlled by high profile fourth generation wine family the Penfold-Hylands. The family's highest profile member had the glorious name of Rebel Penfold-Hyland. She came from a long line of lively women and lived up to her name. Rebel was a budding actress and her salacious exploits made regular and compelling reading in the newspapers of the day.

Fortuitously for Tooheys' shareholders the Penfold-Hyland family's delusions of grandeur led to the rejection of Tooheys' very attractive offer. The Tooheys' directors then shifted their gaze to the smaller, more palatable and much easier target, Wynn Winegrowers. This time they got it right and kicked a goal for their shareholders; in fact, quite a few goals. Wynns went from strength to strength in raising profits sevenfold over the next nine years whereas Penfolds achieved eminence as a public relations darling but little else.

The first reaction of Wynns' executives to the takeover announcement in the Melbourne newspapers was a fear for their jobs. I saw the takeover as an ideal opportunity to extend our field of influence, in particular mine.

The Tooheys' investigative team appointed to search out more and better particulars seemed to be taken aback by our positive approach to being taken over. Having been brought up in the bully boy environment of the brewing industry it clearly expected a far more servile attitude than it encountered.

At a bonding luncheon of Tooheys' and Wynns' executives a couple of weeks later I was boldly holding forth on the subject of product pricing. In an aside to David Wynn, Lloyd Hartigan, Tooheys' CEO whispered; 'I've heard about this young man, you don't really allow him to set your prices do you.' I saw David nod his head. With David's faith in his judgment of people now fully restored he then waxed lyrical, or so he told me later, particularly extolling our premium pricing policy on the Wynns' winecask.

The Australian brewing industry in 1972 was bureaucratic, highly unionised and commanded significant influence in government affairs. Little in the industry had changed for decades. The brewers rarely crossed state boundaries and stuck to their own captive markets. They had full control over the distribution process, owned a large number of hotels, the best of which they managed and a much larger number of which they leased to naïve, optimistic ex-footballers and cavalier opportunists. The lease agreements were usually onerous for the lessees, in other words, one-sided. Other liquor retailers were not much better off and had little choice but to accept the brewers' oppressive terms of trade (payment within seven days) as well as keep their noses very clean in case their beer supplies dried up. It was a highly insulated market and reflected the raw exercise of power. The brewers had rarely if ever operated in a competitive market and the word innovation was not part of their vocabulary. Little had changed in industry product offerings over the previous thirty years and to the brewers the only relevant element of the marketing mix was that of price, which was the exclusive domain of the CEO, hence Lloyd Hartigan's raised eyebrows to the lofty comments on pricing of a thirty-two years old ex-schoolteacher.

Lloyd Hartigan was an impressive man. Almost two metres tall, he had the bearing of a patrician but unlike the smugness of his more self-important executives, had not lost contact with his lower middle class background. For years he conducted business meetings with Tooheys chairman of directors in the kitchen of his modest western suburbs Sydney home. Lloyd, like David Wynn, believed the future trading environment was headed for change. He was keen to explore diversification opportunities as well as prepare his executives for what he felt was the coming challenge of real competition. He was a strong if paternalistic leader and, refreshingly for a brewer, open to opposing views. Well, much of the time. He also had a tendency to fall in love with particular executives — sometimes only briefly — and he was particularly attracted to those he later referred to as 'young Turks'. Despite Lloyd's potential for embracing new and adventurous thoughts and his preparedness to occasionally be challenged the culture at Tooheys at the time of our arrival still reflected that of the traditional, bureaucratic brewing industry.

Unbeknown to me, Lloyd's direct reports had always addressed him not only in public, but also in private, as 'Mr Hartigan'. At my first executive meeting you could have heard a pin drop when, unaware of the prevailing culture, I addressed Lloyd by his Christian name, his direct reports eagerly anticipating the newcomer getting his come-uppance. Their eyebrows rose even higher when Lloyd casually responded with words to the effect, 'well, now that particular piece of ice has been broken, I think we can dispense with the formalities in future,' no doubt giving the longer serving incumbents a case of the dribbling shits. He had taken to me in the same way that older executives consciously or otherwise foster their favoured young.

David Wynn quickly exited the scene, Frank Devine was appointed chairman and my role was upgraded to general manager (effectively chief operating officer) of Tooheys' wine division, trading as Wynn Winegrowers Pty Ltd. Frank's role was now largely symbolic, a role he nonetheless seemed comfortable with, and he spent much of his time on association matters, keeping in touch with his competitors, supervising his large vineyard (which had a handy contract to supply a significant quantity of grapes to Wynns) and giving me the benefit of his advice on the occasions I felt I needed it, which I admit wasn't all that often.

Frank appeared to accept, albeit grudgingly, that Lloyd largely sought my advice on commercial wine matters. It was a classic case of the young bull on the up and the old bull on the down, a situation I should have managed more sensitively. However, I was that pain in the arse, a young man in a hurry. And a young man in a hurry was inclined to ignore complexities that would come back to haunt him later. I was now responsible for the additional functions of finance, winemaking, vineyards and packaging, with the respective departmental heads now reporting to me rather than to Frank. This was the same one-on-one organisational relationship Frank had had with David Wynn.

¶

It was the Seaview brand that first drew my attention to the myth and magic of the wine industry, that difficult to design and implement concept by which a wine brand can seemingly come out of nowhere and become a force to be reckoned with. Before we added the Seaview brand to our sales portfolio Seaview's distributor in New South Wales had done an excellent job in gaining wide coverage for the small winery's products in Sydney's restaurants.

Wine lists in those days, unlike today's wine lists that are as long as encyclopaedias, were limited to a few wines, largely from the wine industry's larger players, so the appearance of a little heard of winery not only attracted attention but also carried with it the implied recommendation of the restaurant. The Seaview wines were nothing special but nevertheless 'good enough' and the Seaview name began to appear in reviews by wine writers, further building the image of the brand. It was an early example of the wine consumer's high and often unjustified belief in the integrity of the small winemaker (or what might appear to be a small winemaker). For some reason the Seaview name and its naïve but distinctive labels caught on with Sydney's smart set, the sophisticates having been susceptible to something different from the tired, plain product presentations offered by Australia's dominant wine companies, Penfolds, Lindemans and Orlando, wryly referred to by all in the industry as 'the PLO'.

The Sydney big-noters started recommending the new chum to their friends, who in turn recommended the brand to their friends and like a snowball rolling downhill the Seaview brand gradually gathered momentum and became fashionable. It quickly brought home to me the power of word of mouth recommendation. We happened to be in the right place at the right time. Assisted by what we had to offer in a sales and marketing sense Seaview's annual sales volume exploded from 250,000 bottles to 2,000,000 bottles within four years, in the process making ourselves look pretty good.

But, as with many fashion oriented industries, rapid sales success and the cascading effect it tends to generate often leads to a tipping in the opposite direction. The big noters, always looking for the next big thing, do not like to see their favourite table wines being consumed by those they see as unsophisticated dickheads. By the end of the decade Seaview's table wine volume had fallen to around 1,500,000 bottles as the early adopters and their followers moved on. Fortunately, we were more than able to cover this sales retracement with the introduction of Seaview 'Champagne' which, by the end of the decade, was exceeding table wine volume.

¶

In 1974 Rod Blake, our national sales manager, decided to move his family to Queensland and take on the state manager's job. I broadened the replacement role to include marketing. Ross Oakley, who later made his name as the chief executive of the Australian Football League, was the successful candidate. Ross did a great job for us over the next three years before moving on in 1977 to run car insurer AAMI, and then Eagle Insurance before his appointment to the AFL.

With Ross having taken the sales managers and the brand managers off my hands it enabled me to focus even more on business development ideas. As the wine cask had successfully challenged the established order what other things could we look at that might achieve the same result? We introduced several new products and line extensions, some of which were highly successful and others which were plain dogs. The market had been starved of new products for so long that anything new had a good chance of being successful even if only short term. We then went round for round with Reckitt & Colman's Orlando, the most dynamic of our competitors, in introducing a range of new products.

In addition to our success with wine-casks and the Seaview brand came an eclectic group of new products; apple wine; a range of carbonated flavoured and unflavoured wines including hock lime and lemon (the forerunner to the one time wonder, Coolers), an alcoholic milkshake, Blackberry Nip, whisky flavoured sherry and a number of conventional line extensions such as Seaview 'Champagne' and Samuel port. The new product program excited the market place and retailers couldn't wait to see what we were going to do next. Many of these products were always going to have a relatively short lifecycle although some are still successful products almost forty years later and our enthusiasm for all things new developed a life of its own. Combined with our wine cask initiative, Seaview successes, brand extensions for our more serious products and a range of more weird introductions our product development program drove profit growth at close to thirty per cent each year over the eleven years to 1981.

¶

In late 1974 the momentum that had been building for the passing of the Restrictive Trade Practices Act finally came to fruition. A key element of the Act was the outlawing of resale price maintenance.

This meant suppliers would be prevented from forcing retailers to maintain a supplier's preferred retail pricing structure. In other words, the practice of discounting, 'specials' and promotional pricing was about to raise its ugly head. The Trade Practices Act would also undermine the omnipotence of the breweries by preventing them from withdrawing supply as a means of enforcing brewery policy on its resellers. As David Wynn had predicted, the wine industry's cosy marketing arrangements came to an end as well and it was a whole new ball game for both industries as we entered uncharted waters.

Lloyd Hartigan felt that a revolution was about to occur so it made good sense to bring in a heavyweight marketer from outside the company to run the beer division. Bill Widerberg, who had an excellent track record at Coca Cola, got the nod. Bill was in his early forties, a fitness fanatic, tough, hard-working and no less ambitious than me. He also took his guidance from an Italian philosopher by the name of Machiavelli who counselled that it was far better to be feared than to be loved.

At one of our executive meetings Lloyd Hartigan was pontificating as to whether Tooheys should appoint a female director to the board. We sat back to ponder such a revolutionary idea, but not Bill. 'No,' he said, unequivocally, 'that wouldn't work.'

'Why not?' responded Lloyd.

'Well,' said Bill, 'everybody knows that women are not as intelligent as men.'

Initially dumbstruck, the rest of us proceeded to fall about in various forms of jocularity. We knew Bill well enough by now to know that he rarely joked but we all thought, apart from its being an outrageously politically incorrect thing to say, that even a misogynist like Bill couldn't possibly believe it were true. But Bill looked at each of us as if we were mad. Mind you, he was in pretty good company. Thinkers from Aristotle to Kant had over the centuries questioned whether women were fully capable of reason. Someone suggested to Bill that perhaps in future he should keep that idea to himself.

Bill might have been hard to love but he certainly kicked his brewing career off with a very big and momentous bang. He quickly cleared the decks of long-serving but non-performing brewing executives that Lloyd, ever the paternalist, had refused to sack. But Bill's key contribution was in instigating an outstanding television campaign created by Mojo, the hot Sydney advertising agency. Mojo was so hot at the time they would have had little trouble convincing you that shit was toothpaste. The 'I feel like a Tooheys' jingle, in association with actual film clips of Test cricket sixes being belted over the fence and famous Rugby League tries made for a sensational TV advertisement. Tooheys Draught sales immediately spiked and ultimately settled down with a verifiable volume increase of more than ten per cent over what would otherwise have been the case. It was a phenomenal result for an old and tired product. The campaign was right up there with arguably the most successful new product launch in Australian marketing history, that of Paul Hogan's Winfield cigarettes in 1974, also a Mojo inspired success. The net result would ultimately boost Tooheys' bottom line by more than thirty per cent over expectations.

Bill was never able to repeat the act but he was definitely the man of the moment and able to dine out on that success for a long time to come, in the process forcing me out of the picture as Lloyd's favourite son.

In 1976, around two years after Bill's arrival, Tooheys' beer sales hit a plateau as had those of its competitors. This was the period of that highly unusual phenomenon known as 'stagflation', a perplexing phenomenon for politicians and economists that had been brought on by world events but fanned to even greater heights in Australia by the highly questionable economic policies of the Whitlam Government. High inflation (up to seventeen per cent a year), high interest rates (about the same), rising unemployment and a slowdown in economic growth, a seemingly unique and conflicting combination, hit the mid to late 1970s with a vengeance.

Bill Widerberg, still bathing in Lloyd Hartigan's particular brand of sunshine, was about to become a thorn in my side from a different perspective. While hardly capable of charming the birds out of the trees Bill was nonetheless a very persuasive debater, a particularly useful ingredient for the ambitious executive. Moreover, he could present his ideas so clearly and compellingly that even intelligent people might come to believe them.

Bill put to Lloyd Hartigan that the now disappointingly flat sales of Tooheys beer could be rejuvenated by a plan to increase the size of his New South Wales sales team (Tooheys' beer sales were still largely restricted to New South Wales). Lloyd was in denial that Bill's spectacular success with Tooheys Draught had run its course and that a level of market equilibrium had been reached. He wanted to believe that Bill's particular brand of magic had more to offer and was more than sympathetic to Bill's plan. It was not a particularly attractive plan from my perspective. Bill had twenty-seven sales representatives in New South Wales and I had ten. Bill argued that if the New South Wales beer and wine sales teams were combined, naturally under him, the result would be more beer sales and more wine sales because of greater efficiency and more coverage. It meant Bill would effectively become my New South Wales distributor. I prepared a long and, I thought, constructive and persuasive paper for Lloyd on all the reasons Bill's plan would be detrimental to the wine division without adding much if anything to the beer business. I would like to report that my paper was instrumental in persuading Lloyd to disregard Bill's plan. It wasn't and it didn't.

By the third month of Bill's now implemented strategy it was with a degree of smugness I was able to report at the board meeting that our New South Wales sales were down by around ten per cent compared to the previous year. Smugness turned to delight when I was able to report that by the sixth month our New South Wales sales were now down by close to twenty per cent whereas our wine sales in all other states continued to show healthy increases. All my predictions were coming to pass, including that of a continued stagnation in beer sales. Bill promised to address the situation.

By the ninth month there was no improvement and a chastened Lloyd Hartigan felt compelled to allow me to reinstate the New South Wales sales team. While there is always something indescribably joyous about witnessing the demise of a rival's strategy, we didn't get our sales representatives back. Bill, never to be underestimated, insisted on retaining my old New South Wales sales team. Lloyd took the fiasco on the chin like the good man he was and by month thirteen we had a new, albeit smaller, New South Wales wine sales team in place and had started to regain the lost ground under a vibrant, energetic manager by the name of Mike Pelly, who was ultimately to become my sales and marketing manager at Mildara Blass in the late 1990s.

Despite the New South Wales hiccup as well as continued high inflation and equally high interest rates the wine division continued to prosper. But the New South Wales debacle weighed heavily on my paternalistic boss's conscience. Human nature being what it is, Lloyd had allowed Bill Widerberg's initial success to blind his judgment, leading to an embarrassing reversal for him in front of the Tooheys' directors. He also felt guilty about how I had been treated and decided to throw me a couple of bones.

In addition to my role as general manager of the wine division Lloyd anointed me with the added role of general manager, corporate development, for the entire Tooheys group. Given its obvious part time status it was more symbolic than real but it made both of us feel a lot better. He reaffirmed that as far as he was concerned only Bill and I were the contenders for his job if and when the time came.

Conveniently, for Dawn and me, Lloyd also thought it was time we became more familiar with the wine industry outside Australia. Getting on aeroplanes in 1977 for eight weeks was still pretty special. Sitting up the pointy end for international flights spoiled us for ever. Holiday Inn accommodation was juxtaposed with first class flight arrangements but we didn't know any different and thought it was all magnificent.

15

The dream run ends

By 1978 I was suffering the second in command blues. Wine division earnings had jumped to a pre-tax profit of slightly more than $5 million, up from around $400,000 in 1970 and return on investment had trebled to a little more than fifteen per cent, at least three times greater than that for the rest of the wine industry. I ran the wine division but vanity had taken hold and I wanted to look like a boss as well as be the boss. I needed a new challenge and my MBA inspired fantasy of embracing a turnaround opportunity was still alive and kicking. Killing two birds with one stone would be good, but killing three birds would be even better. Seeking those rewards would not be without risk.

The previous year my appetite had been whetted by being approached to become marketing director of Queensland United Foods Ltd as a walk-up start to becoming managing director. It was a publically listed company based in Brisbane and the managing director was looking to step down and take on the role of non-executive chairman. I took an option on a large and lovely Queensland property in one of Brisbane's older suburbs. Rolling lawns, a swimming pool and a cricket pitch including nets made it a gem (Brisbane properties were very cheap at the time). However, in the final negotiations over salary I realised my heart wasn't in leaving Melbourne when I pushed for an impossibly high number.

There were other considerations. Jer was in his critical year twelve at Mentone Grammar and Dawn was in the process of landing a top job as chief of staff to a Victorian Government minister. It was a great job, one that would enable her to enjoy her passion for politics. Dawn was later offered preselection for a safe federal seat in Parliament but was deterred by needing to spend time in Canberra away from her family and knocked it back. When the minister's political career imploded a couple of years later Dawn moved on to work with Laurie Kerr, the same Laurie Kerr I had shared a bath with at Carlton in 1956. Laurie, a journalist, had established International Public Relations Pty Ltd, a firm that soon became one of Australia's leading public relations agencies. Laurie, the chief puppeteer, worked in the shadows, pulling the strings of the powerful in sport, business and politics. It was at IPR that Dawn bathed in the sobriquet, 'the thinking man's crumpet.'

By 1979 I was into my ninth year at Wynn's, Lloyd Hartigan was showing no signs of retirement and my need to seek another challenge had not gone away. Jumping the Department of Education fence in 1966 had led to a dream run. Three times the dice had fallen my way; first with Frank Irving at Squibb, then when David Wynn took a gamble on someone with no experience and finally, when, for many years, Lloyd Hartigan, with one notable exception, gave me my head and sporadically thought I was 'the man'. The tide was about to turn, dramatically.

I was shortlisted (one of two) for the marketing director's role at Tooth & Co, Tooheys' major competitor in New South Wales. Again, as at QUF, the real role was that of managing director. The incumbent, Harry Alce, Lloyd Hartigan's ex-deputy at Tooheys at the time of the Wynns takeover, planned to step down within the next twelve months. Harry was an old style tough guy but without Lloyd's intellect and was badly out of place in the beer market's new paradigm. Although Tooth's was still a larger business than Tooheys it was a weak opponent and Tooheys continued to eat into its market share courtesy of Bill Widerberg's well-honed aggression.

Lloyd heard about my having been short listed for the Tooth's job, presumably from Harry, and warned me off. However, I didn't think I had too much to lose so I went ahead with the interview with Tooth's chairman. Following orders was still not my long suit. After a head to toe inspection by the Tooth's chairman the meeting was difficult and negative. It was clear that Harry had succumbed to the pressure from his old workmate and ruled me out with his chairman. The next day Lloyd rang me and said, 'I told you, didn't I.' Lloyd, not without some justification, felt that his paternalistic tendencies had not been appropriately rewarded, my disloyalty sticking in his throat like a fur ball. Naively, I had wanted to believe that Lloyd had nurtured his young in their own interests rather than his own.

Fortunately, the speed with which I was able to refocus was assisted by a distraction that arose in the form of a small Victorian wine business that had run into financial headwinds. The owner was an extremely affable, entrepreneurial type who had established Australia's first virtual wine business. The business had no vineyards, no winery, no packaging line and no warehouse and obviously relied exclusively on purchased wine. Perceived wisdom at the time was that a wine business required credibility and you couldn't have credibility unless you made your own wine, preferably from your own grapes. This one did not tick any of the credibility boxes. It was called Killawarra and its wines (actually, Mildara's wines as it turned out) had gained good coverage in Victorian restaurants. For reasons known only to its small but increasing band of consumers the brand had also developed a strong word of mouth recommendation.

A little like the Seaview brand a decade earlier, Killawarra had quickly struck a chord in the marketplace and its growth had exceeded even the entrepreneur's most optimistic expectations. However, in classic fashion, he couldn't fund the working capital tidal wave that was building ahead of the sales curve. To compound matters he had pulled funds out of the business for his own use and frittered them away. As a consequence, his business and his personal affairs were in something of a mess. It was no coincidence that I had had my eye on the emerging Killawarra brand for a couple of months and was delighted to get a call from his banker. Conveniently for me his banker happened to be Wynn's/Tooheys banker as well and was acutely aware from my attendance at the banker's occasional promotional lunches that I was more than prepared to consider opportunities such as this.

As the banker had hoped, I offered the fatally wounded entrepreneur a deal too good to refuse. It also enabled Mr Killawarra to retain some semblance of pride. I offered $50,000 for the brand and allowed him to collect what he was owed by his customers. Wynn's would pay off his around $200,000 in debts (more than $100,000 of it owed to Mildara which was more than desperate for the money). Again, my offer must have seemed like divine providence for banker and entrepreneur, not to mention the struggling Mildara. My offer was a more generous deal than was necessary but I always felt a quick game was a good game, not always the path to a happy and full life in the world of deal negotiation. I felt I had developed a bit of a nose for identifying brands that had the potential to take off and was confident we could do something worthwhile with it.

Within eighteen months, assisted by Bill Stevens' input, the Killawarra brand was contributing almost $1 million a year in profit for an initial outlay of slightly more than $250,000 and Wynn's was on its way to producing a profit in excess of $7 million, more than one-quarter of Tooheys profit.

¶

In 1980 an inconvenience of some significance occurred. Tooheys and Queensland brewer Castlemaine Perkins agreed to merge. In financial circles mergers are regarded as a myth, inevitably one company emerges and the other company submerges. The new company, now known as Castlemaine Tooheys Ltd, retained Lloyd Hartigan as CEO but Castlemaine Perkins gained a majority of directors on the board as well as the chair, so it was really a takeover of Tooheys by Castlemaine Perkins. It was also the kiss of death for me.

The Castlemaine directors still lived in the dark ages. To some extent I had been lucky not to pursue the opportunity with QUF Ltd because it seemed the last new idea they liked in Queensland was the introduction of the death penalty. And the Castlemaine directors acted as if they still believed in that other anachronism, the feudal system. Their chairman, Ted Stewart, a long term absentee landlord of a number of hotels, had very successfully led the hotel lobby in keeping liquor stores and licensed grocers out of Queensland. He may not have been financially sophisticated nor remembered much about the details of running a business but he certainly knew all about the exercise of power. Even Lloyd Hartigan was now being treated like the hired help and Lloyd soon ceased exuding the confidence that had previously characterised his highly effective unilateral style of management.

The exercise of the beer monopoly and its tendency to display unjustified hubris and arrogance was no better exemplified than in Queensland. For decades, Castlemaine Perkins' directors had taken success in Queensland for granted and had developed the unique perspective that management was not particularly material to the outcome. This was the attitude the directors had brought with them to the merger with Tooheys. In particular, the chairman was less than interested in who ran the wine division, a role he apparently regarded as not being all that important anyway. As far as Ted Stewart was concerned, Frank Devine, albeit the division's titular head, was responsible for all the success that had been delivered over the previous decade and even if that hadn't been the case then he didn't seem to care. In a nutshell, he wasn't interested in the wine business and largely deemed it to be irrelevant.

In contrast to those business leaders who had positively influenced my dream run the new chairman had little time for me and even less time for my style. He particularly did not like what he saw as a radical and irreverent attitude that seemed to question the very foundations of a culture steeped in history. The chairman informed Lloyd he wanted my chief winemaker and subordinate, Mark Babidge, to be promoted over me to head the wine division when Frank Devine retired. My sacking of John Parkes eight years earlier had finally raised its ugly head and had been referred to in the discussion. The chairman made it clear to Lloyd that I was not the sort of person he wanted running 'his' wine division. Lloyd was either powerless to put him straight or wasn't prepared to. Nor was Frank Devine, who continued to hang on year after year until finally retiring in 1985. It was an ignominious and thunderous body blow and there was no amount of Panadol that could take away that kind of ache. The year of 1981 was shaping up very nicely to be another piece of shit.

In 1981, recession bedevilled the globe. It was not a great time to be looking for another opportunity but I was shattered by what I felt was an ignorant stance by the chairman and Lloyd's less than enthusiastic backing. Over the previous decade wine division profits had risen at the enviable rate of almost thirty per cent a year. Profits were now more than $7 million a year and along with a company called Wolf Blass we were producing the best return on investment in the wine industry by far.

But that was irrelevant, according to the chairman of Castlemaine Tooheys. Not for the first time in my life, but certainly for the first time in my business career, I learned that life wasn't always meant to be fair. And there comes a time in just about everyone's life, certainly for those with a lot going on in their head and particularly for those who are risk-takers, that when things start to go wrong they have the potential to go really wrong. It was about to be my turn in that particular barrel and I was to find myself in that terrible place of not having anyone other than myself to blame for my predicaments.

It was the first time since entering the world of business that I had to deal with a sense of wretchedness. In an attempt to divert a burden I had kept to myself I agreed with Dawn to open what was deemed at the time to be a very fashionable and attractive business, a bookstore. It was to be the first of a succession of lousy bets. Foolishly, I had kept Dawn in the dark as to my having become a fallen star at Wynn's. The intent had been honourable but nonetheless inept, failing to honour the letter let alone the spirit of our partnership. Males can be a bit like that when they fall from grace.

The bookshop seemed like a good idea at the time and I liked the idea of being involved in a business in which we had some skin in the game. By that time Danielle and Brook were at private school, Jer was at university and I was a successful and proven businessman with superior ability, at least in my own eyes. I thought that the application of my obvious expertise to the mundane business of book retailing would lead to a very handy supplement to our regular incomes. I had my head up my backside. The application of my previous corporate experience to a small business operation was irrelevant. In any case, retailing is a different, different world altogether.

We took a lease on an excellent property in the suburb of Sandringham. That was my first mistake. The owner of the property was a good friend of our Beaumaris neighbours, the McDonalds. Dawn and I had met the friend at one of the McDonalds' regular barbecues and he seemed like a decent bloke, seemed being the operative word. He was in the process of refinancing the Sandringham property with his banker and the banker needed a new long term lease to support the loan. Naturally, I didn't want to commit to a long term lease, at least not until King's Bookshop was a goer. In any case we had an alternative location, albeit not quite as good, where the owner was prepared to meet our needs.

I made it clear I had no intention of committing ourselves to the Sandringham property for more than three months given the availability of the alternative location. In what seemed like a credible and practical compromise he suggested I should sign his lease to keep the banker happy. He gave me his word that if we needed to cancel the lease at the end of three months he would tear it up. Good intentions at the time or not, it turned out to be bullshit. Taking comfort in his close friendship with my near neighbour and still believing in the inherent goodness of man, I fell for it. Forget about the apparent morals of big business, the world of small business is one of dog eat dog and trust no one.

After an excellent first couple of weeks the shop's takings started to slide and by week ten we were just breaking even. The trend did not look good. In addition to my now depressing day job I was working weekends in the bookshop, checking in new books at night and keeping the accounts without anything to show for it. Holding the dead baby to the breast didn't seem to have a lot going for it. Instead of the bookshop being a pleasant diversion to my Wynn's problem I now had two demons sitting on my shoulders and quickly losing enthusiasm for our new venture.

I informed our landlord we would not be continuing with the lease beyond the twelfth week. I would return all the books to the suppliers (the trading terms were sale or return) and we would close the doors in keeping with the verbal agreement.

'Not so fast', said my new best friend.

I reminded him of our agreement. As easy as pie, conscience no problem, he dismissed his previous verbal commitment. His exact words were: 'That was then, this is now, times are tough and I am going to hold you to the lease you signed'. It was one of the few times in my life that I felt a strong inclination to violence.

I looked and felt pretty stupid. He had baited a trap that was largely of my own making. My word against his didn't look all that clever when he had my signature. But God had been watching. It was at this point that Dawn said she would 'wrap him up in silver paper'. Within a few months our landlord had been diagnosed with stomach cancer and twelve months later he was rotting in his grave. Not in Hell as Dawn had quietly suggested but rather in Cheltenham Cemetery. As well as her other attributes Dawn seemed to have access to wider powers.

I attempted to sublet the property and advertised the business for sale but to no avail. We now had a cash drain which in theory could last for another four years and nine months. Impatient to get the problem out of the way I was about to very neatly compound the problem. The dominoes were only beginning to fall.

Enter Harry the Thief. Harry had been out and about, waiting for something to turn up and something had turned up. Me. Harry's game was deception and it was all class. A young man with the face of an angel and the mind of a villain, Harry had seen my advertisement and arrived licking his lips. He already 'owned' two bookshops and was looking to expand but was, in his own words, 'temporarily, a bit stretched'. On the basis of a $1000 deposit he agreed to sublease the Sandringham property and to purchase the business, largely stock, for $25,000. He agreed to pay us $1000 a week over the next twenty-four weeks. This time I was much smarter. I had it in writing, including a lien over the stock for the amount owing, a second mortgage on his house and a sub-lease for four years and nine months.

There was a chance I had conned him but I soon got the distinct impression it was something entirely different. In the criminal world it is known as being 'found'. It was also very definitely amateur hour. A week later I called at the shop to collect our first $1000. It was empty. I called on his two other shops. They were empty. I called on his home in Marriage Road, Brighton. It was empty. It was a sting of the first order. Silly Raymond had become very silly Raymond. We were now $25,000 out of pocket, an enormous sum in 1982 and enough to buy a house in a decent suburb. To this I had to add the $250 a week rent on which we still held the head lease.

It was now confirmed. On the gullible meter my arrow pointed towards 'very'.

The deficit was more than double the bonus I had earned following my introduction of the wine cask. And just to add insult to injury, more than $23,000 of that was stock which we could have returned to the suppliers under the sale or return principle. Harry had returned the stock, got the cash and disappeared. In attempting to palm our problem off on to someone else I had, as Pierce Cody had suggested in 1970, been too bloody smart for my own good.

Harry, naturally, was never to be seen again. The police went through the motions of tracking him but he was long gone and the file apparently condemned to the bottom of the pile. My sense of self was hardly improved by the Beaumaris Police Station sergeant's droll comment, 'we have been a silly boy haven't we; we have given our business away.' How much shit could you get into? The answer was plenty.

It took a couple of months but I was finally able to sublet the Sandringham property to the National Bank and get into a degree of clear air. It had been an expensive and sobering lesson.

It was another blow to my now increasingly fragile self-esteem. To this point I had known only the kind of doubt that is calculated and secure, never the fearful unravelling that comes when one ceases to trust one's judgment. My career was unravelling, our financial status was unravelling and my confidence was unravelling. And I had made the mistake of playing the bulletproof tough guy.

Just when I thought things couldn't get any worse, they did — and the shit continued to pile up very nicely.

Graeme Galt, an engaging but hyperactive ex-university colleague, had resigned from the Education Department at around the same time as me and had also spent a number of years in the field of market research. He was, courtesy of his sister having married one of Australia's most experienced head-hunters, Eugene Brau, now a principal in Brau Galt & Associates, an executive search firm they had established in 1978. The brothers-in-law had immediate success and by 1981 Brau Galt was Australia's second largest executive search firm by billings to the British based powerhouse, Spencer Stuart.

Eugene and Graeme worked the Sydney market and had one partner in Melbourne, ex-investment banker, Philip Cooper. Graeme and Eugene believed Philip needed help in Melbourne (Philip disagreed but was outvoted) so Graeme approached me to become the second partner in Melbourne.

I was obviously vulnerable to an offer given the circumstances in which I found myself at Wynn's. In favour of acceptance was the pleasant fact that the field of executive search was becoming increasingly dominant in senior level appointments, in fact startlingly so. It was also a highly lucrative business. The fees charged were mind boggling, at least to me, up to forty per cent of the position's annual remuneration plus expenses that were delightfully and ruthlessly padded. Remarkably, clients paid up irrespective of whether or not you were able to find the right executive for them. You were paid to look, not necessarily to find. Well, that was how it worked in those days. I would share in the profits although initially at a lower level than the others. The broad expectation was that I would earn more than at Wynn's and arguably significantly more.

The arguments against were weighty: In 1981 the world economy had plunged into deep recession. Senior executive appointments tend to spike in good economic times and slump in the bad times. And there was something else — the ratio of senior appointments in Melbourne relative to Sydney. Although none of us was aware of it at the time the Sydney market for senior appointments was almost three times the size of the Melbourne market, despite the population of the two cities being roughly similar. Sydney was and still is the central location for a high proportion of Australia's major businesses. The final negative was personal. I had never been much of a networker and the executive search business relied on a network of close contacts in order to generate assignments. It was going to take time for me to develop that network given my natural tendency to be something of a loner. To kickstart things I attended a plethora of business conferences and business association luncheons. Once there, I was to identify the influential executives and invent credible ways of smooching them on the benefits of using Brau Galt if and when our services might be needed. This was not my style, a glad-hander I am not. Finally, I was still relatively young for this rapidly rising specialist business in which the average consultant's age was nearer fifty-five and if things didn't work out it would not be a big plus for my CV.

Graeme Galt connived to convince me it had not been his style either (it was), yet he outlined how he had quickly learned the ropes and believed I was perfect for the job. He believed my successful track record would provide a high level of credibility. The reality was somewhat different. Because Wynn's was only a division of Castlemaine Tooheys its performance had received little, if any, publicity. Very few business people knew who I was.

Dawn advised me against taking the position. She felt the role would not suit my open, candid and creative approach to the business world. Furthermore, she felt I was far better at telling people what to do rather than trying to convince them to do something they may not have felt inclined to do. She was right on both counts. In any case, she couldn't understand why I wanted to make a right angle turn from a career that had been remarkably successful. She was, of course, unaware that it had become a struggle for me to get up in the morning and go to work. My head was not in a good place and I convinced myself this was the new challenge I had to have.

In short, the executive search role was the nadir of my career. I hated it and it lasted a very long eleven months, during which logic would suggest laughs were few and far between and that I had to take them where I could find them. That was far from the case, there being no surfeit of laughs. There were periods of classic brooding and introspection but the more memorable response characterising this period was that the ups were higher and the downs more subterranean than my natural and more measured approach to life's difficulties had previously dictated. The body's defence mechanism seemed to cry out for relief, albeit that dark humour and relief of the comic variety was the more common.

Nevertheless, there were some aspects of the job that I liked. I enjoyed the detective work of seeking out the best candidates for a particular assignment. Executive search means exactly that. There is no advertisement. In those days data bases were pretty skinny so you got on the phone to suppliers and customers in the relevant industry and anyone else who you thought may be able to point you in the right direction. You broadly described the role and sought their advice on who they knew who might be a good candidate for that particular role in that particular industry. In this way you built up a list of prospective candidates, including the duds who were out of work or about to be out of work and those being recommended to you by well-meaning acquaintances. Remarkably, this cold calling on the telephone rarely failed. Business people love to be asked for their advice and with the increasing awareness of the importance of the role of the head-hunter in senior executive appointments, as opposed to advertised positions, executives were happy to be on side with a head-hunter in case they might need help themselves.

Almost without exception, the potential candidates rarely refused to come in for a chat when they received your call. The appeal to the ego was too great to knock back. In that year, on top of thousands of exploratory calls seeking information, I made around six hundred telephone calls to potential candidates. Only one, Peter Bartels, who ultimately became CEO of Foster's Brewing Ltd and later Coles Myer Ltd, knocked me back. However, he was very nice about it. He was at that time one of John Elliott's lieutenants at Elders. All John's lieutenants were on a very good financial wicket and loved working with the charismatic and dynamic Elliott. They were disappointed if they didn't get a weekly call from a head-hunter.

What I didn't enjoy was the other side of the consulting business, trawling for assignments. Touting for business when you are trying not to be seen to be touting for business is a cool art form that takes a long time to develop, if at all. And it takes years to build a network of contacts that will enable you to exploit that art. Watch the eyes of the desperado as he chats with you at a business function. They are flicking everywhere but your face as he scans the room to identify someone more important to him than you. Then watch the true expert in action. For three minutes you will be the most interesting and the most important person in his life. His eyes will not move from your face. Making a slick but credible exit he will move on to the next person and in turn bathe him in sunshine. You smile in admiration. His expertise is a wonder to behold as he works the rest of the room. The title of world champion in this regard must go to long-term friend, business colleague, philanthropist and charity fundraiser Carl Strachan.

Starting from scratch is tough. In one stretch I attended a business lunch forty-one working days in a row. It was time-consuming, it was emotionally exhausting and it was demeaning. But it was necessary. Even though each lunch was only a preliminary skirmish I was only moderately good at it. Again, while I was up for the challenge,

I hated it. Dawn was absolutely correct. It just didn't suit my style or my values. I had become that less than laudatory blowfly buzzing around the arse of power.

After a harrowing nine months I received a telephone call from Peter North, chairman of Mildara (Wines) Ltd. Mildara, a public company, had been around for almost a century but had fallen on hard times. Peter was looking for someone to become managing director of Mildara's marketing and distribution business, Haselgrove Wines Pty Ltd. I said that I would be happy to find someone for him.

'No,' he said, 'I want you.'

At the time I joined Wynn's there had not been a great deal of difference between Wynn's and Mildara in terms of size. In the eleven years that had since elapsed Wynn's had grown its profits by a factor of almost twenty whereas Mildara had gone backwards. Effectively, I was being asked to repeat the Wynn's exercise. Having the opportunity to put my turnaround fantasy into practice with Mildara was not only the best opportunity around, it was the only one around.

16

Mildara: The beginning

In September 1982 Mildara shareholders were not exactly jumping for joy.

During the ten years to 1982 disaster had been piled upon disaster, the company's share price steadily heading south to a level around one-third of where it had been more than a decade earlier.

Mildara had commenced business in 1887 processing wine grapes in Irymple in Victoria's north-west corner in the region known as Sunraysia. Like its competitors in those early days, Mildara produced mainly brandy and fortified wines such as sherry and port, the wines most in demand since the establishment of the Australian wine industry in the early 1800s. It was not until the late 1960s that demand for Australian table wines replaced brandy and fortified wines as the major users of the country's wine grapes.

Mildara's head office, winery and packaging plant, a messy hodgepodge of modern, not so modern and downright antiquated structures in 1982 had moved a few miles from Irymple and were now located on the edge of a sleepy little settlement by the name of Merbein. Merbein had little to say for itself other than it was located on the picturesque banks of the Murray River, ten kilometres west of Mildura, the hub of the Sunraysia region. Mildara's only real treasure in 1982 was its eighty hectares of vines and a winery in Coonawarra in South Australia.

Per capita consumption of wine in Australia had almost doubled between 1970 and 1982 but with few exceptions the rapid expansion of the country's wine industry during this period had not translated into general prosperity. Mildara was not one of those exceptions.

The company had been beset by its own set of problems, some

273

self-inflicted, some not, its profit performance now only a shadow of its former self. Mildara's wine production had grown at the same impressive rate as that of the wine industry over this period but production was not the name of the game. The real game was profitable brand sales. It was an unfortunate fact of life for Mildara shareholders that consumers of brandy and sherry, the key products sold under the Mildara label, simply kept disappearing. One could only presume this was a simple function of natural ageing rather than something more sinister.

The reality was that over the previous decade Mildara had become more of a grape processor than a wine marketer and much of the company's heady growth in table wine production was now being sold in bulk to other wine companies. The fact that the wine industry had routinely been in a state of oversupply for most of its existence made the bulk wine trade a very poor business to be in. It was the domicile of the born losers. Not only was the price of bulk wine set by the market but it also kept oscillating between low and even lower due to the volatility of annual grape yields. Not having control over selling prices nor having any level of certainty as to whether other wineries might have a need for your excess wine was not a great place for any company to be.

Lacking control over bulk wine sales and prices was not Mildara's only Achilles' heel. Since the Second World War Mildara had left the distribution and marketing of its branded products largely in the hands of its thirty per cent major shareholder, the powerful international trading company, Gollin & Co.

Gollin was one of Australia's largest companies, had operations in sixteen countries ranging across a number of diverse activities and its major money spinner was its international commodity trading business. Unfortunately, for Mildara the distribution of wine was an activity of relatively minor importance for Gollin and its sales personnel displayed little if any interest in doing anything more vigorous than merely taking orders for Mildara's traditional products, brandy and sherry. Any focus on business development or on activities designed to exploit the increasingly popular table wine and sparkling wine categories under the Mildara label had either been half hearted or simply ignored. With the exception of some limited marketing activity on its wines from Coonawarra that same passive attitude had prevailed among Mildara's management as well.

In 1976 Gollin's cavalier commodity traders made a number of disastrous calls on the hedging of future steel prices. Those transactional losses were to presage the largest reported loss in the history of the Australian corporate sector up to that time. Gollin was soon declared bankrupt and quickly placed in liquidation. Overnight, Mildara's major distribution system and source of cash flow had sunk beneath the waves and Mildara was in real danger of sinking with it.

Not only was Mildara owed a terrifyingly large sum by Gollin for its wine purchases but Gollin also held significant inventories of Mildara's packaged products, particularly its Coonawarra wines, for which Mildara had been slowly but steadily building demand. The liquidator, in acting in the best interests of the Gollin creditors (in other words Mildara and its shareholders could go and get stuffed), immediately started selling Gollin's inventory of Mildara products at heavily discounted prices. This action not only robbed Mildara of the ability to make further sales and generate cash until the Gollin stock had slowly threaded its way through the market place but also trashed the embryonic but slowly improving image Mildara had been developing for its Coonawarra wines.

Mildara's CEO was Richard Haselgrove. His father, Ron Haselgrove, had run the company extremely well for more than thirty years and was justifiably a local legend. And in the best dynastic tradition he had in 1971 handed the reins to Richard. The Haselgrove family owned less than ten per cent of Mildara shares but Ron Haselgrove's legacy, assisted by the protective influence of long term director and strong man, Bob Hollick, was paramount in the appointment of his successor.

Richard was a St Peter's boy, the Adelaide's establishment's preferred school. He was also Mildura royalty courtesy of his father's stellar standing in the community. A graduate of Adelaide University, Richard had been anointed at a very early age to take over from his father and the Gollin collapse was Richard's first real test as a leader. He acquitted himself well. By all accounts he extracted the last cheque written by Gollin before it closed its doors. Fortuitously, the cheque was not only honoured but also went unchallenged by the liquidator as a preferred payment. Had the liquidator been more aggressive in his duties it is unlikely Mildara would have survived. Richard also managed to gain the sympathetic support of the company's bankers, its creditors and its shareholders. But it was support that was approaching a dangerous level of fragility as Mildara's meagre cash resources continued to leak ominously.

While managing Mildara's disaffected stakeholders was no stroll in the park, Richard had an even more critical ball in the air. A distribution system needed to be quickly put in place to get Mildara products back into the crowded marketplace. As Mildara did not have the financial strength, let alone the luxury of time to establish its own national sales force, Richard had little choice but to attach the distribution of Mildara's product range to an already existing system. This meant adding Mildara's products to the plethora of products already handled by the too few general distributors that were available. It was asking a lot of providence but beggars couldn't be choosers. Mildara limped along from month to month uncertain as to whether the next period's payroll would be covered.

With desperate times beginning to call for even more desperate measures, rarely the prelude to a happy outcome, Richard was approached by Peter North, a Sydney-based management consultant who had had the ailing Mildara on his radar for some time. He had devised a plan in which Mildara would become the lynchpin in a proposed larger wines and spirits business. Given Mildara's dire circumstances Richard and his co-directors felt they had little choice but to at least hear Peter North out.

Peter North was an elite engineer of rocket scientist intellect as clearly evidenced by his having graduated in the top two per cent of his MBA class at Harvard's elite business school. Unfortunately, it seemed Peter fell into that paradoxical category foreshadowed earlier of being just too smart — he had the downside of the super intelligent in not being the easiest person in the world to get along with. His stratospherically high intellect not only made it difficult for him to relate to employees of lesser intellect but also undermined his ability to understand the mindset of the average consumer as well. In other words, Peter couldn't put himself in anyone's shoes other than those of the super bright.

Peter's high profile in the Australian business world at that time was one he would have preferred not to have had. Following an earlier stint in the engineering division of the Ford Motor Company in the US, Peter had been appointed CEO of British Leyland Australia Pty Ltd in 1973 to plan and implement the launch of Leyland's 'Australian' car, the ill-fated Leyland P76. The introduction of the Australian designed and built P76 was to complement British Leyland's already highly successful Australian business which centred on the importation of UK manufactured vehicles. Although the P76 initially sold well in Australia it was burdened by production delays and service complaints, the almost inevitable outcome of a newly commissioned plant. Sales gradually slowed to a trickle as the P76 gained the probably undeserved mantle of being Australia's greatest lemon. Things were not looking good for the CEO. But Peter's unilateral management style and his impatient, fractious nature didn't help his cause either and he was to become an easy scapegoat.

Following the highly publicised visit to Australia by his much younger UK boss, Peter was forced to throw himself on his sword. Within twelve months the P76 had been scrapped, ultimately becoming a much derided collector's item. The P76 and its newly commissioned plant had probably been a bad idea from the outset but Peter, the person in the hot seat, provided the convenient head that such disasters too often call for. Following his highly publicised demise at British Leyland Australia Peter had little choice but to tread that well-worn path of the one-man consultancy. He had to do something to put bread on the table.

William Grant & Sons was a privately owned and up and coming Scotch whisky producer and marketer. In the late 1960s a renegade member of the Grant family had been banished from Scotland by the company's CEO who just happened to be his brother. The banishment was for some unmentionable 'crime' that the family refused to talk about. The black sheep of the family was given the task of establishing an operation in the USA where it was hoped he would remain, gone and forgotten. But the renegade turned out to be a surprise packet. An original thinker and born trader, he developed a successful business trading bulk whisky around the world before successfully establishing Grants' various brands in the US market.

The renegade was an interesting oddball. He was an engaging character and a fearless business builder, albeit a bit on the ruthless and devious side and, it has to be said, a more than slightly sex-obsessed raconteur. Whatever he turned his mind to he seemed to be good at. His path had crossed Peter North's during his Harvard days and following Peter's having to 'do the rounds' after his ignominious fall from grace the Grant family's inglorious bastard had recommended to the other family members that Peter might be of some use.

Grants had already made strong inroads into the Scotch whisky market in Australia. The passing of the Restrictive Trade Practices Act in 1974 had opened up the Australian market to aggressive newcomers such as William Grant and Sons and the wily Scots intended to leave no stone unturned in taking full toll of the opportunistic beachhead they had already established. Their plan was to switch gears and now play 'long bowls'. Peter's availability seemed to be right up their alley and following his appointment to help with the long bowls strategy he spent nearly six months researching and evaluating Australia's alcoholic beverage industry. It was an excellent piece of analysis befitting the intellect of its author, although it included little that common and garden variety industry insiders didn't already know.

Central to the proposal emanating from Peter's analytical study was a plan for a separate wine and spirits entity to be established as the marketing and distribution arm of Mildara Wines Ltd. It was to be a wholly-owned subsidiary of Mildara but be managed independently of the wine production business. It was to trade under the name of Haselgroves Pty Ltd. The underlying aim of the new structure was to give the impression of Haselgroves having complete independence from Mildara's wine production. This plan would encourage the owners of other wine brands to distribute their products through Haselgroves and overcome the recognised limitations of the Mildara brand as well as provide much-needed critical mass. Peter's plan was also a deliberate attempt to separate sales and marketing activities from the control of Richard Haselgrove and to restrict Richard's activities to those Peter thought Richard knew best, the production function.

A key plank in Peter's strategy was for Grants whisky and it's more premium priced brother, Glenfiddich Pure Malt to be distributed by the new Haselgroves organisation and contribute valuable distribution earnings. But the generation of those distribution earnings was not the only objective. The plan, or at least the objective, was for the increasingly high profile Grants and Glenfiddich brands to create added value by attracting the distribution rights for other significant spirits and liqueur brands.

This logic was to be supported by Peter's strong recommendation that Mildara's distribution business be staffed by sales personnel unadulterated by the wine and spirit industry's prevailing bad habits. But as far as those salesmen were concerned there were no bad habits; in fact, it was the contrary. Spirit salesmen were permitted, nay, encouraged to drink on the job. Known widely as 'travellers' they effectively purchased their orders by either having a drink with the proprietor at each call or by leaving the price of a drink with the barman. Hotels were still the most common licensed outlet at the time. Unsurprisingly, 'travelling' was a particularly popular and highly sought-after occupation by the nation's legion of salesmen. Making up to fourteen calls a day these salesmen were rarely in great shape at the close of play, their heavily veined red noses glowing ever more brightly as the day wore on. The spirits traveller in particular was the one to be kept under strict surveillance because he operated on the long-held belief, an accurate one as it turned out, that 'a bottle opened was a bottle sold'. Mind you, wine salesmen were not beyond having a drink or leaving the price of a drink on the counter when collecting their orders either.

It was no great surprise that business expenses accounted for a high proportion of the salesman's costs. He was a one-man promotional band. The established practice of the traveller always ordering a drink from a bottle of one of his brands that was as yet unopened was to lead to an even more creative and even more bizarre scenario. Once a month, as a means of delivering an even greater promotional thrust to his brands, the spirits salesman took full advantage of his employer's generously provided opportunity to shout for the bar at every call. The suburb's or the town's reprobates soon woke up to this happy state of affairs and on their push bikes they stuck to the salesman's wheel like the peloton in the Tour de France as he drove (slowly, to accommodate the pack) from outlet to outlet.

Peter's sensible plan was to free the sales function of these apparent encumbrances and for the Haselgroves' sales team to be recruited from the more professional and better trained food industry.

William Grant & Sons proved to be no 'white knight' and would seek its pound of flesh for the added value it deemed to be bringing to Mildara. It would take a twenty five per cent shareholding in Mildara by way of a highly discounted share placement in order to keep an eye on things. It was a shareholding from which the canny Scots would ultimately do very well. In 1996, eighteen years later, William Grant & Sons would get back around fifteen times its original investment.

An important and key element of Peter's plan was also a share issue to existing Mildara shareholders to fund the acquisition of a yet to be identified branded wine business which, again, was aimed at increasing the company's critical mass.

Having successfully got his foot in the door Peter's plan developed a life all of its own and, given Mildara's dire circumstances, the company's directors felt they had little choice but to go along with it. In so doing Mildara copped Peter's jaw-breaking fee of $250,000, an enormous figure for the times, for a job the company hadn't even commissioned. William Grant & Sons and Peter North had driven a hard bargain. But that wasn't all.

Peter North proposed he should become a director and deputy chairman of Mildara, oversee the implementation of the corporate restructuring and more importantly, chair a new operating policy and planning committee recommended by Peter to drive and approve all major decisions. Peter had at last found himself another job.

Richard Haselgrove, Mildara's managing director and the yet-to-be-appointed managing director of Haselgroves would each report to the board via Peter's committee. This arrangement would put Peter in a very powerful position particularly as Mildara's chairman, Sir Oscar Meyer, was in poor health and in his grave inside two years. Peter had effectively become both chairman and part time CEO, an impractical and potentially dangerous combination. With remarkable prudence, Peter acknowledged that his proposed strategy may not work out for the best if information then not available were to appear in the future but it was clear he thought such a course of events most unlikely.

Like the elite Harvard graduate that he was, Peter had accurately defined Mildara's problems and addressed them with logical plans. He had asked all the right questions and my MBA corporate strategy course leaders would have given him a decent tick. But Mildara, unlike Monash University, operated in the real world where people are an integral part of the equation and where judgment and the efficient and effective implementation of plans are critical to the outcome. Unlike the theoretical environment at Monash University, the answers to the key questions were now as important as the questions themselves and those answers very much relied on an understanding of and an ability to work through ordinary people.

It was hardly astonishing that Peter had a rigid belief in the power of intellect. His choice as managing director of Haselgroves was in line with that belief and he appointed Ken Haylan, an investment banker. Ken was certainly smart. His intellectual apparatus was first class but, again, he was a smart person with no great people skills, a commonly acknowledged weakness of the investment banker. Given he knew little about the subject of marketing or that of running a distribution business those people skill shortcomings would only add to the problem.

It was also no surprise to anyone, with the possible exception of Peter North, that Richard Haselgrove and Ken Haylan didn't get on. Effectively, they were joint managing directors, an organisational structure that has rarely if ever succeeded and Mildara was to be no exception. Richard and Ken, as well as their team members, were soon at each other's throats and in practice the production and distribution businesses operated as separate silos. Not only was there a lack of coordination between the two functions but each blamed the other for the failure of various initiatives. The level of coordination was not helped by the lines of accountability and demarcation not being made clear at the outset and that the two incumbents were simply not compatible. That incompatibility inevitably developed into a healthy hatred. Pretty well all of the potential impediment boxes had been ticked.

To add a bit more fuel to the fire the business now had a public relations problem with the wine and liquor trade as well. Mildara's direct customers, those retailers and wholesalers operating in the wine and spirits trades, felt their intelligence had been insulted by the attempt to portray the old Mildara selling organisation as a horse of a different colour by dint of its new name. Those customers voiced their criticism at the coalface and did so aggressively. In no time the badgered Haselgrove salesmen felt they had little choice but to take matters into their own hands and revert to introducing themselves as representing Mildara.

The owners of other major wine brands and spirits and liquor brands obviously felt the same way. Not one of them came Haselgrove's way in seeking its distribution services. The continuing weak financial status of the Mildara/Haselgrove's group was a strong deterrent in itself. Why even consider switching your distribution to a company that may never pay its bills?

Worse was to come.

Peter North had settled on Hamilton's Wines Pty Ltd as his targeted wine brand acquisition. It is extremely doubtful he could have made a worse choice. After an all but brief period of success in the early 1970s with a product, called Ewell Moselle, Hamilton's had descended into an ailing, low price, low margin business with an image for its mainly table wine flagon business even poorer than that of Mildara, which was saying something. Hamilton's had but two things going for it. It was cheap and it was available. But it was a dog, an unimprovable dog and a dog going downhill. Less than five years later the Hamilton's name would disappear from the market place.

Nor did the distribution profits from Grants Whisky and Glenfiddich Pure Malt prove to be the path to a happy and full life either. There were working capital considerations. Both products carried heavy excise duties that were around three times greater than the cost of the product and these duties had to be paid to the federal government within seven days of a Mildara customer making a purchase. Unfortunately, Mildara's customers did not pay their accounts, including the excise duty, for another seventy-five days, leaving Mildara severely out of pocket in the meantime. The more Grants whisky that was sold the worse those cash flow problems would turn out to be.

The business plan had been hatched in an intellectual vacuum and was purely a theoretical construct. Few of the elements of the grand plan had worked and Mildara continued to die the death of a thousand cuts. But now the company had many more shares on issue and Mildara's share price continued its steady decline.

Under significant pressure from Mildara's shareholders Richard Haselgrove's heritage came to the fore and he decided to take matters into his own hands. He couldn't do much about his chief antagonist,

Peter North, but he still had enough clout to do something about one of the thorns in his side, the combative Ken Haylan. Richard argued that Ken Haylan should be replaced by someone with a track record in the wine industry who might represent a better than ordinary chance of helping restore Mildara to its eminence of a decade ago. A case was made for recruiting me, hence Peter North's approach in July 1982.

I was more than accepting of the approach (in truth I leapt at it) on the basis that the separate divisions be reintegrated under the Mildara name and that I run the company as chief operating officer, reporting to managing director and CEO Richard Haselgrove. I would also take direct responsibility for the sales and marketing function. I pushed for a performance element in my remuneration package which I thought more than reasonable, two per cent of annual profit before tax in excess of Mildara's best ever annual profit, a profit of around one million dollars earned almost a decade earlier.

This didn't seem to be too outrageous a suggestion, at least to me, given that Mildara had incurred an overall loss during the previous five-year period but Peter, as contrary an individual as the century has ever produced, pushed back. He wasn't prepared to negotiate with anyone he thought to be his intellectual inferior or indeed anyone else for that matter. More importantly, Peter still believed he would be Mildara's ultimate rainmaker and he didn't want any part of that contribution going to me. Of course, the bottom line was that I was prepared to accept whatever was on offer to get my life back on track and Peter almost certainly sensed that. It was at this point that I realised the Harvard boy was going to be something of an aggravation. And as it turned out I was not wrong.

17

Mildara audit

I planned my first steps in a gloomy windowless meeting room in Mildara's Victorian sales office in the suburb of Mulgrave. My office furniture was in keeping, a Laminex kitchen table and chair extracted from the denuded office kitchen and a telephone attached by exposed extension cord to the Victorian state manager's office next door.

Despite the ominous shadow cast by the Harvard Boy I was back on top, the turnaround-fantasy now a reality. With the battle cry again ringing in my ears the cavalry was heroically galloping to Mildara's rescue. And while gaining the CEO's title would take a little longer, I was again a 'they', one of 'them' who held the lives of others in his hands. In my mind's eye I had spent eleven years at Wynn's just preparing for the Mildara challenge. I was going to do things and I had a pretty good idea of what they were.

At the time I joined Wynn's in 1970 Mildara and Wynn's had been approximately the same size, albeit Mildara had been doing slightly better than Wynn's from a profit perspective. Eleven years later Wynn's was turning over more than $30 million in sales revenue, had grown earnings before interest and tax at almost thirty per cent a year to $7million, was producing a return on investment in excess of fourteen per cent and was seen by the liquor trade as a force to be reckoned with. On the other hand, admittedly hampered by the Gollin debacle, Mildara had sales revenue of only $18 million ($12 million in branded sales), had lost money over the previous five years and was very much seen in the trade as a lame duck. Wynn's was valued at more than $60 million, Mildara a mere $9 million.

Richard Haselgrove, Mildara's managing director and my boss, had the strength of character to acknowledge he didn't have the business development skills to deliver the company out of the doldrums. Richard was happy to give me carte blanche authority and, in his own words, to 'put my stamp' on the company. It was an encouraging vote of confidence and a testament to Richard's almost religious regard for the legacy of his father and his loyalty to the company. Richard was far less motivated by personal ambition than by his heritage and he was committed to restoring Mildara to its former standing in the wine industry as well as in the local Mildura community.

It was fair to say that the Mildara shareholders were ambivalent about my appointment. Too many times over the previous four years predictions of improvement had fallen by the wayside and with the share price now at an all-time low, the smell of blood was in the air. The irony was that if I were successful in helping to lift the company out of the doldrums there was every chance that at the first opportunity the major shareholders would think about selling to the highest bidder and yours truly would be out of a job. It was another example of that fine line between excitement and terror.

In 1982 the business world was still marking time as it slowly emerged from the 1981 recession. Inflation and interest rates were still in double figures, continuing legacies of the stagflation that had beset the '70s. The economic environment wasn't all that good but it hadn't prevented Wynn's from being successful.

The audit's negatives heavily outweighed the positives.

Mildara's greatest weakness was its significant dependence on selling bulk wine to other wine companies at little or no profit.

Its second greatest weakness was its brand name. The Mildara name was related to old, declining products and had almost negative credibility in those market segments that were growing — table wines and sparkling wines

Thirdly, to minimise unit production costs, the company's strategy had been to maximise throughput. The downside was that it purchased grapes, made wine and carried inventories that arguably it did not need. It was a strategy that was great for local growers and

*Nanna and Pa King.
Wedding day, 1910.*

*Mum and Dad.
Wedding day, 1938.*

Bill Pedie, me, 1947

Bugger of a kid, with the evil 'Tiger', 1943

King's cricket team. Gray Street Primary, 1949.
Me with the tongue, Brasso McGregor distracted

Kings Bakery delivery cart, 1953

Carlton Football Club, Under 19s 1957.
Back Row: B. Holding, B. Lowry, J. Francis, B. Colbert, C. Clark, R. Bent, B. Jordon
2nd Back Row: J. Taylor (Trainer), W. Armstrong (Treas.), G. Job, J. Deftereos, J. Shaw, M. Gardner, J. Scarpella, J. Muir, A Charahous, J. Albrecht (Boot Studder), E. Kiernan (Trainer), A. Thomas (Manager)
Front (Sitting): L. Allen, J. Watson, P. Lyons, S. Silvagni (Captain), K. Aitken (Coach), R. King (Vice-Captain), C. Ridgway, K. Tait, H. Spear (Prop. Man)
Front (on Ground): B. Whelan, R. Job, B. Puglia

Cut like a diamond. With Philip Shirrefs, Puckapunyal, 1958

Thelma, Jeremy, me. Bendigo 1964

The big time, 1967

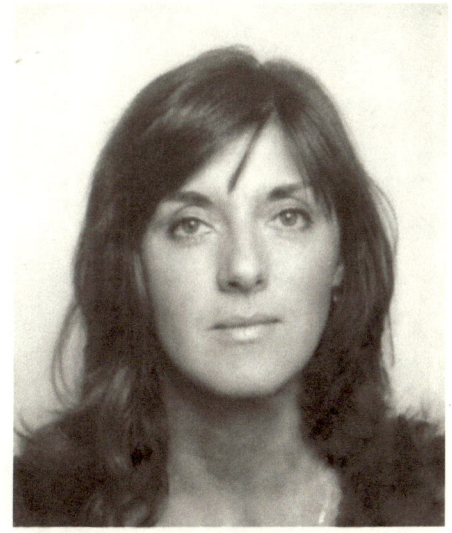

Dawn, 1977

The Brady bunch. King Family 1977, from Dawn's Council Election brochure, 1977

Dawn, election brochure 1977

The author, 1978.

Australian Masters Cycling Champion, 1996

great for local employment, its chief focus being on production rather than demand. Mildara was a company being run along communal lines and in the process was dying the death of a thousand cuts.

The members of the salesforce, burdened by poor leadership and a product portfolio that contained little the market needed, were living a miserable existence. Trading terms followed accepted orthodoxy. There was a theoretical range of prices for each product that was related to the volume purchased. But the trading terms were being largely ignored. Maximum discounts, say for fifty case buys, were being offered on single case buys, a reflection of rock-bottom team morale and confidence. Remarkably, this lack of financial discipline even applied to the sale of Mildara sherry. Because of Mildara's strong consumer franchise for its sherry, one of only two of its products the market felt it needed, these were 'must have' lines for retailers. Offering discounts on sherry was throwing money away and an indictment of the team leaders who were not properly supervising their teams' activities. They either didn't know what their team members were doing, didn't care or were plain incompetent.

As I had anticipated, the information system also left a lot to be desired. The recording and reporting of operating expenses was OK but nobody could tell me a product's real selling price and profit margins. The monthly sales report was a metre high computer print-out of highly detailed information that nobody seemed to read. Rubbing salt into the wounds was an adjustment to the previous month's accounts for promotional and co-operative advertising allowances that had simply not been recorded or accrued the previous month — a practice the frustrated directors had seemingly accepted as normal.

I was delighted to identify so many negatives. It meant we had plenty to work with.

But did we have any positives? It seemed that cupboard was pretty bare although we did have what could be termed some non-negatives. Wine costs didn't appear to be a problem and were largely in line with those at Wynn's. As were selling, marketing, warehousing and administration expenses as a percentage of sales revenue, which were also roughly comparable with those of Wynn's.

With the exception of my positive assessment of the personnel at Merbein I was scratching around trying to find much else that could be applauded. The best I could do was believe there might be an opportunity to turn two negatives into positives. Excess wine inventories might be put to better use other than being sold in bulk to other wine companies and each Mildara salesman had the capacity to sell significantly larger volumes of product as long as their portfolio included products the market actually wanted.

The biggest positive by far was the personnel located at Merbein. Maurice Dean, still in his twenties, was in charge of vineyards, winemaking, and packaging. He was genuinely interested in the business of business, a can-do person and breaking his neck to make a contribution. His positive attitude and enthusiasm was also reflected in that of his first reports, particularly those of his production manager, Ron Treffene, an ex-dead-end kid and an unlikely gem. And chief financial officer, David Smith, a South African import, was like that country's precious stones, an absolute diamond. We all wanted to 'do something' and thirty years later we are still doing stuff together.

18

A bumpy start

The Mildara boardroom was not a happy place.
Board meetings were tiring six-hour affairs starting at 10 am. On top of an early morning flight to Mildura they were far too long for such a small business, in fact for any business, inevitably reducing discussion to matters of minutiae rather than strategy. The Harvard Boy was still acting as if Mildara's operational vacuum, a vacuum created and sustained by his own unworkable organisational structure, was still in existence. He continued to see the board as the main operational decision maker.

Naturally, he was the dominant player. As chairman, he set the agenda, controlled the discussion and made sure the minutes reflected the flavour of his arguments. David Grant, marketing director of Mildara's major shareholder, William Grant & Sons, attended only two board meetings a year but made up for his non-appearances on those two occasions and was the chairman's strong ally. David was ex-Oxford University, lived in a posh, tight house in Chelsea and had that frothy self-importance of the British ruling class. He had been a key and dominant player in Grant's global success over the previous decade but his feel for and excellent understanding of the dynamics of the far more structured and predictable Scotch whisky market did not extend to the wine market. He didn't allow that to get in his way. David Grant had formed a formidable alliance with the Harvard Boy and had contributed to making Richard Haselgrove's life a misery. But I was now the one in the hot seat.

The Harvard Boy and David Grant, alpha males of the first order, had successfully thrown their weight around with little effective opposition for so long it was no surprise they didn't particularly welcome my style or my view of the world. I was pretty keen on getting my own way as well, particularly on a subject I thought I knew a bit about. The one thing on which the Harvard Boy and I did appear to agree was that in an industry with an abysmally low return on investment it was necessary for Mildara's approach to be radically different from that of its competitors. It was the means by which that difference might be brought to bear that was to lead to our long drawn out dogfights.

Apart from the Harvard Boy, David Grant, Richard Haselgrove and yours truly, there were five other directors on the Mildara board. William Grant's second nominee was the sound and capable CEO of the Bushell's Tea Company, David Barnett, also an Englishman, as was David Grant's official alternate, Brian Barber, a finance man. Both had learned to tread a fine line between their natural instincts and their riding instructions. Gray Barnden and Dennis Mills, local Mildura businessmen, welcomed my arrival but were often intimidated into silence. And finally there was Bob Hollick, another local and an ex-Mildara vineyard director who was well into his seventies but still a force to be reckoned with. While Bob didn't take shit from anyone he also had difficulty keeping up on more sophisticated business issues and, like his local Mildura counterparts, didn't like the domineering stance the Harvard Boy and David Grant often adopted. As far as Bob and his local counterparts were concerned, I was, in historical boxing parlance, the great white hope for the future. But they would have to bide their time.

Board meetings became a series of determined exchanges between the Harvard Boy and me on most issues. They were exhausting affairs as I battled his intellect and superior debating skills, a distinct disadvantage when you can no more prove your argument is correct than your opponent can prove that it isn't. And, after all, he was the chairman. He was exceedingly impatient of contradiction and given his intellect and determination, a daunting opponent.

The meetings weren't much fun for the other directors either. The contests between me and the chairman inevitably descended into a game of verbal ping pong, he at one end of the board table, me at the other and the directors' heads swivelling left and right as we belted the metaphoric ball back and forth across the net. My arguments, rather than breaking down his resistance, usually had the opposite effect. A track record in the wine industry didn't seem to count for much with the Harvard Boy. What could you say to, 'that was then this is now?' In any case, trying to persuade peers to your perspective rather than telling subordinates what to do is a much more difficult task, more so if you are trying to convince them of the virtues of the unorthodox. And although the Harvard Boy was prepared to go off road in search of solutions, he much preferred his own particular road.

¶

In 1982, two months before my joining Mildara, the company had won the Jimmy Watson Trophy for its 1981 Coonawarra cabernet sauvignon.

In an industry drowning in trophies and gold medal awards the Jimmy Watson Trophy had become THE trophy to win. The award, named after legendary Lygon Street wine bar raconteur, in whose fine establishment David Dole had introduced me to wine in my student days, is for the industry's best one year old red wine. Given that a one year old red wine is still 'in the tank' or barrel and only part way through its maturation process at the time of the judging, it didn't make much sense, in fact it made no sense whatsoever, for the Jimmy Watson to have become the most coveted winemaking award in the country.

Wolf Blass, having emigrated from Germany in 1961, had established his own wine business in the Barossa Valley in 1966. He was about to make a huge contribution to the Australian wine industry. A gambler in all senses of the word and invariably happy to defy convention, Wolf had introduced Australia to a new style of red wine making: he made premium quality red wines that were softer and 'ready to drink' much sooner than the more traditional Australian red wines that contained higher levels of acid and tannin and needed much longer periods of maturation before becoming palatable.

The fact that Wolf had revolutionised red wine making in Australia was an achievement that largely went unacknowledged by a conservative industry whose leaders envied his success and who turned up their noses at Wolf's unique form of blatant self-promotion. The industry's views on Wolf were aided and abetted by most wine writers. They kept their most strident criticism for his wines, which were generally blends of different varieties, often from different areas. Wolf's critics believed in the 'purity' of wines made from single grape varieties from single regions. On the other hand, Wolf pushed the eminently sensible idea that the wine itself should do the ultimate talking.

The Jimmy Watson had been first awarded in 1962 and not a great deal had been heard of it until 1974 when Wolf won the first of his three consecutive Jimmy Watsons. Wolf, who dresses and acts like a slightly deranged golf professional with a bow tie, is a colourful, flamboyant character, a little crazy but eminently likeable. Despite their often snooty attitude to his blended wines the media loved writing about him and his antics. In the years following each of his Jimmy Watson wins Wolf's Black Label brand bathed in a blaze of publicity that not only kept raising his profile ever higher but also implanted the importance of the Jimmy Watson Trophy in the wine consumer's psyche as Australia's top wine award. It was largely bullshit but masterful stuff on Wolf's part.

The fact that the Jimmy Watson Trophy is won by what some critics describe as a 'half made wine' is only part of the perceived problem for the smug wine buff, a cut-out character often more closely aligned with pretension than expertise. When the winning wine hits the market a year or so later besotted consumers flock to buy it. And with beauty being in the eye of the beholder they are rarely disappointed.

What few consumers realised was the extent of the potential for a bit of skulduggery. These were the days before cellar records provided the details of a wine's provenance, records which today are mandatory. Apart from the actual winemaker, very few of his colleagues and certainly no one outside the company was aware of exactly how much wine in the cellar was representative of the single sample bottle from the single barrel submitted for the Jimmy Watson judging.

Even today, it could be argued that only the single bottle sample submitted from the single barrel in which it is maturing is truly representative of the winner. And the quantity in that barrel is no more than two hundred bottles. But even within those two hundred bottles there will be individual bottle variation, a function of the fact that wine is a living thing, continuing to change over time and to respond to its particular environment. Irrespective of the 'quality' of the wine at the time of the judging it is certainly a different wine by the time it arrives on the market at least twelve months later.

Historically, the quantity available for sale and claimed to be the Jimmy Watson winner has varied each year from as little as a thousand bottles to as many as 300,000. The dollar value of the award to the successful company is obviously determined by how much of that wine has been produced, or is claimed to have been produced, as well as the significant price premium that winners could charge. The temptation for the winning winemaker to maximise the justifiable quantity of the winner, in other words to cheat, is clearly very great. In my own case, I was more than prepared to give winemakers the benefit of the doubt for claimed quantities. Winemakers generally have high levels of integrity, a human value they will usually defend to the death. As a consequence, there is nothing quite as disappointing for a wine boss to accept that in determining the winner's volume his winemaker is more honest than he might be himself.

When a Wynn's Coonawarra cabernet sample was the winning entry in 1977, Mark Babidge, our chief winemaker claimed around 220,000 bottles as being representative of the winning sample when more than plausibly he could have stretched it to a slightly greater number.

Mildara had produced a claimable quantity of around 100,000

bottles for the 1981 winner and we were planning to release the wine to the market in the last quarter of the 82/83 financial year. Without that release the company was headed for another trading loss, the second in three years. But Richard Haselgrove, who sat on the board of the Australian Wine and Brandy Producers' Association, was sensitive to an increasing level of suspicion within the wine industry that some previous winners had compromised themselves on claimed quantities. Although he never said so I suspect he was more than suspicious of the claimed quantities of the Wynn's 1976 winner. Richard didn't want any potential criticism to apply to Mildara, there being perhaps a hint I may have been damaged goods in that department.

Mildara's senior winemaker, the shy, balding, reclusive and vastly underrated Jack Schultz, was adamant that around 100,000 bottles was the appropriate quantity as being truly representative of the winning sample. Jack, as enigmatic a soul as the world has ever produced, was as straight up and down as you could get and what's more, a man of very few words. He either described a wine as 'bloody good' or 'no bloody good'. Given Jack's inherent conservatism and integrity if he said the number was 100,000 then that was good enough for me.

I planned to label the 100,000 bottles as the winner. But Richard wasn't so sure. It was to be the only time he pulled rank on me. We ended up with a compromise and as so often happens with compromises, we designed the inevitable camel. We decided to label 35,000 bottles as the JW Trophy Winner and 65,000 bottles as the JW Classic, with back labels clearly explaining the minor difference. The only real distinction between the two was that at the time of the award there was a timing difference of two months as to the period spent maturing in wood, although ultimately the whole 100,000 bottles would get the same wood treatment. In my preparedness to go along with Richard in order to get along, I had convinced myself that perhaps there was a practical upside to Richard's stance in that wine lovers might purchase one of each of the wines in order to compare them.

As it turned out, my conviction proved to be correct but only for a disappointingly short period of time.

The two Mildara wines were released together, with the JW Classic priced ten per cent lower than the trophy winner. But most retailers placed the same retail price on them and almost certainly didn't bother to draw consumers' attention to the distinction between the two. The front labels were similar but far from identical and the back labels detailed the wood maturation differences at the time of the award — so as far as the retailer was concerned, let the buyer beware. As anticipated, our sales were buoyant.

Around a month later I received a telephone call from the producers of the ABC's *Four Corners* TV program. Wine labelling had been selected as the subject for one of its stories and the ABC wanted to interview representatives of half a dozen relevant wine companies. Dawn had experience with the media and immediately smelled a rat.

'It couldn't be anything more than an attempted expose,' she argued.

I wasn't totally dismissive of her view but I felt that the PR benefit to the struggling Mildara in being on the *Four Corners* program would outweigh any major risk. I wanted to believe that if the dual label were part of any discussion I would be able to present a masterful case supporting the argument that, given the clear explanations on the respective back labels, Mildara's integrity was not only beyond reproach but also of pristine proportions. Dawn felt I was being alltogether too naive and too trusting. But hubris had taken over. And I was going to be a TV star wasn't I, conveniently ignoring the fact that I was not exactly the world's quickest thinker?

The TV crew duly arrived and while they were setting up in my office I had a lovely chat with *Four Corners* presenter, Christopher Sweeney. Dawn's fears were clearly groundless.

Bullshit they were.

The cameras started rolling and my new best friend, Christopher, reached into his brief case, pulled out two Mildara bottles and opened the bowling with a blistering, reverse swinging yorker.

'Mr King, we think you are misleading the Australian wine public.'

Fuck me! I nearly had to call for a change of underwear. Christopher's little old heart must have been going pit-a-pat as the cameras unmercifully recorded for all time my shocked reaction. I bunkered down, now in recovery mode and trying to regain the high ground. I finally convinced myself I had done well enough to make up lost ground and was confident I had more than adequately sold the company's story and given a pretty good account of myself. But I had disregarded the cutting room floor. All my good bits were edited out and the not so good bits, in fact the worst bits (but from *Four Corners'* perspective, the very best bits) were included in the five-minute segment that hit the nation's screens. For the show's producers, my initial reaction must have felt as good as winning the lottery. *Four Corners* opened the program with me and it didn't look too good. In fact it was bloody awful.

I later bemoaned the fact I hadn't pushed more strongly to label all the 100,000 bottles as the winner. As had been the case at Wynn's on the day of the leaking wine-casks I wondered whether my career at Mildara may now be over before it had really got under way. The Harvard Boy and David Grant, who happened to be in Australia for one of his six-monthly board meetings, now heartily sick of my vigorous debates with the chairman, were apparently of that view. I was yet to launch my grand plan for the future and they saw my bad publicity as yet another negative for the company in its continuing struggle to make any headway in the marketplace. They didn't mess about, informing me that instead of my being part of the solution to Mildara's problems as they had initially hoped, I was now seen as a continuing part of the problem. The implication was fairly clear.

But I was worrying unnecessarily. The *Four Corners* program had gone too far in criticising the wine industry's honesty and integrity—criticism that had been levelled not just at Mildara but at all the companies represented on the program, particularly industry figurehead and favoured son Murray Tyrrell. In an unexpected and fortunate turn of events, particularly for me, the reaction from the wine media was vitriolic as to the program's stance. The Wine Press Club, an informal association of wine journalists, counterpunched by promoting the view that *Four Corners* had been more than mischievous in misleading the Australian wine buying public with its biased reporting. And, in a blind tasting of 'those' two wines, the Wine Press Club extolled the virtues of both wines, albeit by then they were the same wine.

Nonetheless, there was a residual odour. Despite the clear evidence of the labelled differences of those two Mildara wines, many people, particularly some of the holier than thou wine journalists, still wanted to believe Mildara had benefited unfairly. And for many years Australia's leading consultancy in executive media training used my *Four Corners* performance as its leading example of TV disaster interviews. But if all publicity were good publicity then I was in excellent shape.

19

The plan

Just pull a few rabbits out of the hat and Bob's your uncle.

Apart from the cerebral challenge offered by a company turnaround opportunity, the stark reality is that the turnaround doesn't have a lot going for it. Empirical evidence suggests the odds of successfully turning an ugly duckling into a swan are not great. The corporate graveyards are full of those who deemed to think otherwise. But if you wanted to look on the bright side then the turnaround had one thing in its favour — the worse the situation the cleaner and broader the canvas you started with.

The Mildara plan began with the end game; my MBA acquired pathfinder of ROI (return on investment).

OBJECTIVE 1 — ACHIEVE A TWENTY PER CENT ROI.
Return on investment became the first item written on our metaphorical clean sheet of paper. In simple terms, ROI is a productivity measure — how many cents profit can be squeezed from one dollar of investment.

There was certainly nothing unique about starting a business plan with an ROI objective but we weren't about to pay lip service to the concept and then park it in some soon forgotten bottom drawer. ROI was to remain front and centre in almost everything we did. It was to be the beacon that would not only guide our way through the minefield of variables requiring day to day operating decisions but also throw light on the specific financial structure Mildara needed to put in place in order to meet that ROI objective in the first place. Into that financial framework we would then attempt to squeeze the flesh of a living, breathing, operating business and, having achieved that objective, fight tooth and nail to keep it there.

For example, imagine setting the following simple financial construct for your business: earnings (profit) before interest and tax to be no less than twenty-five cents for each sales dollar, operating expenses such as selling, marketing, logistics and administration to be no greater than 25 cents in the sales dollar and gross margin to be no less than 50 cents in the dollar (alternatively, cost of goods sold to be no greater than 50 cents in the dollar). Nice idea but impractical and unworkable in the real hurly-burly world of uncontrollable business factors the critics would suggest. To that argument we would produce seventeen years of empirical evidence that proved such an approach was not only achievable but also maintainable.

While there are many definitions of return on investment, the definition is far less important than the use of the concept itself. Our preferred definition was earnings before interest and tax (EBIT) as a percentage of total invested funds (later, after being acquired by Foster's we adjusted it to earnings before interest and tax and amortisation of goodwill (EBITA). We defined invested funds simply as shareholders' funds plus borrowed funds, the two key sources of funds for running a business.

Before having a Eureka moment (or thinking I had a Eureka moment) towards the end of my tenure at Wynn's I had regarded ROI as essentially a guiding philosophical concept rather than the illuminating operational road map it would become at Mildara. At Wynn's we had attempted to optimise ROI by maximising profits and being careful about any unnecessary build-up of assets. In other words, I had, like pretty well everybody else who at least understood the concept, treated ROI as the residual outcome of pursuing a range of other business objectives. As a consequence of that Eureka moment I thought I had during my final year at Wynn's, our approach at Mildara was dramatically different; we would reverse the process. Our ROI objective would determine what those other business objectives should be.

So what was this Eureka moment? Despite being a serial financial doodler and daydreamer (I am a Pisces after all), it was only towards the end of that eleven-year period at Wynn's that the Eureka moment materialised. I had been doodling away, playing with the numbers as was my wont, when it dawned there was a close correlation over time between the growth in Wynn's assets (essentially a proxy for invested funds given that assets are what the funds are invested in) and the company's growth in sales revenue. Like most things on the point of your nose it took almost forever before I actually saw it.

From 1970 to 1981 Wynn's annual sales revenue had grown by a factor of around ten from a little more than $3 million to $31 million and invested funds (in vineyards, wineries, packaging plant, warehouses, working capital etc) had grown by roughly the same multiple — from slightly less than $5 million to around $50 million. In other words, the relationship between invested funds and sales revenue had remained relatively fixed over those eleven years, that ratio being roughly $1.50 of invested funds for each $1.00 of sales revenue, the ratio often referred to as the capital intensity ratio.

Initially, my discovery was a fairly casual observation but I soon realised that its significance was considerably less than casual. With a bit more doodling it became clear that the relationship between investment and sales revenue had dramatic conceptual consequences. And then a bell started to ring down a deep, dark alleyway. The discovery of the relationship was not a Eureka moment after all. The Nobel Prize would not be coming my way. I had seen that relationship before, hidden away in a finance textbook while doing some random reading during my MBA years. Ironically, my MBA lecturers had ignored not only the nuances of capital intensity but also the subject itself, a subject which, if properly understood, is arguably one of the keys to identifying the road to improved business performance. Again, was I the only one in step?

Q. What were the illuminating features of this second-hand discovery?

A. First, if eleven years of history could be considered a guide to the future, then the same ratio between investment and sales revenue would apply. That is, to achieve an additional $1.00 in sales revenue

Wynn's would need to invest another $1.50 in assets in order to achieve that sales growth. In other words, as the relationship between the two variables had been relatively fixed over the eleven-year period, it was reasonable to presume it would remain fixed in the future. Admittedly, in practice, year on year investment growth might be stop-start and lumpy rather than maintaining a perfect straight line relationship with sales growth. But over the long term the evidence clearly suggested that, barring major technological advances or a new brand of thinking that might change the level of capital intensity, the two relevant variables, investment and sales revenue could be confidently expected to grow at approximately the same rate. Mildara's level of capital intensity was similar to that of Wynn's.

The second and even more illuminating consequence of this discovery was that if funds invested and sales revenue grew at approximately the same rate then there also had to be a fixed relationship between the two key profit ratios, EBIT to funds invested and EBIT to sales revenue. In other words, setting a return on investment objective would automatically translate to a return on sales revenue objective and vice-versa.

Q. Why use return on investment as the starting point of the planning process?

A. From a practical perspective, a firm achieving a higher ROI will generally provide a shareholder with what he is, or should be, looking for — higher levels of free cash flow that can be used to pay higher dividends or to fund future growth strategies, the twin paths to increased shareholder wealth.

The ROI ratio also has something to say about the quality of a firm's management. As for me, I wanted to be able to say to investors, 'give me a dollar and I will eventually get more out of it for you than most of my peers.' It may have sounded trite but I was looking to set a genuinely superior performance benchmark against which Mildara and the quality of its management could be measured.

While ROI is only one of the countless balls a CEO might have in the air at any one time and which might influence the company's performance and credibility rating among investors and the money market, it was, in my view, the most important ball by far and therefore the best starting point.

As important and as interesting (or as boring) as the above reflections on ROI may be to the individual, the strongest and most practical reason for focussing on ROI as the key objective was that it provided specific guidance as to what levels profit margins needed to be; and, by extension, the price levels that needed to be in place to turn the company into a superior performer. At Mildara, we did not see price levels and profit margins as passive elements in the business mix or as dynamics dictated by market conditions and largely outside our control. We believed proactively setting price and gross margin targets and then ruthlessly pursuing those targets was the key to superior performance. Conventional wisdom suggested that ignoring competitors and setting price and gross margin objectives as if they were independent variables was utopian and unrealistic, something you would only do at your peril. But ignore our competitors we did. We operated largely on the basis that they didn't exist. And for seventeen years we were able to get away with it.

Q. Why set a ROI objective of twenty per cent?

A. In 1982, according to surveys carried out by the Australian Wine and Brandy Producers' Association, the average ROI for an Australian wine company was between three and five per cent, not much better than putting your money in the bank and that was pretty well risk free. And since 1982 it hasn't got much better. In February 2011, the chairman and CEO of Angove Family Winemakers Pty Ltd, John Angove, was quoted in the *Australian* newspaper as saying, 'the wine industry is too inefficient to provide the returns demanded by public investors. Public shareholdings don't work because the industry has too much capital investment tied up in stock and in equipment we use only once a year. There is insufficient turnover and it's historically a very low profit industry anyway. Why would a shareholder want to invest in that? Only crazy families will do it.' But families were not the only crazy ones.

More recently, Treasury Wine Estates (spun out of Foster's Brewing Limited in 2012) announced an underlying EBIT performance of $206 million for financial year 2013. Foster's had begun its foray into the wine industry with its acquisition of Mildara Blass in 1996 for which it paid $592 million (including $310 million in newly created goodwill). Following some relatively small acquisitions by the Mildara Blass management team initially retained by Foster's, as well as the need to fund the additional investment required for organic growth, Foster's investment in its wine business had risen to around $1.1 billion by the end of the decade. Based on around $150 million in EBITA in financial year 2000 the rate of return was slightly higher than thirteen per cent, not great but not too bad either given the dilution effect of the goodwill component created in purchasing Mildara Blass in the first place.

Ignoring the arguably artificial creation of around $310 million in goodwill, the internal rate of return was running at a heady nineteen per cent. With its wine business in the year 2000 now under new management Foster's dictated an acquisition feeding frenzy of mammoth proportions. By 2005 the wine division's investment bill had risen to more than $6 billion. TWE's rate of return in 2013 of three per cent was no better than that of the wine industry's bad old days. Worse, since the turn of the century, it had invested almost $5 billion for an annual profit increase of $50 million, a return of 1%. The heavy hitters on the board of Foster's had something to answer for. But they were never held to account and continued to draw their not insubstantial fees as if nothing had happened.

Everything is relative. According to the Australian Bureau of Statistics the average ROI for manufacturing businesses, still the most common form of business in Australia in 1982, was around twelve per cent.

Given that Mildara was a public company and competing for funds against all other companies listed on the Stock Exchange we felt in 1982 that the higher return generated by businesses in general was the better yardstick than the abysmal return earned by the wine industry. However, even in this higher benchmark territory, we wanted Mildara to be seen as a superior performer. Fantasising in my ivory tower, I thought that being in the top twenty-five per cent of all manufacturers in terms of ROI was a worthy goal. It may not have been realistic but it was certainly worthy. The top quartile cut-off point at that time was an ROI of around eighteen per cent. Adding a little margin for error we decided on a simple twenty per cent target. We weren't going to slash our wrists if we didn't get there but if we could get somewhere near it we would be deliriously happy.

An ROI objective of this order was obviously a massive challenge given the less than five per cent ROI earned by the wine industry in general. Mildara's earnings had been volatile (two profits and one loss) over the three years to June 1983 and one of those profits had been due purely to the one-off win of the Jimmy Watson trophy. However, if one added a further two years' history then Mildara had actually made a cumulative loss over the previous five-year period once interest payments had been taken into account.

Simplistically, a significant increase in Mildara's ROI could be achieved in one of only two ways. We could reduce investment (for example, by selling Mildara's assets) while holding the profit and loss side of the business roughly constant or we could increase profits by raising prices and/or reducing expenses while holding investment in assets roughly constant. In either case, it would be no easy task and require more than a little imagination and creativity as my corporate strategy leaders had so drolly suggested in 1968.

But as good an idea it might be to reduce investment in either or both fixed assets or working capital, the necessary conversion to the different business model this entailed would take far too long. Our shareholders wanted some fire and action and they wanted it now. Our focus would have to be on the profit and loss side of the business if we were to achieve a rapid enough turnaround to keep the shareholders even remotely happy. In other words, we would have to make more profit out of each sales dollar while essentially maintaining the company's existing asset infrastructure. It was a tall order.

Applying a specific twenty per cent ROI objective to the concept that had struck me all too late at Wynn's would in theory work as follows: Mildara's 1982 level of invested funds (shareholders' funds plus debt) of $22 million suggested an EBIT requirement of $4.4 million (twenty per cent of $22m = $4.4m) in order to produce that twenty per cent. But Mildara's three year moving average EBIT in 1982 was only $1.6 million and most of that was interest. To achieve the targeted $4.4 million our profit would have to rise by another $2.8 million without any corresponding increase in invested funds, seemingly an impossible task. On the other hand (switching from the balance sheet to the profit and loss statement), an EBIT of $4.4 million applied to Mildara's sales revenue in 1982 of $18 million suggested an EBIT to sales revenue ratio requirement of twenty-four per cent compared to our current return on sales of only nine per cent ($4.4m as a percentage of $18m = twenty-four per cent).

In other words, instead of making nine cents profit in every sales dollar we would have to aim to make twenty-four cents profit. Mildara's production costs for each litre of wine were broadly in line with those at Wynn's. So too, were the expenses of running the non-production side of the business (warehousing, selling, marketing and administration), which at the time were running at a ratio of around one quarter of sales revenue. This was the other dynamic that had been a relative constant at Wynn's. Operating expenses as a percentage of sales revenue at Wynn's had remained a relatively constant twenty-five per cent (25 cents in the dollar), despite sales revenue and investment increasing around tenfold over the eleven-year period. Therefore, it seemed unlikely there would be much realistic scope for achieving the higher profit target by cutting production costs or reducing operating expenses.

I was no devotee of strategies based on cutting operating expenses. Strategies based on cutting operating expenses never seemed to work in anything other than the short term. Invariably, those strategies were over-optimistic in assuming that the cost cutting would have no negative impact on continued organisational effectiveness, in other words on the generation of sales revenue. Moreover, it begged a not unimportant question: if you could cut those expenses without impacting on either the efficiency or the effectiveness of the business then why were those expenses there in the first place? Surely, in announcing an expense reduction program anyone other than a new CEO was declaring a past inability to do his job properly in the first place.

To achieve the EBIT to sales objective of twenty-four cents in every sales dollar, gross margin would have to rise from its existing level of thirty-four cents for each sales dollar to forty-nine cents in order to accommodate the twenty-five cents of revenue required to run the warehousing, selling, marketing and administrative operations of the business (forty-nine per cent minus twenty-five per cent equals twenty-four per cent). In other words, gross margin would need to rise from thirty-four cents in each sales dollar to forty-nine cents. And there was only one way that could be achieved. Prices would need to increase by fifteen per cent. Phew!

And there we have it. We had finally arrived at our destination. The lofty, seemingly intangible return on investment objective had been reduced to a simple and tangible imperative — lift average prices by fifteen per cent. It was a tall if not impossible order but as some wise person once correctly said, 'achieving the impossible is just a state of mind.' At least we knew where the focus would need to be. Seventeen years later, in late 1999, we were producing a gross margin of fifty-three per cent, an EBITA to sales ratio of thirty-three per cent and, ignoring goodwill, an ROI of nineteen per cent. Even ex-Treasurer and Prime Minister Paul Keating would have described them as a beautiful set of numbers.

It was clearly unrealistic to believe that one could achieve the required increase in gross margin and return on sales by merely raising the prices of Mildara's existing products by fifteen per cent. The most promising areas that might be exploited were the introduction of new products with higher profit margins and more efficient management of discounts and promotional allowances which, following the passing of the Restrictive Trade Practices Act, could reach as high as twenty-five per cent of sales revenue on some products. Finally, there was my old chestnut of gradually rejigging the product portfolio by having the sales force focus on higher margin products and the gradual deletion of lower margin products.

Although it was handy to know how we might achieve those higher prices and gross margins the far more important piece of information was knowing what those levels needed to be in the first place. Knowing what our prices and gross margins needed to be was the key.

As difficult as the wine market might appear to be for a participant to achieve a high ROI, given the industry's low return environment, it does have a couple of things going for it. First, it is not an amorphous whole but a series of market segments delineated by price as well as various other overlays, more like a checkerboard than a sporting oval. You can select, and change, the market segments in which you would like to play. There is more scope to reinvent a wine business than might first meet the eye.

A less important but nonetheless useful characteristic is the wine market's plethora of products, maybe as many as ten thousand, available to consumers. As opposed to, for example, breakfast cereals, there are so many wine products available it is far more difficult for consumers to keep track of wine price movements than price movements in other industries. This is the contrarian beauty (to the supplier) of the highly competitive, highly fragmented wine market. It provides the scope to edge wine prices to consumers higher without them necessarily being aware of it. Naturally, you need the cooperation of the retailers, which is a challenge in itself, but there are various ways to appeal to their self-interest.

Similarly, due to the constant and variable practice of retailers running specials, the shelf price of a particular product can vary by up to as much as twenty per cent between retailers at any one time, again providing the opportunistic marketer with the ability to push prices up without consumers being fully aware.

Finally, wine consumers do not stick to buying the same product week after week as with grocery items or hair care products. Wine consumers have a changeable portfolio of products, depending on their whim at the time, again making it difficult for them to monitor price changes accurately. You just need the intestinal fortitude to put the theory into practice. It is one of life's great mysteries that many wine products today are being sold at the same or at lower prices than twenty years ago despite the self-evident fact that product costs and operating costs have increased by up to fifty per cent.

Our ROI approach had given us our specific riding instructions as to what prices and gross margins needed to be. They were the bare bones and just the first step. Putting flesh on those bones would be another story altogether and that story would have to revolve, initially anyway, around an aggressive new products program with significantly higher prices and higher gross margins than our existing products.

OBJECTIVE 2 — DEVELOP NEW PRODUCTS THAT WOULD PRODUCE HIGHER PRICES AND HIGHER GROSS MARGINS.

Q. In which waters should we drop our new products fishing line?

A. The wine industry had always published monthly sales volume figures in reasonable detail but they were not quite what we needed. We used some MBA imagination and divided the domestic market into thirteen product/price segments. We projected the size of each market segment eight years down the track in 1990 using projected growth rates and my own feel for the market (effectively, a quantification of ideas). The real twist was that we expressed each market segment not in litres sold or sales revenue but in potential gross margin dollars. There was no point in focussing on sales volume or sales revenue because of the wine industry's wide variance in profitability across products. For example, $1000 in sales of Mildara Coonawarra cabernet produced $650 in gross profit, $1000 sales of Mildara sherry produced $350 in gross profit, $1000 sales of flagons produced $250 in gross profit and $1000 sales of bulk wine produced between $50 and $100 in gross profit.

It was already clear that Mildara's product portfolio was concentrated in the wrong market segments in terms of future market trends but we hadn't realised by just how much until the exercise had been completed.

The final outcome of the quantification of our crystal ball gazing suggested that the domestic wine market's growth by 1990 might be worth close to $90 million in additional gross margin each year compared to what we estimated it to be in 1982. But it didn't really matter what that number was. What was important was projecting *where* within the market that growth was likely to take place. Our projections suggested that more than eighty per cent of the market's profit growth would be accounted for by just four of the thirteen nominated market segments; sparkling wine, wine-casks (bag in box), high priced bottled reds and medium priced bottled whites. The wine-cask segment was the surprise inclusion. It was a low margin, low ROI segment but since its introduction in 1972 it had grown rapidly to around forty-five per cent of the market by volume and would ultimately peak at close to sixty per cent in the late '80s. More critically, five of the remaining nine market segments were projected to produce a lower gross margin in 1990 than currently.

In 1982 only thirty per cent of Mildara's total gross profit was accounted for by products in the market's four major projected growth segments. Ominously, the remaining seventy per cent of Mildara's gross margin in 1982 was accounted for by products in market segments that were actually in decline. Clearly, our new product program (like the bank robber) would need to focus on where the money was likely to be.

This exercise accounted for the big picture aspects of the new product program. We now knew which market segments we should concentrate on. The much more difficult task would be step three, that more esoteric activity of creating the individual products.

From a micro perspective, we needed to develop new products that had more appeal than the almost ten thousand individual products that abounded in the market place. In most industries, targeting superior product appeal means aiming for better quality or better performing products. But the determination of wine quality is so subjective that restricting ourselves to that road would leave too much to chance. In any case, we already had the wine 'in the tank' and had to make do with what we had.

Given the pressure we were under we had little choice but to work on that more nebulous concept, the perception of quality, in other words, the myth and magic of credibility. In the absence of product recommendations by acknowledged wine experts or a wine's creation by a highly regarded winemaker (both of which are rarely available when you need them), the initial perception of quality or credibility for a new product rests largely on two variables; higher prices and product presentation. We had already decided to play on different checkerboard squares by introducing new products with higher prices so, to a degree, that box had already been ticked. Product presentation and branding now had to be the focus.

To my mind, presentation was all about what we called 'appetite appeal'. And my broad definition of appetite appeal was that intangible something which might encourage a consumer to pick up a product from the shelf and admire its presentation. But achieving this objective would not be as simple as it might seem. We were faced with two sub-objectives which were in almost direct conflict with one another.

First, in order to induce a consumer to pick up our product and admire it, the product would have to be sufficiently different from its competitors to attract the consumer's attention in the first place. The point of difference was important not just from a consumer's viewpoint but also from that of the retailer. To get new products on to the retailers' shelves there was little point in giving them more of what looked like those they already had. After all, there were already too many products on their shelves that were substitutes for each other. We therefore had to focus on trying to be different, or at least appearing to be different. But just being different was unlikely to be the sole answer. And this was where the potential conflict came in.

It is one thing to develop a presentation that is discernibly different but it is something else entirely to have a presentation that will encourage consumers to be comfortable enough to actually purchase it. In marketing speak, one has to provide a product that matches the consumer's existing product 'values'. The product needs that intangible something that makes a consumer feel the product looks right. And given that what looks right to consumers is strongly influenced by what they are already familiar with meant that focussing on trying to be different also involved a high degree of risk. Being too different might be as bad as not being different enough. It all came down to exercising good judgment in being sufficiently different to attract consumers' interest in the first place but not so different as to turn them off. It required a deft balancing act of the different and the familiar.

In 1982 the hot grape variety in Australia was the recently introduced chardonnay. It was no surprise to anyone given the lack of regulations at the time there appeared to be a lot more chardonnay being sold than grown.

Wine technocrats at Davis University in California had developed in the 1960s a revolutionary approach to winemaking. Brian Croser, who was to become one of the legends of the Australian wine industry, was one of the first to introduce this new approach to Australia. He introduced the revolutionary approach to budding Australian winemakers at the Wagga Wagga Agricultural Institute in the early '70s where he was justifiably regarded as the guru.

The approach was all about extracting and emphasising the pure flavour of the grape. This was best done by minimising contact with oxygen during and after the wine making process. And that involved a range of new techniques, including the use of stainless steel for winemaking equipment as well as for long term storage rather than the wood and concrete that had been used by the traditional wine producing countries for centuries. The new way revolutionised winemaking approaches, particularly for white wines and paved the way for the nomenclature 'New World' wines.

Consumers saw that adage as meaning wines from non-traditional winemaking countries but within the industry it also meant the 'new way'. As a consequence, white grape varieties, which benefitted enormously from this new process, started to taste better and to become more popular, not to mention fashionable. And the most fashionable variety of all, commencing in the '70s and not plateauing until the late '90s, was chardonnay. This was something of a paradox because the chardonnay grape has a fairly neutral flavour and winemakers tend to rely on subtle wood characters extracted from a short period of maturation in wooden barrels to provide differentiation. This 'neutrality' ultimately paved the way for the extraordinary success of the more flavoursome grape variety, sauvignon blanc, particularly from New Zealand which was better able to leverage the benefits of the new way.

¶

Between 1975 and 1982 the sparkling wine market in Australia, then dominated by Seppelt's Great Western 'champagne' and McWilliams Minchinbury 'champagne', had grown at the express pace of twenty-five per cent a year, but in relative terms was still a small market, accounting for less than eight per cent of all wine sales. In those days, Australian wineries were permitted to use the term 'champagne' on their labels, a term which today is restricted to the labels of sparkling wines made in the Champagne region in France. This was a good place to start our product development program. We coined the name Windsor, a name we felt had image and substance, added the magic name chardonnay and introduced Windsor Chardonnay 'methode champenoise'. By law, the Mildara name had to be mentioned, but we made sure it proved hard to find on either the front or back label.

Mildara had no champagne making process so we approached Yellowglen Cellars, located on abandoned goldfields at Smythesdale near Ballarat. Yellowglen Cellars used the classic French method known as methode champenoise, meaning fermented and sold in 'this' bottle. Although Seppelts and McWilliams also fermented their products in the bottle they used a more cost efficient method to extract the dead yeast cells from the bottles in which the secondary fermentation had taken place. This was known as the 'transfer' method. It still produced a good product but the process lacked the mystique (the myth and the magic, or, if you like, the 'fairy dust') of the far more labour intensive, much slower and more costly methode champenoise.

Yellowglen 'champagne' had been successfully introduced to the Australian market the previous year at around $10 a bottle and been priced midway between Seppelts' and McWilliams' price of around $4 a bottle and French Champagnes of around $18 a bottle.

Yellowglen 'champagne', made at the time by the handsome, charming and well-named French import Dominique Landrigan, soon developed a small but loyal cult following among those consumers who were captivated by its frothy, creamy texture and who were attracted to its higher price positioning and image. It was almost as if Australian consumers had been busting to pay $10 for a bottle of Australian 'champagne'. I was more than sceptical as to how Dominique achieved that differentiating creamy texture but it was a master stroke and the word quickly spread, creating the image for what was to become one of Australia's great wine brands.

Given Windsor Champagne's two features, chardonnay and methode champenoise, we priced our product fifty per cent higher than the two market leaders, Minchinbury and Great Western, but well below Yellowglen's $10. And we stuck as closely as possible to Dominique's coat-tails, looking for reflected glory and regaling every retailer who was prepared to listen that Windsor was being made by the fabled (according to us) Dominique Landrigan.

In also aiming for the Windsor presentation to have the appropriate feel (the appropriate product 'values') I had referred to my copy of Hugh Johnson's *World Atlas of Wine*. It featured all the classic labels of the world's leading wine producers. We fashioned a label that incorporated some of the characteristics of the famous Möet & Chandon label (whose owners later took action against us, ultimately forcing us to make a cosmetic change that few if any people ever noticed) and some of the characteristics of the slightly less famous Chateau Coutet Barsac label (who didn't take action against us). It was overkill but we weren't taking any chances.

Our second new product focus was the medium priced white wine segment. We introduced a range of three wine styles under a name we felt had a good and comfortable feel, Church Hill (although the market seemed to prefer referring to it as Churchill) and again downplayed the Mildara brand name. The coining of fancy names was in its infancy in Australia at the time but the tactic was soon adopted by the rest of the industry and embraced to such a degree that over the next couple of decades catchy names stopped being catchy.

We used chardonnay as the grape variety for the lead product. But that wasn't enough. Although chardonnay was a growth segment there was already a plethora of chardonnays on the market. We would need another hook. And that hook presented itself in the form of a French label that had recently been brought from New York by a colleague. The label had not rated a mention in my wine atlas because it was too new. It was the yet to be introduced to Australia, Georges Duboeuf Beaujolais label. It featured bright and beautifully presented pink and red flowers. I thought the presentation absolutely stunning. We didn't copy it for the Church Hill chardonnay label or the other varieties but went fairly close. Using different colours as well as different flowers we also introduced a fume blanc, a Riesling and later, a lighter-styled red wine.

¶

One of the industry's hot products in 1982 was Brian Croser's premium priced Petaluma Rhine Riesling. It was packaged in a unique amber coloured bottle and had a small but very distinctive yellow label at a super-premium price. I thought it was a great presentation; different, but with the right feel. Mildara was selling only a 'hat-full' of its expensively grown Coonawarra Riesling under the Mildara label. The majority of the high cost fruit was being used in unprofitable bulk blends. I knew we would not sell huge quantities if we drew inspiration from the Petaluma presentation but as the majority of our Coonawarra Riesling was being wasted and there was no chance of confusion in the marketplace (our product was priced at forty per cent less than Petaluma's) I couldn't resist the temptation. I was already being branded the naughty boy of the wine industry so, in for a penny, in for a pound.

It was no great surprise that Brian Croser was hopping mad. He rang Richard Haselgrove and complained bitterly about my lack of ethics. He knew there was little point in taking legal action because he didn't have a legal leg to stand on (he'd already checked it out). The label was similar but far from identical. Strangely, given Richard's sensitivity to ethical issues he was unmoved. But I rang Brian straight back.

There was a long silence after I introduced myself. I admitted I was being opportunistic and, probably sounding a bit on the sleazy side, told Brian I had great admiration for his label, which was true anyway. I explained that once our new product was up and running, say in six months, I would change the presentation, the benefits hardly worth the potential angst. To a degree honour had been served. In a burst of non-characteristic humour Brian was quoted in the press to the effect that Mildara's Riesling was worthy of no better than a two star rating. On the other hand, the label was worthy of at least five stars. Brian and I eventually became firm friends as well as allies and he wrote me a very flattering letter when I retired sixteen years later, referring to me as being as 'straight as a gun barrel'. That was probably because many people thought I wasn't.

¶

The fourth member of the new product brigade was Benjamin port. Port was not one of the identified market growth segments but I felt we could be opportunistic in exploiting our expertise in making fortified wine. We named Benjamin after Ben Chaffey, one of the two famous Canadian brothers whose engineering genius had led to establishment of the Sunraysia and South Australian irrigation areas. I was really only following what we had done at Wynn's when we introduced the highly successful Samuel port, named after Samuel Wynn. The real opportunistic hook in Benjamin's case was a bottle design that was remarkably reminiscent of Australia's famed and very expensive port brand, Seppelts' Para Liqueur. The aim, once again, was to give the product the appropriate feel. This time, the Mildara name was front and centre on the label. Of our four examples of 'imitation being the finest form of flattery' it was the only one that I was potentially worried about from a legal perspective. I felt we had cut the bottle design pretty close. But the lightning bolt did never eventuate. We had obviously stayed on the correct side of the line.

And with all of these new products we priced them to produce a gross margin greater than fifty per cent, around twenty per cent higher than Mildara's average gross margins at the time.

OBJECTIVE 3 — ADDRESS THE MISMATCH BETWEEN PRODUCTION AND DEMAND

The additional sales volume we hoped to generate from Windsor chardonnay champagne, the Flower labels and Benjamin would make a dent in our excess wine supply but not as big a dent as we would like. I decided to return from whence I had come and introduce a Mildara wine-cask. There were twenty-six wine-cask brands already on the market and we were to become the twenty-seventh. Why would retailers want to stock another wine-cask? They wouldn't. But we rationalised that if our four new bottle products struck the chord we were hoping for then the momentum might be sufficient to assist the salespeople to get a reasonable number of retailers to stock a Mildara branded cask. The product would never produce the pricing that would meet our ROI objectives but nonetheless it would provide a far better return than selling bulk wine to other wineries or in two litre flagons. And its introduction might provide sufficient breathing space for further new products to take up the slack in the medium term. If and when that occurred the plan was to delete the wine-cask from the product list.

OBJECTIVE 4 — APPOINT NEW STATE MANAGERS

The key to successfully implementing our strategy in the marketplace was the need for a group of state sales managers with experience and a strong sense of ownership. They needed to be financially disciplined and proactive business developers with good track records. The two major states, Victoria and New South Wales accounted for seventy-five per cent of Mildara's business. Laurie Evans and Gary Byrne had been my Victorian and New South Wales state managers at Wynn's. They were by far the 'best in show', understood and embraced the need for strict financial discipline, took great pride in their role, were highly industrious and, importantly, good leaders. Moreover, they were unhappy working for my successor at Wynn's, Mark Babidge. They were an easy steal.

Mark Babidge had reported to me at Wynn's and been responsible for the winemaking function. He was no slouch in the intelligence department, was extremely affable and an excellent luncheon companion, being highly articulate and able to speak authoritatively on any number of general knowledge topics. He set exceptionally high standards for himself and was super-humanly industrious. But as is often the case with hard-working high achievers he also demanded his own almost impossible high standards from his subordinates. He found it difficult to accept that human beings are rarely perfect and capable of more than the occasional stuff-up, particularly if you encourage them to use their initiative. Ultimately, he was invariably disappointed with his subordinates and found it difficult to award them his confidence or trust, something they quickly picked up on. Without that sense of trust they were never going to go the extra yard that robust, vigorous organisations thrive on (metaphorically turning off the lights when they left the office).

In late 1981, only months after my rash decision to quit the wine industry, Wynn's hit a rocky patch along with the rest of the

Australian economy as the recession worsened. Wynn's was headed for its first profit decline in a decade. And it was a serious decline. Having succeeded me as general manager and needing to believe he was doing everything possible in his new job to generate business, Mark felt sufficiently pressured to yield to the temptation of encroaching on what I always considered to be the state managers' sacred domain, the selling function.

The state managers immediately saw this intervention as questioning their integrity, their strong sense of ownership and their overall effectiveness. In direct contrast to my practice of leaving the sales function exclusively to the state managers Mark began to visit major customers on selling campaigns, sometimes with the state managers, sometimes without. Inevitably, he got himself caught up in something in which he had little experience and even less expertise. Unless you are a natural, a rare attribute in itself, sales negotiation is an art form that can only be honed by years of experience. In any case if you have a dog with a decent bark you shouldn't be trying to do the snarling for him. If you do then he stops snarling. Mark simply gave in to demands for better price deals. Laurie and Gary objected to the intrusion and feeling belittled and frustrated couldn't wait to jump ship. They came aboard Mildara in March 1983. Bill Stevens, a Wynn's veteran of twenty years in marketing services and export development, soon joined the exodus. Just over a year later, another Wynn's stalwart, Vic Patrick, Australia's leading viticulturist, also gave in to frustration (and my strong exhortations) and came aboard as our vineyard director.

Departing from my policy of allowing the state managers to operate with almost complete freedom, as long as they adhered to strict financial guidelines, was far from Mark's major mistake. He had also resorted to conventional wisdom of not raising prices during a lull in sales momentum. Mark had done away with my rigid policy of regularly raising prices at least in line with inflation irrespective of the business cycle (costs and expenses were still increasing at that time by more than ten per cent a year). Failing to increase prices by ten per cent over twelve months not only had the same effect as a ten per cent price reduction in a no-inflation environment but, more importantly, reduced average gross profit margins from around forty-five per cent to thirty-five per cent. Sales volume would have had to increase by almost thirty per cent to compensate for the gross margin reduction, a virtual impossibility. Particularly so given everyone else in the wine industry was dropping their prices as well. With no positive effect on volume Wynn's net profit immediately slumped from twenty cents to 10 cents for each sales dollar, resulting in a halving of total profits. An old adage I had preached to my subordinates was that, 'the price increase you don't put in place now is the one you never get'. Actually, I had stolen that line from my old army friend Philip Shirrefs, the master of the temporary love affair, who had applied that saying to something entirely different. The significance of maintaining pricing discipline had obviously been lost on Mark and following the break in that pricing policy he was never able to get the profit margins back on track. In early 1984 Castlemaine Perkins lost patience with Wynn's performance and began negotiating the sale of the business to Southcorp for less than half its 1981 valuation.

OBJECTIVE 5 — DEVELOP AN INFORMATION SYSTEM THAT WOULD DRIVE BEHAVIOUR

Wine companies, more so than other manufacturers at that time, tended to have product portfolios with a wide range of gross profit margins, most of them towards the bottom end. This was often because of a once a year winemaking season as well as an inflexible supply of grapes. This lack of flexibility inevitably caused demand and supply mismatches, nearly always erring on the side of too much supply rather than not enough. The pressure really came at vintage time when limited storage facilities needed to be emptied to make way for the new vintage. As a result, low price, low margin products would be created in ever increasing numbers or regular products would have their prices slashed to help empty the tanks. It was also another reason wine companies felt compelled not to raise prices in line with inflation — a major reason for the industry's poor ROI. Products created purely to empty the tanks, or standard lines that had had their prices slashed, tended to become permanent fixtures instead of being treated as temporary aberrations.

Mildara's average gross margin was thirty-four per cent, although the margin earned on individual products appeared to range from as high as sixty-five per cent to as low as ten per cent, appeared being the operative word. As at Wynn's in my early days the specific gross margins for individual products were unclear.

We needed to increase our average gross margins from thirty-four per cent to nearer forty-nine per cent. Clearly, we couldn't raise existing prices by fifteen per cent overnight so, initially, we would have to rely on other avenues — the introduction of new products with higher margins, the gradual deletion of low margin products, encouraging the sales force to focus on products with higher margins and, finally, implementing and managing more efficiently and more effectively a new set of discounts and promotional allowances.

I was back to my old obsession, the one that almost cost me my job at Wynn's, of needing to know exactly what each product contributed to the bottom line.

The complicating factor now was the plethora of promotional allowances (discounts) that had arisen in the food and beverage industries following the passing of the Restrictive Trade Practices Act of 1974. These allowances often made it difficult to determine an individual product's actual selling price and therefore its profit contribution.

The simplest allowance was a range of discounts based on case quantities (twelve bottles at the time) purchased by a retailer who was supplied direct from our warehouse — say, $3 a case for a three case buy, $5 a case for a for a five case buy and so on. These discounts appeared on the invoice, effectively reducing the price, and so did not represent a transparency problem.

A slightly more complicated and less transparent allowance occurred when a retailer, who was supplied direct from our warehouse, ran a full page advertisement in the daily newspaper for a range of our products (as well as other companies') and demanded a lump sum promotional fee covering the group of Mildara products being promoted rather than a case allowance. Retailers favoured the lump sum over the case allowance because of its potential for deliberate obfuscation — they could put some of it in their pocket (we would never know how much) rather than devoting all of it to reduced retail prices. The lump sum principle obviously made it more difficult for us to determine our real (net) price for each product in the promotion and, by extension, its targeted gross profit level.

But the real problem of determining net selling prices and accurate gross margins lay with business that was done through the wholesalers and a further step removed from the consumer. The wholesaling channel still represented at least fifty per cent of the market. As well as running their own promotional programs each retailer generally had membership of at least one, and usually more than one, buying or banner group. The stock for these promotions was purchased by the retailer from the wholesaler who arranged the promotions and extracted the relevant allowances from the wine companies. Invariably, wholesalers, like retailers, demanded a lump sum. A proportion of that lump sum was passed on to retailers to compensate for the lower retail price charged to consumers in accordance with the advertised promotion (again, we wouldn't know exactly how much). Again, the lump sum approach gave wholesalers the opportunity to divert a healthy proportion of the supplier's allowance to themselves. Initially, wholesalers refused to supply the details of case quantities purchased by retailers for these promotions in order to maintain a level of camouflage to cover what they were syphoning off. But finally, one wholesaler yielded to Mildara's demands and the other wholesalers ultimately followed suit.

Unlike Mildara, most wine companies solved this problem of blurred net prices in the simplest way possible. They ignored it. They bundled lump sum allowances and case allowances into a separate expense line classified as promotional allowances in their monthly profit and loss statements and regarded gross margins as 'before promotional allowances'. Those suppliers who took this easy way out were kidding themselves as to the real prices and gross profits being earned on individual products. Promotional allowances on promoted products averaged around ten per cent of the selling price and in some instances reached as high as twenty-five per cent. Unless these allowances were allocated to individual products not only would false gross margins be produced but lazy state managers would escape from being made accountable for determining the effectiveness of the promotions they had agreed to.

This was the manner in which Mildara had previously accounted for promotional allowances. But to make matters worse the company had had such a poor system for recording the promotions that it was necessary each month for an adjustment to be made to the previous month's promotional allowances. This was all about to change.

From now on, the rule at Mildara was that every dollar of promotional allowance had to be allocated, even if it were an educated guess, against a product's price in order to produce as accurate a net selling price and gross margin for each product as possible. Recording the most accurate net prices and gross margins was the key to being masters of our own destiny. As a consequence, we would know, if not exactly then certainly within reason, by how much we needed to raise the price of each of our products to cover increasing costs or to achieve profit improvement goals.

Ultimately, the Mildara state managers became highly proficient in dealing with this potential minefield of promotional allowances. They took great pride in effectively wresting control of the process from the wholesalers' buyers, forcing the buyers to rely on the state managers of our competitors for their slush funds. Anecdotally, I estimated that the benefit to Mildara of this rigid discipline and the expertise of our state managers in managing the process was ultimately worth to the bottom line between five and seven cents of every sales dollar.

The other aspect to driving corporate behaviour was the need to finesse the financial reporting system. Companies generally report headline business growth in terms of sales revenue. In some industries, such as in the food and beverage industries, standardised cases of physical product may also be used as a growth rate indicator. Mildara was no exception and we continued to use sales revenue and case sales as performance indicators in our half-year reporting to the Stock Exchange. However, for monthly management reporting we quickly dispensed sales revenue to the dustbin and replaced it with gross margin in absolute dollar terms. With such stark differences in gross margin for each dollar of sales between our various products, continuing to assess management performance by way of sales revenue was bullshit. My main objective was to change behaviour and have the sales teams focus on the gross profit they generated rather than sales revenue, hopefully getting them to concentrate on the higher margin products rather than the easier-to-sell cheaper products in order to hit their gross margin targets.

I was helped in this process of information gathering, analysis and communication by Bernard Saw. Bernard had an intellect of Mensa proportions, was an IT whizz and had established his own computer software business. Known to his very few friends from his earlier days at Scotch College as 'Bernie Briquette', he had inflexible views on life, was more right-wing than Genghis Khan and like so many other highly intelligent people, had come up short in the emotional intelligence department. Bernard's many detractors were more specific. They thought he was more than a bit on the weird side. But Bernard loved the business of business and talked tirelessly and passionately about it. He came from a broken home, had led a sad, lonely childhood and was not helped by having an imperious, less than maternal, independently wealthy mother. One gained the distinct impression she had been dismissive of Bernard for most his life. Adding to Bernard's weirdness, depending on your perspective, was his devotion to being determinedly counter cyclical in dress and hairstyle. He had also developed the disconcerting practice of jogging between business appointments in full business regalia. And of course (much to the derision of my family members) I spent a lot of time with him. For close to twenty years I was probably his closest friend, his regular weekend golf partner at either Royal Melbourne or Kingston Heath and for at least a decade his largest business client.

In 1995 Bernard's business, gradually deserted by its clients, fell into deadly disrepair. In quiet desperation Bernard implored me to act as his personal guarantor for a $200,000 bank loan that would in his view (but not in mine), provide a solution to his problem. As sensitively as possible I tried to explain why I could not meet his request. Bernard immediately terminated our friendship (or whatever it was) adamantly refusing my subsequent attempts at reconciliation. Bernard later sought financial help from an aged uncle, was refused and in a fit of rage Bernard bashed him to death with a lampshade, copping a twenty-seven year sentence for his brain snap. Bernard continues to reside in prison providing financial, tax and other business advice to inmates and prison staff. It seems he is the happiest he has ever been.

20

The turnaround

We held our breath, prayed to the man upstairs and waited on the market's response to our new products program.

The Mildara flower labels led the charge in July 1983. It was a shaky start. Many retailers, often the worst judges of what consumers might embrace, initially refused to stock them on the basis the labels were too arty farty or, in some less articulate cases, a bit poofterish. I also copped criticism from the wine writers for plagiarism (guilty as charged your honour). This was not the first time that had happened in Australia — the original Orlando Jacobs Creek label had a distinct likeness to a French Haut Brion label. However, we were on the money as far as consumers were concerned and were soon selling the range, particularly Church Hill chardonnay, at the rate of a million bottles a year, providing a good lead in for the Petaluma look-alike Coonawarra Riesling, Windsor chardonnay 'champagne' and just before Christmas, Benjamin port. The Mildara wine-cask followed in the newyear. The stars were in alignment and God was kind.

Mildara was voted by Victorian liquor retailers as the wine industry's most innovative company of the year. In financial year 1983/84, despite the new products having been in the market for only part of the year, EBIT jumped seventy per cent from $1.6 million to a company record (hardly something to write home about) of $2.9 million. The momentum was maintained in 1984/85 with EBIT reaching $4.6 million. Huon Hooke, a wine writer with an acerbic turn of phrase, wrote an article in the *Financial Review* headed, 'The Wine Industry's Naughty Boy Turns the Tide for Mildara.'

In two years Mildara's ROI had almost trebled to 17.6 per cent not only because of the surging success of our new higher margin products but thanks to a far more rapid reduction in working capital than we had dared hope. This was largely as a result of the successful new product program drawing down bulk wine inventories more quickly than anticipated. We had succeeded in reducing our level of capital intensity, albeit inadvertently. Although the glorious and seemingly unattainable ROI target of twenty per cent had not been achieved we had managed to get close, and much sooner than we thought likely at the outset. Average gross margin as a percentage of sales revenue was up from its lowly thirty-four per cent in 1982 to forty-two per cent and EBIT to sales revenue had more than doubled from nine per cent to twenty-two per cent because of the greater productivity of the sales force. Operating expenses had fallen sharply from twenty-five per cent of sales revenue to an unsustainable twenty per cent, the ratio gradually working its way back up to around twenty-two per cent over the next twelve months. We were delivering on our ROI-driven strategy. It was at that time we cautiously added a second key objective, growth. We would seek to grow earnings for each share by a minimum of ten per cent a year. The number was more symbolic than an expectation but at least it provided us with a target.

Over the fourteen years to 1996 Mildara proceeded to average an annual growth rate of fourteen per cent in earnings per share, compared to twenty-seven per cent in annual EBITA growth. Although we were to generate reasonable levels of cash from operations, we found it necessary to continually raise funds to finance our high level of growth. The disparity between the two profit growth rates was caused by a few things working against us. Interest rates on borrowed funds were still in double figures and we had to continually raise funds through issuing new shares to keep our debt to equity ratio within parameters acceptable to the ANZ Bank as well as to the share market. Issuing shares may be the safest form of financing but the process obviously dilutes share earnings growth because of the larger number of shares on issue.

¶

Our path to resurrection in those early years also attracted the attention of the opportunists from the bigger end of town.

In 1983, during my brief and unhappy sojourn at Brau Galt and Associates, I had carried out executive search assignments for a guy by the name of Christopher Skase. Christopher was the major shareholder in Qintex Limited, a small holding company that had Christopher's sticky fingers in a number of small operating subsidiaries, the largest of which was prestige retailer, Hardy Brothers.

Before starting down the road to becoming famous Christopher had worked as a stockbroker but apparently recognised the opportunity presented by a relatively unsophisticated Melbourne Stock Exchange. He switched to being a financial journalist with the *Sun News Pictorial,* now the *Herald Sun,* presumably to put his theories into practice. Following some conveniently penned newspaper articles Christopher seemed to be on the right end of the consequent share price movements. He then parlayed these gains into the formation of Qintex before the 'coincidences' attracted serious attention from the relevant authorities. All the gains had been spun in the washing machine and back into the system as clean as a whistle. Christopher had then set himself up very nicely with legitimate business interests, a bit spread here, a bit over there. By the time I met him he had achieved a modicum of legitimacy. It's the same the world over, villains ultimately crave respectability and Christopher was no different. He was charismatic, a born salesman and slow to pay his bills, not to mention the fact that his grasp of the truth was not always secure. But his most distinguishing positive features were his photographic memory, his crystal clear ability to think strategically and to very effectively execute his plans to the letter. Combining those abilities with a bit of skulduggery here and there was always going to make for a heady combination.

Christopher must have regarded our briefing and debriefing sessions on executive search assignments as a source of light relief because they were usually conducted at the end of the working day and invariably accompanied by a bottle of wine. During one of those sessions I must have caught him in a weak moment because he agreed to be the speaker at the next Monash MBA graduates' dinner. On the day of the dinner I rang to make sure he hadn't forgotten.

'Shit,' he said, 'is that tonight?'

'Here we go', I thought, but he didn't let me down. He spoke for an hour and with little or no preparation absolutely laid everyone in the aisles.

Within months of my joining Mildara Christopher had snapped up around five per cent of Mildara's shares at rock bottom prices. Six months later the word was out that we were kicking a few goals with our new products and the Mildara share price had responded to the tune of around fifty per cent. There was even some commentary in the press that we could now be an attractive takeover target and that the Qintex parcel might be on the market. My worst nightmare, that of being taken over, was beginning to galvanise into action.

Christopher, never beyond jumping on the telephone in his quest for inside information, rang me to allay any fears I might have had and told me to disregard what was in the newspaper.

'It's all bullshit,' he said, 'I'm in for the long term.'

Christopher was not exactly weighed down by a heavy conscience because without any apology he sold his Mildara shares the very next day. But that was Christopher. The reality was that Christopher had been up to his old tricks and had initiated both rumours in order to more easily facilitate the earner on his Mildara shares.

By the late 1980s Christopher had seriously upgraded his fantasies. By now Qintex was the owner of a string of luxury holiday resorts, had a controlling interest in television company Channel Seven and had made an offer to buy, of all things, Hollywood's MGM film studios.

The deals had become too big and the funding elastic band was stretched to breaking point. The prudence exercised by Christopher in his early days at Qintex, in getting out before the authorities got busy, had finally gone out the window. Hubris had taken over in spades. He kept betting the ranch and Christopher's judgment disappeared out the window as well. Ever the salesman, Christopher had by 1989 extracted close to $2 billion in financing from an admiring, naïve money market. It was the top of the business cycle and a period of excess for all the entrepreneurs. Banks and anyone else were prepared to risk their hard earned on just about anything

Dawn and I had attended all Christopher's Christmas parties, even that of the inaugural party in 1983 with around thirty invitees — financial journalists Terry McCrann and Robert Gottliebson were also in attendance — and which later became famous, morphing into extravaganzas of excess. The peak was the attendance of nearly a thousand of the rich and famous at the 1988 party, all of whom were flown to Brisbane on Christopher's chartered flights for a party which reputedly cost Qintex $500,000. Before his fall from grace, invitees gloried in advertising the fact they had received invitations to Christopher's parties. Afterwards they were more inclined to keep their mouths shut.

It had become abundantly clear, at least to me, when Christopher bought the controlling interest in Channel Seven, things were not going to end well. It was just not possible for him to have the necessary financial wherewithal. In early 1991, with the credit squeeze well and truly under way, his business empire duly collapsed and Christopher fled to Majorca, Spain, accompanied by two containers of antique furniture, where he proceeded to live in luxury off the funds he had been strategically salting away in Swiss numbered bank accounts in anticipation of such an occurrence.

Christopher had always thought like a guy who wasn't going to be captured, more like a successful criminal than a prison inmate. He famously became the Australian Government's most wanted fugitive. For ten years the authorities tried in vain to have him expedited to face charges arising from $1.5 billion in business debts and around $150 million in personal debts. Christopher had planned his work, worked his plan and outsmarted the authorities but not the great patriarch in the sky. Stomach cancer got him in 2001. God had been following his every move.

It was some time before Huon Hooke wrote his sweet and sour article in the *Financial Review* that I received another telephone call from left field, actually, more from right field. The voice on the other end was as smooth as silk and began, 'Mr King, my name is Marc Besen, I own Sussan Corporation.' I knew who he was. He was the head of one of Melbourne's richest families and one of its most successful businesses.

'I am hoping you will accept an invitation to have lunch with me.'

'Of course Mr Besen, I would be more than happy to,' I managed to stumble out, although it probably sounded more like a collection of garbled vowels. Still, he must have got my meaning because he responded with, 'Call me Marc.'

Earlier in his business career, charmingly courteous Marc Besen had taken action in respect to two troubled companies not in accord with the views of his daughter, Naomi.

Feisty and a rebel apparently without cause, as well as a force to be reckoned with in her own right, Naomi was aggressively antagonistic towards her father's wealth at the time I carried out executive search assignments for the business she ran with her then husband, Fred Milgrom in 1982. Naomi had made it abundantly clear what her political proclivities were at the time and how she really felt about her father's business activities, 'fucking capitalist', being her specific description as I recall. But she couldn't resist Marc's persistent charm offensive nor could she resist her call to greatness and she ultimately made a right angle turn in her career path and became another poacher turned gamekeeper. She has very successfully directed, managed and expanded Sussan Corporation's empire since the early 1990s.

'May I call you Ray', was Marc's first comment as he shook my hand in his private dining room at Sussan's headquarters. 'I know all about you from my old friend David Wynn and I would like to hear how you have managed to turn Mildara around', was his second comment.

One thing led to another and following his second invitation for me to join him for lunch he casually dropped on the table that he would like to buy Mildara as long as I was prepared to stay with the business.

'The way WE do these things,' he said, immediately slapping the metaphorical hand-cuffs on me, 'is you will be given ten per cent of the company's shares with an interest free loan which you will pay back out of profits.'

I was all for it of course but David Grant pushed for an unrealistically high price for his family's twenty-five per cent shareholding and unfortunately for me the deal fell over. But that was not the end of my lunches with Marc. At least once a year until he moved his base to the Yarra Valley, Marc and I would reminisce over what might have been.

¶

As Mildara continued to make its mark the change in morale throughout the company was good for the soul. After the Gollin collapse in 1975 Mildara employees had felt as if the sword of Damocles was poised above their heads. Now they wanted to run through brick walls. The sales teams had developed a swagger and were vociferously dismissive of their competitors' derisive claims that Mildara was nothing but a one-day wonder and reliant on a cheat for its success.

One of the more illuminating side effects of the company's transformation was the Merbein based staff association's unwitting spreading of the gospel of gross margin. On its own initiative the association established a company-wide monthly 'sweep' on estimated gross margin performance against budget. Daily gross margin performance was posted on all the company noticeboards, enabling participants to follow their predictions and exercise any bragging rights that might have been warranted. At the outset, with the exception of the sales and accounting personnel, few had even heard of the term gross margin let alone know what it meant. Within a few months that had all changed.

While the bottling line employees, winery and warehouse staff were unlikely to be word perfect on the definition they had gained at least a rudimentary understanding of what this strange term meant. If they were going to have a monthly bet on the gross margin number they wanted to have some idea of what they were betting on. It added a degree of understanding that a profit oriented company did not necessarily mean the exploitation of its employees. It was an example of the whole company being on the same page. Adam Smith's invisible hand was on the job and we were all enjoying the fun.

Morale received a further boost by the board's decision, in April 1983, to establish an employee share scheme. I had to give credit to the Harvard Boy here. It was an egalitarian scheme and 3000 shares were offered to every full time employee, me included. Surprisingly, given Mildara's record over the previous five years and the legal obligation to repay their interest free loans if Mildara's share price headed south, the share offer was eventually taken up by more than ninety per cent of potential participants. They were feeling particularly good about themselves as well as the company.

With Mildara's share price more than doubling over the next twelve months the lower level employees started to cash in their holdings. This was no great surprise as the $3000 to $5000 potential windfall was, for many of the employees, the largest lump sum to have come their way. For many, the accumulation of $1000 had previously been utterly beyond their powers, the accumulation of $5000 completely beyond their imagination. Gambling that much on the company's continued success was just too much to ask. Within another twelve months less than fifteen per cent of the original participants remained in the scheme. Somewhat mean spiritedly a few of the Mildara directors took a dim view of what they deemed to be the employees' lack of loyalty and lack of appreciation for what had been done for them but the goodwill that had been created would stand us in good stead for a long time to come.

In late 1984 the board finally agreed to an executive share scheme. Following my failed August 1982 remuneration negotiations with the Harvard Boy I had pushed for share options to be the performance element in executive remuneration packages. I didn't believe in bonus schemes, rightly as it turned out, given the way in which that concept has since been rorted and manipulated in giving executives incentives to do what they had been employed to do in the first place. I had always believed the best incentive was to keep your job and that any performance pay should be aligned with the interests of the company's shareholders. Executive share schemes were not all that common in 1982 but Peter agreed with the concept and an agreement in principle was reached that such a scheme, involving a maximum of five per cent of the company's shares, would be made available to executives. Frustratingly, the Harvard Boy's Machiavellian proclivities led to almost another twelve months before the scheme saw the light of day. By that time Mildara's share price had soared by almost two hundred per cent, significantly reducing the potential benefit. Grumbling noises from the senior executives were not insubstantial (I suspect being fanned by me), blame being directed towards the chairman, who was prevented by the company's constitution from participating in the scheme.

When the scheme was eventually introduced it was, again, egalitarian and around forty employees were able to participate in a significant way, almost twenty per cent of the company's personnel. This was in direct contrast to most other company schemes at the time and, it must be admitted, an honourable scheme far ahead of its time. Again, the Harvard Boy deserved a tick.

The Mildara share scheme went all the way down to supervisor level. Even at that level the volume of shares made available was significant. Over the ensuing years further share issues were made to management and by the time we sold out to Foster's in 1996 most had made enough to pay off their mortgages. The scheme was wonderful for morale and Mildara soon became the talk of the wine industry in being the place to work if you were lucky enough to be handed the opportunity.

21

Yellowglen

'Where do we go from here?' enquired the Harvard Boy and David Grant late in 1984.

They still had mixed feelings about my approach to strategic and tactical issues and were not going to let the matter rest. My response, that we should stick with the creative, opportunistic approach that had so far proven to be successful, didn't exactly meet with a roar of approval. The duo believed the longer term required a more orthodox, structured and transparent growth plan. The dilemma that directors would prefer not to have to address had now raised its ugly head — a difference of opinion between some directors and management as to future strategy.

The Harvard Boy and I disagreed on several marketing and strategic issues but one of our more vigorous topics of debate was how much we should be investing in promoting the company's products. For example, Peter felt initiatives to attract consumers via the winery cellar door was important. I didn't. His close colleague David Grant was keen on investing heavily in media advertising, a strategy that seemed effective in the Scotch whisky business. I didn't. What had worked very well for us so far had been a strategy based on new products with appealing names and presentations that departed from the norm but not too far and which in a market of more than 10,000 individual products caught the consumer's eye. Getting a wine writer to say something nice was also more than useful. Admittedly, we were short of a brand franchise but I was working on that, spending lots of time staring out the window.

My two adversaries regarded my supporting argument of Mildara's admittedly short but successful recent track record as proof of the pudding as a one-off event, conveniently disregarding a not unsuccessful track record at Wynn's.

In advocating a contrary course of action the Harvard Boy and David Grant were departing from the maxim, a maxim admittedly not always universally accepted, that directors should not impose a strategy on a company's management. Such is the contrariness of what sometimes goes on in a boardroom of alpha males, females being no exception. If management doesn't believe in the strategy being proposed it is unlikely to put its best foot forward. This is where the judgment of a good chairman is worth its weight in gold. Unfortunately for me, the chairman was my chief antagonist.

In the part-time twilight period of my business career I ended up sitting on a total of twenty boards, ten of them as chairman. I remained steadfastly of the view that the most successful corporate strategies come from management, or at the very least from strategies enthusiastically embraced by management. Unsurprisingly, it was a view I held pretty strongly as a CEO but on balance it was one I continued to maintain as a more objective non-executive director despite a strong temptation to sometimes act otherwise. Non-executive directors are by necessity part-time and rarely have management's intimate knowledge of either the inner workings of the company or the market's changing dynamics. Fighting with the CEO and attempting to impose a strategy on him isn't the answer. Backing him or sacking him is.

In truth, the Harvard Boy was still trying to act more like a CEO than a chairman. Rather than mentoring, counselling, shaping and encouraging he was still vigorously pushing his own view of the wine world. Word was getting back to me from some of the other directors that while the Harvard Boy and David Grant had acknowledged, grudgingly, that I had done a good job in pulling Mildara out of the fire they nonetheless had left little to the imagination in advocating I was not the man to consolidate that success and to take the company forward. Sacking me seemed to be their preferred option and David Grant was waving Grant's twenty-five per cent shareholding around as if it were a giant fist. More worrying was his veiled threat that the Grants' products might be better off being distributed by someone else. Not beyond a bit of moral blackmail was David. Nevertheless, the fact that I was hearing these rumblings from the other directors, including funnily enough one of the Grant directors, was probably a good sign. At least I hoped so.

Then the Harvard Boy made a more than useful suggestion. His concern was risk mitigation. Despite our ongoing feuds I had to concede that often what he had to say did make sense and on the odd occasion, a lot of sense. In this particular case, he believed the security of our source of supply of Windsor chardonnay champagne was at risk. Windsor's sales volume had quickly overtaken that of the Yellowglen brand and become Yellowglen's largest production item. Windsor now held more than seventy per cent and counting of Yellowglen's production output. He believed that funding the rapidly expanding working capital requirements for Windsor would have to be putting financial pressure on Yellowglen's owner, Ian Home. If that were true and Ian were sympathetic to an offer from an outsider then our source of supply for Windsor would almost certainly dry up.

Harvard Boy thought we should at least consider offering to acquire Yellowglen to shore up the future supply of Windsor. But as good an idea as his risk mitigation strategy was in respect to the security of supply for the Windsor brand, I started to salivate at the possibility of getting our hands on the Yellowglen brand. That was an even better idea. Despite its relatively small volume and premium price Yellowglen had struck an early chord with a small group of influential, better heeled wine consumers.

Ian Home was something of an enigma. Extremely nice and honourable as well as an aggressive business adventurer, he was an unusual combination. An ex grocer, he had run Ritchies Supermarkets in Victoria and had also chaired the SSW grocery wholesaling business for many years. In the 1970s Ian had succumbed to that seductive and invariably financially debilitating siren's call of establishing his own vineyard and had purchased fifty-eight hectares of land at Smythesdale, ten kilometres west of Ballarat. His intention was to have one of the local wineries turn his grapes into table wine which he then planned to sell under the Yellowglen brand, an excellent name he had coined one evening when having dinner with his wife, Dorothy. It reminded me of the droll statement made by Burt Bryant, long gone 3UZ race caller and creator of colourful similes and metaphors, that, 'I've never heard of a good horse with a bad name.'

Having built a very nice home on the vineyard site Ian and Dorothy found to their dismay that their vineyard had two problems. Low grape yields made the vineyard less than viable and what grapes were being produced had ripening difficulties, largely because of Ballarat's generally cold, low hours of sunshine climate. Smythedale's low lying micro climate had exacerbated those difficulties. Ian's idea of producing high quality table wines was not looking like much of a winner.

In addressing the problem Ian came up with a creative and seemingly bizarre alternative.

'OK, let's make a right angle turn here. If we can't get the grapes ripe enough to make table wine we can certainly get them ripe enough to make champagne (sparkling wines are lower in alcohol and therefore need less grape sugar, the key determinant of the level of alcohol). Let's establish a champagne cellar and create a premium Australian champagne instead.'

As it turned out, it was brilliantly prescient and one of the rare cases, despite the myth to the contrary, in which a problem has successfully been turned into an opportunity. But the plan to execute his vision was even more incisive. He imported Champagne maker, Dominique Landrigan from France and his intuition was right on the money. Ian's entrepreneurial approach created in Australia an embryonic but potentially highly lucrative new market segment. He had discovered that most elusive of all marketing's gems, creating credibility by being different. His French winemaker seemed to be the key.

But the Harvard Boy's intuition was also on the money. His batting average was improving. The financing of maturing stock had become a real problem for Ian Home's limited financial resources. The more successful he was in creating demand for the Yellowglen brand and the more successful Mildara was in continuing to build Windsor's sales, the greater was Ian's problem of funding the necessary build-up of maturing inventory ahead of the sales curve.

Entering into the contract to produce Mildara's Windsor champagne, which had initially turned maturing inventory earmarked for the Yellowglen brand into cash, had for Ian seemed like a great idea at the time. But Windsor's unexpected level of success and the need for a much larger and more rapid build-up in stock had made Ian's funding problem worse, in fact untenable. He candidly admitted this to me when I arrived, hot to trot, two days after the Mildara board meeting.

The conversation went something like this.

'Ian, we would like to assist your funding issues by taking an equity interest in your business.'

'I might be prepared to consider that,' he said.

'That's good, but how would you feel if we made an offer for at least fifty per cent?'

'I might be prepared to consider that,' said Ian, his face breaking into a cheesy grin.

Feeling pretty cheesy myself I said, 'well, to be honest Ian, we would really like to buy the lot and if that were the case we would also like you to join the Mildara board.'

Ian had obviously anticipated the real reason for my visit because his response was rapid fire. 'OK, but the price would need to be $1 million, plus inventory and I get to keep the house.'

I could have pushed back on that price given the apparent financial pressure that Ian was under but like the Killawarra deal at Wynn's some years earlier I felt that would have been overkill. We had a good deal. Let's not be too greedy.

'Done,' I said.

The whole process took less than three minutes. Ian was delighted but I was delirious. I would need to be very careful driving back to Melbourne. There was only one other deal in my business life that would create a greater feeling of euphoria and that was yet to come. A total price of $2 million for Yellowglen (we later purchased Ian's house for $300,000) turned out to be a steal, although we had no idea at the time how much of a steal. Within four years, admittedly with some modest assistance from Mildara's wherewithal, sales of Yellowglen had exploded from 100,000 bottles a year to more than one million. By then the brand was producing a profit that valued the brand at well in excess of $40 million. Ian's strategic right angle turn had succeeded way beyond his wildest dreams. Unfortunately for Ian he was not the major beneficiary. Mildara's shareholders were.

By the time we had reached the higher sales level the early adopters of the Yellowglen brand had moved on. At social functions whenever my involvement with Yellowglen became known I would get, almost on cue, 'Oh Yellowglen used to be fantastic but it's now not as good as it used to be.'

I would usually smile and say something like, 'well I suppose beauty is always in the eyes of the beholder.' The reality was that the product was far superior to that of its early days but again, in the minds of the early adopters, there were too many dickheads and losers now buying it.

As with Seaview in 1972, and Killawarra in 1981, we were able to exploit someone else's creativity. We had brought capital, distribution strength and financial and marketing nous to the table. But the far more difficult, valuable and elusive task of creating Yellowglen's image had been completed long before we arrived.

Was it possible we had a genuine competitive advantage in being able to recognise and then exploit the creativity of others by turning financially unsuccessful businesses into success stories?

Predictably, the Harvard Boy was again dismissive of my suggestion that we continue to take such an opportunistic and less than structured approach to our future growth targets. Despite our rapid profit growth, the elevation in our ROI and our rapidly increasing market share, not to mention Mildara's escalating share price, the chairman continued to insist we pursue a more conventional and tangible long term strategy for maintaining that growth and the battles between us continued to rage. I had to concede that the probabilities supported his textbook view but intuitively I believed, given the poor profit record of participants in the wine industry, that opportunities would present themselves, we would identify them and hopefully exploit them.

It was at this point that director Bob Hollick assumed the role of board powerbroker. He was about to throw his hole card on to the table, the one already labelled 'the big white hope'. An industry guru on vineyards and a key contributor to the development of the mechanical harvester that revolutionised grape picking Bob had broken the Australian powerlifting record for seventy-year olds and was relentlessly determined when he set his mind to something. As well as being concerned about the possibility of my being wooed by another wine company, Bob felt that insufficient credit had been given to those responsible for the company's success and he had become tired of the chairman's continuing attempts to dominate the agenda and the outcomes. Much to the Harvard Boy's dismay and his cry that the directors just 'didn't understand,' as well as David Grant's indignant opposition, Bob garnered sufficient board support for Peter North to be removed as chairman, Richard Haselgrove to replace him and for me to be formally appointed managing director and CEO.

A few months later *Business Review Weekly*, Australia's leading business magazine, devoted a large portion of one edition to Australia's most wanted executives. The magazine had commissioned Australia's major executive search and personnel placement firms to select and rank Australia's top twelve executives under the age of fifty. There was my name in the top twelve, three places ahead of my old mate from Tooheys, Bill Widerberg. Bob Hollick was very pleased with himself. I was not unpleased myself.

22

Krondorf

Yellowglen was succeeding beyond our wildest dreams and on its way to becoming a famous brand.

It was just as well because two years after the 1983 new products roll-out those new products were slowly hitting the skids, continuing to make progress but with predictably declining growth rates. The major growth was now being generated by the newly acquired Yellowglen. Even at this early stage Yellowglen was far exceeding our most heroic projections and showing all the hallmarks of becoming a superstar.

Yellowglen had also blown Windsor out of the water. Windsor had been our second most successful new product introduction and before our purchase of Yellowglen had been on the way to establishing itself as a significant brand of the future. But as hard as we now pushed retailers to promote both sparkling wine products at their two quite different price points, the retailers' and consumers' preference was always Yellowglen. It was a nice problem to have because Yellowglen's bottle gross margin was almost three times that of Windsor.

It was a good example of the importance of credibility in the wine market enhanced by some myth and magic. The beautiful irony was that despite our best efforts for them to do otherwise consumers wanted to pay sixty per cent more for Yellowglen.

Yellowglen was priced at around $10 a bottle and Windsor around $6. The preference of retailers and consumers was always Yellowglen rather than Windsor yet it was compellingly ironic they were exactly the same product. Naturally, we kept that piece of information to ourselves. But it hardly mattered because the market wanted

Yellowglen and consumers couldn't get enough of the higher priced product or, more accurately, the label.

Yellowglen's huge success was masking the disappointing but not unexpected realisation that further market penetration by our earlier new products could no longer be relied upon. We all know a new product will not keep growing forever. After a while it isn't a new product any more. What we don't know and therefore cannot plan for is at what point in the growth cycle is it likely to stop. Mindful of this phenomenon we had tried introducing further new products and some line extensions but had largely come up empty handed. We were beginning to show the worrying signs of becoming a one trick pony and the Harvard Boy's criticism of our opportunistic approach was becoming more difficult to deflect.

We were also faced with the marketer's classic dilemma. Did we attempt to rejuvenate those ageing new products by throwing money at them — often the conventional tactic following a product's market appeal having gone off the boil? My view was a simple one. Given the existing set of market dynamics it seemed equilibrium had already been reached with our now not so new products. The market was delivering a message that would require kicking against the wind to change that equilibrium. I didn't like the odds. In any case, I felt we had other options or, perhaps more to the point, I wanted to believe we had other options.

The conclusions drawn from my contemplative staring out the window thinking time were about to be tested. As my old boss at Wynn's, Frank Devine used to say, 'some people sit and think and others just sit.' Our major need was for a table wine brand that would not only provide further profitable growth but one with potential for substantial longevity. We either had to introduce our own new brand that would strike a chord in the market place or acquire an existing one. To that end, I had my eye on three potential acquisitions; the Barossa Valley-based Krondorf, Adelaide's Woodley and the Hunter Valley-based Tyrrell's. These were all marketing successes but not performing to anywhere near their financial potential. It seemed a much better bet to acquire one and to work on making the brand financially successful.

Woodley was owned by Ron Brierley's Industrial Equity Limited. Brierley, one of Australia's original corporate raiders, was forever on the lookout for undervalued companies, particularly those that were going through short-term financial difficulties. Until the 1970s takeover bids for Australian public companies had invariably been friendly but Ron Brierley broke that mould. He got down and dirty by making on-market offers to dissatisfied shareholders rather than the more popular, genteel and behind the scenes approach of talking to the directors. His strategy was to replace tired or incompetent management, restore value and then on-sell the company at a profit.

Industrial Equity had picked up Woodley Wines by default when acquiring Moran and Cato, a poorly performed Australian grocery chain. Apparently, Ron Brierley had not been aware that Moran and Cato even owned a wine business. Historically, Woodley had been known for its Three Roses sherry but a table wine brand, Queen Adelaide had been introduced which, without much or any initiative from its new owner, had started kicking a few goals and was now on the way to becoming a success. It was another example of a name and label that happened to strike the right note with wine consumers. I felt Queen Adelaide had significant potential and might be a good clip on for Mildara but I wasn't sure as to how I might go about approaching the awesome Brierley.

Having spent a morning in Sydney with Gary Byrne, our New Sales Wales manager, I had arranged to see my old Castlemaine Tooheys boss, Lloyd Hartigan, early that afternoon to chat about old times. Strolling along Macquarie Street considering what I might do about lunch I was about to pass a building displaying the Industrial Equities logo. On impulse, I swallowed hard, squared the shoulders, effected a neat right angle turn and marched up to reception. It was no surprise to anyone that executive chairman Ron Brierley was not in. The reality was that he was in but because he was a surprisingly shy and reclusive man he rarely made himself available to anyone let alone some cheeky young bugger who had walked in off the street. As I turned to leave, the receptionist casually mentioned that deputy chairman, Bill Lowenthall, Brierley's chief operating officer, might be available. If so, would I like to see him? Is the Pope a Catholic? She walked me through a door marked private. Everyone likes to walk through a door marked private. Ushered into Bill Lowenthall's cavernous office I stammered out an introduction and, trying to effect 'cool' but in reality shitting my pants, blurted out that I would like to make an offer to buy Woodley. He threw his head back and laughed but it was either one of his slow days or his response was not without agenda because he glanced at his watch and said, 'I'm just about to go out for lunch (to the nearby Australian American Club) why don't you come with me.'

Predictably Mr Lowenthall, now my friend Bill, said that Woodley was not on the market but added that he was always interested in offers for any of Industrial Equity's businesses. Remarkably, he gave me a price range he thought the business might be worth as well as three weeks to do some due diligence and then make an offer.

'How easy is this,' I said to myself.

I had really hit the big time, rubbing shoulders with such headline grabbers as Brierley and Lowenthall.

Three weeks later I arrived in Sydney to stitch up the deal. Bill and I had developed an excellent relationship and I couldn't wait to get the deal done at my generous offer of $3.5 million, cleverly pitched slightly above Bill's earlier top of the range value of $3.3 million. Fully satisfied with my reflection in the gilt-framed mirror in Industrial Equity's reception area I bounded up to the receptionist with more than a decent spring in my step. I could already see next day's business headline, 'King gets himself a Queen.'

'What a wonderful thing it is to play the role of the great businessman,' I laughed to myself.

Bill Lowenthall was of the old school and believed there was no good way to deliver bad news other than in person and that it should be delivered quickly. Having immediately asked for the value of my generous offer, he didn't stuff about but got straight down to business. Withdrawing his rapier from its scabbard, he neatly slipped it between my ribs and casually drove it all the way home. Holding out his hand (shades of 'here's your hat what's your hurry') he observed in the drollest of tones, 'well Ray, it looks like this is going to be a very short meeting.'

Fortunately, my reaction, unlike that of the *Four Corners* thunderbolt, was not recorded for posterity. Surely he was joking. He wasn't. The meeting lasted every bit of thirty seconds. Another thirty seconds later I was back on the Macquarie Street pavement looking for a taxi back to the airport. The Lord giveth and the Lord taketh.

The next day Karl Seppelt, the CEO of Seppelt Wines, announced that he had agreed to purchase Woodley for $5.2 million. Bill had chewed me up and spat me out. He had either blind-sided me by shopping the deal to another potential buyer or had used me as a lever to increase Seppelt's offer price. There had to be a lesson in there somewhere and it was loud and clear. I was playing outside my league. And my now erstwhile friend, Bill Lowenthall, was sitting in his office smiling the smile of the gander that got the goose.

¶

Krondorf Wines Limited had been established in the late '70s by two highly ambitious young South Australian winemaking tyros, Grant Burge and Ian Wilson, who had met up at Roseworthy Agricultural College. They didn't want to work for anyone but themselves. Having established their own business they had immediate success in the market place. They were joint managing directors, one of the rare instances in which that structure appeared to work, and were known as the Simon and Garfunkel of the wine industry. Grant did the winemaking and Ian did the marketing. In one of the wine industry's few successful advertising campaigns they had used the songsters' hit record, *Bridge over Troubled Waters* as the theme for a highly successful Krondorf radio commercial. This success had been underpinned by the publicity surrounding their Jimmy Watson Trophy win in 1980. They were kicking goals from every angle. Then reality set in.

Grant and Ian had listed Krondorf on the South Australian Stock Exchange in 1983 to attract funds to finance the inevitable problem of working capital, in the process diluting each of their shareholdings to around twenty per cent. But despite a stream of tantalising and puffed up press releases Krondorf was not delivering from a financial perspective. It seemed to me that the Krondorf shareholders who had generously responded to the puffery in the float prospectus had to be decidedly unhappy with the company's languishing share price.

In June 1985 I telephoned Grant and suggested the three of us meet for lunch. He was reticent to do so but persistence won out and he ultimately agreed. As it happened, the lunch was a laugh a minute affair and went on a lot longer than any of us might have anticipated, causing me to miss my flight back to Melbourne. I now felt I was playing in the proper league, Grant and Ian being far more my cup of tea than Bill Lowenthall. During lunch I warmed up with some medium paced remarks extolling what they had achieved. As there was no simple way of saying I would be happy to talk to them if they were ever interested in selling the business, I came straight out and said as smooth as silk that 'I would be happy to talk to them if they were ever interested in selling the business.' Not unexpectedly, they were dismissive of my suggestion. It is probably fairer to say they were insulted, pointing out to me in no uncertain terms that Krondorf was an infinitely superior business to that of Mildara. A smiling Ian Wilson then fired back a biting jibe mischievously asking whether Mildara might be for sale.

From my perspective, the get-together had two purposes: what could I learn about the Krondorf business I didn't already know and to drop a large enough pebble in the pond to see what might eventuate. Intuitively, I felt, or at least hoped, that Krondorf's financial under-performance would ultimately lead its independent shareholders to force the sale of the business. Krondorf's listing on the Stock Exchange had provided valuable working capital but the potential downside had always been the business's exposure to the whim of the other shareholders. If and when that occurred I wanted to be at the head of the queue.

As with the Queen Adelaide brand I felt that Krondorf would be an excellent clip on for Mildara. Not only would it give us access to another major price segment of the table wine market but it would provide identification with South Australia's highly regarded Barossa Valley. It would also provide instant brand strength and growth potential. Our sales teams still had plenty of capacity to handle the brand. My back of the envelope guesses suggested that there was an excellent chance we could meet our twenty per cent ROI target if the opportunity came to fruition.

I was far more convinced of Krondorf's compatibility and potential value after our enjoyable lunch. As I had hoped, neither Grant nor Ian was overly familiar with the tricky subject of financial dynamics. Both were focussed on sales revenue and market share, pursuits in which they had done very well, but the dynamics of gross margin and profitability seemed to be something of a mystery. Following a couple of Ian's candid comments I now had a much better fix (or so I thought) on what their sales volumes were. It was a fairly simple exercise to apply what prices and gross margin a bottle I thought the brand was capable of and, by extension, determine the total gross profit Krondorf might bring to the party. I made a conservative estimate of the additional operating expenses that might be required to support the additional volume of business and applied my standard but simple valuation criteria of multiplying the net contribution number by five. This was the price Mildara would be prepared to pay for the business in order to meet our ROI target of twenty per cent.

Critics of this approach would suggest a purchaser shouldn't have to pay for the value that he might bring to the table. But I believed that apportioning where value might come from was irrelevant as well as a distraction. The relevant question was; is there a benefit to be had or not? Our shareholders wouldn't care where the value came from as long as it ended up in their pockets. I had quickly, if conveniently, come to the conclusion that in negotiating a deal your only concern should be what is in it for you and to ignore the distraction of what the other party might be getting out of it. If there happened to be more in it for him than might have appeared to be equitable so much the better if you were getting what you wanted. At least you would be able to get the deal done. This was the philosophy I had applied in acquiring seventeen businesses over a seventeen year period, each of which it must be said were not always world beating successes. In the acquisition game you pay your money and you take your chances.

The only strategic negative was that Krondorf appeared to be largely a white wine brand. Grant Burge was yet to make his name as an excellent maker of Barossa shiraz. If we wanted a red wine brand we would have to look elsewhere.

In the meantime, I convinced myself there was a red wine opportunity in the form of a small winery by the name of Balgownie. Balgownie had been established by ex-pharmacist Stuart Anderson some ten years earlier on seventy-seven hectares near Bendigo. Like that of Yellowglen, the site of Balgownie's vineyard was an old gold mining tenement. Stuart Anderson had developed an awesome and enviable reputation for his red wines which, being a Francophile, he made in the austere French style. Again, the word on the street was that he wasn't making much if any money. Stuart was close to sixty years of age and the word was that he might be susceptible to an approach. I loved the Balgownie name and its classically designed French inspired label but the products were priced at the ultra-premium end of the market (around $20 a bottle, a pretty robust price in 1985) and Stuart already sold all the wine he could produce from the less than thirteen hectares of vineyard planted to vines. His annual production capacity was less than 40,000 bottles and could not be increased in the short term. I had speculated that the Balgownie brand might be capable of being successfully leveraged to a second label (using Mildara red wine) to compete in the much larger, more commercially priced red wine market.

Stuart's asking price was $1.5 million. Within reason the price we might have to pay was not the issue. The issue was whether we could creatively use the Balgownie brand to build a much bigger presence in our target market (around $8 a bottle). And that outcome would be in the lap of the gods. If we were successful the purchase price (as with Yellowglen) would be totally irrelevant. So far, our batting average on accurately predicting the response of the wine consumer had been pretty good. I was confident that, given Stuart Anderson's credibility and stellar standing in the market place, we would have all the appropriate intangibles in place.

As well as being an excellent wine maker, Stuart Anderson was impressively handsome, a patrician, a dilettante and a collector of antique sports cars. He was also extremely strong willed, prickly and something of a snob.

Journalist Philip White wrote in the *National Times*, a now defunct Melbourne Sunday newspaper under the headline, A TOUCH OF SILVER FOX MAKES FOR AN INTERESTING BLEND,

> 'Stuart Anderson and Ray King are chalk and cheese, old lace and arsenic, north and south, east and west. One could never imagine the twine entwining. But somehow they did. Anderson, the Bugatti besotted, bassoon playing ex-pharmacist with the pukkah handlebar moustache, just a flash of gold on the correct tooth and the cultured voice playing its cozy, anecdotal style of conversation sold his beloved Balgownie to King. Ray King, 'the silver fox,' is your classic wine marketing ace. King was the man who created Mildara's Jimmy Watson Classic, the wine which would have won the Jimmy Watson trophy had it been the same wine as the very similar one from just up from the cellar which did win but was available only in limited quantity. He is the fellow responsible for the Mildara Coonawarra Rhine Riesling with the Petaluma lookalike label. King's presence in the manager's chair will send the odd twinge of fear through the wimpy purists but the accountants and shareholders love him; he gets the money rolling in quickly and steadily.'

I had arranged for Stuart to spend time with Maurice Dean, Mildara's manager of operations and his winemakers to sample our better wines that were in the tank at Merbein. This was a prelude to my plan for Stuart to develop a superior red blend he would be happy to put his name to and spearhead the thrust into our target market.

But there were too many cooks in the kitchen.

The get-together proved little short of a disaster. Stuart was overtly dismissive of the wines he tasted and I soon learned why. Some of the Mildara winemakers had met Stuart in other circumstances and they hadn't liked him, not one little bit, leading to more than a whiff of conspiracy. The Mildara boys had protected their best red blends and made available to Stuart only their less than better wines. I should have anticipated their inclination to do exactly that irrespective of whether they liked Stuart or not.

Winemakers are creative types. They also have a strong disposition to behave like prima donnas, particularly if they feel their integrity is in danger of being compromised. I hadn't thought all the possibilities through. Now on the horns of a dilemma, did I insist the Mildara winemakers take one on the chin for the greater good by giving up their better wines to someone they felt looked down upon them? I decided to defy the odds and gamble on Stuart's image and reputation carrying the day with retailers and consumers in the hope he would be prepared to play my game. It was a glorious but vain hope.

Feeling beholden to no one, Stuart made it more than clear he felt he had been compromised. The wine writers duly damned the wines with faint praise. Without the overt support of Stuart and to a lesser degree the wine writers, the gamble wasn't going to pay off. I had to accept I had stuffed it up.

As it became increasingly obvious our Balgownie play wasn't going to work we would now have to look elsewhere for a successful red wine brand. I wasn't particularly brave about dealing with the Balgownie failure and began treating Stuart like a bad smell. This made us about even because Stuart had quickly arrived at the position that I was pretty much on the nose myself.

With the relationship at low ebb I made it easy for him to walk away from his five year commitment and to create another life for himself. Predictably, Stuart never forgave me for turning my back on him and his beloved brand and he made certain my actions were cast in the least attractive light to his band of followers

The Balgownie failure was a blow but I conveniently rationalised that, as in American baseball, 'nobody bat's a thousand'. With some gnashing of teeth I was quickly drawn to what routinely became my default option — accept the truth and try to move on as quickly as possible, which I was happy to do with the speed of a startled gazelle. Moving on was facilitated by a light appearing at the end of the tunnel — the Krondorf train was about to arrive at the station.

Four months after our enjoyable lunch the wine industry tom-toms were again beating out their rhythm and the message was that Krondorf's creditors were unhappy and crying out to be paid. That was the thing about the wine industry. Industry matters were an open secret and there was an awful lot of loose talk with people knowing stuff they shouldn't by rights know about. In October 1985 joint managing director Ian Wilson, always a whimsical character, offloaded around half his Krondorf shareholding to O'Connor Investments, a South Australian-based family investment company. Shortly afterwards, the Krondorf directors made a ten per cent placement of new shares to O'Connor Investments at fifty cents a share, lifting the family's shareholding to eighteen per cent.

The *Financial Review* quoted a Krondorf spokesman as saying that the capital raising was required to support a Krondorf export initiative, a furphy if ever I had heard one. The Krondorf board of directors were obviously hoping the O'Connor family's shareholding would provide a strong defensive bulwark in keeping potential marauders at bay. But the directors had pulled the wrong rein, South Australian sentiment in this particular case not counting for much. We received a telephone call to the effect that O'Connor Investment's parcel of Krondorf shares might be for sale and were we interested. Were we what? Of course we were interested. Ian Wilson had, helpfully as it turned out, spilled the beans as to my motive for our enjoyable lunch in order to add a bit of sizzle in supporting the sale of his parcel of shares to O'Connor Investments in October. When we returned the call we learned the family was decidedly pissed off. They apparently believed they had been misled by Wilson and then by the Krondorf directors as to the reason for the share placement. O'Connor was now a seller and seeking to offload the Krondorf investment at 60 cents a share, in the process producing a neat and tidy twenty per cent earner in less than two months.

Following a hastily arranged telephone hook-up the Mildara board approved the purchase of the O'Connor parcel after which our CFO, David Smith, started making frantic calls to the ANZ Bank to see if we could pay for it. The following day, Richard Haselgrove and I arrived on Grant Burge's doorstep. Despite Grant being quoted in that day's *Adelaide Advertiser* to the effect that the Krondorf directors, who had their foot on sixty-five per cent of the company's shares, would not be sellers Grant was clearly shaken by the company's increasingly rumoured financial problems and his joint managing director's decision to apparently head for the exit. Grant's Krondorf shares had been pledged as collateral for bank loans that financed his significant personal vineyard holdings and he was now under pressure. We offered him 60 cents a share. He countered with sixty-five cents. As with O'Connor Investments we didn't stuff around by trying to nickel and dime him and agreed to his price. We probably could have done a better deal but I was still confident we could make it work. The other Krondorf shareholders quickly caved in and we had Krondorf for $6.16 million. It was our third acquisition in eighteen months but more importantly we now had a presence in the Barossa Valley, the Wall Street of the Australian wine industry. David Smith's calls to the ANZ bank became even more frantic. A month later Krondorf released its first half results. To nobody's surprise the directors announced a significant loss for the six months to December.

The *Financial Review* led with, 'KRONDORF COUP SHOWS MILDARA A FORCE TO BE RECKONED WITH'.

Mark Shield wrote in the *Age* under the headline, 'YEAR OF THE BATTLE FOR THE WINE INDUSTRY':

'One of the few who will probably survive the battle is Ray King from Mildara. Mr King is one of the new breed, high profile marketing men. As a measure of his star he rejoices under the sobriquet of the silver fox. The silver refers to his shock of white hair and the fox is supposed to be a mark of cunning. But there is much more than cunning in his make-up. He's a chameleon with an astute business brain and a ruthless streak. There is a healthy quantity of ego but it remains in control and never gets in the way of business. There is an ability to get on with the people who matter.

He's a great defuser of arguments — try to pick a fight and he'll derail you by agreeing with you and admitting he was wrong. That can be exasperating. He has caused more than exasperation amongst his competitors. Some of the Mildara labels bear a striking resemblance to other companies' labels.

When I tackled Mr King about his copycat labels he tipped the usual bucket of cold water on the subject by saying, 'in retrospect I don't think they were all such a good idea.'

So when I met Mr King the other day to hear the news about the Krondorf acquisition I was under no illusions about a probing in-depth interview. It was more a case of listening to what he wanted me to hear. There is no way Ray King would ever let a secret slip, as the control and the delivery is flawless. There is just the right amount of confidentiality in the tone, a wisp of flattery and the odd expletive to illustrate he can be one of the boys. It was masterly stuff worthy of the silver fox and I came away from the meeting believing that the Krondorf move was very astute indeed, particularly as in future it will have the marketing talents of Ray King.

Perhaps the most galling thing about the carpetbagging Mr King is that he is easy to like. Every purist bone in my body dictates we should be implacable enemies but that is impossible because he is urbane and witty company with a sense of humour. You get the impression that he is playing a grand game by his own set of rules and loving every minute of it because he is winning. Even in Australia we are learning to like winners.'

The moment in the sun was nice but now came the harder part. To meet our twenty per cent ROI target we needed Krondorf to make an EBIT of at least $1.2 million. Given its dismal half year profit result that task was going to be a bit tougher than I originally had in mind. Krondorf's branded annual sales volume of just under 1,200,000 bottles was almost twenty-five per cent less than the figure I had been led to believe by Ian Wilson at our lunch six months earlier.

Nevertheless, irrespective of whether I had been the victim of an Ian Wilson sting, I believed we might still be in the ballpark to meet our ROI target. But we would have to be more ruthless on operating expenses than originally estimated. I figured that with some price increases we could lift Krondorf's gross margin on each case to around $15 but this meant we could only afford around $300,000 in additional operating expenses. A bit more downsizing was called for than I had originally estimated. Ninety per cent of Krondorf's sales, marketing and administration staff were let go over the next four weeks and the Mildara sales teams added the Krondorf sales and distribution activities to their existing product portfolio. It took us around four months to renegotiate Krondorf's inefficient trading terms with major retailers and wholesalers and bring them into line with our own. By the beginning of the 1986/87 financial year the financial dynamics of the acquisition were within our parameters.

Despite little or no contribution from three months' ownership of our new acquisition Mildara reported a thirty-one per cent increase in profit before interest and tax to $6.0 million for the year to June 1986.

Eighteen months after our acquisition of Krondorf, Grant Burge, still only in his mid-thirties, came to the conclusion that he was neither fish nor fowl within the Mildara organisation. As had been the case with Stuart Anderson I agreed to let Grant off the hook and allow him to go back to doing his own thing. Grant then established the Grant Burge brand and has operated very successfully ever since. These days, Grant Burge Barossa Shiraz is a constant companion in Dawn's and my wine cellar.

As for Ian Wilson, I was curious as to what I might be able to learn from him so I offered him a six months contract to provide consultancy services on a needs basis. That largely amounted to his coming to Melbourne every fortnight to have lunch. He was excellent company. He was well put together, square jawed, finely chiselled, now all leather pants and mandarin jackets and letting it all hang out; gay. It was 1986 and the AIDS epidemic was all the rage in the world media. I received a lot of raised eyebrows from our restaurant companions at adjoining tables. That was their problem, not mine. Sadly, after a lingering illness, Ian died of a rumoured AIDS related problem before the decade was out.

23

Jamiesons Run

On a magical autumnal day in 1986 Hugh Cuthbertson strolled into my office to ask for a job.

I had finally relocated from the Spartan surroundings in Mulgrave and established a small head office in Dundas Place, Albert Park, above a then struggling restaurant by the name of Ricardo's. Chief financial officer, David Smith had relocated from Mildura and had brought with him some key accounting personnel. Judy Hacker, an FMCG specialist, had joined as marketing manager now that Bill Stevens was spending an increasing proportion of his time on exports. It was a lean and hungry collegiate group with each member devoted to his/her autonomous piece of the business, our in baskets invariably overflowing. I was available for problems they couldn't solve but largely the team was left to its own devices, a situation everyone seemed comfortable with.

Hugh Cuthbertson hadn't asked for a job. The cheeky bugger had presented a case as to why Mildara needed him. This was convenient for me because, unknown to Hugh, I had finally conceded that the pips were squeaking to such a degree we did need more marketing support. Hugh had studied winemaking and marketing at Roseworthy Agricultural College and on graduating had immediately established his own business selling, of all things, the dinosaurs of the wine industry, premium fortified wines. Impressed by his initiative but less so by his choice of product I ignored the likelihood that Hugh's fledgling business was kicking shit uphill as well as his more than apparent and desperate need for a real job to support his young family ('rent up to date is it Hugh?'). One of the subjects we discussed was the style superiority of the Wolf Blass reds and Hugh was delighted to offer his thoughts — never short of a point of view was Hugh.

In the 1970s Wolf Blass had revolutionised red wine making in Australia, producing red wines that required less bottle age than the more traditional Australian red wines. They were softer wines with less acid. Wolf used American oak in the maturation process rather than the Australian wine industry's practice of using more traditional French oak barrels. American oak, particularly Kentucky blue grass oak imparted a sweeter and less astringent wood character. In simple terms, his range of red wines tasted better to the average wine consumer than those of most of his traditional competitors and the Wolf Blass brand, selling across a range of price points, had become by far Australia's largest selling brand of premium and super premium red wines.

I suggested to Hugh he might travel to Coonawarra and discuss with Gavin Hogg, our senior Coonawarra winemaker, whether Wolf's highly successful red wine style could be matched. Gavin Hogg was a high achiever on the bullshit scale and it seemed immediately apparent that Hugh may be no slouch in that department either. If something came out of Hugh's discussions with Gavin there may be a job for him. As I had suspected, they got on very well and were enthusiastic about the project. After playing around with a number of blends and different wood treatments they were in agreement we could more than meet the objective. Hugh had his job.

Hugh's involvement in the ultimate success of Jamiesons Run was to be his most significant contribution to Mildara's fortunes. It would be a contribution difficult for anyone to surpass let alone Hugh. But over the years it would not be his only idea that proved valuable: he was good at ideas. But often what Hugh was personally charged with didn't work out all that well. After a while you realised others had to mould his ideas into practical shape. Then they did work. His contribution to Mildara's success by way of ideas stood the test of time because by the time of my retirement in 1999 Hugh was still presenting them.

23 Jamiesons Run

The search for a red wine brand to complement our success with Yellowglen and our solid share of the white wine market with the acquired Krondorf brand had already seen the failure of the Balgownie project. And my promising early discussions with Murray Tyrrell to buy his Hunter Valley-based wine business had also led nowhere. The fact that Murray was equally as keen as me to get his own way was probably not all that irrelevant as to the reason for his discontinuing our talks. Increasingly, it looked as though we would have to seek the answer to a red wine brand internally.

For more than two years, like a security blanket, I had kept a new product idea locked away in my bottom drawer, nervous about testing its veracity. Each time I was tempted I rationalised that I was waiting for the right opportunity. While it remained in my bottom drawer I could continue to dream. Hugh's arrival tipped me over the edge and I decided it was shit or bust time to let the genie out of the lamp.

Bill Stevens had come in more than useful from a slightly different standpoint. He had arranged for Dawn and me to spend time with John Gay, a Californian-based wine consultant during our February 1984 trip to the US. Fifteen years later John Gay was hired by Keith Lambert to spearhead Australia's Rosemount Wines' highly successful export thrust into the US.

Dawn and I spent a few days skiing in the Rockies and then joined John for a couple of weeks during which he introduced us to the better Californian wineries as well as some of the movers and shakers in the US wine industry. The US wine industry was going through a particularly tough time. Rumour had it that the Bank of America had fifty-seven wineries on its books that were either in administration or in the process of being liquidated. The Californians suffered from the same diseases that afflicted most Australian wine companies except that at that time their problems appeared to be more terminal. They had succeeded in turning wine company failure into an art form, an observation I had somewhat artlessly made in a rush of blood at a wine industry luncheon and which unsurprisingly earned me the undying enmity of the US wine press.

One of the Californian wineries that had closed its doors, never to reopen them, was Ehlers Lane. I had asked John Gay to provide us with what he thought were the top ten US wine label designs (you can't teach an old dog new tricks) and the Ehlers Lane label was among them. The label showed a misty, impressionist pastoral scene that to all intents and purposes could have been set in Australia.

There was nothing like it on the Australian market and to me it was the standout in a clutch of very interesting labels. The Americans were already well ahead of the Aussies in having moved on from their previous traditional label designs. The Ehlers Lane label was highly original and had what I thought was a lovely feel. I had filed it away in my ideas file where it sat for more than two years waiting for its call to greatness. That file — of course, other peoples' ideas — was a particularly thick one, a more than useful practice I had picked up from David Wynn and Bill Stevens.

¶

Ray Barraclough, a Jack of all trades, had been employed by Mildara all his working life. In 1986 Ray was spending most of his time on a variety of logistics and marketing services issues. Unlike Hugh Cuthbertson, Ray didn't have much flair. However, despite not having a creative bone in his body, he was doggedly determined and if you wanted anything done to the letter Ray was your man. He also possessed an extensive library of publications on the wine industry, particularly those of a historical nature and when visiting Merbein I usually dropped into his crammed and untidy office to have a yarn with him.

On this day, as usual, papers spilled out of Ray's carelessly stacked manila folders, indiscriminate dog-eared documents and memorandums obliterated the surface of his large desk and fat computer reports were randomly and precariously stacked around his small office. Ray was the sort of bloke who worked best in a little chaos. I removed the folders resting on his straight-backed visitor's chair, picked up the book hidden underneath and began leafing through it while Ray regaled me with the details of his latest transport problem.

I found the book far more interesting than Ray's transport problem which I was more than happy to leave in his capable hands. The book focussed on the historical trials and tribulations of the Sunraysia region. I thought it looked interesting enough to browse through on the flight back to Melbourne. During the flight I was struck with a bolt of lightning — of the metaphorical variety. The 1890s had been a particularly difficult period in Australia's economic history. It had been an era of unseasonal heat and drought and Australia's boom and bust economy had descended into one of its regular deep recessions. One of the Sunraysia region's business failures had been its largest sheep station, Jamiesons Run. I felt the name had huge potential as a wine brand. The next day I put Mildara's foot on it by registering the name with the Patents Office. I had a name to go with the label concept that had been biding its time in my ideas file.

This was not to be the last time that Mildara would benefit from serendipity. In 1994 Dawn and I were having dinner in our hotel in San Francisco. Having been brought up to date at lunch by our US president, Peter Perrin, neither of us was particularly hungry and we had decided to make do with a glass of wine and some cheese. We studied the cheese menu and immediately looked at each other, eyes shining and eyebrows high.

'That's a good name,' I thought I said, although Dawn's recollection of the epiphany suggested this was one of those times when I was not the first 'to see the sea'.

Pepperjack, a local cheese, was the 'cheese of the week'. It was still working hours in Australia so I rang Peter Thomas, our company secretary, and had him register the name in Australia. Given the peppery nature of Barossa Valley shiraz we both thought it was an ideal name for a wine from that region. A year later in Frankfurt, dog tired after our long flight from Australia, we were both taken by an advertisement on TV for Yello, a sparkling wine with a ceramic label printed directly on to the bottle. Again, I was immediately on the phone to Peter Thomas to register Yellow, which was to become our highly successful understudy to Yellowglen.

Following Hugh Cuthbertson's chance appearance in Dundas Place we now had a wine concept to go with the name and the label. Bench testing the blend that Gavin Hogg and Hugh had ultimately decided on got us pretty excited as well. We added a few sheep to the Ehler's Lane pastoral scene to make it look Australian and released Jamiesons Run in early 1987 with four months' bottle age.

Everything appeared to hit the mark and Jamiesons Run was an instant success despite my alarm four months before release. As the wine was going through the bottling process I did something you should never do. I removed a bottle from the production line for a quick tasting. In stark contrast to the smooth eclectic blend that had lifted our hearts in the laboratory I was startled to find the wine thin and astringent. We all knew it normally took a few months for a wine to settle down after the bottling process but Jamiesons was my baby and I couldn't help myself in committing this cardinal sin. Perhaps the stars were not going to line up after all.

Maurice Dean shared my concern. Could the wine really improve that much to meet our hopes and aspirations in such a short time? The litmus test was the ageing, slightly balding, enigmatic winemaker, Jack Schultz.

'What do you reckon Jack,' I asked somewhat pensively.

'Well,' he said, rolling his eyes at his managing director's misdeed, 'you wouldn't expect it to be any bloody good at the moment would you?'

The non-committal rebuff by the man of few words successfully put his managing director in his place and I could do little else but take my punishment, silently shaking my head in response. For the next few months I remained edgy, apprehensive, trying not to think about it. We waited, impatiently, for the wine to do the right thing and turn the corner.

In October 1987, James Halliday, Australia's leading wine writer at the time, wrote in the *Weekend Australian*,

'The 1985 Jamiesons Run is going against the trend. Initially it was possible to pick it up for about $6.99 and a few outlets still have it at that price. More probably you will have to pay at least $7.99 but at this price the wine is still an absolute bargain. Grown and produced by Mildara from its Coonawarra vineyards it is a blend of cabernet sauvignon, cabernet franc, merlot and shiraz and has into the bargain been accorded some sophisticated and very successful oak treatment. The architect was Mildara's managing director, Ray King.

From the moment I first tasted the wine I felt that the Mildara winemakers had exceeded themselves. It is, in other words, almost too good. The warm, vanillan American oak flavours certainly support the drink now style of the wine. And it seems even better things are in store, with the 1986 version winning the trophy for the best wine at the 1988 Perth Show.

Poor old Ray King, he comes up with a brilliant idea, his winemakers do everything he asks of them and more and suddenly he has a product on his hands which not only doesn't need discounting but will by its own sheer quality force up the price. Life can be tough at the top sometimes.'

Such superlatives from Australia's most influential wine writer were worth a fortune to us in establishing the credibility of the brand. In combination with what I thought to be a highly suitable and seductive Australian sounding name in Jamiesons Run and a label design unique to Australia the stars had indeed moved into alignment.

But there were more things in store for the good guys.

In 1989 Jamiesons Run won the coveted Jimmy Watson Trophy. By 1990, now priced well above $10 a bottle, Jamiesons Run had supplanted Wolf Blass Yellow Label as Australia's highest selling individual premium red wine. The product had been on the market for less than four years. It was another example of the kaleidoscopic nature of the wine market and the tendency for a new wine brand to occasionally capture the imagination of consumers and rocket to success.

Gavin Hogg, front and centre the night the trophy win was announced, was asked by the media throng at the Coonawarra pub why a wine made in Coonawarra was named after a long gone sheep station in Sunraysia almost 600 kilometres away. Gavin, the bullshitter's bullshitter, had already put away a couple of early looseners and as usual was quick on his feet in stroking the journalist's question to the boundary (Gavin was an elite cricketer and had represented a South Australian country side against the MCC tourists in 1963). Somewhat less than authentically, Gavin pointed out that Jamiesons Run was a particularly large sheep station in the 1890s and stretched all the way from Sunraysia to Coonawarra and beyond, making it the biggest sheep station in Australia, if not the world.

Twenty-five years later, Jamiesons Run survives, but only just. The retail price of my baby is now trashed and its label also trashed into boring mediocrity by the simpler, cleaner lines aimed at modernisation as recommended by a succession of anaemic brand managers at Foster's. Its cachet gone, Jamiesons Run now sits among a plethora of characterless lightweights languishing in despair among the other losers at the bottom end of the market. It's hard to let go even thirty years later.

24

The eclectic period

In 1987 the entrepreneurs in Australia came out to play. And they played hard.

It was believed by just about everyone that Mildara's financial success to date was attributable to its strong brands, Yellowglen, Jamiesons Run and Krondorf. Conveniently ignored was the fact that our early success had been achieved without strong brands. There had even been a suggestion of something slightly sinister.

Having been variously described by the wine media as a hard head, a cheat, a plagiarist, a carpetbagger and the naughty boy of the wine industry, there had also been more than a just a whiff that some sleight of hand had embellished our bottom line. What wine industry cynics had in mind was the possibility that Mildara had manipulated the accounts of some of its acquisitions. A number of our competitors apparently believed, perhaps in order to assuage any feeling of inadequacy on their own part, that the profit ratios we were achieving were less than legitimate.

What they didn't realise or perhaps deliberately ignored was that taking advantage of the existing regulatory loopholes that enabled the restructuring of financial accounts of companies about to be acquired was a game too dangerous to play. That is, a game too dangerous to play unless you were the sort of guy who intended to head for the exit sooner rather than later. As others had found to their chagrin, that sort of accounting manipulation, referred to at the time as financial engineering, only came back to bite you on the bum, or more to the point your shareholders' bums, sometime later.

A glaring example of someone who played that game and played it extremely well, or badly depending on your perspective, was leading

Australian businessman Alan Jackson. Jackson added to his legitimate fame as an elite businessman by breaking the jaw of his chief operating officer at the company Christmas party in 1999, interrupting his second in command's speech to the gathered throng, bringing the speech and the chief operating officer's job to a hasty and violent end.

Jackson, CEO of industrial conglomerate BTR Nylex in the 1980s, had generated adoration little short of religious fervour from an admiring investing public. Someone had calculated that in the preceding decade Jackson had turned a shareholder's initial investment of $1 into an impressive $350. So it was with little surprise he was perceived to be a businessman somewhat out of the ordinary. Business friend Ray Horsburgh, a successful CEO, non-executive director and one time president of the Essendon Football Club, had worked for Jackson earlier in his career. He told me he thought Jackson one of the best businessmen he had come across. A consequence of Jackson's outstanding record was his being offered the CEO's role at BTR Nylex's much larger parent organisation, BTR Plc in the United Kingdom. It was in the UK that the first hint of trouble arose. A feeling of omnipotence had raised its ugly head. To the surprise of the Australian business world Jackson, who could do no wrong as far as his Australian supporters were concerned, ever so suddenly decided to call it a day and returned to Australia.

A press release stated this was a mutual decision but press speculation had it that his crass Australian style had rubbed the staid British directors the wrong way. The jungle drums suggested something else. Following his speedy return to Australia in early 1994 a number of investment opportunists, not the least being Jackson himself, were motivated to raise an initial sum of $100 million from a still adoring Australian public. Incredibly, the capital raising was to fund the acquisition of a yet to be identified group of manufacturing businesses upon which Jackson was to breathe his special brand of magic. The vagueness of the proposal beggared belief but such was Jackson's reputation that the capital raising was quickly and heavily over-subscribed, none other than business leader Kerry Stokes becoming the major investor.

Ultimately, over a period of four years, Jackson was to acquire thirty-six disparate, largely unrelated manufacturing businesses, many of them in fast-declining rust bucket, metal bashing industries. Most of these purchases occurred in Jackson's first few years as CEO. It begged the question as to how it might have been possible to carry out proper due diligence on so many companies in such a short time let alone integrate them into some sort of rational financial and operational structure.

But Jackson was a living legend. Perceived wisdom at the time was simply that with Jackson at the helm the whole would be worth significantly more than the sum of the parts. This view seemed to be supported in the market place. Three years later the shares of the company, now named Austrim Nylex, were trading at a price approximately three times greater than that of the original issue price. Everything was going to plan and, even more surprisingly, underlying profit performance appeared to justify the rising share price. But some observers were more than sceptical. The non-believers were of the view that a degree of alchemy had been at work and things may not have been as they seemed.

Even just a moment's thought suggested Jackson's due diligence on his acquisitions could only have been cursory at best and he almost certainly overpaid. How else could you turn the owners of thirty-six businesses into sellers in such a short time unless you overpaid or the vendors were busting their backsides to ride off into the sunset with their money as quickly as possible and probably both? Many of the vendors were apparently more than happy to consider coming to Jackson's party by sweetening the deal for him.

Given the more laissez faire corporate regulatory regime at the time a popular ploy of buyers of businesses was to pressure prospective vendors into writing down the value of trading stock and any land and buildings before the sale took place. As a consequence, as if by magic, as soon as the ink was dry on the acquisition's sale contract its profits registered a remarkable and significant improvement. And that improvement came courtesy of the write-downs before acquisition rather than any productivity improvements. The written down trading stock was sold at normal prices, producing much fatter profit margins than those being achieved by the previous owners. The apparent application of fairy dust lasted only until the written down stock had been depleted, usually no longer than three or four months for each acquisition. As long as one kept buying new businesses the profit momentum was forever underpinned. At an acquisition rate of one every three or four months you were in the money but at one a month you could be rolling in it.

However, there was a drawback to this course of action. Not only did it lead to initially misleading positive profit results but it was akin to riding a tiger. As soon as you stopped buying businesses the profit momentum would not only stop, it would start reversing at a hundred miles an hour and shareholders would want to know the reason. In other words, having gotten on that particular tiger's back it was just as dangerous to think about getting off. It was a tiger's back akin to a Ponzi scheme.

The opportunity for a bit of skulduggery also applied to fixed assets. Any written down land and buildings could be on-sold to third parties (sometimes back to the vendor) at inflated prices, with the acquirer leasing them back on long-term leases that reflected the inflated sale price. This practice had three effects. First, it enabled the inflated, largely illusory one-off profits on the sale of fixed assets to be brought to account in the profit and loss account as if they were trading profits, the claim being at the time that the buying and selling of fixed assets was so regular it was effectively a trading activity. Second, it provided cash to support further acquisitions and finally, and more insidiously, it undermined the viability of the continuing businesses in the longer term thanks to inflated non-commercial rental rates and lease back expenses.

Subsequent events suggested Jackson's record was a Jekyll and Hyde performance of dramatic proportions and one can only wonder as to whether the brain tumour that led to his death only a few years later had been a contributing factor. However, the pain suffered by Jackson's successors and particularly by long-suffering Austrim Nylex shareholders was not due solely to questionable restructuring of accounts before acquisition. The much bigger and unfixable problem in the longer term was that the majority of these acquired businesses were simply duds. At their time of purchase they were already being subjected to strong competitive pressures from more efficient Chinese and South East Asian manufacturers and these competitive pressures would keep escalating to such a degree they would ultimately account for the demise of the businesses that had been bought with such heady optimism.

In reality, Austrim Nylex was a house of cards and an extremely messy and complicated house of cards at that. It would take close to another decade for the house to finally collapse but it was really just a matter of time. Even the company's auditor, leading accounting firm at the time, Deloitte's, couldn't fathom out the accounts because of the patchwork of different accounting systems that had accompanied the acquisitions and which were apparently incapable of being unified.

In 1997, with few further acquisitions on the horizon, Jackson decided it was time to take his money off the table. He sold his Austrim Nylex shares at very healthy prices, returning him a cool $43 million, providing more than a hint as to what was lurking around the corner. Following the sale of his shares Jackson was permitted to continue to hang about as CEO by an indulgent board apparently oblivious to his obvious lack of faith in the future of Austrim Nylex as well as his increasingly bizarre personal behaviour. But the delivery of his right jolt to the jaw at the Christmas party was the final straw and he was dismissed in the year nought of the new millennium, leaving behind a legacy of financial pain as well as undermining the reputations of many well-intentioned executives and directors who heroically followed him in attempting to clean up the mess. Nylex Limited ultimately closed its doors and was placed in liquidation in 2009.

My knowledge of and familiarity with Jackson's moves was almost at first hand. In 2004 forty-two years old Glen Casey had been appointed CEO of the renamed Nylex Limited. Glen was a colleague of mine on the board of AFL Club, St Kilda where I chaired the board meetings for the seven years I was a director, seven years in which we turned an initially bankrupt St Kilda around, reversing a balance sheet deficit of $4 million and producing regular annual profits of around $1 million.

Normally, the presidents of AFL clubs chair the board meetings but St Kilda's president, the wealthy, self-made businessman Rod Butterss, deferred to my greater experience and requested I do the job. Rod was mercurial, colourful and loved the limelight, his touch of Hollywood forever coming to the fore. He was generous of spirit, exciting company and engagingly lovable but frustrating as well, his confidence knowing no bounds, nothing beyond his reach. When his lovely wife, Evelyn, finally lost patience with him — she'd been a football widow for long enough — he bestowed a volunteered, generous divorce settlement on her and with fate conspiring against him during the global financial crisis he saw the rest of his fortune go down the drain following some highly leveraged and lousy bets.

It was always believed that running an AFL club was a life or death experience but football club presidents disagreed. They thought it was more important than that. It was not even the most important thing in their lives; it was the only thing in their lives and Rod was no exception. His failure to focus on other things led to the loss of his marriage as well as his wealth. Rod was just another member of that very large club seduced by hubris, booze, recreational drugs or the presidency of an AFL club.

'Easy come easy go,' said a seemingly unfazed Rod. 'Twice I've made it and twice I've lost it and I'll make it again,' he vowed.

He then joined Alcoholics Anonymous and became a regular counsellor for AA in resurrecting his life before resuming his business life. At the time of publication Rod has been off the booze for 1,859 days, recreational drugs for 1,507 days and cigarettes for

275 days, no mean feat for a guy who liked to push the boundaries. 'Giving up cigarettes was the toughest,' he said. Rod still attends AA meetings a couple of times a week as well as counselling 'lost souls' on a regular basis.

Rod and the rest of us had walked from the St Kilda boardroom in late 2007 after a challenge organised by two of Rod's dissident directors. They were lawyers and had been unhappy with their treatment by a president who hadn't made it beyond year ten at technical school. They effectively organised a coup to unseat Rod, along the way attempting to air some alleged dirty linen in public. They had approached me to join their 'ticket' but after seven years I had had enough of the paranoia, the ego, the infighting and the time devoted to a role that anachronistically is still an unpaid role despite the AFL being a multi-billion dollar industry. It was an easy and resounding 'no'. The coup was Victoria's sports story of the week, successfully sensationalised by the TV media throng gathered at St Kilda's offices that ensured the event was front and centre of that day's national news bulletins. Sharp-tongued sports journalist, Caroline Wilson led the charge, her opening gambit an explosive, 'Rod there are strong rumours of substance abuse surrounding your life. Can you throw any light on that?' There was an even more explosive intake of Rod's breath as his face turned a ghastly shade of grey despite the bright lights of the cameras. It was unusual for Rod to be lost for words, an unflattering 'ughhhh' the best he could manage. In his understandable panic Rod's brain had resorted to its natural default option, ignoring the fact that I was supposed to be the official spokesperson. I placed a quick and hopefully comforting hand on Rod's arm, invisible ink for, 'don't say a word'. Some colour returned to his face. While Caroline Wilson's blistering question was not totally unexpected it was nonetheless a trifle more lethal than any of us thought even Caroline was capable of. I raised myself to my now age-reduced maximum height of 169 centimetres, looked her in the eye and said, 'Caroline you don't really expect Rod to dignify that question with an answer do you?' It must have looked and sounded pretty impressive and even if I do say so myself I was more than pleased with my cool response. There are few things more pleasurable in life than people believing you are better than you actually are. Particularly when you are on TV. It certainly made up for my disastrous Jimmy Watson TV interview in 1983. But of course I was not that glib. I had sort of cheated, finally learning that 'winging it' was not the path to a happy and full life when you were in the media spotlight. Anticipation and preparation always the better answer. But Caroline, never to be underestimated, was not to be deterred either. She had also done her homework. She followed up with a smiling, cleverly disguised question with the same thrust as her earlier missile. I was even more pleased to deliver that smart-arsed response, 'asked and answered Caroline', successfully giving her a decent dose of the jimmy brits and bringing a smile to the faces of those who envied her ballsy style. There was an audible sigh of what might have been relief from a small minority of those present but it was largely one of disappointment for those who were eager to see some blood, which, human nature being what it is, was of course most of them. The coup d'etat didn't turn out to be a great outcome for the St Kilda Football Club. By 2014 the club was back in financial crisis, potentially bankrupt and reliant on the good graces of the AFL Commission for survival. The club announced an operating loss of $4 million for the 2014 year and an excess of liabilities over assets that had risen to a daunting, seemingly unsustainable $9 million.

Glen Casey had encouraged me to take on the role as chairman of directors at Nylex to help and support him in his endeavours to turn the ailing company around. By this time the company's share price had more than ominously collapsed from around the $3 a share received by Alan Jackson when he sold his shares seven years earlier to less than 20 cents. This inevitable collapse was accompanied by equally inevitable asset write-downs of almost $1 billion, essentially written-off goodwill that had been created to balance the books for the inflated prices that had been paid for the various acquisitions in the first place.

The goodwill that had been created in Nylex's balance sheet following the acquisitions (the difference between the price paid for each acquisition and the book value of its assets) was illusory, about as substantial as a bag of wind, purely an accounting entry. Glen's and my roles, as well as those of the stream of directors who preceded and followed us, were poisoned chalices of the first order. I remained as chairman for less than two years before being pressured to resign by the tame directors appointed to the Nylex board by major shareholder Kerry Stokes to look after his interests. Kerry had not been pleased with me, disagreeing as to what was proper process in what amounted to a conflict of interest.

As far as Kerry was concerned I had blotted my copybook by preventing National Hire Limited, a company in which Kerry had a majority shareholding, from purchasing Nylex's only successful business, AH Plant Hire, at what in my opinion was a give-away price. It would have been a very bad look for all concerned, irrespective of the legal technicalities, and would not have passed the pub test.

I had insisted on an independent valuation being undertaken to remove the possible allegation of what might have been seen as insider trading. Kerry by this time was, unsurprisingly, trying to salvage something from the Nylex ruins — after all, he had lost a small fortune over the long unpleasant journey in, one had to admit, admirably trying to keep Nylex afloat. Naturally, he felt a little quid pro quo wouldn't have gone astray given his losses.

Actually, I had done his reputation a favour, one which he was never to acknowledge. He threatened to call an extraordinary general meeting of shareholders to have me and Glen removed but relented when I told him I would be delighted to outline the conflict of interest circumstances at the meeting. National Hire Limited was ultimately forced to increase its offer by around fifteen per cent.

I was glad of the excuse to head for the exit. Glen, who had aided and abetted my defiance of Kerry Stokes' plans, followed a few months later. It had become increasingly obvious that the sins of Nylex's past, sins I had become increasingly familiar with, were looking more and more likely to bring the company to an untimely end. Three years later it was placed in liquidation.

In taking on that appointment I had allowed sentiment to get in the way of good sense but sometimes it's good for the soul if you take one on the chin for the good guys. I couldn't blame anyone else for the position I found myself in because I knew in my heart of hearts that Nylex was a can of worms at the outset. Before taking on the role of chairman to 'quarterback' Glen I had studied four successive years of Nylex annual reports. It was impossible to reconcile one year with the next, the accounts little better than gobbledegook and an ominous presaging of the future. Those four annual reports should be made required study for every budding chartered accountant.

Meanwhile, back at the Mildara ranch.

Wine market observers believed strong brands had been the path to our happy and full Life.

What nobody was aware of, other than those in Mildara's inner sanctum, was the critical contribution made to our track record by our obsession with a numbers driven strategy and particularly by the relationship between the two ratios, EBIT to funds invested and EBIT to sales revenue. The company's operational activity, of which our current brand strength was only part, was the flesh attached to the financial framework that remained our guiding light.

Despite changing market circumstances over the previous eight years and slight adjustments to the target ratios to cater for the inevitable changes to and expansion of the business, the key financial ratios and the operational and organisational structures underlying them formed the first step in each year's planning process. But because this process was little understood by outsiders (as well as many insiders) our discipline in taking them so very seriously was given little or no credit for their key role in guiding Mildara's success. Our marketing and business development skills were always given pride of place by market observers as the keys to Mildara's successful track record. They were clearly very important but they would not have been nearly as effective had we not stuck so zealously to our largely inflexible financial framework. Over the seventeen years from 1982 to 1999 EBIT grew each year by an average of twenty-seven per cent despite being severely hindered by two periods of serious recession. Seventeen years of superior performance suggests our return on investment and numbers-based approach had to stand for something.

But while our dedication to financial based planning was inflexible our operating strategies were less so.

Between 1982 and 1987 Mildara had gone through two strategic phases. The first two years were all about survival and had been based on a mix of sound market analysis, opportunism, desperation and good fortune. The second phase was the establishment of a more conventional foundation based on the acquisition of brands and the development of our own brands. A third phase, a three-year period beginning in 1987, could only have been described as eclectic.

The late 1980s in Australia was a period of exuberance, opportunism, business development and share market volatility. Borrowings financed a larger proportion of that expansion than normal, a not unusual occurrence at the top of any business cycle and the swashbuckling entrepreneurs and their feats were continually in the headlines. We all wanted to believe a new paradigm had arrived that transcended rational thought, conveniently ignoring our dashed hopes when we had thought exactly the same thing in 1968, in 1974 and again in 1981.

The regularity of these historical downturns contradicted our optimism and heady sense of adventure but we were yet again saying to ourselves, 'this time it's different.'

Most of the entrepreneurs making headlines in the Australian media were not Australians. There were some Australians among them such as John Elliott and Christopher Skase but many were foreign born. Robert Holmes a Court and Alan Bond were English, Ron Brierley and Bruce Judge were from New Zealand, John Spalvins was Latvian and Abe Goldburg was Polish. Most of them eventually bankrupted their companies. Some, like Alan Bond, ended up in jail, some, like Christopher Skase, fled the country in disgrace and proved too clever for the authorities to expedite back to Australia and some, like Bruce Judge, simply disappeared into obscurity. By 1990

John Elliott had lost his personal fortune and almost bankrupted Foster's but still retained the chutzpah to keep his head above the trenches. When you are making money in the telephone number category — and John had been making plenty — it's handy if you can keep your hubris in check. He apparently couldn't. Having dealt in mega-millions in his heyday big John was by now down to borrowed fifties and feeling for coins down the back of every sofa.

It was the period of the conglomerate, financial engineering, unfriendly takeovers and share market volatility. Anything appeared to be acceptable in business as long as it made money. The market bears continually claimed that history would repeat itself, that the music would inevitably stop and you wouldn't be able to find a chair to plonk your bum on. But no one was listening. We were all too busy having a good time. But stop the music did, on Black Monday 17 October, 1987.

On that day the Australian Stock Exchange all ordinaries index plunged twenty-five per cent, the market's biggest one-day fall ever, a plunge even greater than that registered in one day either during the Great Depression of 1929 – 1933 or the global financial crisis of 2008. By the end of October, in less than two weeks, the Australian stock market had fallen a mammoth forty-two per cent. The sky had fallen and most investors were in a state of panic, not to mention company CEOs who were in shock and numb with fear, me among them. Those investors financed by margin loans were soon wiped out and suddenly it was a good time to buy second hand Maseratis.

Melbourne sharebroker Russell Keating was still capable of some black humour. He postulated that at this rate of market decline all the companies listed on the Australian Stock Exchange in another three weeks would be worth exactly nothing. Incredibly, the market recovered all of that forty-two per cent loss and then some within eighteen months. Black Monday, instead of being a portent of things to come had been despatched to the trash can and quickly forgotten as an aberration.

Obsessed with maintaining Mildara's high growth rate and not uninfluenced by the exciting environment, we darted here, there and everywhere searching for ways of keeping profit growth momentum at the highest possible level.

Between 1986 and 1990 we acquired Morton Estate, New Zealand's most successful premium wine brand at that time. We acquired Island Cooler, the market's number two brand during the all too brief wine cooler phenomenon of the '80s and we acquired Mark Swann, a small but budding exporter to the fast developing US market for Australian wine.

We entered into a joint venture with a large Japanese trading company, Sanraku, which took a ten per cent equity interest in Mildara and we began exporting wine in significant quantities to Japan.

We captured the Australian distribution rights for Cascade Beer, and lost it again three years later. We sought and gained the bottling rights for Jim Beam Bourbon, and were happy to relinquish it four years later to provide capacity to package our surging wine business. We introduced our own brand of bottled cooler, Hula Cooler and we pioneered the market for wine coolers in wine-casks with a brand called Half and Half. Most of what we did made some sense, at least to me, and if we thought there was money in it we looked at it. I considered, thankfully only briefly, buying pubs, drilling for gold on Balgownie's and Yellowglen's goldfield vineyards and even investing in the rampant Japanese stock market. Two years later the Japanese stock market had plunged by sixty per cent, the same outcome as the Australian stock exchange index during the global financial crisis twenty years later.

Some of the non-core activities we contemplated were pretty mild compared to what the headline entrepreneurs were up to. Like them, we were prepared to consider departing from our core business — but not from the guiding hand of our financial model.

It was during this period that the Australian wine export phenomenon got under way, ultimately leading to our next strategic phase. Until 1986 selling Australian wine overseas was hard work. For decades Australian export managers enthusiastically and diligently kept knocking on overseas doors but struggled to make much impact. Wine exports accounted for less than seven per cent of all Australian bottled wine sales at the time of the wind change. There was little doubt that overseas distributors were impressed with Australia's wine style and its quality but they were concerned their consumers new little about Australian wine and would be loath to buy it. In those dark early years Australian companies such as Brown Brothers did some wonderful pioneering work in the UK market for what ultimately became known as Brand Australia, as did the free thinking, entrepreneurial Mark Cashmore in the US market with his Black Opal brand.

As far as I was concerned the export business was too difficult compared to the opportunities still abounding in the domestic market. That did not deter Bill Stevens from his lonely, painstaking and ever-resilient proprietorial efforts in what amounted to a lone crusade for Mildara as he roamed the world in the face of market adversity and my lack of anything more than moral support.

Bill, a free agent and only 160 centimetres tall, admired women, particularly those with dusky skin. It was an admiration that would not go unrewarded, so his wandering the world was not without its compensations. But when the export winds turned from headwinds to tailwinds Mildara was not only carried along by the momentum but I also transformed my thinking and made a right angle turn in our growth strategy. Suddenly, exports had become an area worth pursuing.

Again, we tried to be a little different. Instead of focussing on Australia's historical key export market, the United Kingdom, we concentrated on the US market, a much smaller market for imported wine than the UK but potentially far more profitable.

It was no surprise that the golden period for Australian wine exports coincided with the floating of the Australian dollar in December 1983, which was then trading at around ninety US cents. Before the float the value of the Australian dollar was pegged to the trade weighted index and the value was determined each day by the Reserve Bank of Australia in consultation with the government. However, the boom in Australian wine exports did not get under way until 1986 after a precipitous fall in the Australian dollar from around seventy-seven US cents to fifty-seven cents over a period of a few months. The price of petrol to Australian drivers jumped by thirty per cent but Australian wine was now twenty-five per cent cheaper than a few months earlier. Overseas retailers and distributors were finally encouraged to take a chance with the wines from down under. Attracted by the lower prices, their consumers were more than pleasantly surprised. By 1990, in less than four years, Australia's annual wine exports had jumped by more than four hundred per cent to a level equal to around thirty per cent of the volume of bottled wine sales in the domestic market. By 2009 Australian wine exports had increased a further tenfold to a level equal to more than three times that of the domestic market for bottled wines. It was a wonderful success story in terms of volume but, as usual in the Australian wine industry, not so in respect to profits.

Initially, it took me a while to get my head around the principles one should adopt in export pricing. At that time, as Paul Keating had implied, export markets had generally been regarded by Australian businessmen as little more than an afterthought and merely a passive add-on to their largely protected activities in the domestic market.

This was in direct contrast to the view of hardened, professional exporters such as the Scandinavian countries and Germany who saw export markets as crucial to their future prosperity and who had developed proactive and discrete marketing and pricing strategies to that end. The popular pricing approach adopted by the average Australian exporter at the time, an approach certainly not exclusive to the wine industry, was to charge lower prices than in the domestic market. Those lower prices generally excluded consideration of all of the business's cost structure, in particular fixed costs. As long as export prices exceeded variable costs and made some sort of contribution to profits everything was seen to be hunky-dory.

Then the Harvard Boy, still my nemesis on the Mildara board, came in handy again. What he advocated was a philosophy that not only appeared to be arrestingly simple, but was arrestingly simple. He advocated that export markets should be treated in exactly the same way as the domestic market in respect to pricing: we should make the same level of profit on an exported bottle of wine as one sold in the domestic market. The vast majority of Australian exporters, particularly those in the wine industry, didn't subscribe to that policy. They were in love with growth and that was what they got. Unfortunately, they got little else.

For more than twenty years Australian wine exports rose by more than twenty per cent a year. It was a phenomenal period of sustained growth and a unique opportunity to improve wine industry profitability but at the end of those twenty years most Australian wine exporters had much less to show for that good fortune than should have been the case. They took advantage of the low Australian dollar and worked on far lower profit margins than were necessary. By the turn of the century, with the Australian dollar back up above US eighty cents, the market was looking far less rosy and about to be further encumbered by a global oversupply of wine. The pips were beginning to squeak. Australian exporters, loathe to increase their prices to compensate for the higher Australian dollar, had not left sufficient room in their pricing policies to respond to a rising currency. When the Australian dollar kept rising, as a consequence of the new millennium's mining boom, to above parity with the US dollar the majority of Australian wine exporters were dying the death of a thousand cuts as they fought for survival on wafer thin and often unsustainable profit margins.

From 1986 onwards exports increasingly gained importance in Mildara's profit growth aspirations and ultimately became a key plank of the fourth phase of our strategic journey. But not until after our next major acquisition, a delight that was yet to be savoured.

25

Mr Audacious

'I'll give you $60 million for it', I said. For a while he looked as though he had swallowed something he found difficult to digest.

In January 1990 the conglomerate, Adsteam, formerly known as Adelaide Steamships Limited, purchased Australia's second largest wine company, Lindeman's, from global tobacco giant Philip Morris. Under nearly twenty years of stewardship by Philip Morris the profit performance of Lindeman's had been unrelentingly poor.

A year earlier I had met the CEO of Philip Morris Australia Pty Ltd with a view to making an offer for Lindeman's. He was pompous and self-important, wore a striped tie with little elephants on it and spoke in such a precise, clipped manner it suggested he felt he was being marked on diction. He was less than impressed with my exploratory offer of $60 million for such a great brand as well as irritated by my query as to why, if Lindeman's were such a great brand, it wasn't making much if any money. The jibe on my part was not all that smart but I had decided from the outset that I didn't like him all that much and had yielded to temptation.

Adsteam already owned Australia's largest wine business, Penfolds, which it had bought in 1986 from Sydney brewer Tooth & Co. Adsteam's CEO and driving force was John Spalvins who, in the '70s and '80s, had turned that company into a thriving and successful corporate raider. His bank borrowings topped $4.8 billion, an enormous figure even by today's standards. Among a number of other leading businesses his stable included Woolworths, National Foods and David Jones stores so it is easy to understand why there was a consortium of more than 200 banks involved. Loan to value ratios during this period were at record levels and the banks were prepared to lend for almost anything.

The media sought my view on the wisdom of Penfolds and Lindeman's being merged into the one business although I wondered why they even bothered to ask. Apparently, they didn't get from me the sound bite they were looking for. Apart from believing the price Adsteam paid to be far too high, I predicted that the merger of the industry's two largest companies wouldn't work. Despite Penfolds and Lindeman's being seen by almost everyone, except for me, as great businesses, most people were either unaware of or ignored the fact that both companies had a majority of low price products that were ready substitutes for one another. The exception was the Penfolds premium bin wines that in any case accounted for less than five per cent of the merged companies' sales revenue. The risk of a high level of cannibalisation of the lower priced products if both brands were handled by one sales team was immense. It was no great surprise, given John Spalvins' leviathan standing in the business community, that my contrarian views, seen to be little more than sour grapes, raised little or no comment in the media.

In 1989, less than two years after Black Friday on world stock exchanges (Black Monday in Australia), the Australian and global economies were again becoming overheated. Business and consumer confidence had again leapt into the stratosphere, inflation was on the increase, house prices were booming, as were the prices of all other asset categories. The game of musical chairs and pass the parcel on share markets and asset classes in general was again in full swing and the imminent danger of another sharp downturn was beginning to focus the minds of the members of Adsteam's banking syndicate.

The banks began putting pressure on Spalvins to pay down some of Adsteam's enormous debt load. Spalvins clearly believed that the acquisition of Lindeman's would make it easier for him to hive off the Penfolds business and to leverage its value by selling the two businesses as a pigeon pair. In his view, the combined value of the two companies was greater than the sum of the parts. This was also the view of most others in the business world, including the financial journalists.

I was again the spoilsport. I thought that with proper management the two major brands could generate far greater value if kept separate. Moreover, I believed the ultimate combined value could be even greater if the companies were broken up into even smaller pieces.

I wanted desperately to believe there was an opportunity somewhere in there for Mildara. The key hurdle was the rumoured asking price of around $400 million. But if the two largest wine companies in Australia could be split into say, six to eight logical pieces, the combined value to the individual purchasers could conceivably be well in excess of $400 million. Frankly, I didn't care whether that turned out to be the case or not. What I did believe, or more to the point wanted to believe, was that whichever piece Mildara might end up with under such a scenario could be made to work significantly better than was currently the case and produce our targeted twenty per cent ROI.

I jumped on the 'phone and rang Wolf Blass, Robert Hill-Smith at Yalumba, Gunter Prass at Orlando and Don McWilliam at McWilliam's. They probably thought I had been smoking an illicit substance but none rejected the idea out of hand and each agreed to discuss an in-principle arrangement. Once I got down and dirty on the details of what would have to take place for a successful bid I realised I must have been smoking an illicit substance. My hazy plan was to sell off the vineyards and wineries for around $100 – $150 million and enter into long-term contracts for the supply of wine, leaving half a dozen $40 – $50 million chunks to be paid for the various sub-brands.

Selling the vineyards and wineries was the easier bit — in 1989 buyers were lining up to acquire vineyards and wineries because grape and bulk wine prices had gone through the roof. But would the consortium members go for it after they had really thought the exercise all the way through? They no doubt wondered how it would all work when we got there. I was kind of interested in finding that out myself.

At that time, the idea of not being directly in control of your own wine supply stood conventional wine industry wisdom and accepted practice on its head. But over the next decade and particularly into the new millennium this is what ultimately happened. To reduce capital intensity and increase return on investment wine companies started to give up that control and to outsource wine supply as well as activities such as packaging and storage. Supplying all your own wine needs became the exception rather than the rule. It hadn't been such a silly idea after all.

The more than tricky issue was always going to be the basis on which the brands and the various sub-brands might be shared among the consortium members as well as that of gaining agreement on generic promotion of the two key umbrella brands. I planned to divide the businesses into logical bite sized pieces and ask each consortium member to effectively value each piece by bidding for them. My back of the envelope calculations had the intrinsic value well in excess of $400 million. This was based on the assumption the various pieces were appropriately managed.

The break-up would be a nightmare to plan, implement and get general agreement on given some of the bidders would probably prefer the same bits but I wanted the impossible dream to last for as long as possible. I didn't want to even think about how the overall deal might be financed, a not irrelevant piece of the jigsaw puzzle.

The investment bank handling the sale leaked to the press that I was heading up a consortium to bid for the two companies. For a couple of days the media was all over me but then it soon became fairly clear that the lead investment banker, Geoff Hill, didn't take the consortium seriously (he had a point) and was only using me as a stalking horse to maximise the price he could get from his real target buyer, South Australian Brewing boss, Ross Wilson.

When the deal with SA Brewing was eventually announced some weeks later I voiced my outrage that the sale process had been poorly handled but it was largely theatre and my sense of relief was palpable. I had finally gone cold on the idea of going through the time-consuming funding nightmare and the herding-cats process that would have been required to pull the deal off. The chances of ever pulling a workable deal together even in the event SA Brewing had not gone ahead would have been at cricket score odds. And although the still friendly wine industry provided a better chance of success of such an arrangement than most other industries, joint ventures with one partner are tough enough let alone a consortium of six members. It had been a pipedream, admittedly a nice pipedream, from the beginning. And we got lucky because potential disaster was just around the corner.

In 1991, the economic downturn and resultant credit squeeze trashed asset prices. Australia's entrepreneurs would pay the price for their boldness. John Elliott effectively bankrupted Foster's and ultimately himself. Adsteam's share price collapsed in one day from $5 to less than $1. The company descended into liquidation, shareholders lost their socks, Spalvins stepped down in disgrace and like many of his entrepreneurial peers, simply disappeared.

26

Wolf Blass

'Wolf, I think it's time we got together,' I ventured into the 'phone. 'How about I come to Adelaide and we have a spot of lunch?'

For almost a decade and a half following the first of his Jimmy Watson Trophy wins Wolf Blass, the man, had continued to kick goals from eighty metres out against the wind and his company had been an outstanding success. But by 1988 Mildara had overtaken and passed it, the process assisted by a plateauing of the Blass business's previous momentum.

Blass marketed a small range of premium priced products and to have reached an annual sales volume of more than seven million bottles and sales revenue close to $50 million had been worthy of generous acclamation for a single brand company. However, by 1989 the brand had gone off the boil — too often the fate of the single brand business in an industry with more than a semblance of fashion consciousness.

Fashion conscious wine consumers were now deserting the Wolf Blass brand. Its remaining core consumers were largely those fearful of making a mistake with their wine purchases. These were the security conscious and those only just beginning to embrace wine as a regular purchase. As these consumers made up the majority of the market the confidence provided by the brand was still a definite plus from this perspective. The question no one could answer was, which of the two countervailing forces might win out in the future? While fashion conscious consumers made up less than ten per cent of the market they nonetheless were the opinion leaders and wielded a high degree of influence over their less knowledgeable and less confident peers.

This dismissive attitude towards the Blass brand, erroneous or not, appeared to have developed a life all of its own as it filtered resolutely and unflinchingly down the hierarchical pyramid, with its very large rump of consumers in need of constant reassurance. But there was strong evidence emerging that the Blass business was not being well managed. If this were true a good repair job might outweigh the negative vibes of the opinion leaders.

Wolf Blass, the executive chairman, had been a dynamic force in establishing and developing the Blass business. In his early winemaking days he had revolutionised red wine making in Australia but by the early 1980s Wolf was no longer directly involved in making wine and by the mid-1980s he was spending a lot of time overseas. In Australia, he had initially been a great hit with retailers and consumers as a result of his promotional stunts but now there were worrying signs this was wearing out. The publicity surrounding his ownership of a large stable of generally slow racehorses probably wasn't helping matters. Wine consumers prefer to believe their favourite winemakers have the arse out of their pants. Worse, others had copied the Wolf Blass winemaking approach and the brand had lost the unique style advantage that had driven its earlier success.

The Blass directors were faced with a dilemma even more uncomfortable than the increasingly disappointing performance of the business. And that was what to do about their executive chairman and sixty per cent shareholder. Wolf had always been a crash or crash through leader. Problem solving and people management skills, those prime requirements for dealing with an organisation's changing and more challenging environment, were not always Wolf's key strengths. Moreover, Wolf's quixotic and increasingly autocratic approach (often the outcome when a company's performance starts to slip) had either discouraged more capable executives from joining the company or quickly intimidated those not so discouraged into becoming nothing but tame bureaucrats. This was a market that required positive, intuitive energy.

Understandably, Wolf was impatient to have his previous level of success restored but his increasing frustration seemed to be making matters worse. Not improving matters was human nature. Wolf had arrived at that stage in his life where he was displaying periods of disinterest in the business, no doubt hastened by the bewildering and depressing burden of the disappearing success that had seemed so easy only a few years earlier. He had been pleasantly distracted by a new and lovely lady whom he would ultimately marry and the couple was spending up to four months each year in overseas markets. Alarmingly, Wolf's absences had seen decision making at head office grind to a halt. Wolf's increasing habit of countermanding decisions when he returned to the business had been an unintended but nonetheless debilitating blow to morale and to organisational effectiveness. The business had had four chief operating officers in four years.

From my own three to four week absences from home base I had soon learned a valuable lesson. In more relaxing circumstances away from the daily cut and thrust one's well-seasoned stress threshold soon crumbled. A return to the coal face saw minor irritations taking on more daunting proportions. I quickly learned to bite my tongue and try to get through that first week without making any major decisions or adopting extreme stances for which I might be sorry afterwards. By then, one's stress threshold and equanimity had usually returned to their well-honed former levels.

Cracks were appearing in the Wolf Blass business and it looked as though the time was about right to drop another stone into that metaphorical pond to see what might eventuate. Or was it too late?

In January 1990, not long after SA Brewing Limited had acquired Penfolds and Lindeman's, rumours were running rife about other possible wine industry amalgamations, rumours fanned if not invented in the first place by sensation seeking journalists. I had telephoned Wolf and suggested it was time we got to know one another. Wolf agreed that having allies made good sense. It was really a repeat of the Krondorf play five years earlier. As I tended to avoid wine industry functions the opportunity had never arisen for Wolf and me to meet, let alone to have a conversation.

Despite our contrasting personalities and apprehensions as to what might eventuate, our mutual sense of adventure prevailed and we had an enjoyable lunch. We aired our most candid views on life as well as on the wine industry and agreed to keep in touch pending further developments.

In late 1990 the recession that had been looming on the horizon hit the global economy with a vengeance and Blass's sales were off ten per cent. But the Blass business was suffering the double whammy of declining profit margins as well. In the six months to December 1990 Blass profits had slumped more than sixty per cent compared to the same period the previous year. Whether the Blass business was permanently crippled or merely crippled at the moment was difficult to say. What I hoped was that Wolf's concerns would have had him staring at the phone and playing will I or won't I games with himself. He duly picked up the phone and I agreed to resume our previous discussion.

We had decided to go cloak and dagger and meet at a pub deep in the Adelaide suburbs away from prying eyes and accidental encounters. It didn't work out that well. We had a nice bit of lunch and a most constructive chat but the pub happened to be the venue for the quarterly meeting of the Australian Wine Federation. The cat was out of the bag.

During our lunch, Wolf, volatile as ever, railed against the forces of darkness and evil that were working against him: the Federal Government was hopeless, retailers were getting too greedy, his competitors were becoming too powerful, some members of his team were letting him down and he was no longer on speaking terms with his joint venture distribution partner, the French cognac producer Remy Martin with whom he shared his brand's distribution profits and losses.

Wolf invoked his German heritage, complaining that he should never have entered into that distribution arrangement. 'The fucking French had always been piss weak and could never be trusted to stand up when the going got tough'. The reality was that Remy Martin was a good distributor of spirits and liqueurs but the distribution of its traditional spirits products and that of wine were different games altogether. Remy Blass was a babe in the woods in dealing with the increasing and rapacious power of the retail trade in respect to the far more competitive wine industry with its large array of substitute products. This was particularly so in the 1990–91 economic downturn which had resulted in a buyer's market. Predictably, retailers were subjecting wine suppliers to enormous pressure to lower their prices and most suppliers were buckling under the onslaught. Remy Blass, being new to the cut and thrust of wine price negotiation, more than aped their wine competitors in simply giving too much away for too little reward.

Wolf was obviously shaken by the increasingly disappointing performance of his business because he and I quickly shook hands on an in-principle merger agreement which would be effected by a takeover of Wolf Blass by Mildara. The new company would be called Mildara Blass.

At that point I decided I liked Wolf even more. The amalgamation was to be presented as a merger to avoid spooking Wolf Blass consumers but the Blass directors would also be looking to save face as well. The financial terms and board representation numbers were to be finalised between me and Bob May, Wolf's personal financial adviser and a director of the Wolf Blass Company. The agreement reached with Wolf was that I would run the merged operation and Wolf would be a roving global ambassador for the Blass brand as well as become deputy chairman of the Mildara Blass board. But there was trouble around the corner. Bob May didn't think our merger plan was such a great idea.

For the next four weeks Bob May and I went backwards and forwards on the details. And soon enough I didn't like the sound of what I was hearing or more to the point what I was not hearing. By now, I had been around the block often enough and long enough to recognise trouble when I saw it. Then I heard that Wolf and Bob had met with the giant US liquor supplier Seagram. The Australian branch of Seagram had a contract to package the Blass products so there was a good reason for Wolf to be talking to them about unwinding their bottling contract given our proposed agreement. But the word on the street was that the deal was slipping away. It was again shit or bust time and my turn to pick up the 'phone. As it happened the stars were in alignment and Wolf agreed to see me first thing the next morning in his Adelaide office.

When I arrived I was even more delighted to see Bob May wasn't present. But Wolf didn't appear to be sharing my delight. After sleeping on it, he had apparently come to the practical realisation he had now positioned himself somewhere between the devil (me) and the deep blue sea (Bob). I had some work to do.

Fortunately, I had worked on a merger paper for most of the night. The paper set out what I thought were the full profit and loss benefits of the merger and more importantly the impact on Wolf's personal net worth. The paper was a repeat in principle of the exercise that had won David Wynn's heart on the wine-cask project so many years earlier. Mildara would offer Blass shareholders the alternative of a straight share swap or a cash and shares deal worth approximately $50 million. When Wolf saw my estimates as to what the ultimate benefits of the deal would be on a straight share swap his eyes nearly popped out of his head. But it was a risky approach.

Not only was I taking something of a chance in revealing all my assumptions as to the additional value to be created by putting the two companies together but the approach also transgressed all the principles adopted by professional merger and acquisition practitioners. I had presented Wolf with the opportunity to seriously up the ante. However, I had guessed correctly. Wolf was more than happy with the certainty of his net worth being doubled overnight.

Within minutes, Wolf telephoned Bob May and suggested in no uncertain terms he should get around to Wolf's office quick smart.

'Bob,' yelled Wolf when Bob's startled face appeared through the doorway, even more startled when he saw mine. 'Stop all this other bullshit. I'm going to do the deal with Ray,' were his exact words.

Bob was far from happy with this sudden turn of events and remonstrated with Wolf for making yet another agreement without his being present. Wolf by now had developed a full head of steam. He was adamant this was the best deal. He kept waving my paper around with his arm at full stretch as if it were the tablet of stone. Bob, less than pleased that his influence had been undermined, genuinely believed Wolf would be much happier without, what he believed, would be my intimidating presence. Wolf probably would have been happier elsewhere but I was certain his net worth in an alternative deal would turn out to be only a fraction of what the potential outcome would be in a merger of our two businesses.

Bob had little choice but give up in despair. Wolf was cock-a-hoop, already counting his reviving fortune and I was at least trying, albeit unsuccessfully, to stifle my cat that got the cream grin. It was a pretty emotional five minutes and I couldn't wait to get home with the bacon and celebrate with Dawn. If I'd had a tail it would have been wagging.

It turned out that Bob May had explored alternative deals with BRL Hardy and US-based Seagram. And while Wolf later declared he would never have done a deal with either there was no doubt as to what Bob's strong advice had been. He wanted Wolf to do a deal with Seagram, a spirits company, and it appeared that little had been learned from the Remy Blass disaster. Seagram might have saved some bruising to Wolf's ego but it would also have provided him with a second grade financial outcome.

I had rolled the dice and God had again been kind. The Blass brand joined Yellowglen, Jamiesons Run and Krondorf as another jewel in our crown in the domestic market. Within four years Mildara Blass was the third largest profit earner in the global wine industry. As I had foreshadowed to Wolf, putting the two companies together did indeed turn out to be a bumper financial result for him. It was not quite the bonanza it would have been had he accepted the all-shares offer instead of cashing out thirty per cent of his original Blass shareholding, but the outcome wasn't all that bad either. By the time we agreed to sell Mildara Blass to Foster's in 1996 Wolf's residual investment in the combined business had increased fivefold, equal to a tenfold increase on its value before the merger, known in the financial markets as a ten bagger.

The Mildara/Wolf Blass merger announcement on 16 April, 1991 was the Australian media's lead business story of the day and almost all the financial commentators were positive as to the likely outcome. But the far better informed James Halliday wasn't so sure. He wrote, in the *Australian*:

> 'It would be unfair to suggest that the Mildara-Wolf Blass marriage was a shotgun affair but it stretches the imagination to suggest it is a marriage made in heaven. Indeed, one must wonder whether it is a marriage at all.
>
> Over the past seven or so years the two companies have been the most consistently profitable in Australia thanks to the acumen of their respective Chief executives. Ray King and Wolf Blass are tough, street smart and have been single minded in their pursuit of profit. Each has exerted the maximum possible influence over the management, philosophy and strategies of their companies.
>
> Successful chief executives of this calibre do not normally wish to see their company taken over. For make no mistake this is a takeover by Mildara.
>
> Where did things go wrong? Some will point to Wolf's wish to step back from the day to day running of the business: he put in place a structure to deal with that but it failed. Likewise he foresaw the need to control his own distribution: the Remy Blass joint venture was supposed to do that but it too failed.
>
> But arguably, the greatest failure was in the area in which he had shown such brilliance. It is in the marketing of the wines that the wheels have fallen off. In a frighteningly short period of time the Blass brand has become old fashioned. Sure, it is still a valuable brand with a virtually guaranteed sales base but it will not carry the fight through the 90s.
>
> It is here that the strategy of Ray King will be crucial. In order to

save, let alone restore, the goodwill the Blass brand has (or had), he will have to hasten slowly in his modernisation plans for the impossibly gaudy, ornate labels that defy conventional wisdom and that happily obscure the multi-regional, multi-varietal blends.

Yet one wonders whether Mildara has the luxury of time on its side. And how will Ray King deal with the fact that each company's major success stories, Jamiesons Run and Blass Yellow Label are natural competitors? Ray King is known as the Silver Fox — he will need all his cunning to make sure he avoids the sour grapes'.

It was at this point that the Harvard Boy got his revenge, not on me, but on the man who had helped facilitate his replacement as chairman five years earlier, Richard Haselgrove. Richard may not have held a candle to the Harvard Boy in terms of business acumen (naturally an extremely sore point with the ex-chairman) but Richard did know how to get the best out of me and that was to let me run. Richard's chairmanship ended up being far more effective as well as making my life so much more pleasant.

However, driven by the Harvard Boy's unrelenting belief that I had been allowed to run with too much freedom (he had never strayed from that particular line), there was now a growing groundswell among the directors, fanned by the Harvard Boy, for a change of chairman. That groundswell was based on the rationale of Mildara Blass's prospective doubling in size and presumed increased level of complexity. While I thought it was probably overkill I was nonetheless comfortable with the plan for leading executive search firm Spencer Stuart to search for an A-grade chairman under the Harvard Boy's sub-committee chairmanship. Peter North was not to know that I had developed a good relationship with Kerry McGinnis, the boss of Spencer Stuart, from my old days at Wynn's.

Kerry McGinnis knew which side his bread was buttered on and he was to keep me up to date every step of the way. While it was going too far to suggest I chose my own chairman, Kerry, unlike Peter North, was a member of the old school that believed a good relationship between the CEO and the chairman was one of the more important ingredients for success.

Brian Healey had left school in Yorkshire aged fourteen and had worked his way up the business ladder before coming to Australia at age twenty-eight as sales and marketing manager of UK small appliance maker, Hotpoint. After a successful stint running the Australian operations of US biscuit and cereal supplier Nabisco Inc., Brian was sent to London to run Nabisco Inc. Europe. He was then head-hunted back to Australia as CEO of Nicholas Kiwi, one of Australia's few multi-national companies at that time, which Brian ultimately sold to US company Sara Lee, making the Nicholas family very happy as well as very rich.

Brian knew his onions but he was more the statesman type and, in his own words, a far better operator in large bureaucratic organisations than getting down and dirty as I had done and continued to do at Mildara. So we complemented one another pretty well. This was his first public company role as chairman and the role was to put him on his feet as a professional company director. He believed his key role as chairman was to encourage and support the CEO in the further development of the business. We got on very well, again the Harvard Boy thought too well, but Brian and I agreed with the philosophy that said 'never employ anyone with whom you are not prepared to go out to lunch'.

Brian's approach provided the model for me when I ultimately took on chairman's roles. Ours was a transparent relationship and we would meet at least once a week for lunch for a 'fireside-chat' about problems and opportunities within the business. The reality was that the Harvard Boy's plan had backfired. Brian not only continued to allow me to run free but encouraged me to become even more adventurous.

Within six months of the Wolf Blass acquisition, Australia's third largest wine company by volume, the privately owned Thomas Hardy, was on the block. The business was only marginally profitable, the consequence of a still struggling world economy emerging ever so slowly from the 1991 recession. The owners, the Hardy family, had finally blinked and agreed to put the nearly one hundred and fifty year old business on the market. Hardy's CEO, Wayne Jackson, a popular figure and an honourable man (who ultimately succeeded Ross Oakley as CEO of the Australian Football League) encouraged me to explore the Hardy's opportunity, believing Mildara Blass to be the only potential buyer.

Wayne and I had a number of meetings that culminated in our reaching an agreement in principle to add Hardy's to our shopping list. Unfortunately, the timing was not exactly great. We were yet to get on top of the Wolf Blass acquisition and the challenge of solving Hardy's problems, while not a particularly complicated one, would stretch our resources and split our focus.

The financial and operational risks were not to be sneezed at and neither were the strategic risks. We were not entirely comfortable with Hardy being a major player in the wine-cask market or with it being a significant exporter of low priced product to the UK. But these were the company's major activities and would not only need to be retained but also require us to flex our exclusive focus on the premium end of the market.

Nevertheless, Hardy's was a seductive prize and not wishing to look a gift horse in the mouth I decided to give it a go, hopeful rather than confident we could achieve our targeted twenty per cent return on investment at Wayne's suggested price of $90 million. The purchase would effectively quadruple the size of our business compared to our pre-Wolf Blass days, a not insignificant challenge in itself even without the additional risks. Despite a degree of nervousness on my part as to whether we might be biting off more than we could chew we settled back and waited for the Hardy family to come to the party. It was the one that got away.

Wayne Jackson rang to say there had been an unanticipated turn of events, in other words a spot of bother. Team South Australia had decided to get involved.

The South Australian Government had evidently not been overjoyed with Mildara's earlier purchases of two key South Australian businesses, Wolf Blass and Krondorf, and then redeploying their activities to Victoria. The much larger Hardy's business would see even more South Australian jobs lost to Victoria. But that wasn't all. Yachtsman Sir James Hardy, a much-lauded and admired South Australian who had played a key role in famously and sensationally winning the America's Cup yacht race in 1983, wanted the Hardy business to remain in its ancestral home and had given the government a decent needle in encouraging them to do exactly that. It just wouldn't do.

The government decided that the state's largest wine company, that went all the way back to 1854, had to be kept in South Australia at all costs and the rapacious Mildara taught a lesson into the bargain. Berri Renmano, a large and plodding South Australian fruit cooperative, was encouraged by significant government funding support as well as annual tax breaks exceeding $4 million to exceed Mildara's offer.

This new turn of events would require us to stump up at least another $15 million to top Berri Renmano's offer, a sum that might not be enough to get us across the line anyway given the apparent determination of the SA Government to keep us at bay. It was the straw that broke the camel's back. Having been rocked back on our heels we allowed the opportunity to go begging. Nevertheless, it had also been time to get philosophical. We had been fortunate to get our hands on Wolf Blass, albeit that we were still struggling at the time to get on top of that business's problems. Perhaps taking on the Hardy's opportunity was asking too much of divine providence.

As it turned, out the newly named BRL Hardy performed very well during the 1990s under the energetic management of an initially underrated ex-brush salesman by the name of Stephen Miller, who turned out to be something of a surprise packet.

It was perhaps not without some relevance that the ex-brush salesman was given a walk-up start by having employed my former marketing and business strategy analyst of three years, Chris Day, a clever, hard-working livewire now living in Adelaide. Chris had become pissed off with me because I wouldn't allow him to take six months off to complete his MBA full time, in the process absconding with a filing cabinet full of more than useful Mildara information as people were generally permitted to do in those days.

Ironically, Stephen had called me to get some sort of feeling for my attitude to Chris's pending appointment. I suspected that, as well as doing some due diligence on Chris, Stephen was more than a little concerned at the time that Chris may have been a conveniently planted mole.

27

Wolf Blass merger outcome

'Bloody Hell, that's not good', I said to David Smith, our chief financial officer. A very nasty feeling was developing in the pit of my stomach.

Our profit projection for the next year was now down the drain to the tune of a very heady $9 million and, to quote a phrase, I was suddenly feeling very Uncle Dick.

I had originally estimated the merger synergies with Wolf Blass to be of the order of $8 million. More than half that sum was not to come from economies of scale but from the added value we thought we could bring to the Blass business — the intangibles of distribution strength, pricing discipline, the greater efficiency and effectiveness of our trading terms and our sales teams' well-honed negotiating skills with retailers. Some guts and determination were not going to go astray either.

It soon became abundantly clear that the challenge of achieving the profit levels we had projected was, yet again, going to be tougher than we would have liked. This should not have been too much of a surprise. Invariably with an acquisition, you find rattlesnakes where you least expect them. Unpleasant surprises or the 'known unknowns' of the takeover business are an unfortunate fact of life. However, with this one we were to find a few more serpents than we had bargained on and one very large and very nasty bastard in particular.

Once all the information was in, we projected the combined profit before interest and tax for the two companies in financial year 1991 at no more than $14 million. It was almost $3 million less than the number earned by Mildara on its own the previous year. More worrying, was that it was $4 million less than the profit base we had planned on when we put the deal together. Without wishing to be too unkind to ourselves, we had just paid $50 million for the pleasure of purchasing a still declining, loss making business.

Australia's and the world's serious recession of 1990–91 had resulted in licenced retailers reducing their stock levels by between ten and twenty per cent, equal to about three weeks' sales volume. No surprise there and nothing more than classic retailer behaviour during a business slowdown. Mildara, in also being caught up in the downturn in retailer confidence, suffered its first profit downturn, albeit slight, since my arrival in 1982. But the Blass trading performance between the date we began merger negotiations and when we completed the consolidation had been an unmitigated disaster. The severe sixty per cent profit downturn suffered by Blass in the six months to December and on which we had based our projections had considerably worsened in the second half; performance had plunged into serious loss-making territory. Worse was to come.

When David Smith looked into the details of the Wolf Blass accounts he discovered something else that set his alarm bells ringing. He knew I didn't like nasty surprises and he assiduously worked his department's backside off to ensure this happened as little as possible. David was neat and tidy and he sweated bullets if he had to be the bearer of bad news.

What he had found was something he wasn't looking forward to telling me. He had turned his discovery upside down, around and every which way in his mind but finally had come to the inescapable conclusion it was a problem for which even the most creative accounting hocus pocus couldn't find a solution. And that was the basis on which the Blass business valued its wine inventories, in other words, its cost of goods sold. Whereas Mildara valued its inventories on the basis of averaging its wine production costs over the preceding three years, Blass used a single year's costs as the basis for its cost of goods sold and embraced an inventory system known as first in first out (FIFO). In simple terms, this meant that the earliest produced wine (of its two to three year stock holding) was deemed to be the first sold. And the oldest wine, particularly during this period, was by far the cheapest because increasing demand for Australian wine in overseas markets had grape prices escalating at more than ten per cent a year.

During a period of rapid inflation the FIFO method produced a higher profit (or a lower loss) than the more conservative averaging method. To non-accountants, and sometimes to accountants as well, it seems nonsensical that the size of a firm's profits or losses could be dependent upon seemingly arbitrary decisions and definitions. The fact remains that rules intended to provide a degree of flexibility for businesses with different characteristics often turn out to provide results unintended by the rule makers. While the users of FIFO were not always motivated by sinister thoughts you could be forgiven for raising an eyebrow or two when you found you were on the rough end of the stick.

It was open to debate as to whether the FIFO method produced misleading annual financial results because of what were arguably out-of-date production costs. Given our now feverish, panicked state of mind we didn't think there was any debate about it all, they were misleading. The most galling thing was that that the accounting rules did not require companies to explicitly disclose the basis on which they valued their inventories. Human nature being what it is we were now looking for someone to blame. The only conclusion we could reach was that it was our own stupid fault; we hadn't asked enough questions or, more correctly, the right questions. We were left with the inescapable conclusion that the Blass business's loss in its 1990 financial accounts had been seriously understated by being based on 1988 production costs at around twenty per cent lower than those existing in 1990, a potential negative impact on our bottom line of around $5 million. This was the manure that was yet to hit the fan because we had no choice but to change the Blass stock valuation method to make it consistent with Mildara's method. It meant the projected 1991–92 Mildara Blass profit performance would have an even bigger black hole, which was now $9 million. We had some very serious work to do.

Gary Butler was an energetic, loud, laughing bumble bee with a colourful sense of the ridiculous. Only 164 cms tall, he had had two seasons at Melbourne Football Club in the early 1960's before being given his marching orders by iconic Melbourne coach, Norm Smith for being too short. Banished to Prahran Football Club in the then Victorian Football Association he had the doubtful pleasure of proving Norm Smith wrong by winning that competition's best and fairest award. I met him in 1968 during my MBA studies at Monash University and we became firm friends. He was to play a key, if unusual role in solving the Wolf Blass conundrum.

Gary was an industrial psychologist and had helped establish a successful business carrying out psychological testing and personnel placement services. Having split with his business partners in order to buy a transport business he was for a few months at a loose end. 'Come and give me a hand' I suggested, 'I need someone to spend time in the retail trade so I can get a fix on how retailers view the Blass takeover'.

The debriefing sessions were riotous affairs and my subordinates could have been forgiven for believing I had resorted to the taking of banned substances given the guffaws of laughter that emanated from my office. The Blass issue was clearly far from a laughing matter but our sessions were good therapy for dealing with Gary's unpopular findings. That is, findings that were unpopular with me. Retailers were adamant they would need extra discounts to renew consumer confidence in the Blass brand. It just shows how a bit of self-interest by respondents has the potential to lead you up the wrong path. Clearly, price reductions would only dig us deeper into the mire, so fortunately, my degree of self-interest more than outweighed theirs. I dealt with Gary's findings as simply as I could. I ignored them. I had also benefited from Dawn's participation at the evening dinner table as I kept bouncing ideas around as to what to do, in the process releasing the pressure and dissipating that debilitating, paralysing state of mind called uncertainty. Having the opportunity to kick around 'on the one hand but then on the other' ideas in a collegiate, unintimidating environment was, as always, worth its weight in gold. Consultants all over the world would ultimately be making small fortunes from providing such pressure releasing services to CEO's.

In 1992–93, as if by magic, the combined Mildara Blass EBIT was back on plan at $28 million and the Mildara/Blass 'merger' turned out to be one of the few major consolidations in the wine industry to produce its anticipated benefits. It was another one for the good guys.

Proponents of mergers of companies with strong brands invariably believed aggressive cost savings could be achieved without diminution in the revenue line. There was this erroneous belief that the brand strength of the merged business would transcend the power of the retailers to determine which products they would carry on their shelves. Following the consolidation of Seppelt's, Penfolds and Lindeman's in 1990, South Australian Brewing (later to be renamed Southcorp) found to its profound surprise that retailers believed they didn't need all those products on their shelves. But nothing was learned from that experience. Worse was to come when those brands were combined with Rosemount following the disastrous merger of Southcorp and Rosemount under Keith Lambert and even more disastrously when those four brands were further combined with those of Mildara Blass under Trevor O'Hoy's stewardship at Foster's in 2005. The captains of industry deluded themselves into believing brands would transcend all and their shareholders suffered the consequences.

So, why did the Mildara Blass consolidation work when the others failed?

First and foremost was our almost paranoid focus on the numbers. We had determined the size of the black hole, albeit a very nasty and much bigger black hole than we had anticipated. The solution was very simple: we just had to find a way to fill it. Our directors, particularly the ex-Blass directors, thought we had gone stark raving mad when we announced our intention to immediately raise Blass prices by around ten per cent across the board. But there was method in our apparent madness.

The 1990/91 recession had caused our competitors to significantly lower their prices, seemingly almost a reflex action when times turned tough. But of all the major wine brands at that time Wolf Blass had probably been the worst in caving in to retailers' demands for discounts. Our madness in raising Blass prices had merely brought Blass consumer prices back to where they had been twelve months earlier. But our sales teams had also delivered and we achieved the very tasty double whammy of increased sales volumes as well. At the end of the first twelve months Blass sales volumes had increased by ten per cent, recovering the ten per cent volume loss incurred by the struggling Remy Blass sales team the year before. Increased prices and increased volumes had delivered an additional and very tasty $10 million to the bottom line in the space of twelve months.

At first glance, one might have argued from a strategic perspective, that the merger succeeded because Mildara Blass, with a combined turnover of $100 million, was much smaller and more focussed at the premium end of the market than Southcorp's $420 million business. The fact that Blass had a small range of high volume lines with very strong consumer and retailer franchises certainly helped our cause. The combined product range of Mildara and Wolf Blass was not so large that it could not still be handled efficiently and effectively by one, albeit larger, sales force. No. The major reason for the merger's success was much simpler. In the domestic market we had merely returned the Blass brand to essentially the same level of profitability it had had when it was in its pomp five years earlier with an EBIT of around $12 million.

In other words, the major reason we succeeded was because Wolf had failed to continue to pursue his historical profit maximising policies. If we had put the two businesses together when the Blass business had been at its height it is unlikely we would have done all that much better than what the two businesses were achieving as separate entities. Again, it seemed a victory for a targeted, numbers-based approach.

To put it in numerical terms, before the merger, and the 1990/91 recession, Mildara's EBIT to sales revenue ratio had been running at around twenty-six per cent. In the mid-1980s Wolf Blass had been able to achieve a similar ratio. But by 1991 the Blass profit to sales ratio had fallen to zero and then into negative territory. By 1993, two years later, we had merely raised the combined EBIT to sales ratio back to slightly more than twenty-six per cent (by 1999 it was running at thirty-three per cent). Our move on Blass had been well timed. It was the timing, as well as our understanding of the financial dynamics, that had been the key to the merger's success.

However, the $28 million in EBIT that we produced in FY 1993 was not solely because of our efforts in rejuvenating the Wolf Blass business. As is always the case in a dynamic world, other things were happening. Jamiesons Run continued its rapid and profitable penetration of the domestic premium red wine market and was awarded Wine Brand of the Year by the wine media, we were able to cash in on the burgeoning international market for Australian wine and sales of Yellowglen resumed their upward path after suffering a brief period of stagnation.

¶

In the four years following its acquisition in 1984 Yellowglen's annual sales volume increased from around 100,000 bottles to more than a million bottles but by 1988 the sales curve had begun to plateau. While the Yellowglen brand had created and then very successfully dominated the premium market segment for Australian sparkling wine, it was now attracting the inevitable competition. BRL Hardy's Sir James and the French-owned Chandon in the Yarra Valley were making life more difficult for us along with a bevy of pretenders who were also trying to get in on the act. The premium segment was still growing strongly but interlopers were stealing much of that growth.

In the wine industry, it was not unknown for husbands and wives to have key management roles in the same company. It was far more common practice in privately-owned wine companies, although

Brian and Fay McGuigan worked together very successfully at Wyndham Estate Limited in the Hunter Valley when it was still publically listed.

In 1989 Dawn and I committed the sin of joining that exclusive club. Yellowglen needed a change in tack and I had convinced Dawn against her strongly voiced better judgment to become the marketing manager for the Yellowglen brand and to employ her public relations skills and experience in bringing about a rejuvenation of the brand.

Dawn had initially recommended we bring in someone else to execute her belief that public relations was the way to go. But I convinced myself and Dawn that she was the best person to do the job. It was self-indulgent on my part for many reasons, not the least of which was the simple pleasure of having her nearby on a daily basis. But in most people's view it not only defied convention but also common sense.

And as Dawn kept emphasising to me it would place her in an almost impossible position in relation to other Mildara staff members. But Dawn's successful strategy for the Yellowglen brand and its steadfast implementation did the ultimate talking.

Having overcome the initial and inevitable emotional hurdle of being the boss's wife, although that burden like Damocles sword did never quite go away, she eventually became a respected and accepted member of the marketing team. With the Yellowglen brand having been successfully rejuvenated, Dawn then took on the role of corporate affairs director in 1994 (together with some specific marketing challenges) and we continued to work closely together until our retirement in December 1999.

This included our last four years following the sale of Mildara Blass to Foster's. When the Foster's directors, not unreasonably, questioned the wisdom of employing a husband and wife team, my chairman, Brian Healey, was quick to point out that Dawn was the really smart one.

As I had anticipated, or maybe just hoped, Dawn's high standards and highly developed people skills enabled her to overcome most if not all the conventional criticisms of the unenviable position she found herself in. The subject of Mildara in all its rainbow colours became our major topic of conversation at meal times where we argued our respective cases as to how the business might be better run.

Nor, was she happy with her salary. Hardly a surprise. While she understood full well we were playing a team game she occasionally bristled at a pay grade she felt demeaned her contribution and which I deliberately set at least one and arguably two levels lower than was clearly justified. There were few secrets as to what people at Mildara received by way of remuneration and it was my way of paying lip service to the symbolic price that had to be paid for the unconventional arrangement I had put in place.

But I have digressed yet again.

A major contributor to added shareholder value following the merger was the power of the Blass brand in export markets. Again, we were able to extract every advantage provided by the opportunity that presented itself.

Whereas most Australian wine companies pursued a volume first, profit second policy in an export market growing at twenty per cent a year, Mildara Blass didn't. We adopted the same policies we adhered to in the domestic market. Our export prices were thirty per cent higher than the average for all Australian bottled exports; we continued to focus only on the top twenty-five per cent of the market by price; and we stuck to our policy of regular price rises to at least maintain our record of achieving higher year on year gross margins for each bottle sold.

28

Too many brands

Could a wine company have too many brands?
In 1993 our export business was being carried along very nicely by the surging demand for Australian wine and the domestic market was also doing the right thing. However, I was concerned as to how long we would be able to continue to grow our share of the domestic market.

Consumers of most food and beverage products largely stick to one or two favoured brands, but not wine consumers. They like to chop and change and to churn their favoured brands; hence our strategy of having a broad portfolio of brands and a belief in the need to keep refreshing that portfolio. For such a strategy to be effective our sales teams needed to continue retaining the attention of retail buyers before overload and tedium had them staring off into the distance thinking of better things to do. Attempting to fully satisfy the needs of consumers with a broadening range of brands would ultimately conflict with the time constraints of the gatekeepers, the retail buyers. Determining the maximum number of brands/products one salesman could handle effectively before the law of diminishing returns took hold was impossible to predict. You would not know until you had stepped off the cliff and by then it would be too late. But in 1993, following our acquisition of Wolf Blass, I felt we must have been getting pretty close to the edge.

The idea of some sort of conceptual limit to the number of products a salesman can handle with maximum effectiveness is one with which just about everyone is prepared to agree. In principle that is. But in practice, it is a problem that has almost always been universally ignored; and for good reason. Establishing a second distribution force and then reallocating the company's product range between them is a nightmarish logistical conundrum and the additional cost likely to reduce profits, at least in the short term. It was a pill too bitter to even contemplate. Better to ignore it.

My description of one of the key reasons for Southcorp's problems being the limitations of a single sales force was a broken record that journalists, wine writers and my co-directors were heartily sick of hearing. I was getting closer and closer to being beholden to putting my money where my mouth was.

In 1993 we established a second sales team in each state under the name Southern Cross — hardly original but, having agonised for long enough, we wasted no more time trying to think of something better. We switched some brands from the existing Mildara Blass sales team and the Southern Cross team took a higher proportion of new brands and acquisitions as they came on stream. The two teams had separate sales offices but used the same warehouse, delivery infrastructure and marketing support structure.

A benefit of going down this road was the pressure it imposed on me to acquire new brands and on our marketing team to introduce new brands to spread the cost of the dual team strategy as well as to more quickly use the greater fire power we now had at our disposal. This pressure pushed the boundaries and unsurprisingly our proportion of new product failures rose, although not to the point at which it negated the effectiveness of the two team strategy.

Before implementing our strategy, we soon realised there was a related hurdle that seemed like a serious one. Our decision to go with two sales teams was an idea not welcomed with open arms by our first line customers. Retail and wholesale buyers argued they didn't want to waste time by having to deal with two salesmen. They were categorical they would not buy any more Mildara Blass product from two salesmen than they would from one salesman, irrespective of the number of products. It was a convenient argument that defied human nature. The law of diminishing returns had had almost universal application to merged wine companies in the past and would inevitably raise its ugly head again when one sales team had too many products. So we ignored the trade's views and stuck to our guns. Conventional wisdom (and some of our board members) suggested that acting in defiance of our major customers' views would be at our peril.

Between 1992 and 1995 Mildara Blass sales revenue, admittedly assisted by a buoyant export market, increased by thirty-four per cent from an annual rate of $108 million to $145 million, EBIT increased by sixty-one per cent from $26 million to $42 million, our EBIT to sales ratio increased from twenty-six per cent to thirty per cent and share earnings jumped by eighty-eight per cent from twenty-five cents a share to forty-seven cents a share. It appeared the proof of the pudding had been in the eating.

The only number to go into reverse was return on investment although that was for different reasons. EBIT to funds invested dropped from twenty-two per cent to sixteen per cent due to the $70 million we had invested over that three-year period in yet to be needed new vineyards. The vineyards needed to be put in place in order to ensure our projected demand requirements would be met seven years down the track. Paradoxically, in more than twenty years in the wine industry, it was my only long-term planning project. By 2000 the wine world was in the process of changing and by 2005, long after I had gone, it was clear that because of the world's over-supply of wine, it had been an unnecessary investment. Still, as we all know, when you make a forecast, particularly a long-term one, the only thing you can be certain about is that you will be wrong. It's just a matter of how wrong.

29

Pre Foster's

The last decade of the twentieth century saw grape growers turning cartwheels, throwing their hats in the air and buying new motor cars. It was a rare decade of prosperity for a group that for the previous hundred years had been on the bones of its backside.

Two other factors characterised the Australian wine industry throughout the 1990s: the inexorable, insidious expansion of Coles and Woolworths liquor retail chains and the almost insatiable demand for Australian wine in overseas markets.

¶

In 1991, the year Mildara took control of the Wolf Blass brand, the export business accounted for less than twelve per cent of the two companies' combined wine volumes. Despite continuing good growth in the domestic market that proportion had jumped to thirty per cent only three years later. As one of our key strategies was to restrict our focus to the top priced twenty to thirty per cent of both the domestic and export markets, we had to fight tooth and nail in a very tight spot market for premium grade grapes. This obviously meant paying higher prices than we would have otherwise preferred.

With the company's own vineyards projected to produce less than thirty per cent of future requirements (compared to around sixty per cent five years earlier) we had embarked on a significant vineyard planting program, as had all the other major companies. The huge increase in new plantings was exacerbated by the unintended consequences of the Federal Government's tax laws which gave rise to the infamous tax avoidance MIS schemes.

These schemes saw investors piling into grape planting projects (as well as forestry, tea tree oil, almonds and olives) to generate tax deductions from their initial investment, with no concern for whether there would be any demand for the output when the investments came on stream five to six years down the track. The 1990s' short-term shortage of grapes turned into a raging surplus a little more than a decade later. It was another example of the boom and bust characteristic of primary production and which, it can be argued with twenty-twenty hindsight, was always likely to be another example of history repeating itself.

To help fund our investment in grape supply, we divested in 1993 our New Zealand business, Morton Estate. We also sold the vineyards in the Marlborough region of New Zealand that had come with the Blass purchase. We had had five poor vintages in a row in New Zealand and I decided it was not a good place to grow grapes compared to Australia even though the timing of these divestments did leave something to be desired. Within months, initiated by the success of the intensely flavoured Cloudy Bay sauvignon blanc from the Marlborough region, New Zealand sauvignon blanc began taking the world by storm and soon challenged the almighty chardonnay as the preferred glass of white wine. It was an opportunity that would go begging, but quitting New Zealand had seemed like a good idea at the time.

The traditional export market for Australian wine had been the UK, a market that had waxed and waned for more than a century. But when UK consumers again embraced cheaper Aussie wines, following the helpful floating of the Australian dollar, they found to their consummate and surprised delight that Australia's New World wine styles tasted far better than they might have remembered and, even more surprisingly, better than the French, Italian and Spanish wines that had for years exclusively graced their tables. Unfortunately, there was a downside for the Australian exporters. The British retail chains had learned the art of the rapist and mugger sooner than their brethren in other countries and most Australian exporters were led like lambs to the slaughter. The retailers from the Old Dart were able to extract better and better deals as they played one Australian winemaker off against one other. Only Brown Brothers, Brian Croser's Petaluma and Mildara Blass showed much resistance.

Fortunately for Mildara Blass, US consumers had also discovered Australian wines and started a vigorous love affair. The US retail wine market was far more fragmented than that of the UK and US retailers were unable to exercise the same degree of unilateral power. Initially stimulated by Paul Hogan's film *Crocodile Dundee*, North Americans had developed a soft spot for all things down under. Many Americans still saw Australia as a more modern version of their own Wild West frontier and were delighted to apply the blissful, but erroneous, romance of that period in American history to the little Aussie battler. While they drew the line at Vegemite and John Elliott's Australian meat pies, neither of which were able to get off the ground, the affection of North American and Canadian consumers for Australia was quickly reflected in the speed with which they adopted Australian wines.

As the US produced around seventy per cent of its own wine needs, Australia's export volume was never likely to reach the dizzy heights achieved in the UK, a market that relied almost exclusively on imported wine. But the US prices (thirty per cent higher) and profit margins (eighty per cent higher) were far more attractive and this was where Mildara Blass concentrated its major export thrust. As a result, the far more profitable US market ultimately accounted for around fifty per cent of our exports whereas the much larger but less price effective UK market accounted for less than twenty-five per cent, the reverse of the position held by most Aussie wine exporters.

It would be hard to think of a more overlooked character in Mildara's success than export manager Bill Stevens. In addition to Bill's tireless efforts I had flirted more aggressively with the US export market in 1988 by acquiring the Mark Swann group of brands from Robert Hesketh, an Australian wine industry opportunist who also had a penchant for doing things differently.

Robert's Australian wines were early entrants to the US market, with one brand, Roo's Leap, being predicted by leading wine writer Robert Parker and influential US magazine the *Wine Spectator* to be a hot brand of the future. One couldn't help but wonder whether Robert Hesketh's engaging persona had had something to do with the *Wine Spectator's* enthusiastic accolades because he certainly did far better out of the deal than we did, the brands failing to fulfil the *Wine Spectator's* predictions.

Roo's Leap, unsurprisingly, had a bounding kangaroo on the label that was a little before its time. I ate my heart out when another Australian brand, Yellowtail, also with a kangaroo on the label but far better designed, was introduced to the US in 2002 at a disappointing and unnecessarily low price and absolutely smashed the market, selling more than 80 million bottles a year. Yellowtail's low entry price was a disaster for other Australian wine exporters who caved in to their distributors' demands for deep discounts so as to be more competitive with Yellowtail.

Giving in on pricing pressure at the first whiff of grapeshot was a familiar stance for Australian winemakers and totally unnecessary given that the wine market is really a series of market segments demarcated by price (and a number of other classifications) rather than one amorphous whole.

¶

Throughout the '70s and '80s the retailing of alcoholic beverages in Australia had remained highly fragmented. There were a few entrepreneurial retailers such as Theo's in Sydney and Dan Murphy in Melbourne who owned multiple stores and extracted sizeable discounts from favoured suppliers. But the majority of retailers at that time were single store mum and dad liquor shops and hotels that largely relied on their membership of wholesaler banner groups for their regular weekly specials.

In this environment the performance based trading terms of

Mildara Blass continued to stand us in very good stead. While the more entrepreneurial retailers drove a hard bargain for discounts they did support their favoured suppliers and as a consequence punched well above their weight in terms of performance. Being prepared to meet the seemingly rapacious demands of the likes of Theo's and Dan Murphy was still well worthwhile.

As Coles and Woolworths gradually acquired liquor stores they soon outstripped the entrepreneurs in terms of volume of business but were nowhere near as savvy or as effective in their ability to appeal to consumers. The simple reason for this was that the liquor departments of Coles and Woolworths were run by middle ranking bureaucrats who did not have a creative bone in their bodies. They had risen through the ranks by being able to follow the rules, by keeping their noses clean and applying a bit of thuggery which appealed to their bosses even more. As a consequence, we were offering Coles and Woolworths discounts of only seven and a half per cent whereas we were offering as much as twelve and a half per cent to the entrepreneurs who were much better value despite their much smaller size.

Woolworths turned out to be far more successful than Coles in venturing into the booze business. This success can be attributed to it having acquired the then relatively small Dan Murphy operation. It had quickly become starkly obvious to Woolworths management that Tony Leon and the Dan Murphy name were assets that generated far greater activity than the outlets managed by their own bureaucrats. Woolworths had the sense to throw its considerable financial resources behind the acquired management in pursuing its apparently personal, entrepreneurial approach in building Australia's most successful liquor chain. Twenty years later the vast majority of Dan Murphy's customers still think they are purchasing from Dan the man. On the other hand, Coles has stuck with its rigid, bureaucratic formula apparently believing that its impersonal Liquorland offering ticked all the boxes.

In their drive for increased coverage Coles and Woolworths naturally focussed on acquiring the bigger independent stores and in particular owners with multiple stores. Mildara Blass faced the possibility they would acquire stores that were getting a better deal from us than they were. If and when that occurred they would be ferociously unhappy. The very least they were likely to do would be to give us a lengthy and costly holiday from their promotions as well as force us to give them the maximum discount. I was particularly concerned about Theo's, owned by Theo Karidis (eventually purchased by Coles), who was receiving a twelve and a half per cent discount. Although it was technically not against the law to offer different discounts to different customers the Corporations Act required a rationale to justify such differences.

This was not a problem in itself. The greater problem was that Coles and Woolworths would not be interested in any fancy arguments justifying variable discounts. They would always want the top discount as a matter of course. Because Coles and Woolworths accounted for less than twenty per cent of the national market (they would have a seventy per cent share by 2014) an extra five per cent discount would deliver a $1.5 million blow to our profits, something I was not exactly turning cartwheels over.

Theo was Greek and, like his forebears, a born trader who played a mean game of poker. Theo and I had lunch every six months or so and got on very well. But, as it turned out, not well enough. Sentiment was not in Theo's make up. In a rush of ill placed bonhomie I explained my potential predicament to him. He was sympathetic in principle but steely eyed about any potential reduction in his discount. I nevertheless decided to test his resolve. Despite the fact that his seven stores accounted for around eight per cent of our business in New South Wales I told him I had no choice but to reduce his discount to ten per cent. He warned me what would happen.

We shook hands and returned to our respective corners. His resolve was unshaken. For the next nine months he did not buy a single bottle from us. I estimated it cost our bottom line more than $1 million — not much less than the annual cost of having given the higher discount to Coles and Woolworths in the first place. I threw up my hands in defeat, went back to Theo cap in hand and reinstated his twelve and a half per cent discount. We were now mates again and he insisted on taking me out to lunch.

Ironically, my about-turn in throwing in the towel with Theo could now be financially justified on the basis of solving our looming problem with Coles and Woolworths. By resuming business with Theo we would generate the profit that would now be lost by voluntarily giving Coles and Woolworths the additional discount. The argument was a bit Irish because we would always be around $1.5 million worse off than if we had been able to maintain the original arrangements. But then again, the status quo was always an unrealistic longer term outcome given the appetite for expansion by Coles and Woolworths.

The real lesson to emerge from this minor fracas was that a strong retailer like Theo didn't need our brands or indeed any other particular brands. By now, Mildara Blass had some of the strongest brands in the market place but because of the number of products available to retailers, Theo proved more than conclusively that strong wine brands were in themselves not worth a pinch of billygoat manure. There were too many substitutes. To believe otherwise was delusional. It was a realisation best kept to myself.

¶

Our perceived cavalier approach of continually pushing up prices and profit margins was matched by our belief in the finite life cycles of most wine brands. This was not to suggest when their time was up that wine brands disappeared, rather they plateaued then gradually declined.

By 1993, seventy per cent of the Australian market for upper middle, premium and super premium priced wines was held by brands that had not existed twenty years earlier. The underlying factor was wine consumers' tendency to regularly add to and delete brands from their preferred portfolio. This made older brands increasingly vulnerable.

Interestingly, that attitude does not apply to sparkling wines. Sparkling wine buyers approach their purchases with a totally different perspective. They are positively influenced by the popularity of a product whereas the more sophisticated table wine consumers do the reverse, are usually derisive of popular wines on principle and and more likely to be on the lookout for new wines from adventurous winemakers, known as 'discovery' wines. This contrast makes the sparkling wine market far more conducive to conventional media advertising and PR campaigns.

Opponents of our thinking on table wine brand life cycles argued that adopting a fatalistic attitude was ultimately self-fulfilling. Irrespective of whose argument was correct the most bizarre example of how counter-productive a promotional campaign can be occurred in 1975. Lindeman's Ben Ean moselle had been a huge success story in the Australian market. It was an inoffensive, slightly sweet white wine in the German moselle style, a name that can no longer be used unless the wine is sourced from the Moselle region in Germany. Ben Ean was Australia's largest, individual wine product by a country mile and by 1974 had reached a sales level equal to a rumoured seven million bottles a year, a huge volume even by today's standards. At this level, Ben Ean's sales volumes had stalled. Philip Morris, Lindeman's owner since 1972, decided to show Lindeman managers how it was done by throwing marketing money at the brand.

The biggest TV campaign in the history of the Australian wine industry was launched. The rumoured spend was $3 million, an enormous figure for a wine product at the time and equal to around thirty per cent of total wine industry profits. The thrust of the campaign was that Ben Ean was the biggest selling wine in Australia and, by implication, the best. Suddenly, wine consumers were alert to the suggestion that 'everybody' drank Ben Ean. The brand was suddenly seen as ubiquitous and common. Within two years sales volumes of Ben Ean had plunged to only a third of the level that existed before the beginning of the campaign. It was a lesson not to be forgotten.

Given that table wine consumers tended to seek out new brands logic suggested it was better to keep refreshing our own brand portfolio. This was a policy we continued to pursue with great gusto. Naturally, not all were successful. Pepperjack, Robertson's Well, Annie's Lane, Half Mile Creek and Yellow were all successful home grown introductions (if plagiarised ideas) and, with the exception of Half Mile Creek which was later to be killed stone dead by Foster's, all are still successful brands today. Yarra Ridge, Andrew Garratt, Galway Port and Director's Special Port were more than useful acquisitions, Tisdall and Tolley were acquisition duds and Phantom's Lake and Flanagan's Run were notable new product failures that joined a lengthening queue.

Our continued success attracted the attention of the mighty Foster's Brewing Limited which, having displayed exemplary restraint for more than twenty years, decided it was time to get in on the wine act.

30

Sold to Foster's

Never get between between a shareholder and a sandwich at an annual general meeting.

In late 1995 the share price of Foster's Brewing Limited was little changed from three years earlier and chief executive Ted Kunkel was under pressure to find a growth strategy. Ted had made no small contribution to saving the company's shareholders from being wiped out following John Elliott's tragically timed, abortive privatisation attempt in 1990 but shareholders being shareholders they were now jumping up and down about Foster's lack of growth; selfish and hard to please are shareholders, greedy as well.

The word on the street was that Foster's would make a move on the buoyant wine industry and that it had its eye on either Mildara Blass or BRL Hardy. It was perhaps no coincidence that Mildara Blass chairman Brian Healey was now also a director of Foster's. But an important question for Foster's should have been whether Mildara Blass's performance record was likely to continue into the future.

Over the thirteen year journey from 1982 the Mildara Blass EBIT growth had averaged twenty-seven per cent each year and share earnings growth had averaged fourteen per cent a year. Including annual dividends, shareholder value had grown by close to eighteen per cent a year over the same period. Mildara Blass was in exclusive company. It was not unusual for an organisation to have a burst of superior performance for five or six years but to meet what I thought Foster's objectives were likely to be Mildara Blass would need to extend its superior thirteen year growth and efficiency record to at least twenty years. Empirical evidence on long-term historical corporate performance suggested the likelihood of a superior growth record being achieved over a twenty-year period by one entity to be somewhat remote, particularly in an industry as competitive and as changeable as the wine industry. A further factor that should have counted against Mildara Blass was its thirty per cent EBIT to sales revenue ratio, suggesting that every ounce of productivity had already been wrung out of the business. Most other businesses had ratios of somewhere around ten per cent with a few as high as twenty per cent. On both counts, BRL Hardy looked like it should have been the superior bet. Its run of success was only five years old and its productivity level, measured by return on sales and return on investment was significantly lower, suggesting far greater potential for improvement than Mildara Blass.

Foster's most cerebral non-executive director was Fred Hilmer, ex-boss of highly rated McKinsey Consulting and later a highly criticised CEO of Fairfax Limited before becoming a much more lauded vice-chancellor of the University of New South Wales. With good reason he favoured BRL Hardy as the better choice. However, a majority of the Foster's directors chose to place what I would have thought was a long-shot bet on Mildara Blass. Long shot or not, the Mildara Blass bet turned out to be a good one, at least for a while. Over the next five years Mildara Blass's earnings before interest, tax and amortisation of goodwill rose from $47 million to more than $150 million. Return on investment on additional invested capital more than maintained its eighteen per cent historical rate and EBIT to sales revenue rose to an even headier thirty-three per cent. Foster's Ted looked like a genius. Underpinned by Mildara Blass' profitable growth Foster's share price doubled over the next four years. However, the continued solid performance by Foster's well run beer division, Carlton and United Breweries, had not been completely irrelevant to that outcome.

From the time of Mildara Blass's half-year profit announcement in March 1995 its share price had been strong, increasing from $5.60 to $6.60 at the time of the full year results announcement in September. It was no illusion as the company's underlying performance had more than justified the escalating share price, although the possibility of a takeover as regularly aired in the media had helped add a bit of sexiness to the equation.

On a bleak and windy Melbourne morning in November 1995 Mildara Blass chairman Brian Healey's unannounced smiling face appeared through the open door of my Albert Park office. Needing more space to accommodate our expanding marketing and accounting teams we had in 1991 elevated ourselves from the pokey rooms above Ricardo's restaurant to the other side of Albert Park's busy Bridport Street. We were now located in the nicely refurbished former Albert Park picture theatre next to one of that suburb's historical landmarks, the classic Victorian building, the Biltmore. For almost a week the jungle drums had suggested that Foster's chairman, John Ralph, and CEO Kunkel were about to make an offer for Mildara Blass. It was now official, well sort of. Foster's had finally broken cover and discussions were to take place at 2 pm that day at the Foster's office in nearby Southbank.

John Ralph had made his name as finance director and then CEO of mining giant CRA (now Rio) but had since moved on and become an even higher profile professional director of a number of heavyweight companies. John was Australian Prime Minister John Howard's favourite businessman. Straight up and down was John, never a hair out of place, chairman of the board of management at the Jesuit Xavier College and an elder in the Catholic Church. Goody Two Shoes wouldn't have got a look in with John around. But John's religious affiliations didn't fool those who knew him. John was a tough customer, highly capable and a rare taker of prisoners, extremely bright as well. On the other hand, Ted Kunkel was more your common or garden variety rough and tumble, straight ahead half back flanker of the 1970s.

It wasn't that I necessarily wanted to enter into a mine is bigger than yours contest but I did feel it was a bit rich asking Brian and I to meet them at their office. It seemed another example of the high and mighty attitude that had been ingrained in the brewing industry for more than a century and the current incumbents obviously had no intention of breaking that particular mould. At first thought it seemed like intimidation and to show us whose foot the shoe was really on. However, I suspect the simpler answer was that they just hadn't thought about it, merely taking for granted that the mountain should come to Muhammad.

Brian Healey dismissed my questioning look, believing we should be generous towards our suitor. It is said that hypocrisy is the tribute that vice pays to virtue and that in a world less than perfect hypocrisy is sometimes the best that can be managed. Brian, a master of the quote, particularly Latin quotations, felt this was one of those occasions. Irrespective of Brian's motives my initial sensitivity to the two brewers was soon overcome by a healthy dose of self-interest, which can come in handy at times. I found I was more than capable of playing the hypocrisy game. Dawn and I held between one and two per cent of Mildara's issued shares, a figure much less than most people imagined but still very significant to us and I conveniently concluded that having to meet at Foster's office was perhaps not such a big deal after all.

I was unintentionally but fashionably late for the meeting by close to fifteen minutes. I had not been offered a spot in Foster's executive garage and had to park four blocks away, adding another dimension to my initial reaction of being somewhat on the peeved side. Neither had I been brought up to speed on the security arrangements in the Fort Knox like Foster's building and on a need to know basis no one on the door knew who I was. To most people the whole thing was still supposed to be a big bloody secret. I then ran into a tall intimidating security bloke with shoulders the width of an axe handle.

'Help you mate?' he fired at me.

'Yes, I'm here for a meeting.'

'Oh yeah,' he said, evidently not all that captivated either by my look or my tone. He followed up with, 'with whom?' which I thought was pretty impressive for a security bloke.

'John Ralph and Ted Kunkel,' I said, maybe a little jauntily.

'I take it you're Ray King,' ventured the giant glaring down at me while stealing a quick glance at his wristwatch.

Successfully intimidated, I waited for, 'you're bloody late you are' but he didn't say another word and quickly walked me through a door marked private. I hoped it would turn out better than that first time.

Like John Ralph, Brian Healey was a pretty neat and tidy sort of bloke. He didn't like messy or noisy, loud mouths or big-headed braggarts. He diligently shined his shoes every morning and was usually ten minutes early for every appointment. He certainly didn't make an exception to that discipline for our two o'clock meeting with the Foster's heavies, particularly as he fancied a crack at the Foster's chairman's role if and when John Ralph ever stepped aside.

Having finally found a parking spot I had hurried along Southbank's footpath. In my mind's eye I could see Brian beginning to bristle at what seemed like my lack of respect and how it might be reflecting on him. Initially a bit hot and bothered as to the impression my apparent tardiness might be making on my potential employers I had then thought, 'oh what the hell' and got a fit of the giggles, fantasising how my non-appearance might be going down with the three amigos as they kept looking at their watches.

'So where the fuck is he Brian,' demands the church elder finally, nerves starting to get the better of him. 'Is he trying to tell us something?'

'I can't answer those questions,' says Brian, starting to lose the plot and becoming dangerously frivolous. 'Ask me an easier one, say, on football.' (Brian was on St Kilda's board at the time).

'Don't be an arsehole, Brian. Is he normally on time?'

'Normally he's right on the button.'

'So where the fuck is he?'

Fighting to remove the grin before being ushered into the meeting room I am met with very dark looks.

After some muttering and evil eye on Brian's part we padded up together to open the batting. No thunderbolts or late swinging yorkers from John or from Ted. Just on the spot, straight up and down medium pace stuff really, no problems.

After a bit of argy bargy Brian and I agreed to take Foster's final offer of $7.75 a share (they had started at $7.50) to the Mildara Blass board. Months later when we were more comfortable with each other Ted chided me for being a poor negotiator by accepting the $7.75 when they were prepared to go to $8.00. In a fit of what I thought was whimsical good humour I replied I would have been more than happy with the $7.50.

Over the thirteen year journey the Mildara Blass share price had increased from 60 cents in 1982 to the equivalent of more than $10.00 a share after allowing for bonus shares and rights issues. This sixteen fold increase in value compared more than favourably with the Australian Stock Exchange's all ordinaries index over the same period which had registered a more pedestrian threefold increase. The price earnings ratio of the Foster's bid was 16.6 times Mildara's after tax earnings, equivalent to around twelve times EBIT, significantly better than global wine industry valuation multiples at the time. For example, BRL Hardy's P/E ratio was around nine and its EBIT multiple, around 6.5. Foster's offer was a twenty-five per cent premium to the average price Mildara Blass shares had traded at over the previous six months, so it looked like a good deal for Mildara Blass shareholders, all of whom were now jumping for joy and throwing their hats in the air. The smarter ones immediately sold their Mildara shares at close to the offer price and piled into BRL Hardy whose share price had immediately jumped by ten per cent. Over the next few months Hardy's share price rose by a further forty per cent and the smarties were soon on the grin again.

What about the interests of the Mildara Blass executives? The requirement for me to stay on for at least three years suggested that as long as I didn't desert my colleagues and give them the short back and sides they would be well catered for and Mildara's smooth running culture kept intact.

Irrespective of what the impact of a Foster's takeover might be on their employment prospects my top troops, as well as the foot sloggers further down the line, were probably happy to collect the spoils of war now that their Mildara shares were at record levels. As indeed was I. Approaching fifty-seven years of age and feeling as if I were running out of gas as a CEO it provided the unique opportunity to perhaps have my cake and eat it at the same time.

Accounting firm, Ernst &Young got the job to determine whether the offer was fair and reasonable. This legal requirement was supposed to assist the Mildara directors in making a sensible recommendation to our shareholders at an extraordinary general meeting. It was money for jam as far as Ernst & Young was concerned and a complete waste of time and shareholders' money given our shareholders were already licking their lips and waiting impatiently to count their money. But the Corporations Act and the rules of the Stock Exchange had to be complied with to protect any shareholders whose intellectual apparatus was not quite up to snuff. Predictably, the valuation came in at between $6.80 and $7.20 a share, approximately ten per cent less than the offer price so it was fairly obvious what our less than necessary recommendation to shareholders would be.

Overcome with a feeling of fairy flossed goodwill towards my fellow man in the after-glow of the Foster's offer, I didn't use my potential leverage. Although Foster's financial advisers had apparently been adamant that I was essential to the success of the deal I didn't bother to nail down beneficial remuneration and share option arrangements. I still wanted to believe in the goodness of man despite life's earlier experiences. I was evidently one of God's children doomed to repeat past mistakes. People believe that studying history teaches us not to make the same mistakes but we do, over and over, as if stuffing up is one of our basic needs.

On the face of it Ted Kunkel was not the sort of executive I would have chosen as my master but then I suppose I would have found it difficult to choose anyone as my master. Ted assured me when we discussed remuneration matters that I would be well looked after and that my remuneration would be in keeping with the importance of my role. I read a bit more into Ted's comment than he evidently had in mind at the time. On the basis of his handshake that was good enough. Silly old me. Apparently, Ted didn't think my role was all that important. When disclosure regulations on senior executive remuneration were introduced three years later I learned that my annual remuneration remained up to thirty per cent less than Foster's other divisional managers, at least until I took the gloves off and threatened to get down and dirty. It seemed Ted couldn't get his head around my Mildara Blass payout. He apparently felt the windfall (it was obviously no windfall) justified a discount in my future remuneration arrangements.

Foster's was offering $592 million for Mildara Blass, including its $110 million of bank debt. Not bad for a company with an annual sales revenue of less than $150 million. The $592 million was certainly more than a bull's roar from the $9 million the company had been valued at in 1982 and the capitalisation value of the offer now placed Mildara in the largest hundred and twenty public companies listed on the Australian Stock Exchange.

Simon Jemison, a journalist with the Financial Review who wielded an acerbic pen and was no great personal admirer of mine over the years squared off the next day with:

'KING THE KEY TO FOSTER'S BID.'
'Brewing shareholders may well ask, why Mildara Blass? A large part of the $590 million answer is one man: Ray King and his marketing sense for what makes money in the wine industry. Quite simply, Mildara — like the car that King drives — is the Porsche 928 of the Australian wine industry. The 'Silver Fox' has succeeded where so many others have failed.'

Apparently Ted Kunkel wasn't quite so sure. He was quoted in the

Financial Review as saying Foster's would leverage its strengths in manufacturing, distribution and brand marketing. Was this an echo from the '70s and '80s or was it the ghost rising from the ashes of Ben Ean Moselle? As it turned out it was both. Real time evidence would later confirm Ted had given more than a fleeting thought to folding some key parts of Mildara Blass into Carlton and United Breweries, Foster's smooth running, well performed beer division run by his trusty first lieutenant, Nuno D'Aquino.

Within weeks, publicly listed wine companies around the world were re rated by the financial markets and their share prices surged by up to sixty per cent. Foster's move on Mildara Blass underpinned wine company share prices for at least the next decade.

For the first few weeks we enjoyed the handshakes and slaps on the back that are an essential part of the obligatory honeymoon period. It ended abruptly when Ted suggested it would be a good idea to close our head office in Albert Park and relocate more than forty marketing and financial staff to Foster's headquarters at Southbank.

I was about to give Ted some unexpected grief.

'Sorry Ted can't do that,' was my response.

It was exactly what I and the team had feared and I launched into my well-rehearsed speech.

'Ted, I will move heaven and earth to help you make Foster's investment work but, as we discussed during the negotiations, it will have to be my way. The beer industry has a totally different culture to ours. If we move to Southbank we will lose our sense of identity, morale will suffer and so too will performance.'

I had the Tooheys experience to back me up. Nevertheless, it was not totally irrelevant that at Albert Park the very nice couch in my office provided the opportunity for a daily after lunch snooze, sometimes five minutes, sometimes more. It was an indulgence likely to go out the window if we moved to Southbank, my now daily two-hour training ride on the bike before breakfast adding to a life-long natural tendency to be a serial cat-napper. While no cycling superstar I was nonetheless a handy bike rider, having over the years won nine

Masters state championships, four national road titles and placed sixth in the world road championships in Austria in 2014.

I liked my creature comforts and had no intention of giving them up. Nonetheless, Ted, never one to be under estimated, counter punched by installing Duncan Fraser at Albert Park as an unofficial, official mole. Duncan was a senior finance executive without portfolio at Foster's who Ted didn't quite know what to do with. At least one member of the blue blood Fraser family had been employed at the brewery since the year dot as if it had been a requirement of the company's constitution. Duncan's brief was to keep abreast of any particularly good or bad stuff that Ted thought I might want to keep to myself and to report it in timely fashion.

However, we gave Duncan a real job — or at least much more of a real job than he had at Foster's — and in no time he came to the pleasant realisation, certainly from our perspective, that he much preferred Mildara's easy-going atmosphere to the edgy, competitive and highly political environment at Southbank. Duncan's existence soon morphed into that of the double agent, a role from which we arguably received the better value given we had nothing to hide anyway.

Ted was not used to his suggestions let alone his directives being refused and certainly not by a newcomer whose services he felt he had just purchased with thirty pieces of silver. Initially, in the nicest possible way but then not so nicely, he pointed out the error of my ways. Most of the time Ted was a likeable and easy-going sort of bloke but as with most brewery bosses he had learned to be a bully on the job. We butted heads a couple of times and then squared off for the debate. My final comment was, 'Ted, over my dead body,' which probably didn't give him any ideas he hadn't already thought about. Following a decent staring contest Ted, sufficiently street smart to know when to stop being a bully, smiled. First round to me. But it was a knowing smile and that was not to be the end of it. He could be duplicitous at times and he filed this one away for Ron. As in later on. He would try me on for size again around eighteen months later.

In his book *10 Best and 10 Worst Decisions of Australian CEOs 1992 – 2002* business journalist and analyst Robert Gottliebsen wrote,

> 'the transformation of the Australian brewing giant, Foster's, into a global beverage powerhouse began with the purchase of Mildara Blass. Ted Kunkel's stroke of genius was to get on side Ray King who had run Mildara Blass brilliantly. Many people expected King to leave after the Foster's takeover but he worked with Kunkel until his retirement in 1999. By keeping the wine business under King, Kunkel was able to keep the Foster's beer and wine cultures separate.'

Robert was not even remotely aware of how hard I had had to fight to make sure that actually happened.

Ted Kunkel might have been easy-going but he was also tough, extremely resilient and one of the coolest guys under fire I had come across. He had done a good job for a Foster's joint venture in Canada in the late 1980s but had still been a surprise appointment as top dog in 1992. His meteoric rise followed the debt-led and ultimately abortive expansion of the Foster's business in the late 1980s. The then incumbent, John Elliott, had learned his wheeling and dealing craft at McKinsey & Co, the highly regarded consulting business run by Fred Hilmer. By the late '80s Elliott had not only been welcomed into the pantheon of Australian business but had also become president of the Australian Liberal Party and was being touted as possible prime minister material if he made the move into federal politics. That move would have provided only a fraction of what he was earning as a businessman but was one that Elliott ultimately would have rued not having taken given the way things eventually turned out. He also occupied the high profile post of president of the then extremely successful Carlton Football Club.

Unfortunately for Elliott, the ill-timed credit squeeze that hit the Australian and world economies in 1991 like a thunderbolt brought his ambitious debt funded play to privatise Foster's undone. It ruined him financially and he was ultimately declared bankrupt in 2005. But his real and unfortunate legacy had been to leave Foster's in financial tatters. Among many famous Australian business failures, John Elliott's and Foster's demise was probably the century's most surprising and ignominious fall from grace. Elliott had had had an outstanding track record over a twenty year period as a charismatic leader, original thinker and highly successful businessman but his previous good judgment and good luck deserted him in his final throw of the dice. He had fallen victim to the businessman's ever present seducer, hubris, and Big John was the latest in history's litter of powerful people undone by it. Elliott bet the ranch and lost it, including his job and his personal fortune. But give him his due, for the rest of his life he kept popping up, large as life, as if nothing had happened.

Crippled with debt Foster's was in serious danger of sinking beneath the waves. Peter Bartels, a highly capable chief operating officer but a not as successful CEO, succeeded John Elliott as CEO. He had then been easily spirited away to run retailer Coles Myer under the vigilant eye of key shareholder, Solomon Lew. No self-respecting local candidate for the boss' job was prepared to take on either the business risk or the personal risk of presiding over the potential demise of Australia's most famous beer brands. Ted Kunkel was apparently the candidate of last resort and to the surprise of many observers got the job. Ted duly delivered and was able to steady the Foster's ship and ultimately restore its fortunes.

Given the inherent strength of the Foster's brands, the rebuilding task was probably a lot easier than a lot of people realised but Ted's cool head justified his becoming the man of the moment, albeit that he had relied on his prescient appointment of Nuno D'Aquino as managing director of Carlton and United Breweries. Like Ted, Nuno had been lifted from relative obscurity. However, despite Ted's solid contribution Foster's would not have been able to keep their bankers at bay had it not been for a significant capital injection from Australian heavyweight BHP, which had taken on the role of white knight and in 1996 controlled a little over thirty-seven per cent of Foster's shares.

As well as high profile chairman John Ralph, Ted Kunkel, Fred Hilmer and former Mildara Blass chairman Brian Healey, the Foster's board included two BHP heavies, the very pleasant former senior partner of major accounting firm Arthur Anderson, Geoffrey Cohen, and the highly regarded ex Cadbury Schweppes CEO Frank Swann.

Over the next fifteen years the track record of the Foster's board descended from good to lousy despite an infusion of high profile heavy hitters.

Ted Kunkel's corporate strategy man was Canadian Keith Lambert who had been his chief financial officer in Canada. Ted believed he would need allies in his new role in Australia and had invited Keith to join him as chief financial officer but BHP had other ideas — it wanted its own man in the job in order to keep an eye on the unproven Ted and to protect its investment.

Ted was less than happy with BHP's stance but he had little choice in the matter. If Keith Lambert couldn't be his CFO then he would find another role for him so he handed Keith the corporate strategy portfolio. Keith was the spitfire pilot of the alcoholic beverage industry, something of a loner, brilliant at times but predictably unpredictable. He was smart and hard-working but frenetic, hyperactive, aggressively demanding of his small staff and not the best people manager in the world. I liked Keith and enjoyed his boisterous and loud company, apparently one of a small minority of his Foster's colleagues who felt that way. His lack of sensitivity and a tendency not to keep his thoughts to himself led to fractious relationships, his never ending poisonous feud with CUB chief, Nuno D'Aquino being the stand out example.

Keith ultimately resigned from Foster's in 1998 to run Rosemount Wines, owned by his mega rich father-in-law Bob Oatley and had significant early success, particularly in the USA export market. It may have been beginner's luck. In 2003 Oatley added to his not insignificant personal fortune when he orchestrated a reverse takeover of the perennially disappointing Southcorp Limited. Keith was handed the poisoned chalice, the CEO's job.

Unfortunately for Keith, he was successful in arousing the passionate interest of the business world just twice in his life; first when he got the top job at Southcorp and second when he was sacked less than two years later. Keith paid the price for Oatley's (and I suspect his own) erroneous belief that their success with Rosemount, a medium sized business, could be replicated at Australia's largest wine company. They clearly believed that the already bloated Southcorp could not only be rejuvenated but also benefit from being made even larger with the addition of the highly successful Rosemount business.

Following its absorption into the Southcorp empire it was no surprise that the highly successful Rosemount brand immediately started losing ground. It was simply lost in the sluggish monolith that was Southcorp. Nothing had been learned from decades of ponderous, largely unsuccessful Southcorp management. The same ineffective strategies had been repeated time and again and Keith's approach was to be no different. He soon fell into the same old trap of embarking on a discounting spree in an attempt to expand (or more likely to maintain) the sales volumes of the too many brands handled by Southcorp's single distribution system. He had also enthusiastically embraced the associated strategy known as 'channel stuffing', the practice of pushing as much stock as possible into the company's various distribution tiers (generally just before the end of the financial year) in the hope that the stock pressure would force sales out the other end. It didn't.

Practicing it once might have worked but Keith was merely following the bad habits of his predecessors. The unproductive practices had become ingrained and once you started on that particular treadmill you found it difficult to raise the strength of mind to get off. Under the circumstances, Keith's having to resort to such strategies to prop up sales revenue had been as predictable as night following day. The special sales deals aimed at building volume smashed a bottom line that wasn't all that flash to begin with and the sales channels, already stuffed with stock and now stuffed with even more stock, ground to a halt. In a headline grabbing sacking Keith was gone after less than twenty-four months in the job. Keith joined a long list of heavy hitters who hadn't exactly covered themselves in glory at Southcorp, that list including the high profile and now Reserve Bank director, Graeme Kraehe and more recently David Dearie.

I had a soapbox from which I could deliver a dozen sermons on the evils of Southcorp and Dawn and my colleagues had heard every one of them. Like the others who had initially listened patiently to my Southcorp monologues, Dawn was rarely in a hurry to hear any of them again.

By 1999 Mildara Blass, with less than half the sales revenue of Southcorp, was within a whisker of challenging Southcorp as the then world's second largest wine industry profit earner.

Meanwhile, back at the Foster's ranch, Keith Lambert was still a couple of years away from seriously blotting his copybook. But he was about to foreshadow what was just around the corner. At my first Foster's board meeting Keith gave a presentation on how he saw the future unfolding for the new wine business, the self-satisfied Foster's directors sitting back to enjoy the show.

Although Mildara Blass had averaged an eighteen per cent return on investment as a stand-alone business, Foster's would initially earn less than an eight per cent return based on the $592 million purchase price which included the newly created $310 million in goodwill (the price paid in excess of the value of Mildara Blass's net assets).

In his presentation Keith projected that by 2001 Mildara Blass sales revenue would double to $300 million and earnings before interest and tax and amortisation of purchased goodwill would increase from $47 million to $100 million. He also projected that additional investment over the period would need to be no more than around $30 million and that ROI would gradually increase from eight per cent to around sixteen per cent over the period, a better than respectable return.

With a sinking feeling I pondered whether I should speak up or forever hold my peace. You would have thought that Keith might have covered his backside by running his presentation by me to check the facts. I compounded Keith's oversight with a less than diplomatic interruption, a common scenario in which my brain descended to its default position called, 'shooting your mouth off'.

'Sorry Keith but I'm afraid that's not quite correct.'

Silence pervaded the boardroom. I went on, launching into my mantra.

'I've got no problem with the profit projection of $100 million in absolute terms in five years [it would actually reach $150 million] but given Mildara Blass's historical capital intensity ratio of around $1.50 of investment for each dollar of sales revenue and the assumed $150 million growth in sales revenue over the five year period, there will be a need for further investment of at least $155 million (after allowing for our already implemented vineyard expansion scheme). ROI in five years will be little more than twelve per cent.'

Fred Hilmer, who had been on the good money from the outset, preferring the much cheaper and less operationally efficient BRL Hardy, was now nodding his head. Chairman John Ralph tried to debate my grand theory of fixed capital intensity but as this subject was one of my better ones he was on a hiding to nothing. I was never to be forgiven for having provided the chairman with the gratuitous lesson. The stunned realisation round the table was that the Mildara Blass purchase looked as if it may have been based on a false premise.

The next day Ted had me in his office pressuring me to get the eight per cent return on investment back up to the eighteen per cent that Mildara had been earning before the acquisition. Initially, it was not clear whether Ted was deliberately playing dumb but I soon realised numbers were not among Ted's salient strengths. Nor was he used to the submission of scientific evidence. Although Foster's rate of return on its newly acquired business was now only eight per cent (thanks to the $310 million newly created goodwill figure included in the purchase price), the Mildara Blass EBITA to sales ratio was still a very high thirty per cent compared to between eight and twelve per cent for most other businesses. To get the ROI up to eighteen per cent in the immediate short term would require the EBITA to sales ratio rising to sixty-eight per cent, clearly a practical impossibility. It would have required an immediate price rise of thirty-eight per cent and an impossible to achieve gross margin of 88 cents in the sales dollar.

It's always a bit tricky trying to teach your new boss his two times tables but I forged ahead and explained what was possible. As with John Ralph the day before it was not the best way to generate warmth in an audience. I explained to Ted that the problem of Foster's low rate of return on its wine purchase would be best dealt with by aiming for profitable expansion of the business. Based on our track record it was reasonable to presume we could earn an eighteen per cent return on the additional funds required to finance that expansion and over time progressively increase the weighted average return on Foster's initial investment.

'Okay, okay I get the picture; you don't have to bloody go on about it,' groaned Ted finally.

It turned out that was pretty well how things went down. By the time of my retirement four years later the Mildara Blass EBITA was approaching $150 million. The additional $105 million in annual EBITA since our selling out to Foster's was being earned on additional investment of around $500 million, a return of slightly more than twenty per cent on that additional investment. By that time the weighted average ROI of close to thirteen per cent was slightly better than my original projection and on the borderline of acceptability. Profitable growth was the more logical rationale on which the acquisition should have been based in the first place.

¶

Foster's business had originally revolved around it beer division, managed by the extremely capable but sometimes wary and suspicious Nuno D'Aquino. Most people at the top are a bit edgy and paranoid because it's such a long way down but Nuno was often wound up pretty tight. He was not easy to work with or for, but he still produced excellent results. Nuno, like Ted, had been an industrial chemist and Ted had plucked him from obscurity to take on the important CUB management role. It was one of Ted's really good management decisions.

While Nuno was a highly capable and successful executive it appeared he was impatient as to how he might get his fingers on some of the newly acquired wine business. The background to what was about to unfold was Ted's acknowledgement to me in an unguarded moment that he had always felt beholden to Nuno for something that had happened in their past; a something which Ted had no intention of expanding upon and never did. The outcome was that whatever Nuno wanted Nuno got, and mainly for good reason. Most of his ideas worked, but not this one.

Following the failure of a proposal put to the board by Foster's chief financial officer Trevor O'Hoy, a proposal in which parts of the wine division's operations would have been merged with those of CUB, Nuno decided to go the direct route and launch a wine brand of his own.

For numerous reasons, a CUB wine brand didn't make much sense, particularly to me, but Ted defended a strategy that any logical analysis suggested was somewhat on the bizarre side. That's the problem with loyalty. It can be an admirable thing but it can blind you to certain truths. And the problem with doing things with pals is that while you can maybe trust them with your life you can't always rely on them to be right.

CUB's simplistic approach saw wine marketing as not requiring any special properties over those needed for any other consumer commodity. The campaign was the heaviest in the history of the wine industry. Like that of the Ben Ean campaign in the 1970s it would be a complete flop, albeit for far different reasons. The brand was withdrawn from the market less than twelve months after release. Nothing was to be learned from that debacle. In the first year of the new century CUB conscripted one of the Mildara Blass brands, Half Mile Creek (at the time selling around 600,000 bottle a year) that had been created by long-term Mildara marketing manager, Judy Hacker. The conscription of Half Mile Creek was to provide the CUB team with its still unsated obsession of snaring a wine opportunity.

Unlike the earlier heavily researched new product introduction, the Half Mile Creek brand did have an appropriate level of feel but was nonetheless very successfully killed stone dead within twelve months because the beer sales force lacked any sort of credibility in selling wine. The wine retail trade took itself very seriously and saw wine knowledge as important. It felt CUB's move to be merely going through the motions and taking retailers for granted. It was another example of a successful brewing company believing its success came from a special marketing presence rather than a dominant market position.

¶

For the first three years of his role as CEO Ted Kunkel had come up trumps. His cool head had steadied the Foster's ship. He had kicked a goal from outside the fifty metre line with his appointment of Nuno D'Aquino. Ted taking Foster's into the wine business via Mildara Blass had put another score on the board.

In his pressured pursuit of growth Ted had also decided to establish brewing businesses in Vietnam, India and China. It was not one of his better moves and one he should have forever kept in reserve. Foster's Asia was managed by my name sake Jim King. Jim was ex Kraft International Limited and a good operator in a structured and disciplined business but not so suited to the complicated, rough and tumble, corrupt brewing environment of South East Asia. He very much relied on his twenty-six year old chief operating officer Geoffrey Bainbridge for the cut and thrust. Geoffrey was something of a tearaway; dynamic, entrepreneurial, creatively capable and perfectly suited to an unstructured environment but even he was battling mountainous odds. And Foster's had been doing things arse about. It didn't start checking things out until it realised the venture had a problem. And the problem was that more than sixty per cent of the Asian beer market was in the hands of government-owned breweries. The managers of government-owned breweries were not only playing in the first division in their ability to initiate and exploit corruption but were also not yet interested in making a profit. Jim's business had no hope of competing effectively with indigenous managers who knew how business was transacted in South East Asia and who, even more importantly, were apparently not interested in making a profit. Ted finally pulled the pin in 2002 by which time Foster's Asian beer division had incurred losses of more than $500 million.

¶

Within months of the Mildara Blass acquisition Ted was under pressure from financial journalists and brokers' analysts to leverage his Mildara Blass purchase with further acquisitions. The acquisition was something of a problem in this regard. The purchase had significantly boosted the price earnings ratios and share prices of wine companies all over the world. Higher purchase prices would make it extremely difficult, if not impossible, to make an appropriate return from an acquired wine business. Growth by acquisition was no longer a sound or practical idea. By acquiring Mildara Blass Foster's had unwittingly removed, or at least made it far more difficult, to maintain the source of half of the previous Mildara Blass profit growth.

Ted encouraged me to look at Len Evans' 'Rothbury Estate in the Hunter Valley. Rothbury Estate was publically listed and historically had been a poor performer. Len Evans, an ebullient Sydney-based raconteur, had been a professional golfer and journalist in the UK. After migrating to Australia he had great success as a Sydney wine retailer, author and wine publicist before establishing a small but successful wine club and mail order business. He had then planted the Sydney elite's obligatory vineyard in the Hunter Valley and compounded the error by building the inevitable edifice, an expensive and designed to impress, but as it turned out, highly inefficient winery.

The Rothbury brand had never made it in the marketplace (retailers were pissed off by the mail order business which they saw as a competitor) but along the way Len had acquired the Saltram wine business in the Barossa Valley and St Hubert's in the Yarra Valley. These were brands that I thought had significant potential, particularly Saltram which had an excellent winemaker in Nigel Dolan

At best, I was ambivalent about the proposal to acquire Rothbury. Rothbury's share price was already artificially high because of Foster's move on Mildara Blass. The prospect of getting our trademark twenty per cent ROI if we acquired Rothbury would not be easy. I stalled at being prepared to offer the price that Len was looking for. Uncharacteristically, Ted, buoyed by the good publicity surrounding the Mildara Blass purchase, was impatient to do a deal. He intervened in the negotiations and agreed to Len's high price. This was one acquisition I was not confident would produce the desired return. It didn't. But ultimately it sort of washed its face with a return of around fourteen per cent and not much damage was done. Rothbury nevertheless turned out to be a complicated and messy organisation and proved difficult to integrate into our smooth running structure.

¶

In 1997 BHP sold its Foster's shares and its two directors stood down. Foster's chief financial officer, an ex BHP employee, had been appointed to protect BHP's interests. But Ted saw the appointment as being motivated by BHP's desire to keep an eye on him, a situation over which Ted was not entirely happy. Following BHP's sale of its Foster's shares Ted immediately sacked him and sent him back to BHP. He then appointed Trevor O'Hoy, a long term Foster's accountant in his place, an appointment that ultimately led to Trevor becoming Ted's successor as CEO.

Trevor was far more proactive than his more passive BHP

predecessor and with good intentions set out to use the finance function as a vehicle for greater corporate efficiency and profit generation. Trevor turned to his accounting background for inspiration and focussed on cost reduction as the key dynamic for improving profitability. He was a particular devotee of the concept of shared services that had become fashionable at that time.

At a board meeting in early 1997 Ted announced that Trevor O'Hoy would make a presentation of some importance. Trevor got to his feet and delivered a thunderbolt. And that thunderbolt was fired straight at me. He proposed that a number of Mildara Blass' financial, administrative and logistics functions and some sales functions be integrated with those of CUB on the basis of the significant savings Trevor estimated could be achieved.

'That's a bit out of order' I thought, although if I remember correctly the adrenalin spike inspired more colourful thoughts. Ted had bided his time well. It had taken almost two years for him to again challenge my independence but this time he was fishing for some board support. It was pretty evident to all present that day that Trevor's presentation, aided and abetted if not inspired by Ted, was news to me.

With great difficulty I resisted the initial impulse to spit the dummy and stalk out of the boardroom in moral outrage or initiate some other equally unproductive response. The eyes around the table were all focussed on little old me. I tried for unconcern and the inscrutable Chinaman but underneath the table my knees were bouncing up and down like pistons. 'A bit of tactical treachery there Ted', I mused as I gradually cooled down.

I made a reasonable fist of the response, repeating all the cultural reasons as to why Trevor's plan wouldn't work, the same rationale I had given the Tooheys board when my old comrade in arms, Bill Widerberg, had proposed the integration of the wine and beer sales forces in New South Wales twenty years earlier. Although the two proposals were far from identical they were similar in thrust;

well-meaning but flawed integration that would undermine wine division independence and effectiveness.

Wine and beer cultures were like chalk and cheese. While Trevor could logically point to the projected savings he could not guarantee that the wine division's future revenue streams would remain unaffected. It was the same flaw that was to get him into so much trouble and cost him his job as CEO after the acquisition of Southcorp in 2005. Everyone around the table, with the exception of Ted and Trevor, was nodding his head at my chalk and cheese rationale.

It was fair to say that any integration threat was now dead and buried for at least as long as I remained on parade. Ted's rejoinder that I was being overly defensive and it was just an idea, not a firm proposal, was a smooth tactical withdrawal. Ted took his failed ploy on the chin and did not try the integration thing again until after I had retired in late 1999. Within a month of my retirement the Mildara Blass head office was closed down and all staff moved to Southbank. It was the beginning of the wine division's descent into hell.

¶

With the financial markets now affording the value of wine EBIT a multiple of twelve, almost double that of the period 1980 to 1995, maintaining an expansion strategy based on acquisition seemed largely out of the question. The best return you could get on an acquired business was an eight per cent ROI unless there was significant potential for profit improvement. This return was no better than the cost of capital and would not boost share earnings or shareholder value, so why bother? With the Australian wine industry going through its one prosperous decade of the century even the poorly run businesses were doing OK. But even in a tough environment if you looked hard enough you could sometimes find something that might tick the boxes.

We focussed our attention on buying a business called Cellarmasters, an undervalued mail order wine clubs business I had flirted with buying in 1992. It was run by one of the three most capable businessmen I had come across. His name was Terry Davis. Terry had been a champion rower in his early days. This was no surprise given that he was built like a brick shithouse. Terry was a bit on the thin-lipped side but could clown around like the rest of us. Then in a twitch of his shaggy eyebrows he could transform from a waggy-tailed St Bernard into a six feet four poisonous cobra. A bit on the intimidating side was Terry. He went on to run Coca Cola in Australia for more than a decade and in 2011 his annual remuneration was in the vicinity of $9 million.

Cellarmasters Pty Ltd, rather than being a conventional wine business ran wine clubs, recommending and supplying wine to the members of the variety of wine clubs it managed. Wine clubs satisfied two separate needs, the convenience of home delivery and the need of inexperienced wine consumers to keep their ignorance of wine, real or imagined, well hidden. Cellarmasters was a highly sophisticated business befitting the intellect, discipline and determination of Terry Davis. It exploited, via regular telephone calls to its members, the detailed knowledge contained in its huge consumer data base. Cellarmasters had a panel of experts who extolled the virtues of various wines and made monthly recommendations in the company's newsletter. The majority of these wines just happened to be produced in Cellarmasters' own winery, a piece of information it naturally kept to itself.

The necessary credibility was provided by including in each mixed dozen one or two commercially recognised brands that provided the appropriate level of comfort that everything was hunky dory. And because it was an unconventional and little understood business Cellarmasters did not command the same purchase multiple of twelve times EBIT that applied to traditional wine companies. In 1998 we paid $160 million million for $ $26 million of EBIT, a multiple of only six times, around half what it would have cost to buy more orthodox wine earnings. Cellarmasters had a captive audience and its earnings were just as secure, if not more so, than those of a traditional wine business and in my opinion significantly undervalued.

Because the financial markets valued the additional Cellarmasters earnings at a multiple of twelve times, rather than the six times we had purchased them for, we added $ 160 million million of value to Foster's share price overnight. I thought I had a right to feel pretty pleased with myself.

'A touch of gratitude wouldn't have gone amiss,' I bellyached to myself, but no one at Foster's appeared to understand what had been done for their shareholders and I had to enjoy the achievement in silence.

By applying Cellarmaster's sophisticated marketing systems to the existing Rothbury mail order business as well as to the Foster's shareholders wine buying scheme we quickly added sufficient value to get our return on the Cellarmasters investment to our targeted return of twenty per cent.

Within another six months we paid around $100 million to acquire, for a similar earnings multiple of around six times, two direct marketing wine businesses in Europe, Pallhuber in Germany and The Wine Exchange in Belgium. At that point we estimated we held around thirty per cent of the world market for the direct marketing of wine and began exploring similar opportunities in North America.

Under Terry Davis's astute management the direct marketing businesses continued to prosper, including the period following my retirement in late 1999, when Terry took over from me in running the wine division. However, upon Terry's absconding to Coca Cola in 2002, the still little understood (certainly within Foster's) and now leaderless mail-order business went into steep decline and was sold in 2005 to Archer Capital, a private equity outfit, at what appeared to be a give-away price. Woolworths later recognised what Cellarmasters had to offer and bought the business in 2011 for a significantly higher price than Foster's had sold it for six years earlier, making Cellarmasters the cornerstone of its online wine and liquor strategy, a sales channel that had gone through the roof over the previous five years. Foster's had missed an opportunity.

Following our acquisition of Cellarmasters I had encouraged Terry Davis to remain with the business. He was not only the logical person to take over from me but, in my view, also the logical one to take over the running of Foster's from Ted Kunkel. It was obvious to all at Foster's with the possible exception of the board that during the latter period of his stewardship Ted was beginning to think about other things, a not unusual phenomenon for ageing CEOs. But Foster's board was asleep at the wheel. By 2002, two years after I had retired, an impatient Terry Davis was approached by chairman David Gonski to take on the top job at Coca-Cola. When the directors did wake up Ted's job was quickly promised to Terry but by then he was committed to Coca-Cola. It proved to be a disastrous outcome for Foster's shareholders who saw billions wiped from the company's potential share value over the ensuing decade.

¶

With exports booming and now accounting for more than a third of Mildara Blass earnings, our wine business was becoming increasingly global. By 1998 our EBITA had jumped to almost $90 million and we employed around 2000 people in seven countries. I was finally able to plagiarise Brian Healey's comment that I now had 2000 people working for me whose major task in life was to make my life easy.

Ted's recommendation that Foster's buy Mildara Blass was making him look pretty good as well as deflecting attention from the haemorrhaging beer business in South East Asia. And he was impatient to up the ante. He and Keith Lambert had encouraged me to carry out due diligence on the USA's second largest wine business, Beringer Wines, whose annual earnings were not far behind those of Mildara Blass. The Beringer business had done well since being acquired by Texas Pacific Partners, a private equity outfit, and they were now looking to exit for around $1.5 billion. When private equity interests are selling it's a good reason to keep your hands in your pocket or run a mile, preferably both. Private equity outfits are blood-suckers. Having successfully squeezed every last cent out of an acquired business they then flip it. Flipping is something the private equity guys are remarkably good at and the amazing thing is that they generally keep getting away with it.

Ted felt we should make a bid but the return on investment would have been lousy. Beringer was already well run and there were few potential synergies given its location. It didn't make financial sense, at least to me. With little chance of any upside it would not have been share earnings positive for Foster's for a long time, if ever. Again, Ted either didn't understand the numbers or didn't want to understand them. Apparently, nor did his board of directors. Ted accused me of being a wimp as did Stephen Bartholomeuz, the then senior financial writer for the *Age* newspaper, albeit less directly, who felt my 'clip on' approach of making relatively small acquisitions was too conservative. Still, Ted was sufficiently deterred by my negativity not to push the envelope.

Ted and John Ralph had also been keen to bid for Australia's largest wine company, Southcorp, a potential move they had decided not to share with me until I learned of it purely by accident. We had then had had a similar conversation. A year after I was out of the way Foster's went ahead and acquired Beringer and in a blaze of publicity in 2005 as to its excellent strategic fit purchased Southcorp for $3.2 billion. History records that both acquisitions proved to be unmitigated disasters and by 2008 Trevor, who was made to carry the can for the company's strategic malfeasance, was no longer there.

The acquisition of Beringer and Southcorp had both been bad ideas in the first place but Trevor was forced to take one on the chin for the good of the team on the basis of poor strategy implementation. Trevor was not completely blameless but the non-executive directors, all of whom survived, blithely eschewed any responsibility. By 2009 Foster's had written down its investments in those two companies by $2.7 billion, more than fifty per cent of their original acquisition prices.

Ted and his high profile directors couldn't get their heads around the idea that purchase multiples for wine acquisitions were just too high and that potential synergies could not possibly make up the difference. However, Ted's persistence got me thinking about a fourth leg to Mildara Blass's growth strategy. Our exports were booming, the domestic market was producing high single digit growth rates and the concept of direct marketing of wine through the existing mail-order business was a coming force to be reckoned with given the soaring potential for online business. I thought we could perhaps add a fourth string to our bow.

From the mid-1980s traditional wine producing countries France, Italy, Germany and Spain had increasingly lost ground not only to wines from Australia but also to those from South Africa, Chile and Argentina, the so called 'new world' winemakers. Wines from the new world employed the techniques originally developed at Davis University in California that extolled the virtues of the grape and produced fruity, more flavoursome wines.

But it was Australia's winemakers who had led the band up Bourke Street in first exploiting those techniques most effectively. In fact, to such a degree that by the mid-90s Australia was not only exporting wine all over the world but also exporting winemakers as well, even to France and Italy. Despite being a relative newcomer Australia was teaching the world how to make wine.

I began to flirt with the idea of establishing winemaking operations in overseas countries, an idea that was clearly not without risk.

It was becoming increasingly evident that Chile and to a lesser degree Argentina were exhibiting the potential to produce wines equally as good as those made in Australia but at a significantly lower cost because of low labour rates. There was a small but growing market for South American wines in the US and in the UK and I felt South America was where we should focus our attention.

Despite Brand Australia still being hot I couldn't help but think that Australia's share of the US and UK wine markets was close to saturation level. Perhaps there was an opportunity to use our strong and effective US and UK distribution networks to establish our own South American brand and negate any future slow-down in the momentum for Australian wine in overseas markets. Under no circumstances did I want to invest real money in South America as there was still a strong element of volatility in South America's economic and political climate. There had to be a way that involved less risk, particularly with our initial thrust.

The concept that evolved in my head was to aim at establishing a joint venture with a South American wine company. Mildara Blass would invest its intellectual property — its winemaking, marketing and distribution expertise. The South American joint venture partner would provide the real investment, in other words, production and packaging infrastructure and the investment in bulk wine inventory. The Mildara Blass distribution operation in the US and the UK would take a normal distributor's margin and the joint venture's profits (or losses) would be shared equally. It was a highly ambitious approach given the (favourable to us) one-sided nature of the risk/reward ratio. Its elegance was that Mildara Blass could develop a profit stream without having to make a major financial investment, in fact very little investment. If the concept happened to be acceptable to a potential South American partner and we were successful in developing a worthwhile brand then the return on investment for Mildara Blass would be almost infinite.

I chose Chile.

Chile is a country blessed with natural resources. It has significant mineral wealth, an excellent climate for high quality agricultural production and a culture that embraces hard work. Its potential had been repressed by the well-intentioned but disastrous socialist policies of the Allende government in the 1970s and then released (let loose was probably a better term) by the contrasting free market policies of General Pinochet's army junta in the 1980s. The economic policies of Pinochet's government had been implemented following the advice of a number of leading US economists, including the Chicago School's, high profile free marketeer Milton Friedman.

The result had been almost two decades of high growth and rapidly improved living standards for the average Chilean. Chile had become the success story of South America. Unfortunately, there had also been a dark side to Pinochet's regime. He wasn't too keen on opposition and a rumoured 3000 socialist leaders and sympathisers had disappeared into torture chambers and lonely graves. By the time Dawn and I arrived in Chile the general had been ousted and replaced by a more moderate, democratically elected government that still embraced economic growth and strongly encouraged investment in joint ventures with foreigners.

Our Chilean idea turned out to be a wonderful adventure, even though that feeling of adventure might have been boosted by our own colourful imagination and also by the fairly long odds of actually pulling it off. It was also not without an element of self-indulgence. The sun had almost set on my full-time business career and this was going to be the last hurrah in again trying something different.

Dawn and I arrived in Santiago, Chile's capital city in February, 1998, interspersed by a very pleasant three days in Tahiti. We had no idea what to expect other than knowing that Chile was at that time the fastest developing economy in South America. We learned that Bruce Kemp, Southcorp's second in command, had arrived the day before, presumably with the idea of checking the place out for opportunities.

As planned, still dishrag limp with jetlag despite a stopover in Tahiti, we spent the first three days in Santiago doing nothing more than seeking some form of recuperation from the long eastwards flight. Being the jetlag champion of the world I needed it. And dozing by the hotel pool in the warm sun is highly recommended.

At meal times the hotel restaurant was dominated by business types speaking a medley of different languages. Those who spoke English did so in different accents. One sensed that those around us were pursuing opportunities, doing deals and hatching alliances.

The carpetbaggers were out in force and everyone was keen to get in on the act.

All the major Chilean wine companies were either family owned or family dominated and had been members of Chile's ruling class for generations. Most of them still had portraits of the now disgraced General Pinochet in pride of place in their boardrooms. As far as they were concerned, Pinochet had been Chile's saviour. Perhaps given Pinochet's proclivity for violence they had merely wanted things to look that way.

To my pleasant surprise, we were very well received and Dawn and I were wined, dined and feted in luxurious fashion. None of the six wine companies we introduced ourselves to was prepared to reject our more than self-interested proposition outright and three were prepared to seriously consider a joint venture despite the tangible benefits being heavily weighted in our favour. They were all well aware of Mildara Blass's track record and were keen to learn from our reputed expertise.

We ultimately chose Santa Carolina, the third largest wine business in Chile, as our joint venture partner. Santa Carolina dedicated a small winery 100 kilometres south of Santiago to the project and we sent Paul Gardner, one of our two Victorian state managers, to manage the project, along with Adam Marks, one of our young winemakers. For them the adventure was very real.

Paul was a physical fitness fanatic. On his first visit to Santiago, he took an evening run along the banks of the Mapocho River that neatly dissects the city into two halves. Having crossed one of the many bridges spanning the river he jogged steadily towards the next bridge but was disconcerted by a small group of figures blocking the pathway ahead of him. His sixth sense smelled a rat. He turned, retracing his steps towards the bridge he had only recently crossed. The rat suddenly gotten bigger and smellier. There, in front of him, stood another group blocking the pathway. His antagonists had chosen well. No sign of side streets put paid to any conventional means of escape. Discretion was to become the better part of valour.

Paul, a good salesman was also a quick thinker. It was also handy that he was a good swimmer. He whipped off his runners, stuck them up his fortunately tight singlet and jumped into the river. Despite the strong flowing river he made it to the other side long before his new acquaintances could devise a successful plan B. Quickly donning his runners, laces flying, Paul sprinted back to his hotel. Having reported the incident to the hotel manager Paul was informed that Santiago was rumoured to be a significant supplier to the world's lucrative body parts market.

Adam Marks, having completed his first vintage in Chile, learned that when he routinely checked his bulk wine inventories he found to his dismay that the ullage levels in his wine tanks (the empty space at the top of the tank) were often far bigger each morning than they should have been. Either Chile had a unique and very high evaporation rate or someone was stealing his wine. The same was happening to the expertly tended grapes yet to be picked in the nearby vineyard.

Having made further enquiries Adam learned that wine and grape theft was endemic in rural Chile. He purchased two shotguns and posted signs around the property to the effect that trespassers would be shot on sight. Stuart and his assistant then slept by the tanks and at night routinely toured the vineyard in a jeep until things returned to normal and the wine was transferred to Santiago for longer term storage.

We started marketing wine in the US under the Dallas-Conte label and easily hit our first year targets. Japan also became an attractive market but that was where the adventure ended. By late 1999 I had become dead-man-walking and Terry Davis was in the process of taking over from me. In his opinion the Chilean project was too remote, too small and would take too long to come to full fruition. In any case he had bigger ambitions.

¶

In his teenage years Ted Kunkel had been a very promising golfer, so promising he thought he might take up the game professionally.

Ted's hard working German parents thought otherwise. They refused to sponsor him and counselled a career path in industrial chemistry and, as parents sometimes are, they turned out to be right. It led to his first job at Foster's as an assistant brewer. By the early 1990s Foster's had become a regular sponsor of golf tournaments in Australia and it was inevitable that Ted and Greg Norman, the number one golfer in the world at the time, would come in contact.

Ted decided it would be helpful to Foster's if Greg became the ambassador for the Foster's beer brand in the US where, conveniently, Greg now lived. Greg liked the idea of easy money, difficult money as well and put an annual price of US$1 million a year (A$1.3 million) on his head, a figure a bit more than what Ted had in mind. Not helping matters was the fact that Greg's price was not much less than the annual royalty Foster's was receiving from having sold the USA licence for the Foster's brand almost a decade earlier.

Ted had a bit of a problem. It was little known to outsiders that the burgeoning overseas sales of the Foster's brand, initiated by John Elliott's earlier proud boast that he would 'Fosterise the world', produced paltry profits despite the press releases extolling the virtues of its extraordinary sales successes. The world was indeed now in the process of being Fosterised but unfortunately for Foster's shareholders the company's financial collapse following the Elliott era had required the brand to be licensed to overseas brewers at a minuscule ongoing royalty rate in order to achieve the hefty upfront cash sums that had been required to keep the banks from putting Foster's into receivership.

Ted and I crossed swords at my first executive meeting on the wisdom of the public relations puffery that extolled the virtues of the burgeoning overseas Foster's business when so little substance was being contributed to the bottom line. Surely, someone was going to wake up to the apparent inconsistency. Ted turned his steely eyes on me and suggested in no uncertain terms that in future I should stick to my own back yard and keep my trap shut on matters that didn't concern me.

Nonetheless, it was clear that Ted couldn't afford Greg, an

inconvenience Ted was not keen to share explicitly with his new friend other than to imply that Foster's directors thought Greg's price was a trifle steep. But Greg Norman's business mind was more than fertile. He suggested a beguiling alternative. What about a Greg Norman wine brand?

Ted immediately loved the idea given it might get him off the hook. He put it to me in January 1998. I gave Ted a decent dose of the Jimmy Brits by immediately pouring cold water on it. There had been numerous attempts by celebrities and wine companies over the years to create such alliances and they had all failed. My argument was that the credibility factor, so important to the serious wine consumer, was always the missing link so why would this be any different? The brand was certainly not going to be a goer in the Australian market and I was circumspect as to whether it was even worth pursuing in international markets.

But this time Ted was not to be denied, he was facing the prospect of a serious loss of face. To fob Ted off I conceded I would discuss the opportunity with long-term Wolf Blass and Mildara Blass export executive, Peter Perrin, by then president of the Mildara Blass operation in the US. It turned out that Peter was not as pessimistic as me and having discussed the project with some of his US distributors he thought it was at least worthy of consideration. As the average US wine consumer was a decidedly less sophisticated and less knowledgeable animal than his Australian counterpart I began to think that maybe I had been a bit on the premature side in being so dismissive of Ted's, or more correctly, Greg's grand plan.

I agreed to meet Greg and his representatives for a preliminary discussion. We booked a private room at Silks Restaurant in Crown Casino in Melbourne, where Greg had been provided with the presidential suite for the week at mate's rates. Greg's name had already been leveraged into a dozen businesses at the time and his non-golf earnings were estimated to be around $60 million a year. Greg was keen to raise the number even higher and waxed lyrical about what he thought his name could do for a wine brand.

Greg had little idea about the dynamics or the culture of the wine industry but felt there was nothing special about the wine business that would prevent the project from being a success. As it turned out he was right. Despite my reservations (which I shared with Greg and with which the great man took bristling umbrage) I agreed to proceed to the next step and discuss with his management company what the financial arrangements might look like. In the meantime, Peter Perrin came back to me with the slightly irritating news of a heightened level of enthusiasm from his US distributors.

Greg's management company had put a royalty proposal to me based on a fixed dollar sum for each bottle which essentially meant we would be sharing the profits on a 50/50 basis at the price level I thought the brand could stand in the US market (but which I had not declared to them). In relative terms, our profit share would be less than what we were earning on our major selling US brand, Wolf Blass, a clearly unsatisfactory outcome.

Somewhat mischievously, I proposed that we work on a market price around seventy per cent greater than that for Wolf Blass, which in all likelihood would be considered too expensive, torpedo the project altogether and get rid of what I saw as an unnecessary distraction. But Greg immediately fell in love with the idea of a significant premium price, he being a premium price kind of guy. The upside for Mildara Blass was that in the event the premium price ploy happened to be successful all the increase would end up in our pocket and produce a bottle profit that was almost double what we were earning on Wolf Blass. Greg's representatives agreed to the proposal and I immediately decided I quite liked them after all.

Much against what I thought to be the likely odds the brand turned out to be uniformly providential for all concerned. It was a resounding success in the US and also in Japan. Although the brand was always going to be relatively short lived, in line with Greg's inevitable demise as the world's number one golfer, in its best year it earned Greg $5 million in royalties and in the same year the Mildara Blass bottom line was boosted by around $9 million. Greg had been right and I had been wrong or maybe I got it right for all the wrong reasons but who cared?

By July 1999 I had been written out of the script, now on gardening leave. By December I was gone. I was nervous about the next chapter or whether there would be a next chapter but I knew I no longer had the energy or the resilience necessary to be effective as a full time CEO. It was time to go. As is often the case in such circumstances Foster's systematically set about expunging my contribution from the record. And the expunging didn't take very long. Not only did the bugger of a kid no longer exist, he had never existed.

31

Second prize

Never speak ill of the dead.

On 1 December it was time to go and I quietly faded away from full time employment to generous newspaper comment. Finance journalist Terry McCrann wrote a long and flattering piece in the *Australian*.

It was not unusual for CEOs in their final year to be permitted to take on one or two external directorships as a walk-up start to their new business life. However, it was not all that usual for a CEO to take on the role of chairman of another company, particularly a publically listed company. In the twelve months before retirement I was offered three directorships, two of which involved becoming chairman of Stock Exchange listed consumer goods companies and one as a director of an electricity supplier.

Ted was generous enough not to stand in my way. Well, that was one way of putting it. In reality, Ted was more than happy to see the end of me and clearly felt some grease on the wheels might expedite the process. McPherson's Limited, and the King Island Company, a premium brand cheesemaker, both offered positions as chairman of directors. The electricity supplier was Powercor, spun out of the Victorian State Electricity Commission during the Kennett Government's privatisation program.

My involvement at McPherson's and at King Island was to set the tone for the future. I was drawn to businesses with serious challenges. McPherson's, a manufacturer and marketer of housewares items, had been on a long slippery slope for decades and the King Island Company, while producing an excellent product, had a fractured and dysfunctional board as well as serious environmental problems at its inadequate and outmoded dairy on King Island in Bass Strait.

Board invitations had made the thought of transition a little easier but not having the roar of the crowd in your ears took some getting used to, the constant adrenalin rush of treading that fine line between excitement and terror now only a memory. But my energy levels and resilience at almost sixty years of age were no longer up to snuff. There comes a time when you realise that the idea of doing the job seems to generate greater pleasure than actually doing the job. And I had been a 24/7 obsessive, filling my nights and weekends with thinking time as to how the business could be further improved.

On the first day of retirement the business pages of the newspapers had suddenly lost their interest. As it turned out, adjustment to life without full-time employment was ultimately more seamless than I had feared. Most human beings have an in-built mechanism to adapt and I was no exception. Business life not only became more varied but also took on a completely different dimension. And while it was definitely second prize it wasn't a bad second prize.

Within eighteen months, in addition to my existing chairmanships, I was chairman of directors of another four organisations; a group of thirty-two hotels, an IT business, an AFL club and a fledgling wine business. Approaches continued over the next decade. At last count, in 2012, I had had the somewhat dubious pleasure of having been a director of twenty companies, ten of them as chairman. Most people don't lose too much sleep over how boardrooms work and even for the average investor the dynamics of the boardroom are a mystery, its selection processes, its politics, its fractious interfaces a gladiatorial arena and viper's nest of ego.

Dawn had counselled me to focus on the big end of town in respect to potential directorships. I hadn't been so sure, my style unlikely to endear me to the formal, conservative directors of big business. Nor as it turned out did it always endear me to the informal adventurous types in small businesses either. In any case, I still had that romantic, naïve and erroneous belief that as a director I could make a difference and that I would be more relevant to a smaller organisation.

Finally, I wanted to believe that Dawn and I could prosper from my board involvements (an even more erroneous belief). I wanted to be involved in businesses in which we had the opportunity to invest. It didn't exactly turn out to be such a great idea but over time our wins outweighed our losses, slightly.

My maximum number of board seats at any one time was seven. The Australian Shareholders' Association (ASA) argued that was far too many directorships at any one time, particularly when a number of those directorships also involved being chairman. The potential rejoinder to the ASA's argument was a comment that I was always happy to plagiarise.

I had met Dick Holdaway in 1970 when Wynn's was in the process of being prepared for listing on the Melbourne Stock Exchange.

Dick was notable for deriving a great deal of pleasure from debating and from argument. He was particularly good in a hypothetical, abstract debate and his strange enthusiasm for this endeavour was reinforced by his small circle of high profile intellectual friends who thought it highly amusing. He was approximately my age, ex private school, had an ebullient supercilious persona, dressed in exaggerated pinstripe suits complete with fob watch and chain in his matching waistcoat and invariably had a colourful and contrasting handkerchief jutting from his breast pocket. He smoked huge cigars and did so with great flourish. But one gained the distinct impression that Dick's affection for the tobacco torpedo had as much to do with the opportunity for emphasis it provided as for the pleasure of the habit. He often held the cigar between his teeth unlit yet was still able to speak out of the side of his mouth with remarkable authority and clarity on a myriad of fascinating subjects. And if it were a vanity he was trying to create then not only did he prove to be highly successful at it but he also knew he was creating it extremely well. He was naturally pompous and self-important but also quick of wit, with a great turn of phrase, making him a wonderful entertainer and great company.

He often lounged with his fingers laced across his generous girth as if daring the world to spring something on him he didn't already know. Dark wavy hair and a full face replicated that of his soul mate, Oscar Wilde. Dick was an analyst with the stock broking company Guest and Bell which had been retained by Wynn's to advise on the company's prospective Stock Exchange listing in 1970. During the 1980s, Dick gained great notoriety as Australia's leading and most respected expert on the Australian banking system.

Dick indulged himself by keeping 'gentleman's hours'. Arriving at Wynn's late one day a little before morning tea, he strolled into the office he shared with me. In those days the working day was defined by traditional stoppages; morning tea, lunch and afternoon tea breaks in the company's cafeteria.

'Jesus Dick, what's your bloody story, this is not afternoon shift,' I ventured.

Treating me with overt and exaggerated disdain, Dick ignored my biting jibe, settled into his chair, extracted a Cuban Montecristo (God knows how he got them given the trade embargo with Cuba) from his suitably engraved silver cigar case, struck a match with great flourish, lit the tube and proceeded to suck a vacuum cleaner volume of smoke into his lungs. Languidly, despite or perhaps because of his large frame, he lent back in his chair and sent a plume of smoke jetting towards the ceiling. Finally breaking the silence, he spoke.

'Well Ray,' he said, in rounded vowels as condescending as he could muster, 'it's like this. It's not the number of hours that's important it's the quality of thought that counts.'

Appendix 1

Mildara Wines Limited
Earnings before interest & tax ($m)
1981–1990

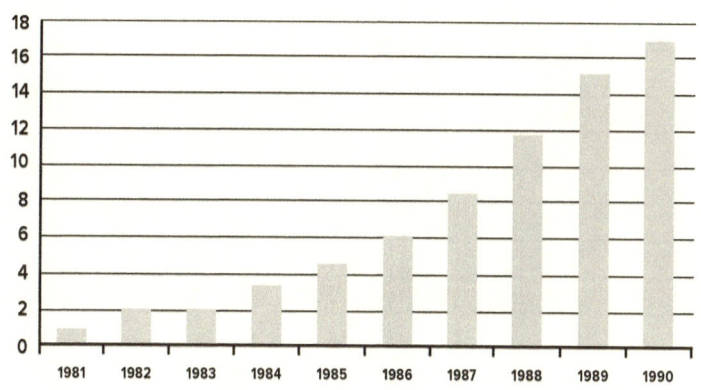

Appendix 2

Mildara Blass Limited
Earnings before interest & tax ($m)[*]
1991–2000

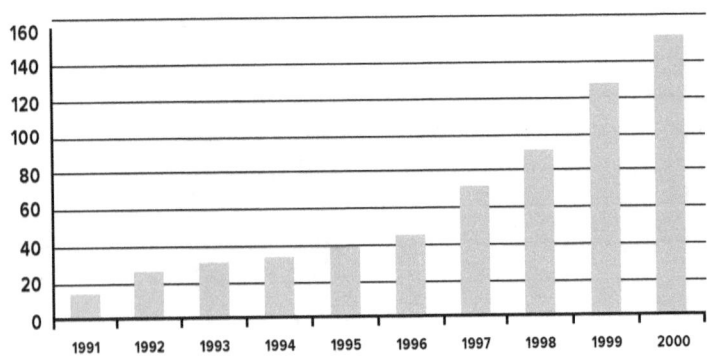

[*] Earnings before interest and tax and amortisation 1996 – 2000.

Appendix 3

Mildara Wines Limited
Return on investment
EBIT as a % of funds invested*

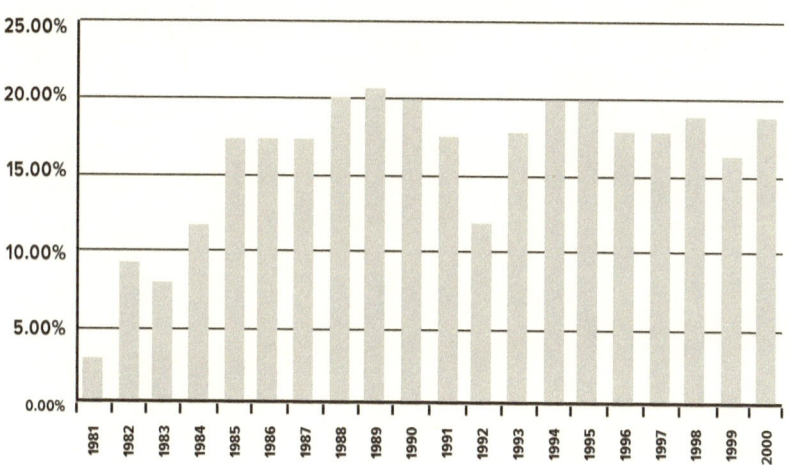

* 1996–2000 Actual funds invested are less $310m goodwill created in Fosters' purchase of Mildara Blass

  The above returns also approximate Mildara Blass' after tax return on equity based on debt funding of 40%, interest rates of 10% and a corporate tax rate of 30%.

Acknowledgements

My thanks to:

Maurice Dean for providing strategic documents, management papers and Mildara annual reports he had squirrelled away over a twenty year period;

My wife Dawn for her patience and advice while the memoir took shape;

Our son in law David for processing photos and charts;

Our son Brook for encouraging me to write the history at the outset;

Our son Jeremy and daughter Danielle for reading the manuscript and providing advice; and

My editor Tony Berry for his patience and sound advice.

www.ingramcontent.com/pod-product-compliance
Lightning Source LLC
Chambersburg PA
CBHW030258080526
44584CB00012B/361